Lecture Notes in Computer Science 6994

Commenced Publication in 1973
Founding and Former Series Editors:
Gerhard Goos, Juris Hartmanis, and Jan

Services Science

Subline of Lectures Notes in Computer Science

Subline Editors-in-Chief

Subline Editorial Board

Witold Abramowicz   Ignacio M. Llorente
Mike Surridge   Andrea Zisman
Julien Vayssière (Eds.)

Towards
a Service-Based Internet

4th European Conference, ServiceWave 2011
Poznan, Poland, October 26-28, 2011
Proceedings

 Springer

Volume Editors

Witold Abramowicz
Poznan University of Economics, Department of Information Systems
al. Niepodleglosci 10, 61-875 Poznan, Poland
E-mail: w.abramowicz@gmail.com

Ignacio M. Llorente
Complutense University of Madrid
C/Prof. Jose Garcia Santesmases s/n, 28040 Madrid, Spain
E-mail: ignacio.m.llorente@gmail.com

Mike Surridge
University of Southampton, IT Innovation Centre, Gamma House
Enterprise Road, Southampton SO16 7NS, UK
E-mail: ms@it-innovation.soton.ac.uk

Andrea Zisman
City University London, Department of Computing
Northampton Square, London EC1V 0HB, UK
E-mail: a.zisman@soi.city.ac.uk

Julien Vayssière
Smart Services CRC, Australian Technology Park, Locomotive Workshop
Suite 9003, 2 Locomotive Street, Eveleigh, NSW 2015, Australia
E-mail: julien.vayssiere@gmail.com

ISSN 0302-9743   e-ISSN 1611-3349
ISBN 978-3-642-24754-5   e-ISBN 978-3-642-24755-2
DOI 10.1007/978-3-642-24755-2
Springer Heidelberg Dordrecht London New York

Library of Congress Control Number: 2011938791

CR Subject Classification (1998): C.2, D.2, H.4, H.3, C.2.4, H.5

LNCS Sublibrary: SL 2 – Programming and Software Engineering

Typesetting: Camera-ready by author, data conversion by Scientific Publishing Services, Chennai, India

Printed on acid-free paper

Springer is part of Springer Science+Business Media (www.springer.com)

Preface

It is our pleasure to welcome you to the proceedings of the 4th European Conference ServiceWave 2011, held in Poznan, Poland, October 26–28. ServiceWave 2011 was the fourth edition of the ServiceWave conference series and the second edition to be part of the Future Internet week. The ServiceWave conference series is the premier European forum for practitioners, researchers, and educators to discuss the most recent innovations, trends, experiences and concerns and to set the agenda for research on the future converged Internet of content (IoC), services (IoS), things (IoT) and related network of the future (NoF) technologies. ServiceWave fosters cross-community excellence by bringing together industrial and academic experts from various disciplines such as cloud computing, business process management, distributed systems, computer networks, wireless and mobile communication networks, grid computing, networking, service engineering, service science and software engineering.

This year's scientific track especially sought reports of novel ideas and techniques that enhance service-oriented computing as well as reflections on current research and industrial practice towards a future converged Internet by scoping the Call for Papers around the following four topics:

- Business Services: dealing with ideas and techniques that allow expressing, understanding, representing, and managing business processes in a service-oriented manner
- Cloud Computing: discussing the potential of emerging techniques and technologies to contribute to a European Cloud Computing Strategy
- Security, Privacy and Trust: taking us from a fragile current Internet to a trustworthy Future Internet bridging the virtual and physical worlds
- Service Engineering Fundamentals: dealing with topics around fundamental engineering techniques that allow us to move toward a Future Internet Service Infrastructure

The ServiceWave program features high-quality contributions from the above-mentioned research areas. In addition to the presentations of the peer-reviewed papers (each submitted paper was reviewed by at least three reviewers) the ServiceWave program included 14 invited scientific track presentations and three invited presentations held in a dedicated FI-PPP session. The papers of both types of presentations are included in these proceedings.

Moreover, there was a joint ServiceWave, FIA and FIRE demonstration evening, for which 14 demonstrations were accepted based on a two-page extended abstract as well as a short video of the actual demonstration. Reviewers found the videos especially helpful in forming an opinion about the scope and maturity of each demo. Accepted demonstrations cover a wide spectrum of technology and application domains.

Above all, ServiceWave was a collaborative effort. First of all, we would like to thank the authors for providing the content of the program. We would like to express our gratitude to the Program Committee and external reviewers, who worked very hard in reviewing papers and providing suggestions for their improvements.

We would also like to thank the organizers of the two full-day workshops EDBPM and OCS as well as the four half-day workshops CT4CS, NESSOS, MONA+ and WAS4FI, which were held on the last day of the conference, for their effort. We also thank Michel Cezon and Andreas Metzger for managing the workshop selection process, Josema Cavanillas for serving as Industry Track Chair, the organizing team from Poznan for hosting the Future Internet week and helping us in setting up the next edition of ServiceWave and last but not least the NESSI team which again did a great job in promoting the event.

Finally, we thank all the sponsors of ServiceWave 2011 who contributed generously to the smooth running of the working conference itself. We hope that you will enjoy reading the proceedings as much as we enjoyed preparing them.

October 2011

Andrea Zisman
Ignacio Martin Llorente
Mike Surridge
Witold Abramowicz
Scientific Track Chairs

Julien Vayssière
Demonstration Chair

Klaus Pohl
General Chair

Organization

General Chair

Klaus Pohl   University of Duisburg-Essen, Germany

Program Comittee Chairs

Witold Abramowicz   Poznan University of Economics, Poland
Ignacio M. Llorente   Complutense University of Madrid, Spain
Mike Surridge   IT Innovation, UK
Andreas Zisman   City University London, UK

Industry Program Chair

Jose Maria Cavanillas   Atos Origin, Spain

Workshop Chairs

Michel Cezon   INRIA, France
Andreas Metzger   University of Duisburg-Essen, Germany

Demonstration Chair

Julien Vayssière   Smart Services CRC, Australia

Scientific Program Committee

Witold Abramowicz   Poznan University of Economics, Poland
Marco Aiello   University of Groningen, The Netherlands
Alvaro Arenas   IE Business School, Spain
Rosa M. Badia   Barcelona Supercomputing Center and CSIC,
                                  Spain
Juan Bareno   ATOS, Spain
Luciano Baresi   Politecnico di Milano, Italy
Abdelmalek Benzekri   University of Paul Sabatier, France
Peter Burgess   VUB, Belgium
Manuel Carro   Universidad Politecnica de Madrid, Spain
David Chadwick   University of Kent, UK
Joris Claessens   Microsoft, Germany
Jim Clarke   WIT, Ireland

Brian Coghlan	Trinity College Dublin, Ireland
Andrew Cormack	JANET, UK
Frederic Desprez	INRIA, France
Theo Dimitrakos	BT, UK
Elisabetta Di Nitto	Politecnico di Milano, Italy
Karim Djername	University of Leeds, UK
John Domingue	Open University, UK
Schahram Dustdar	University of Vienna, Austria
Erik Elmroth	Umeå University, Sweden
Dieter Fensel	University of Innsbruck, Austria
Agata Filipowska	Poznan University of Economics, Poland
Bogdan Franczyk	University of Leipzig, Germany
Wolfgang Gentzsch	HPC Consultant, DEISA, Germany
Christian Geuer-Pollmann	Microsoft, Germany
Lucio Grandinetti	University of Calabria, Italy
Stephan Haller	SAP Research, Switzerland
Seif Haridi	SICS, Sweden
Manfred Hauswirth	Digital Enterprise Research Institute (DERI), Galway
Jean Herveg	CRID, Belgium
Valerie Issarny	INRIA, France
Borka Jerman-Blazic	Josef Stefan Institute, Slovenia
Monika Kaczmarek	Poznan University of Economics, Poland
Dimka Karastoyanova	University of Stuttgart, Germany
Claudia Keser	University of Gottingen, Germany
Christos Kloukinas	City University London, UK
Joanna Kolodziej	University of Bielsko-Biala, Poland
Ryszard Kowalczyk	Swinburne University of Technology, Australia
Marek Kowalkiewicz	SAP Research, Australia
Dieter Kranzlmüller	LMU and LRZ Munich, Germany
Marcel Kunze	Karlsruhe Institute of Technology, Germany
Patricia Lago	University of Amsterdam, The Netherlands
Martine Lapierre	THALES, France
Antonio Lioy	Politecnico di Torino, Italy
Fabio Massacci	Università di Trento, Italy
Philippe Massonet	CETIC, Belgium
Peter Matthews	CA Labs, UK
Andreas Metzger	University of Duisburg-Essen, Germany
Ruben S. Montero	Complutense University of Madrid, Spain
Christine Morin	INRIA, France
Syed Naqvi	CETIC, Belgium
Bassem Nasser	University of Southampton IT Innovation Centre, UK
Burkhard Neidecker-Lutz	SAP AG, Germany
Nikitas Nikitakos	University of the Aegean, Greece

Karsten Oberle   Alcatel-Lucent, Bell-Labs, Germany
Andreas Oberweis   Universität Karlsruhe, Germany
Aljosa Pasic   ATOS, Spain
Dana Petcu   West University of Timisoara, Romania
Marco Pistore   FBK, Italy
Iman Poernomo   King's College, UK
Antonio Puliafito   University of Messina, Italy
Omer Rana   Cardiff University, UK
Stephan Reiff-Marganiec University of Leicester, UK
Matthieu Roy   LAAS-CNRS, France
Shazia Sadiq   The University of Queensland, Australia
Virgilijus Sakalauskas Lithuania
George Spanoudakis   City University London, UK
Mike Surridge   University of Southampton IT Innovation
                        Centre, UK
Domenico Talia   ICAR-CNR and University of Calabria, Italy
Wolfgang Theilmann   SAP, Germany
Robert Tolksdorf   Free University Berlin, Germany
Vasilis Tsoulkas   KEMEA, Greece
Julien Vayssiere   Smart Services CRC / INRIA, Australia
Michael Waidner   FhG, Germany
Stefan Wesner   HLRS, Germany
Yaron Wolfsthal   IBM Haifa Research Laboratory, Israel
Ramin Yahyapour   TU Dortmund University, Germany

Demonstration Program Committee

Alessandra Bagnato   TXT e-solutions, France
Markus Brunner   NEC, Germany
Marcelo Cataldo   Carnegie Mellon University, USA
Francois Charoy   University of Nancy, France
Jean-Yves Delors   Google, Switzerland
Keith Duddy   Queensland University of Technology, Australia
Axel Kieninger   Karlsruhe Service Research Institute, Germany
André Ludwig   University of Leipzig, Germany
Norman May   SAP AG, Germany
Alex Norta   University of Helsinki, Finland
Jennifer Pérez   Technical University of Madrid, Spain
Hamid Reza Motahari Nezhad HP Labs, USA
Davy Van Deusen   Ghent University, Belgium
Ingo Weber   University of New South Wales, Australia
Miguel Jimenez   Technical University of Madrid, Spain
Christos Kloukinas   City University London, UK
Piet Demeester   University of Ghent, Belgium

External Reviewers

Bayuh, Ewnetu
Bertoli, Piergiorgio
Celesti, Antonio
Degeler, Viktoriya
Henriksson, Daniel
Hernandez, Francisco
Jiménez, Miguel
Kaldeli, Eirini

Knittl, Silvia
Razavian, Maryam
Serrabou, Belen
Tamburri, Damian Andrew
Toma, Ioan
Truong, Hong-Linh
Watzl, Johannes
Xu, Lei

Sponsors

Platinum Sponsors

Silver Sponsors

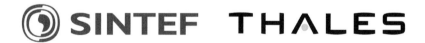

Table of Contents

Service Engineering Fundamentals

Business Services

FI-PPP

Demonstrations

Integration of an Event-Based Simulation Framework into a Scientific Workflow Execution Environment for Grids and Clouds

Simon Ostermann, Kassian Plankensteiner, Daniel Bodner,
Georg Kraler, and Radu Prodan

University of Innsbruck, Austria,
Institute of Computer Science
{Simon,Radu,Kassian.Plankensteiner}@dps.uibk.ac.at,
{Daniel.Bodner,Georg.Kraler}@student.uibk.ac.at

Abstract. The utilisation of Grid and Cloud-based computing environments for solving scientific problems has become an increasingly used practice in the last decade. To ease the use of these global distributed resources, sophisticated middleware systems have been developed, enabling the transparent execution of applications by hiding low-level technology details from the user. The ASKALON environment is such a system, which supports the development and execution of distributed applications such as scientific workflows or parameter studies in Grid and Cloud computing environments. On the other hand, simulation is a widely accepted approach to analyse and further optimise the behaviour of software systems. Beside the advantage of enabling repeatable deterministic evaluations, simulations are able to circumvent the difficulties in setting up and operating multi-institutional Grid systems, thus providing a lightweight simulated distributed environment on a single machine. In this paper, we present the integration of the GroudSim Grid and Cloud event-based simulator into the ASKALON environment. This enables system, application developers, and users to perform simulations using their accustomed environment, thereby benefiting from the combination of an established real-world platform and the advantages of a simulation.

1 Introduction

Scientific computing has an increasing demand for fast and scalable execution environments to deliver results for growing problem sizes in a reasonable time. Few years ago supercomputers were the only way to get enough computation power for such tasks. Afterwards, the high performance sector moved from expensive special supercomputer architectures to more affordable and easier to expand clusters and computational Grids. Recently, a new trend called Cloud computing introduces a new operational model by which resource ownership is moved from individual institutions to specialised data centres from which resources are rented on-demand only when and for how long they are needed. This

W. Abramowicz et al. (Eds.): ServiceWave 2011, LNCS 6994, pp. 1–13, 2011.

shift has the potential of significantly lowering the operational costs of occasionally used resources and eliminates the burden of hardware deprecation. In previous work [11], we have shown that a combination of Grid and Cloud systems can represent a reliable and powerful hybrid platform for scientific computing.

ASKALON [6] is a software middleware that eases the use of distributed Grid and Cloud resources by providing high-level abstractions for programming complex scientific workflow applications by using either a textual XML representation or a graphical UML-based diagram. Beside this, different middleware services support the user with sophisticated mechanisms for transparent scheduling and execution of the applications on the underlying Grid and Cloud hardware resources. All important events that characterise each application execution are logged into a data repository used for postmortem analysis and visualisation.

Besides execution of applications in real Grid and Cloud environments as supported by ASKALON, simulation is an alternative technique to analyse a real-world model which has several important advantages: it delivers fast results, it allows for reproducibility, it saves costs, and it enables the investigation of scenarios that cannot be easily reproduced in reality. To support such simulations, we developed in previous work GroudSim [10], an event-based simulator written in Java that provides an improved scalability compared to other related approaches [2]. GroudSim supports modelling of Grid and Cloud computational and network resources, job submissions, file transfers, as well as integration of failure, background load, and cost models. In this paper we present the integration of the GroudSim simulator into the ASKALON environment to allow the user to execute simulation experiments from the same environment used for real applications. This allows a unique interface to be used for these two tasks which significantly facilitates this dual experimental process.

The paper is organised as follows. We start with a short introduction of the used software packages in Section 2 followed by architectural details about the combination of these parts in Section 3. Experimental results from real and simulated workflow executions are presented in Section 4 and related work is given in Section 5. Section 6 concludes the paper.

2   Background

In this section we present in more detail the two main components of the presented integrated approach: the GroudSim simulation framework and the ASKALON workflow execution system.

2.1   GroudSim

GroudSim is a Java-based simulation toolkit for scientific applications running on combined Grid and Cloud infrastructures. GroudSim uses a discrete-event simulation toolkit that consists of a future event list and a time advance algorithm that offers improved performance and scalability against other process-based approaches used in related work [14]. The developed simulation framework supports modelling of Grid and Cloud computational and network resources, job submissions, file transfers, as well as integration of failure, background load, and cost models. A sophisticated textual and visual tracing mechanism and a library-independent distribution factory give extension possibilities to the simulator: a new tracing mechanisms can be easily added by implementing new handlers or filters in the event system, and additional distribution functions can be included by adding a new library and writing an appropriate adapter. GroudSim focuses on the Infrastructure as a Service area of Cloud computing and is easily extendable to support additional models like Cloud storage or Platform as a Service.

Previous work [12] has shown the usefulness of this simulation package for investigation of provisioning optimisations for Cloud computing. The drawback, however, was that the simulation experiments had to be programmed using a different interface than the one used for real applications, which required additional effort in the design and execution of experiments. These drawbacks are eliminated with the integration into a workflow system presented in this work.

2.2 ASKALON

ASKALON is a Grid application development and computing environment. Its aim is to support application developers by providing a set of high abstraction tools that shields them from the complexity of the underlying infrastructure such as Grid and Cloud technologies.

ASKALON supports primarily the workflow programming paradigm describing a graph of activities or computational tasks encapsulating atomic functionality and interconnected through control flow and data flow dependencies. For the composition of such a workflow, ASKALON provides a graphical user interface, as shown in Figure 1, through which application developers can conveniently assemble activities, define their execution order, and decide which activities can be executed in parallel.

Once the workflow has been created, every individual installation on a Grid or Cloud site (called activity deployment) has to be registered in a software management module. Finally, the user can execute the workflow transparently without taking care about where and how each activity is executed. It is the task of the ASKALON middleware to determine the available hardware resources with corresponding deployments and to transparently create job and file transfer executions to gain the "best" overall performance. These decisions can depend on the number of free CPUs, their clock speed, network bandwidths, authorisation, and many other parameters.

UML Modelling and AGWL. ASKALON provides a graphical user interface to create workflows in an intuitive and user-friendly fashion. A workflow is represented as an Unified Modelling Language Version 2.0 diagram that supports elements specific to Grid computing. The format to store information about a workflow is defined in the XML-based Abstract Grid Workflow Language (AGWL). Supported constructs include basic activities and sub-activities, control flow (sequence, if, switch, while, do, for, parallel, parallel for) and data flow constructs (input and output ports). For the UML representation, a model

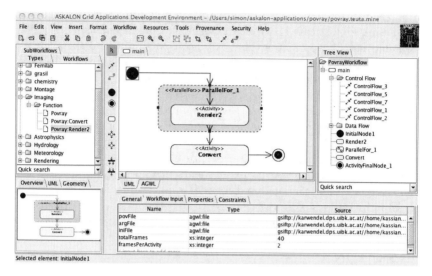

Fig. 1. The user interface of ASKALON using to create UML based workflows and to execute and monitor them

checker for testing its correctness and a model traverser which finally creates an AGWL description which can be handed over to the execution engine is provided.

Execution Engine. The Execution Engine (EE2) is the central service capable of distributing the workflow activities to available resources in their correct order. To provide the required functionality, it uses performance prediction and scheduling services for optimised mapping of the workflow activities on the available Grid and Cloud resources. The scheduling is done just-in-time, meaning that each activity is scheduled to a free resource when all of its dependencies are resolved and a resource capable of executing it is available. This just-in-time scheduling is possible due to the usage of the EE2's internal queue that postpones the execution of tasks with unsolved constraints.

GridARM. Grid ASKALON Resource Manager (GridARM) is responsible for managing physical resources. It provides mechanisms for Grid resource discovery and selection by performing state and capacity checking. Furthermore, it supports reservation, co-allocation, negotiation, and notification mechanisms.

GLARE. While GridARM focuses on physical resources, the Grid Level Activity Registration, Deployment and Provisioning Framework (GLARE) is a service for managing software resources, which supports the registration of software components along with build and installation scripts. This enables automatic deployment on resources and simplifies the use of new hardware into the Grid. In order to separate the description of the functionality of an activity from and the actually deployement, GLARE distinguishes between *activity types* and *activity deployments*. Activity types are a high-level description of the functionality,

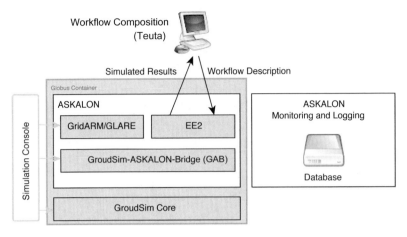

Fig. 2. Single container architecture of the simulation-based ASKALON services

defining its name and input and output parameters with their corresponding data types. Activity deployments contain information specific to an actual deployment on a machine, for example installation paths or concrete names of input files. The application developer is shielded from these low-level information and can concentrate on the high-level activity types.

3 Architecture

Figure 2 shows the architecture of the workflow simulation system integrated in the ASKALON environment. The workflow composition tool connects to a regular execution engine, requiring no changes on the end-user's side. When simulating large workflows, the ASKALON services and GroudSim exchange a large amount of messages for jobs, their execution states and the resources available. Hence, a single container architecture for ASKALON and GroudSim is used when possible to reduce Web service communication overhead between the components, while otherwise all messages have to be sent through Web service calls as it is done in real executions. For each main ASKALON service (i.e. GridARM/GLARE and EE2), we added a thin adaptor responsible for the communication between the existing implementation and the new simulation package in the single container mode. One of the key features of the integrated simulation is the transparent processing of all involved ASKALON events leading to simulated results with the same system state and accessible with the same interface as for real workflows. The existing monitoring mechanisms and the used data repository for tracing and logging executions can be used for the analysis of simulated workflows. Their execution is stored in a separate database to avoid influence on any prediction services that rely on historical data of real executions.

Figure 3 shows the simulation module and its connection to the ASKALON services in detail. The most interesting part of this architecture is the modular structure leading to a new encapsulated simulation package and several

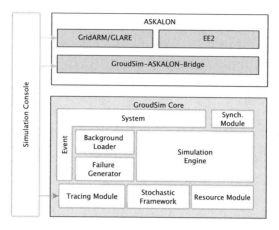

Fig. 3. GroudSim core and adapted ASKALON services

additional adaptors for transferring relevant data streams to the simulator. This results in minimal changes to the ASKALON source code and minimises the side effects to the regular execution mode. The GroudSim core and the GroudSim-ASKALON-Bridge (GAB) are the new components of the system, which are tightly coupled to enable a fast and scalable simulation. The interfaces between the GAB and the adaptor functionality in ASKALON are realised using the Singleton pattern. As the enactment engine and the simulation module are running in the same Java Virtual Machine, Singleton-objects can be accessed by both of them. Furthermore, this allows the usage of reflection mechanisms to avoid creating hard dependencies between the different software modules, especially when using the non-simulation mode. On the left hand side of Figure 3, the simulation console monitors and configures the properties of the simulation environment. As all components to be monitored are executed within a Globus [13] container, the information processed by the simulation console has to be transferred via SOAP messages.

The architecture of the GroudSim core consists of several modules depicted in the bottom of Figure 3, which collaborate internally and act as interfaces to communicate with the GAB. The two central parts of the simulation framework are: (1) the *event system* stores information about what events should happen and when they should happen and (2) the *simulation engine* is responsible to let the events happen at well-defined moments in time. Events can simulate job executions, file transfers, availability of resources (including failures), and background load. The other components of the GroudSim Core are:

Resource module that manages the simulated resources and communicates them to GridARM/GLARE;

Synchronisation module which allows synchronisation of the simulation time and the time used by the execution engine. When the EE2 is generating new tasks and submits them to the simulator, the simulator must wait until all current tasks are submitted before the simulation time can be advanced;

Background loader adds additional load to the resources if necessary wither by using traces from the Grid workload archive [8] or synthetic distribution functions;

Failure generator which handles the failure rates for jobs, file transfers and resources following stochastic distributions;

Stochastic framework that offers different stochastic distribution functions, which can be used for calculating queuing times, submission times, execution times, failure rates or background loads.

Tracing module which is used to store the simulated execution events to a file for analysis or debugging.

4 Evaluation

We evaluated the integration of the GroudSim simulator into ASKALON by first testing it with a synthetic workflow consisting of a *parallel for* loop with different number of iterations. The simulation was set up to show the possible extreme cases of executions with a minimum and maximum number of messages exchanged between the EE2 and the simulator. The evaluation continues with comparison of real workflow executions with simulated ones, conducted to match as close as possible the original executions but within a much shorter period of time. The simulations were executed on a Dual-core Opteron processor with 2.6 gigahertz running Java 1.5 and Linux.

4.1 Simulation Times

GroudSim has a module to measure execution times, installed as a listener to the enactment engine's workflow status events. The times measured in the ASKALON and simulation modules running in the Globus container can be split into three time phases:

ASKALON: The time which can be uniquely assigned to the ASKALON services. This includes the time consumed by the enactment engine, the workflow processing and scheduling, as well as its calls to the GridARM and GLARE services.

GroudSim: The time spent in the simulation of the hardware and the task execution, including the time spent on processing events. These events are responsible for staring, stoping, or failing tasks and resources and for controlling when the simulator has to pause and give the control back to ASKALON.

Synchronisation: This time is needed for synchronisation, which is necessary for a correct simulation. In the real world, a Grid site can start executing a job as soon as it is submitted. Due to synchronisation, the simulation has to be paused until all work that can be scheduled just-in-time is injected into the simulation, otherwise the time would be advanced too early and jobs would reach the simulator at the wrong point of time. Without this synchronisation, the simulation would start running as soon as a job is submitted to the simulator. This would not simulate a parallel execution, as the simulation of

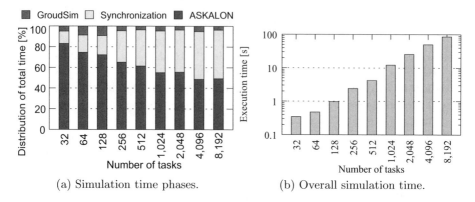

(a) Simulation time phases.   (b) Overall simulation time.

Fig. 4. Performance results for a sequential Grid site

the first job is already finished before the enactment engine can submit the next job, which might be executable in parallel. This time phase therefore represents the execution time of ASKALON when the simulator has work to perform, but it is not allowed to.

4.2 Sequential Grid Sites

The experiments shown in Figure 4 were run on a simulated Grid site with one CPU. The intention of this experiment is to analyse the performance of ASKALON's services and its simulation overhead for sequential execution of a workflow. This test shows the worst possible case for the simulation integration, as for each job a synchronisation of the engine and of the simulator is needed. The simulator never has more than a few events to process and works therefore rather inefficient. The experiments were run for 32 to 8,192 iterations of the parallel loop, which implies the simulation of up to 8,192 tasks and the same number of context switches between the enactment engine and the simulation module.

Figure 4a shows that ASKALON uses the dominant part of the overall execution time. With increasing number of executed tasks, the share stabilizes to 50% while GroudSim uses less then 10%. The other big part is spent doing synchronisation, which would not be needed for this special scenario as jobs are executed sequentially and the simulator could immediately start each job request it receives. This sequential scenario is untypical for execution of workflows and was therefore not optimised allowing this overhead analysis. The evaluation of this experiment shows the linear increase in execution time proving the scalability of the simulation for this special case of sequential execution (see Figure 4b).

4.3 Parallel Grid Sites

The setup for the second experiment series assumes a sufficient number of CPUs in the Grid to execute the workflow with maximum parallelism. This allows

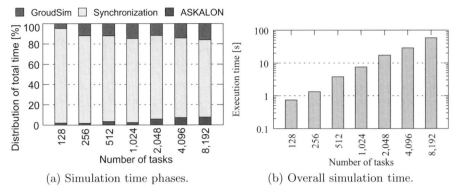

(a) Simulation time phases.   (b) Overall simulation time.

Fig. 5. Performance results for a parallel Grid site

the execution engine to submit all jobs of a parallel for loop to the simulator
before the simulation starts. Therefore, the number of synchronisations between
the engine and the simulator is minimum for this setup. The experiments were
repeated between 128 and 8,192 iterations of the parallel loop, which implies the
simulation of up to 8,192 tasks and a static number of two switches between the
enactment engine and the simulation module.

Figure 5a shows the time spent in the different simulation phases. The huge
amount of synchronisation is due the large amount of parallel tasks. When the
first task is submitted for execution, the simulation could start, but needs to
wait for the EE2 to finish submitting the current batch of submittable jobs.
In this experimental setup, the synchronisation time is hiding most of the time
used by ASKALON. The GroudSim time, on the other hand, stays below 20%
for all workflow sizes. The execution time displayed in Figure 5b shows again a
linear increase. Overall, the execution times for this scenario are faster than the
previous ones as less context switches are needed for the simulations.

4.4   Simulation versus Execution

The previous simulation experiments have shown that it is possible to use the
combination of ASKALON and GroudSim in a scalable way for two simple parallel workflows and different resources. To verify the correctness of the simulation
environment, we executed a real-world workflow called Montage with 649 activities in the Austrian Grid and a private Cloud-based on the Eucalyptus middleware and hardware that has a performance similar to Amazon EC2 *c1.medium*
instances, and compared the real execution trace with the simulated one.

Figure 6 shows Gantt charts of the real and simulated executions of a subset of the Montage workflows containing 27 activities (for readability reasons)
generated using the ASKALON monitoring tool. The real execution took 1,180
seconds (about 20 minutes), while the workflow simulation needed four seconds
to simulate the same execution and had a simulated runtime of 1,290 seconds
(21.5 minutes). The experiment shows that the scheduling and the execution
of the simulated workflow is comparable with the real execution. The runtime

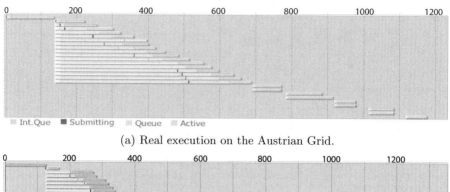

(a) Real execution on the Austrian Grid.

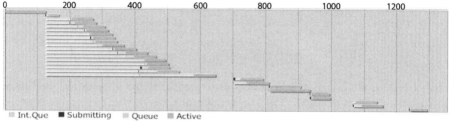

(b) Simulated execution.

Fig. 6. Comparison of a Montage workflow execution and simulation

Table 1. Run-times of all executed workflows and their simulated executions

Workflow name	Number of runs	Total number of activities	Average activities per run	Real execution time [hours]	Simulation time [min.]
Blender	432	131,501	305	41.20	17.2
LinMod	62	100,042	1,620	24.89	12.1
Montage	158	359,946	2,300	78.40	58.5
PovRay	182	78,402	430	1,156.98	9.4
WIEN2k	673	207,256	310	108.21	29.3
Total	1,507	877,293	580	1,409.68	126.0

difference of 110 seconds is due the inaccuracies of the prediction service used for deciding the activity and file transfer execution times used in the simulation, whose inaccuracy is within a 10% range.

The real workflows executed using the ASKALON environment last several hours in most cases. Many of these executions are synthetic runs for tuning the middleware and the underlying methods, which could be significantly improved if simulation would replace all expensive executions done on real hardware. Table 1 provides a summary of the execution of several workflow applications submitted to the Austrian Grid using ASKALON. A submission of about 900,000 activities to GroudSim leads to a simulation duration of 20 seconds when a simple simulation is run without any other overheads, i.e. scheduling and resource management. Executing the same amount of workflows and activities using ASKALON and simulating their execution has a higher duration of about two hours. The major part of the execution is consumed in the EE2 and its communication with the other services, and only a marginal part of this execution (30 seconds) represents simulation overhead. As the simulator does not get all activities of a workflow execution simultaneously as it has to execute them in the order given by the workflow and wait for EE2 and the scheduler, it cannot reach its peak performance and requires 50% longer than when using synthetic jobs.

As all workflows executed were different and of many different sizes, we approximate the simulation workflow size for our evaluation matching the average number of activities per workflow, as listed in Table 1. Analysing the sum of all executions leads to an total average of 580 processed activities per executed workflow and 310 to 2,300 activities for the individual workflows. Simulation of these executions took 2.5 to 19 seconds leading to an overall simulation runtime of 126 minutes for the complete set of workflows (more than 1,500 workflow runs). This results in a speedup of about 700 compared to the real execution on the Grid and Cloud, which took more than 1,400 hours (58 days). The presented approach can therefore significantly reduce the time to validate new research ideas in the area of scheduling or resource provisioning and it closes the gap of developing simulation scenarios which are normally evaluated and, if successful, ported to the real system.

5   Related Work

GridSim [14] is a simulation toolkit for resource modeling and application scheduling for Grid computing. It uses SimJava [9], a process-based discrete event simulation package, as its underlying simulation framework. As it runs a separate thread for each entity in the system it has a poor runtime performance compared to GroudSim [10]. Evaluation results show that the toolkit suffers from memory limitations when simulating more than 2,000 Grid sites concurrently on a certain machine. CloudSim [2] is an extension of GridSim for modeling and simulating Cloud infrastructures and shows the same scalability problems.

SimGrid [4] is a framework that provides the core functionality for the simulation of distributed applications to evaluate peer-to-peer algorithms and other heuristics on Cluster and Grid environments. SimGrid's approach is comparable to the one used in GroudSim, but uses C instead of Java as the main development language, which does not allow a simple and effective integration into the ASKALON project written in Java. Moreover, SimGrid does not address the simulation of Cloud infrastructures.

GridFlow [3] is an agent-based Grid middleware that supports execution and simulation of workflows which has important limitations compared to our approach. GridFlow simulates a workflow before it is executed to estimate the schedule time and it has no support for Cloud resources or modification of the scheduling scenarios as the environment parameters are used. Our approach allows to read the system state from an information service (like the Monitoring and Directory Service) to provide similar scenarios and to customize the resource set using a graphical user interface.

The simulation framework presented in [7] is used for trace-based simulations, does not support Cloud environments, and is not related to a real execution framework. The framework provides no easy possibility to prove the correctness of the simulations results, as opposed to our approach.

There are many more Grid-related simulation frameworks like OptorSim [1], CasSim [15] and GangSim [5] which are more specialized than our generic approach which covers a broader range of possible simulation scenarios including Clouds and real executions.

6   Conclusion

Scientific workflows often have execution times of multiple hours, days or even mounth, even when using a large number of cores from several Grid and Cloud systems. Simulation of these executions, which is decoupled from the execution system itself, is a common technique to allow an easier and faster application development and optimisation of the target middleware system. With the integration of a simulation framework into an existing development and execution environment, we close the gap between synthetic simulations and real executions. The presented combination of a scalable simulation framework with a real-world scientific workflow environment is a novel approach helping at simplifying the research process of new scheduling and resource management mechanisms for Grid and Cloud computing through simulations complemented by real world executions. The user is faced with a single user interface and no longer needs to create a separate simulation environment for the targeted real application execution to evaluate new optimisation and tuning ideas.

Acknowledgement. This work is partially funded by the European Union under grant agreement number 261585/SHIWA Project and by the Austrian Standortagentur Tirol with the Project Raincloud.

References

1. Bell, W.H., Cameron, D.G., Millar, A.P., Capozza, L., Stockinger, K., Zini, F.: Optorsim: A Grid Simulator for Studying Dynamic Data Replication Strategies. Journal of High Performance Computing Applications 17(4), 403–416 (2003)
2. Calheiros, R.N., Ranjan, R., Rose, C.A.F.D., Buyya, R.: CloudSim: A Novel Framework for Modeling and Simulation of Cloud Computing Infrastructures and Services. Computing Research Repository abs/0903.2525 (2009)
3. Cao, J., Jarvis, S.A., Saini, S., Nudd, G.R.: GridFlow: Workflow Management for Grid Computing. In: IEEE/ACM International Symposium on Cluster, Cloud, and Grid Computing, pp. 198–205. IEEE Computer Society, Los Alamitos (2003)
4. Casanova, H.: Simgrid: A Toolkit for the Simulation of Application Scheduling. In: First IEEE International Symposium on Cluster Computing and the Grid, Brisbane, Australia, May 15-18, pp. 430–441. IEEE Computer Society, Los Alamitos (2001)
5. Dumitrescu, C., Foster, I.T.: GangSim: A simulator for Grid scheduling studies. In: 5th International Symposium on Cluster Computing and the Grid (CCGrid 2005), Cardiff, UK, May 9-12, pp. 1151–1158. IEEE Computer Society, Los Alamitos (2005)

6. Fahringer, T., Prodan, R., Duan, R., Nerieri, F., Podlipnig, S., Qin, J., Siddiqui, M., Truong, H.L., Villazón, A., Wieczorek, M.: ASKALON: A Grid application development and computing environment. In: Proceedings of 6th IEEE/ACM International Conference on Grid Computing (GRID 2005), Seattle, Washington, USA, November 13-14, pp. 122–131. IEEE, Los Alamitos (2005)
7. Hirales-Carbajal, A., Tchernykh, A., Röblitz, T., Yahyapour, R.: A Grid simulation framework to study advance scheduling strategies for complex workflow applications. In: Parallel & Distributed Processing, Workshops and Phd Forum (IPDPSW), pp. 1–8. IEEE, Los Alamitos (2010)
8. Iosup, A.: The Grid Workloads Archive. Future Generation Computer Systems 24(7), 672–686 (2008)
9. McNab, R., Howell, F.: Using Java for Discrete Event Simulation. In: Twelfth UK Computer and Telecommunications Performance Engineering Workshop (UKPEW), pp. 219–228. Univ. of Edinburgh, Edinburgh (1996)
10. Ostermann, S., Plankensteiner, K., Prodan, R., Fahringer, T.: GroudSim: An Event-based Simulation Framework for Computational Grids and Clouds. In: CoreGRID/ERCIM Workshop on Grids and Clouds. Springer Computer Science Editorial, Ischia (2010)
11. Ostermann, S., Prodan, R., Fahringer, T.: Extended Grids with Cloud Resource Management for Scientific Computing. In: Grid 2009: IEEE/ACM International Conference on Grid Computing, pp. 42–59 (October 2009)
12. Ostermann, S., Prodan, R., Fahringer, T.: Dynamic Cloud Provisioning for Scientific Grid Workflows. In: The 11th ACM/IEEE International Conference on Grid Computing (Grid 2010), pp. 97–104 (October 2010)
13. Sotomayor, B., Childers, L.: Globus Toolkit 4 Programming Java Services. Morgan Kaufman, San Francisco (2006)
14. Sulistio, A., Cibej, U., Venugopal, S., Robic, B., Buyya, R.: A toolkit for modelling and simulating data Grids: an extension to GridSim. Concurrency and Computation: Practice and Experience 20(13), 1591–1609 (2008)
15. Xia, E., Jurisica, I., Waterhouse, J.: CasSim: A top-level-simulator for Grid scheduling and applications. In: Erdogmus, H., Stroulia, E., Stewart, D.A. (eds.) CASCON, pp. 353–356. IBM (2006)

Large-Scale Multidimensional Data Visualization: A Web Service for Data Mining

Gintautas Dzemyda, Virginijus Marcinkevičius, and Viktor Medvedev

Vilnius University, Institute of Mathematics and Informatics,
Akademijos str. 4, LT-08663 Vilnius, Lithuania
{Gintautas.Dzemyda,Virginijus.Marcinkevicius,
Viktor.Medvedev}@mii.vu.lt

Abstract. In this paper, we present an approach of the Web application (as a service) for data mining oriented to the multidimensional data visualization. The stress is put on visualization methods as a tool for the visual presentation of large-scale multidimensional data sets. The proposed implementation includes five visualization methods: MDS SMACOF algorithm, Relative MDS, Diagonal majorization algorithm, Relational perspective map, SAMANN. A cluster for parallel computation is used by Web service for the visual data mining. The service is of free access to the user community for data visualization.

Keywords: Web Service, Large-Scale Multidimensional Data, Visualization, Data Mining, Parallel Computing.

1 Introduction

Interaction between humans and machines is one of the areas in computer science that has evolved a lot the last years. Progresses and innovations are mainly due to increases in computer power and technology of interactive software. It is also the result of new ways of considering the interaction with computers and the role of computers in everyday life. Real data of natural and social sciences are often high-dimensional ([1], [2]). It is very difficult to understand these data and extract patterns. One way for such understanding is to make visual insight into the analyzed data set ([3], [4]). To analyze multidimensional data we often use one of the main instruments of data analysis – data visualization or graphical presentation of information. The fundamental idea of visualization is to provide data in the form that would let the user to understand the data, to draw conclusions, and to influence directly a further process of decision making. Data visualization is closely related to dimensionality reduction methods that allow discarding interdependent data parameters, and by means of projection methods it is possible to transform multidimensional data to a line, plane, 3D space or other form that may be comprehended by a human eye.

Objects from the real world are frequently described by an array of parameters (variables) $x_1, x_2, ..., x_n$. Any parameter may take some numerical values. Let us have m points $X^i = (x_1^i, x_2^i, ..., x_n^i)$, $i = 1, ..., m$ ($X^i \in R^n$). Denote the whole analyzed data

W. Abramowicz et al. (Eds.): ServiceWave 2011, LNCS 6994, pp. 14–25, 2011.
© Springer-Verlag Berlin Heidelberg 2011

set by $X = \{X^1,...,X^m\}$. The pending problem is to get the projection (or visualization) of these n-dimensional points X^i, $i = 1,...,m$ onto the plane R^2. Two-dimensional points $Y^1, Y^2,...,Y^m \in R^2$ correspond to them. Here $Y^i = (y_1^i, y_2^i)$, $i = 1,...,m$. In Fig. 1, we present an example of visual presentation of the data table (initial dimensionality n=6) using Multidimensional scaling method [3]. The dimensionality of data is reduced from 6 to 2. Here points X^4, X^6, X^8, X^{19} form a separate cluster that can be clearly observed visually on a plane and that cannot be recognized directly from the table without a special analysis. It is much easier for a human to observe, detect, or extract some information from the graphical representation of these data (to detect the presence of clusters, outliers or various regularities in the analysed data) than from the raw number. Therefore, the goal of the projection methods is to represent the input data items in a lower-dimensional space so that certain properties of the structure of the data set were preserved as faithfully as possible ([5], [6]). The projection can be used to visualize the data set if a sufficiently small output dimensionality is chosen [3].

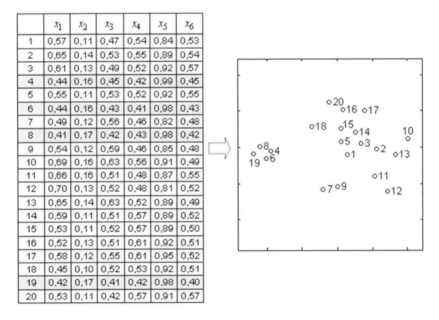

	x_1	x_2	x_3	x_4	x_5	x_6
1	0,57	0,11	0,47	0,54	0,84	0,53
2	0,65	0,14	0,53	0,55	0,89	0,54
3	0,61	0,13	0,49	0,52	0,92	0,57
4	0,44	0,16	0,45	0,42	0,99	0,45
5	0,55	0,11	0,53	0,52	0,92	0,55
6	0,44	0,16	0,43	0,41	0,98	0,43
7	0,49	0,12	0,56	0,46	0,82	0,48
8	0,41	0,17	0,42	0,43	0,98	0,42
9	0,54	0,12	0,59	0,46	0,85	0,48
10	0,69	0,16	0,63	0,56	0,91	0,49
11	0,66	0,16	0,51	0,48	0,87	0,55
12	0,70	0,13	0,52	0,48	0,81	0,52
13	0,65	0,14	0,63	0,52	0,89	0,49
14	0,59	0,11	0,51	0,57	0,89	0,52
15	0,53	0,11	0,52	0,57	0,89	0,50
16	0,52	0,13	0,51	0,61	0,92	0,51
17	0,58	0,12	0,55	0,61	0,95	0,52
18	0,45	0,10	0,52	0,53	0,92	0,51
19	0,42	0,17	0,41	0,42	0,98	0,40
20	0,53	0,11	0,42	0,57	0,91	0,57

Fig. 1. Visual presentation of the multidimensional data

Visualization of a large-scale multidimensional data can be combined with new ways of interacting with a computer using Web service. It leads to the study of the visualization process and to the development of new computing architectures and software tools for the visual display and exploration of such data. Web services are typically application programming interfaces that are accessed via Hypertext Transfer Protocol and executed on a remote system hosting the requested services.

Web services are self-contained, self-describing modular applications that can be published, located, and invoked across the Web ([7], [8]). Web services refer to a set of software applications or components developed using a specific set of application programming interface standards and Internet-based communication protocols. The objective is to enable these applications or components to invoke function calls and exchange data among themselves over the standard Internet infrastructure. Web services provide a standard means of interoperating between different software applications, running on a variety of platforms and/or frameworks. The Web services architecture is an interoperability architecture: it identifies those global elements of the global network that are required in order to ensure interoperability between Web services. By integrating new powerful technologies into multidimensional data visualization systems, we can get higher performance results with additional functionalities. The basic idea behind Web services is that a specific functionality of software running on one machine of an enterprise is accessible to another machine running at another enterprise using specific protocols over the Internet. Providing seamless access to systems functionality without downloading the software is the main concept behind Web services.

In this paper, we focus on the idea of the Web application which provides multidimensional data visualization functionality. We try to combine the well-known visualization methods with modern computing possibilities including Web-based architectures and parallel computing.

2 Background of the Web-Based Service for Visualization

Nowadays, computer systems store large amounts of data. Due to the lack of abilities to explore adequately the large amounts of collected data, even potentially valuable data becomes useless and the data of databases dumps. Visual data exploration, which aims at providing an insight by visualizing the data and information visualization techniques, can help to solve this problem. A human being can comprehend visual information easier and more quickly than the numerical one. Data visualization allows people to detect the presence of clusters, outliers or regularities in the analyzed data.

Several systems are proposed that provide web-based distributed visualization methods, e.g., Weka4ws (http://grid.deis.unical.it/weka4ws/), Faehim (http://users. cs.cf.ac.uk/Ali.Shaikhali/faehim). These systems are rather powerful and include different data mining techniques. However, these systems require a specific knowledge and need to be installed on user's PC. The work with these systems is rather complicated, especially if we want to get a visualization of the data set analyzed without installing specific software and using only the Internet. In our approach, the access to the visualization service is possible from any location with internet connectivity independently of the used platform. The computational work is done using a high-performance parallel cluster, with only user's interaction with the client (without downloading and installing the system).

The Web application for multidimensional data visualization provides a web-based access to several visual data mining methods of different nature and complexity that, in general, allows a visual discovery of patterns and their interpretation in multidimensional data. The developed software tool allows users to analyze and visualize large-scale multidimensional data sets on the Internet, regardless of time or location, as well as to optimize the parameters of visualization algorithms for better perception of the multidimensional data.

To achieve a high performance in large-scale multidimensional data visualization, the parallel computing has to be exploited. Parallel applications, including scientific ones, are now widely executed on clusters and grids. For the large-scale multidimensional data visualization, a high-performance parallel cluster has been used in our implementation. The cluster differs from the network of workstations in security, application software, administration, and file systems. The important feature of the cluster is that it may be upgraded or expanded without any essential reconstructions.

The proposed Web application simplifies the usage of five visualization methods and makes them wide-accessible: MDS SMACOF algorithm [3] – a version of Multi-dimensional scaling (MDS), Relative MDS [9], Diagonal majorization algorithm [10], Relational perspective map (RPM) ([11], [12]), SAMANN ([5], [13]). The Web application is evolving from its first version [14] by extending functionality and capabilities.

3   Visualization Methods

We use nonlinear dimensionality reduction methods as a tool for visualization large-scale multidimensional data sets. Several approaches have been proposed for reproducing nonlinear higher-dimensional structures on a lower-dimensional display. The most common methods allocate a representation of each data point in a lower-dimensional space and try to optimize these representations so that the distances between them are as similar as possible to the original distances of the corresponding data items. The methods differ in that how the representations are optimized.

Multidimensional scaling (MDS) [3] refers to a group of methods that is widely used. The starting point of MDS is a matrix consisting of pair wise dissimilarities of the entities. In general, the dissimilarities need not be distances in the mathematically strict sense. There exists a multitude of variants of MDS with slightly different cost functions and optimization algorithms.

The goal of projection in the metric MDS is to optimize the projection so that the distances between the items in the lower-dimensional space would be as close to the original distances as possible.

Denote the distance between the points X^i and X^j by d_{ij}^*, and the distance between the corresponding points in the projected space (Y^i and Y^j) by d_{ij}. In our case, the initial dimensionality is n, and the resulting one is 2. An objective function (stress) to be minimized can be written as

$$E_{MDS} = \sum_{\substack{i,j=1 \\ i<j}}^{m} w_{ij}(d_{ij}^* - d_{ij}).$$

(1)

Usually weights w_{ij} are used as follows:

$$w_{ij} = \frac{1}{\displaystyle\sum_{\substack{k,l=1 \\ k<l}}^{m}(d_{kl}^*)^2} , \quad w_{ij} = \frac{1}{d_{ij}^* \displaystyle\sum_{\substack{k,l=1 \\ k<l}}^{m}(d_{kl}^*)^2} , \quad w_{ij} = \frac{1}{md_{ij}^*}.$$

The weight may be chosen depending on the visualization goals. For example, the second weight is used when we focus on small distances in original space R^n.

Various types of minimization of (1) are possible ([3], [15]): a Gradient Descent, SMACOF (Scaling by MAjorization a Complicated Function) [3], Conjugate Gradient, Quasi-Newton Method, Simulated Annealing, Combination of Genetic Algorithm and Quasi-Newton's Descent Algorithm [15].

The problems with the classical MDS algorithm are faced when we have to visualize a large data set or a new data point needs to be projected. In the standard MDS, each point needs to be compared with all other points (in each iteration). Thus, the MDS method is unsuitable for large datasets: it takes much computing time or there is not enough computing memory. Various modifications of MDS have been proposed for visualization of large datasets: Steerable multidimensional scaling (MDSteer) [16], Incremental MDS, Relative MDS [9], Landmark MDS [17], Diagonal majorization algorithm (DMA) [10] and etc. In the Web application proposed, the metric Multidimensional Scaling SMACOF algorithm has been used.

The MDS algorithm does not offer a possibility to project new points on the existing set of mapped points. To get a mapping that presents the previously mapped points together with the new ones requires a complete re-run of the MDS algorithm on the new and the old data points. The main idea of the Relative MDS method [9] (which can be easily used for visualizing new points) is to take a subset of the initial multidimensional data set (basic data set) and then map the basic data set, using the MDS. As a second step, the remaining points of initial data are added to the basis layout using the relative mapping.

Various types of minimization of the stress function (1) are possible. It is possible to use the Guttman majorization algorithm based on iterative majorization and its modification so called diagonal majorization algorithm. Guttman majorization algorithm is one of the best optimisation algorithms for this type of minimization problem ([3], [18]).

Diagonal majorization algorithm (DMA) was proposed in [10]. DMA attains slightly worse projection error than Guttman majorization algorithm, but computing is faster. Iterative computations of two-dimensional coordinates $Y^i = (y_1^i, y_2^i), i = 1,...,m$ are based not on all distances d_{ij}^* between multidimensional points X^i and X^j. This allows us to significantly speed up the visualization process and to save the computer memory essentially.

The relational perspective map (RPM) method ([11], [12]) visualizes multidimensional data onto the closed plane (torus surface) so that the distances between data in the lower-dimensional space would be as close as possible to the original distances. The RPM method also gives the ability to visualize data in a non-overlapping manner so that it reveals small distances better than other known visualization methods.

The combination and integrated use of data visualization methods of a different nature are under a rapid development. The combination of different methods can be applied to make a data analysis, while minimizing the shortcomings of individual methods. The MDS got some attention from neural network researchers ([13], [19]). A feed-forward neural network is utilised to effect a topographic, structure-preserving, dimension-reducing transformation of the data, with an additional facility to incorporate different degrees of associated subjective information. A specific backpropagation-like learning rule (SAMANN) has been developed to allow a normal feed-forward artificial neural network to learn Sammon's mapping in an unsupervised way ([5], [13], [20]). The network is able to project new multidimensional points after training. The architecture of the SAMANN network is a multilayer perceptron where the number of input vectors is set to be the input space dimension, n, and the number of output vectors is specified as the projected space dimension.

The analyzed visualization algorithms are iterative or partially iterative which means that parallelization of these algorithms is not effective because of the expensive costs of data transmition between the processors of a parallel computing cluster in these algorithms. It was suggested to use a sequential version of algorithms and to apply MPI (Message Passing Interface) technology in order to make possible the usage of multiple processors of the cluster. Each processor runs the algorithm from a different starting position.

4   Web Service for Multidimensional Data Visualization

The Web service architecture ([21], [22]) for multidimensional data visualization is a three-layer model (Fig. 2): Client Interface, Web service Middleware and Data Visualization Component. The Client Interface and Data Visualization Component layers are the main parts of the system.

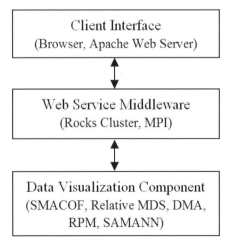

Fig. 2. The Web service architecture

The Client Interface provides a way to define the processing routine for the given data in order to manage the visualization process. The client is responsible for the presentation of the data set to be visualized. Data Visualization Service is responsible to process data according to the created processing routine.

The Data Visualization Component layer contains the algorithms meant for multidimensional data visual presentation. Since the visualization typically involves large-scale data sets, the efficiency saving can be extremely important. A computational cluster has been provided as the hardware system meant for performing visualization processes. In our case it is possible to run parallel visualization components that communicate through MPI. MPI is a significant component of the programming and execution application on clusters.

The analyzed visualization methods are based on iterative algorithms whose parallel versions are not effective. Using a cluster we can run the algorithms simultaneously on different computers from different random starting solutions. In this paper, we suggest to use the design and implementation of the Web Service Middleware that connects the Client Interface and the Data Visualization Component running on a computational cluster. The Web Service Middleware structure is presented in Fig. 3. It includes Frontend Node (Server) and the local computer network controlled by the Frontend Node. In our realization, the function of the local computer network is allocated to the computer cluster (for parallel computations). Such architecture gives us an opportunity to solve large-scale data visualization problems, where a client does not care for computational resources and their proper usage.

At first, a client sends the data to the Data Visualization Component. In our case, five methods are included for visualizing multidimensional data: MDS (SMACOF algorithm), Relative MDS, DMA, RPM and SAMANN. These methods have been chosen for testing the architecture. Relative MDS, DMA and SAMANN are designated to visualize large-scale multidimensional data. In future, the set of options for visualization would be extended.

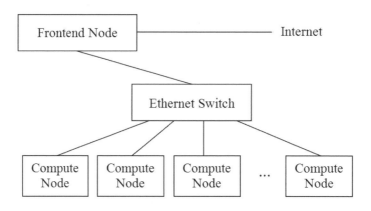

Fig. 3. The Web Service Middleware structure

In the Client Interface (Fig. 4), it is possible to choose (and to change) such parameters:

— Number of processors (in our realization we can use 1–16 processors);
— Maximum number of iterations;
— Method for a multidimensional data visualization (MDS SMACOF algorithm, Relative MDS, DMA, RPM, SAMANN);
— Strategies of forming and initializing the set of basis points (on the line, random, maximal dispersion, principal component analysis);
— Maximal computing time (sometimes it is important to fix the computing time working with a large data sets);
— Upload the client's dataset for visualization (a text file containing table of real numbers – m rows and n columns);
— Maximal number of visualization cycles (the current problem may be solved several times with different initial data and the best result is presented to the client).

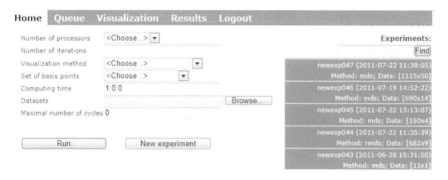

Fig. 4. Client interface: visualization methods and settings

In the Client Interface (Fig. 5), user also can check the status of his task.

Fig. 6 demonstrates the visualization results. User can get a more information about the analyzed dataset:

• Distribution of the projection error on the basic of the fixed number of experiments. We can see the data set projection error distribution and its changes with an increase in the number of iterations of the projection algorithm.
• Dependence of the projection error on the iteration number. In the exploration of projection error distribution, it is important to see the error distribution boundaries when the number of iterations increases.
• Dependence of the computing time on the iteration number.

Home	Queue	Visualization	Results	Logout

job-ID	prior	name	user	state	submit/start at	queue	slots	ja-task-ID
20251	0.60500	experiment	Regimantas	r	07/14/2011 11:23:56	all.q@compute-0-0.local	16	
20247	0.50500	experiment	Regimantas	qw	07/14/2011 11:23:31		8	
20248	0.50500	experiment	Regimantas	qw	07/14/2011 11:23:31		8	
20249	0.50500	experiment	Regimantas	qw	07/14/2011 11:23:31		8	
20250	0.50500	experiment	Regimantas	qw	07/14/2011 11:23:31		8	
20252	0.00000	experiment	Regimantas	qw	07/14/2011 11:23:57		16	
20253	0.00000	experiment	Regimantas	qw	07/14/2011 11:23:59		16	

Fig. 5. Client interface: a status of the tasks (visualization process)

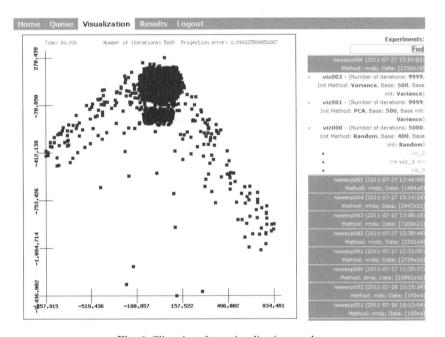

Fig. 6. Client interface: visualization results

More experiments (see Figures 7–8) are carried out with the following two data sets:

— Ellipsoid dataset (20 50-dimensional spheres) [23], where $m=1115$, $n=50$ which contains 20 clusters. The dataset have been visualized using MDS SMACOF algorithm (Fig. 7);
— Thyroid Disease dataset [24], where $m=7200$, $n=21$. The dataset have been visualized using Relative MDS using 10% of the basis points (Fig. 8).

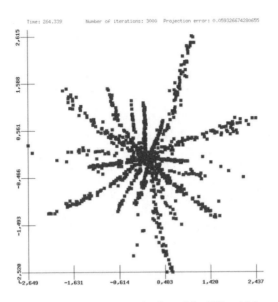

Fig. 7. Visualization result: projection of the Ellipsoid dataset

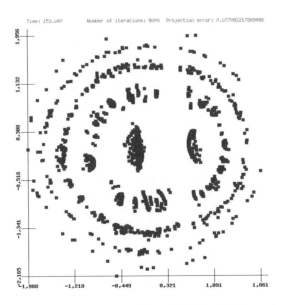

Fig. 8. Visualization result: projection of the Thyroid Disease dataset

5 Conclusions

In this paper, an approach and architecture have been proposed for visualization of large-scale multidimensional data, using Web service technologies. This should extend the practical application of multidimensional data analysis and, particularly, visualization techniques.

The paper focuses on visualization methods as a service for the visual pattern recognition in large-scale multidimensional datasets. The proposed service simplifies the usage of visualization methods that are often very sophisticated and include a lot of the know-how of their developers. In our case, five methods for the multidimensional data visualization are included: MDS (SMACOF algorithm), Relative MDS, DMA, RPM and SAMANN. These methods have been chosen for testing the architecture and approach. In future, the set of options for visualization should be extended. For example, recently new directions in multidimensional data visualization became popular and find applications: various architectures of neural networks ([4], [5]) and nonlinear manifold learning methods [25]. The service is of free access to the user community for data visualization.

Depending on the data set and visualization methods the computations may take the sufficiently large amount of time. The advantage of the service is that the user may not wait for the visualization results online. When computations are completed, the user can download the results at any time he wants.

The main advantage of the proposed approach is that it stimulates the visual data mining and pattern recognition in large-scale multidimensional datasets. It may be integrated into some service oriented architecture environment that enables dynamic, interconnected business processes, and delivers highly effective application infrastructures for all business situations, e.g. using WebSphere [26] software.

References

1. Bernatavičienė, J., Dzemyda, G., Kurasova, O., Marcinkevičius, V., Medvedev, V.: The Problem of Visual Analysis of Multidimensional Medical Data. In: Torn, A., Žilinskas, J. (eds.) Models and Algorithms for Global Optimization. Optimization and Its Applications, vol. 4, pp. 277–298. Springer, Heidelberg (2007)
2. Dzemyda, G.: Visualization of a Set of Parameters Characterized by Their Correlation Matrix. Computational Statistics and Data Analysis 36(10), 15–30 (2001)
3. Borg, I., Groenen, P.: Modern Multidimensional Scaling: Theory and Applications. Springer, Heidelberg (2005)
4. Kohonen, T.: Self-Organizing Maps, 3rd edn. Springer Series in Information Science. Springer, Heidelberg (2001)
5. Dzemyda, G., Kurasova, O., Medvedev, V.: Dimension Reduction and Data Visualization Using Neural Networks. In: Maglogiannis, I., Karpouzis, K., Wallace, M., Soldatos, J. (eds.) Emerging Artificial Intelligence Applications in Computer Engineering - Real Word AI Systems with Applications in eHealth, HCI, Information Retrieval and Pervasive Technologies. Frontiers in Artificial Intelligence and Applications, vol. 160, pp. 25–49. IOS Press, Amsterdam (2007)
6. Dzemyda, G., Sakalauskas, L.: Large-Scale Data Analysis Using Heuristic Methods. Informatica 22(1), 1–10 (2011)

7. Khan, K.M.: Managing Web Service Quality: Measuring Outcomes and Effectiveness. Information Science Reference (2008)
8. Booth, D., Haas, H., McCabe, F., Newcomer, E., Champion, M., Ferris, C., Orchard, D.: Web Service Architecture. W3C Working Group Note (2004), http://www.w3c.org/TR/ws-arch
9. Naud, A., Duch, W.: Interactive Data Exploration Using MDS Mapping. In: Proceedings of the Fifth Conference: Neural Networks and Soft Computing, pp. 255–260 (2000)
10. Trosset, M.W., Groenen, P.J.F.: Multidimensional Scaling Algorithms for Large Data Sets. Computing Science and Statistics, CD-ROM (2005)
11. Xinzhi, J.L.: Visualization of High Dimensional Data with Relational Perspective Map. Information Visualization 3(1), 49–59 (2004)
12. Karbauskaitė, R., Marcinkevičius, V., Dzemyda, G.: Testing the Relational Perspective Map for Visualization of Multidimensional Data. Technological and Economic Development of Economy 12(4), 289–294 (2006)
13. Mao, J., Jain, A.K.: Artificial Neural Networks for Feature Extraction and Multivariate Data Projection. IEEE Trans. Neural Networks 6, 296–317 (1995)
14. Dzemyda, G., Marcinkevičius, V., Medvedev, V.: Web Application for Large-Scale Multidimensional Data Visualization. Mathematical Modelling and Analysis 16(2), 273–285 (2011)
15. Mathar, R., Zilinskas, A.: On Global Optimization in Two-Dimensional Scaling. Acta Aplicandae Mathematicae 33, 109–118 (2001)
16. Williams, M., Munzner, T.: Steerable, Progressive Multidimensional Scaling. In: IEEE Symposium on Information Visualization, INFOVIS 2004, pp. 57–64 (2004)
17. de Silva, V., Tenenbaum, J.B.: Global Versus Local Methods for Nonlinear Dimensionality Reduction. In: Becker, S., Thrun, S., Obermayer, K. (eds.) Advances in Neural Information Processing Systems, vol. 15, pp. 721–728. MIT Press, Cambridge (2003)
18. Groenen, P.J.F., van de Vaelden, M.: Multidimensional Scaling, Econometric Institute Report EI2004-15 (2004)
19. van Wezel, M.C., Kosters, W.A.: Nonmetric Multidimensional Scaling: Neural networks Versus Traditional Techniques. Intelligent Data Analysis 8(6), 601–613 (2004)
20. de Ridder, D., Duin, R.P.W.: Sammon's Mapping Using Neural Networks: A comparison. Pattern Recognition Letters 18, 1307–1316 (1997)
21. Hagel, J.: Edging into Web services. The McKinsey Quarterly 4 (2002)
22. Hagel, J., Brown, J.S.: Your next IT strategy. Harvard Business Review 79(9), 105–115 (2001)
23. Handl, J., Knowles, J.: Cluster Generators for Large High-Dimensional Data Sets with Large Numbers of Clusters (2005), http://dbkgroup.org/handl/generators/
24. Frank, A., Asuncion, A.: UCI Machine Learning Repository. University of California, School of Information and Computer Science, Irvine, CA (2010), http://archive.ics.uci.edu/ml
25. Karbauskaite, R., Dzemyda, G.: Topology Preservation Measures in the Visualization of Manifold-type Multidimensional Data. Informatica 20(2), 235–254 (2009)
26. WebSphere. WebSphere Software, http://www-01.ibm.com/software/websphere

Blueprint Template Support for Engineering Cloud-Based Services*

Dinh Khoa Nguyen, Francesco Lelli, Yehia Taher, Michael Parkin,
Mike P. Papazoglou, and Willem-Jan van den Heuvel

European Research Institute in Service Science (ERISS)
Tilburg University, The Netherlands
{D.K.Nguyen,F.Lelli,Y.Taher,m.s.parkin,mikep,wjheuvel}@uvt.nl

Abstract. Current cloud-based service offerings are often provided as
one-size-fits-all solutions and give little or no room for customization.
This limits the ability for application developers to pick and choose offerings from multiple software, platform, infrastructure service providers
and configure them dynamically and in an optimal fashion to address
their application requirements. Furthermore, combining different independent cloud-based services necessitates a uniform description format
that facilitates their design, customization, and composition. Hence, there
is a need to break down the monolithic offerings into loosely-coupled
cloud services offered by multiple providers that can be flexibly customized and (re-)composed in different settings. We propose in this paper
the *Blueprint* concept - a uniform abstract description for cloud service
offerings that may cross different cloud computing layers, i.e. software,
platform and infrastructure. Using the proposed Blueprint Template for
engineering cloud service offerings will solve these shortcomings and subsequently lower the barrier to entry for cloud computing.

Keywords: Cloud Service Engineering, Uniform Design Template,
Blueprint for Cloud Computing, Interoperability and Portability.

1 Introduction

Recently, the field of *cloud computing*, where computational, infrastructure and
data resources are available on-demand from a remote source, has become hugely
popular. One of the reasons for its popularity is because cloud computing gives
the option to outsource the operation and maintenance of IT tasks, allowing
organizations and their employees to concentrate on their core competencies.

The US National Institute of Standards and Technology (NIST) defines three
delivery models for services in the cloud, or cloud services [1]: 1) Software-
as-a-Service (SaaS), 2) Platform-as-a-Service (PaaS), and 3) Infrastructure-as-
a-Service (IaaS). By combining different cross-layered, independent networked

---

* The research leading to this result has received funding from the Dutch Jacquard
program on Software Engineering Research via contract 638.001.206 SAPIENSA;
and the European Union's Seventh Framework Programme FP7/2007-2013 (4CaaSt)
under grant agreement n 258862.

W. Abramowicz et al. (Eds.): ServiceWave 2011, LNCS 6994, pp. 26–37, 2011.

cloud service offerings from one or more providers we can compose Service-Based Applications (SBAs) to perform a desired end-to-end function. Cloud services and SBAs are ideally matched since the flexibility of cloud computing provides the fabric through which SBAs can be constructed and deployed.

However, despite these advantages, there are a two main issues that need to be considered carefully when migrating (parts of) a SBA to 'the cloud'. The first problem concerns the issue of multi-tenancy of the cloud services used to compose a SBA; current cloud services are often provided as one-size-fits-all solutions and give little or no room for customization. For example, this well-known vendor lock-in issue prevents the customization of the cloud platform and infrastructure through which SaaS applications are provided and monolithic SaaS offerings are likely to be ineffective in meeting the business requirements of several consumers. Therefore, there is clearly a need to provide a more effective and flexible method for SBA developers to select, customize and aggregate cross-layered cloud services, i.e. software, platform and infrastructure services, offered by several providers in the cloud.

Secondly, creating SBAs in the cloud and integrating them with other cloud service offerings is a sophisticated task. When designing, deploying and operating a SBA across several cloud service providers, difficulties can arise due to the inconsistency of cloud resource descriptions and interfaces and the fact that proprietary technologies are an entry barrier, especially to Small-and-Medium Enterprises (SMEs), due to the lack of IT staff dedicated to cloud computing development and operations. Consequently, cloud computing remains largely within the domain of established players.

To allow the flexible design and deployment of customized SBAs in a timely manner, we envision a common foundation to address the way cloud services are designed, engineered and provided though the cloud. Our work revolves around the *Blueprint* concept - an abstract description of cloud service offerings that may cross different cloud computing abstraction layers, i.e. SaaS, PaaS and IaaS offerings. We believe that the barrier to entry for cloud computing can be lowered and SMEs-empowered through a common standardized *Blueprint Template* that provides a common structure, syntax and semantics for cloud service providers to abstractly (i.e., independent of implementation) and unambiguously describe their offerings on multiple abstraction layers. Such a template will allow a cloud service to be designed, engineered, and provided in a uniform way, and hence to be composed across several providers. Our ultimate aim with the proposed template is to provide a tool that supports the SBA developers to select, customize and compose various cross-layered cloud service offerings according to their application requirements, rather than just proposing 'yet another standard' for cloud computing.

The rest of this paper is structured as follows: Section 2 presents a scenario to be used as an example for defining the blueprint. In Section 3, we review the related work and describe how the lack of a uniform representation for cross-layered cloud services fails to meet the scenario's requirements. Section 4 proposes a blueprint template as the approach for developing cloud service offerings. Finally, Section 5 draws some conclusions and future issues.

2 Motivating Scenario

This section presents a simplified version of an enterprise computing scenario developed for the EC's 4CaaSt project[1]. As the scenario shows, it requires a uniform description for cloud service offerings to exist so the design, configuration, and deployment of a cloud-based SBA can occur. The scenario contains a number of information entities and we refer to a particular one using a Universally Unique IDentifier (UUID). As will be seen in Section 4, the UUIDs will be used for identifying particular information entities in our sample blueprints. The scenario in Figure 1 contains four actors, each of which is now described.

CE1 and **CE2** are two providers of an open source *composition engine*. The offering of CE1 (uuid=CE1-PaaS) is already a complete PaaS, i.e. the engine is hosted on an in-house JEE platform and Linux server, and connected to the outside through a 3Gbit Ethernet link. Furthermore, the engine supports the SOAP and REST protocols for Web Service communications, as well as SIP protocol for telecom interactions. The offering of CE2 (uuid=CE2-PaaS) has a similar configuration, except they use Windows server and their Ethernet is only 2Gbit. However, both these offerings are monolithic, since they are already preconfigured and no customization of the underlying resources is allowed.

The telecom service provider, **Tele1**, provides a basic *SMS Delivery SaaS* (uuid=SMS-Delivery-SaaS) through two alternative configurations. They provide a *binary artefact* written in Java (uuid=art-sms-delivery) and requires a *composition engine* for the deployment. Tele1 has set up business with both CE1 and CE2 by signing a contract to use both the CE1-PaaS and CE2-PaaS. Their system integrators are responsible for deploying the *art-sms-delivery* on one of these two external PaaS, depending on the customer selection.

AutoInc is an established SME and has spotted a business opportunity providing fleet vehicle management in the Netherlands. They plan to deploy their business functions as a *Vehicle Management (VM) SaaS* (uuid=VM-SaaS), since this provides ubiquitous and common access for their prospective customers, e.g., logistics companies and car-hiring providers. To implement the solution, AutoInc has contracted a software consultancy who wrote the vehicle management software in Java. The software requires a *JEE application server* (uuid=AutoInc-Req01) including a *Servlet v2.5 container* (uuid=AutoInc-Req02) for the web interface, and *2 instances* of *MySQL database* (uuid= AutoInc-Req03) for recording the vehicle's location together with its characteristics, such as to which company it belongs to, its type and capacity. The software hence contains 3 main artefacts: the *application core binary* (uuid= AutoInc-Art01) as a jar file and a *configuration file* (uuid=AutoInc-Art02) to be deployed on the prospective JEE application server, and a *configuration and setup file* (uuid=AutoInc-Art03) for the prospective MySQL database.

---

[1] EC's 7th Framework project 4caasT: http://4caast.morfeo-project.org/

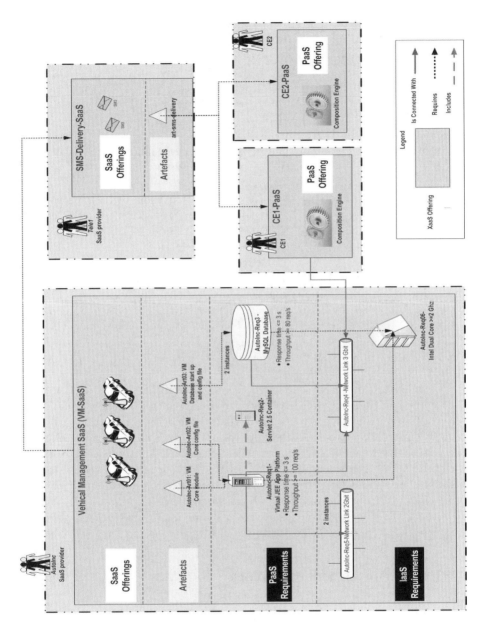

Fig. 1. Cloud Service Offerings Scenario

To maintain the predefined Quality of Service (QoS) level, AutoInc has also QoS requirements for the prospective platform's resource requirements. The JEE application server should ensure a *throughput ≥ 100 req/s* and a *response time ≤ 3s.* For the prospective MySQL DB, throughput requirement is relaxed to

$\geq$ *80req/s* while the response time requirement remains the same. AutoInc has also derived several infrastructure requirements for the machines hosting the platform resources and the connecting network links. It requires the prospective JEE Application server to be connected to the outside through *2 lines* of *2Gbit network link* (uuid=AutoInc-Req05), and with the MySQL database through a *3Gbit network link* (uuid=AutoInc-Req04). Both the JEE Application Server and the MySQL DB must be deployed on *Intel Dual core machine with the processor $\geq$ 2Ghz* (uuid=AutoInc-Req06).

AutoInc also has some invariant constraints prescribing that the whole end-to-end system must have *throughput $\geq$ 80 req/s* and *availability $\geq$ 99%* on *24/7*, and *all the data must be stored only within the Netherlands.*

Furthermore, in the future AutoInc foresees that some of their prospective customers will prefer an SMS service for dispatching new work to vehicles, and decide to include this feature in their VM-SaaS offering. They cooperate with the telecom company Tele1 for acquiring its SMS-Delivery-SaaS. In order to seamlessly interact with the SMS-Delivery-SaaS, AutoInc needs to understand the required APIs and the communication protocols specified by Tele1. Furthermore, due to some performance and economic reasons, AutoInc chooses the first configuration offered by Tele1, in which the underlying composition engine and its required resources are actually provided by yet another provider, the CE1 PaaS provider. As AutoInc also wants their VM-SaaS to interact with the SMS-Delivery-SaaS, the CE1-PaaS is required to be connected with the prospective AutoInc-Req04 network link of AutoInc.

In summary, AutoInc has designed their VM-SaaS offering as a SBA, since the required platform and infrastructure resources and the SMS delivery software service are not under their direct control. This is the distinguishing characteristic of a SBA from a component-based application. Furthermore, in order to enable the further development and deployment of this SBA, AutoInc needs to specify the to-be architecture definition that describes which artefacts should run on which resources and how the resources are connected to or deployed on each other. Figure 1 visualizes also the to-be architecture definition.

In the next section we demonstrate how existing approaches lack the ability to complete this scenario, which leads to the motivation for our *Blueprint* concept.

3   Evaluation of Related Work

The motivating scenario described above indicates the need for a uniform representation that can accurately describe the capabilities, resource requirements, and architecture definition of cloud infrastructure, platforms and software services across different vendors. However, cloud computing is a relatively new research area and very little existing research addresses our research objective. We first review some related work addressing the lack of standardization for describing cloud services that results in the well-known vendor lock-in problem. [2] addresses the vendor lock-in problem that prevents the interchangeability and interoperability between cloud services and presents a state-of-the-art in both standardization efforts and on-going projects. Similarly, the ability to manipulate, integrate and customize cloud service descriptions across different cloud providers has also been recognized in [3], which has IaaS, application and deployment orchestrators, but falls short of proposing a solution for the problem at hand.

Much recent work on standardizing the description of cloud services concentrates mostly on the infrastructure level, and does not cover the complete cloud computing picture. As an example, the DMTF has exhibited proven standards, such as the Open Virtualization Format (OVF)[2] that provides open packaging and distribution formats for virtual machines. [4] uses the OVF to define a service definition language for deploying complex Internet applications in federated IaaS clouds. These applications consist of a collection of virtual machines (VM) with several configuration parameters (e.g., hostnames, IP and other application specific parameters) for software components (e.g., web server, application server, database, operating system) included in the VMs. Similarly, [5] targets the interoperability between the federated clouds by providing a collection of proposals for 'Intercloud' protocols and formats. However, these approaches target only the interoperability and portability between data centers, i.e. only on the infrastructure level.

Approaching the standardization for cloud services from the different perspective, the Model Driven Engineering (MDE) research community has realized the benefit of combining MDE techniques with SaaS development and suggested combining MDE with cloud computing [6]. As the article describes, there is no consensus on the models, languages, model transformations and software processes for the model-driven development of cloud-based SaaSs. Following the MDE vision, [7] proposes a meta-model that allows cloud users to design applications independent of any platform and build inexpensive elastic applications. From their point of view, a cloud application is a software provided as a service that should avoid the vendor lock-in problem concerning the underlying platforms. This meta-model however describes only the capabilities and technical interfaces of the cloud application service. Similarly, [8] presents a different customer-centric cloud service model. This model concentrates on aspects such as the customer subscription, capability, billing, etc., yet does not cover other technical aspects of the cloud services including the technical interfaces of the cloud services, the elasticity, the required deployment environment, etc. Other existing models, e.g. [9], also lack a formal structure and definitions (reducing their usability and reusability) or are not explicit and assume tacit knowledge.

Apart from the need to have a uniform description for cloud service offerings to avoid vendor lock-in, another requirement is to specify in the description the resource requirements and constraints necessary for cloud service development, as shown in the scenario in Section 2. The Cafe application and component templates in [10] are maybe the most relevant approach for cloud-based application development that provides templates for ad-hoc compositions of physical cloud resource components. However, this approach requires the developers to

---

[2] DMTF Open Virtualization Format (OVF), http://www.dmtf.org/standards/ovf

possess deep technical knowledge of the physical cloud topology on which their applications may be composed and deployed. Furthermore, resource discovery in Cafe cannot retrieve resource components that satisfy end-to-end policy and quality-of-service (QoS) constraints. In practice, an attempt to provide template for utilizing cloud services for application development is available from Amazon through their AWS CloudFormation product[3]. This template provides AWS developers with the ability to specify a collection of AWS cloud resources and the provisioning of these resources in an orderly and predictable fashion. Nevertheless, this template works only for AWS cloud platform and infrastructure resources and thus lacks interoperability and portability.

In summary, existing work mostly aims to propose standards for only certain aspects and thus fails to cover the full picture of cloud computing , e.g. providing models and formats for only infrastructure resources, or describing only the functional specification. Furthermore, these standardization efforts do not aim to assist the cloud-based SBA developers to select, customize and compose various cross-layered cloud services across vendors according to their application requirements. We propose the *Blueprint* concept in the next section as a uniform representation to capture the comprehensive knowledge of a cloud service offering to support SBA developers during the various development phases.

4   Blueprint Template for XaaS Offerings

We define a Blueprint as a uniform abstract description of a cloud service offering that abstracts away from all specific technical details and complexities to facilitate the SBA developers with the selection, customization and composition of cross-layered cloud services across various vendors. The proposed Blueprint Template is located on the left-hand side of Figure 2. Using the template, the blueprint provider can describe (instantiate) blueprints that capture their cloud service offerings. In the middle of Figure 2, two sample instantiated Blueprints are introduced that capture the offerings of AutoInc and Tele1 in the motivating scenario from Section 2. The right-hand side of the figure describes some blueprint extensions, which are the add-on data structures, the *QoS profile* capturing the QoS properties and the *Policy profile* capturing the policy properties for the blueprints. These add-on extensions can be described using a variety of existing languages or templates such as the RuleML[4], WS-Policy[5], SLAng[6], etc., and will not be discussed further. The Blueprint Template is divided into template sections, each has a set of proposed properties. Please note that the template is extensible, i.e. if more properties are needed in a particular section, they can be added using the following data structure {property name, property type, [property value range]}. In the following, each template section is dissected with a proposed set of properties.

---

[3] Amazon: Aws cloudformation, `http://aws.amazon.com/de/cloudformation/`
[4] `http://ruleml.org/`
[5] `http://www.w3.org/TR/ws-policy/`
[6] `http://uclslang.sourceforge.net/`

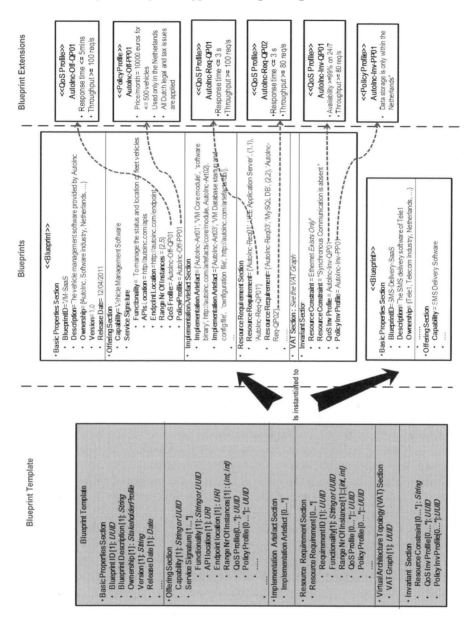

Fig. 2. The Blueprint Template and Sample Instantiated Blueprints

4.1 Basic Properties

Most importantly, the Basic Properties section contains an id (*BlueprintID*) using the UUID type for uniquely identifying a blueprint. This id is used for indexing a blueprint in the blueprint repository as well as referencing the included blueprints in case one would like to offer a blueprint containing a bundle of other included offerings. Apart from the id are the *description, ownership, version information,* and *release date* of the blueprint. While other properties can be described using primitive types, the ownership may need a more sophisticated data structure, e.g. a *StakeholderProfile* complex type that contains the name of the blueprint provider, its industry sector, location information, etc.

4.2 Offering Section

We assume there is only one cloud service offering in each blueprint. However, a bundle of offerings can still be described in a single blueprint that references to other included ones. Inclusion references are specified in another template section (see section 4.5).

The functional capability of the cloud service offered in a blueprint should be described in such a way that the consumer can fully understand and query it from a blueprint repository. Initially, the *capability* follows a simple string-based approach that allows only simple search and selection of blueprints. To enable a more accurate categorization of blueprints in the repository supporting more accurate search and matching, we suggest using the OVF standard for PaaS and IaaS offerings, and the service capability description template in [11] for SaaS offerings, instead of a simple string-based capability description.

The *Service Signature* is included in the blueprint to describe information for each functionality of the offering: the functionality description, the technical interfaces exposed to the blueprint consumers, the elasticity offering, the QoS offering, and the policy rules that constrain the offering. *Functionality* can be described by a simple string-based text or using external templates. Technical interfaces include the *API location* to download necessary APIs and an *endpoint location* for programmatic interactions with the cloud service. The APIs include not only libraries but also documentation for programming the client-side such as which protocols can be used to access the cloud service. Elasticity is specified in terms of the minimum and maximum number of instances of the cloud service (*Range Nr Of Instances*) provided to consumers. QoS properties of the cloud service can be specified in a number of separate profiles (*QoS Profile*) using an add-on templates or external languages, e.g. WS-policy, SLAng, etc. Hence, the blueprint template allows the specification of the UUID pointers referencing these separate profiles. Similarly, the policy rules that constrain the cloud service offering can be specified in existing rule languages in a separate policy profile (*Policy Profile*) that can be referenced using the UUID pointer.

4.3 Implementation Artefacts Section

This section is not used by the blueprint consumers, but is important for the system integrators who are responsible for the deployment and provisioning of this blueprint, as it contains the technical information of the artefacts that implement the cloud service offering. Each artefact has the following information: an *artefact id* for uniquely identifying an artifact, an *artefact name*, an *artefact type* indicating whether this artefact is a software binary, a composition script, a database startup file or some other kinds of configuration files, an *artefact location* for downloading, and some *artefact dependencies* pointing to the other artefacts that have to be executed before executing this one.

Examples of implementation artefacts can be found in Figure 2. *AutoInc-Art01* is the UUID of a software binary called *VM Core module* that can be downloaded from a given URL. However, it depends on another artefact *AutoInc-Art02*, which is a provided configuration file that has to be executed before one can actually deploy the *AutoInc-Art01* artefact.

4.4   Resource Requirements Section

A list of cloud resource requirements needed for deploying a blueprint is specified in this section. This specification guides the system integrators to search for the necessary cloud services offerings in a blueprint repository. Each resource requirement is specified with a *resource ID*, the required *functionality*, the required *Range Number of Instances*, and a set of references pointing to *QoS Profiles* and *Policy Profiles* that contain the QoS properties and the policy constraints of this resource requirement. Similarly to the offering section, the required *functionality* can be described using a simple string-based text or, in a more expressive way, using the external add-on templates, and the associated *QoS and Policy Profiles* can be described using an existing external language.

As an example of resource requirements in Figure 2, the *VM-SaaS* blueprint needs *1 instance* of the resource *JEE Application Server*. This requirement has a unique id *AutoInc-Req01* and is associated with some required QoS properties defined in the *AutoInc-Req-QP01* profile, which prescribes that the required resource should respond faster than 3s and provide the throughput greater than 100 requests per second.

4.5   Virtual Architecture Topology (VAT) Section

The VAT section specifies the to-be architecture definition of a blueprint using the graph data structure that captures the following relationships:

- *Inclusion* relationships: This relationship describes the nesting relationships between blueprints. There exist also inclusion relationships between the resource requirements indicating that a required cloud resource should be provided together with another cloud resource.
- *Link* relationships: A Link relationship in the VAT describes an abstract link between two elements, e.g. between two resource requirements or between a blueprint and a resource requirement, in the architecture topology. This topology helps the system integrator with the provisioning of the to-be system architecture, i.e. how to organize the available cloud resources.
- *Requirement* relationships: This relationship indicates a deployment dependency between two elements, e.g. an implementation artefact needs a required resource for its deployment.

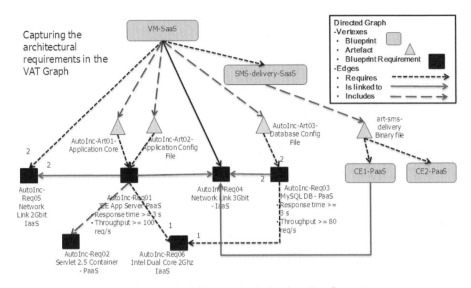

Fig. 3. A sample VAT graph of the AutoInc Scenario

Figure 3 illustrates the VAT graph of the VM-SaaS blueprint of AutoInc in the scenario from Section 2. This graph indicates:

- The *VM-SaaS* blueprint requires the *SMS-Delivery-SaaS* blueprint of Tele1.
- The *AutoInc-Art01* artefact requires a JEE application server (*AutoInc-Req01*) that includes a Servlet v2.5 container (*AutoInc-Req02*).
- The required JEE application server (*AutoInc-Req01*) is connected to two lines (i.e. two instances) of network link 2Gbit (*AutoInc-Req05*).
- AutoInc decides to use the *SMS-Delivery-SaaS* with a configuration that uses the external *CE1-PaaS* offering of CE1. Hence the *CE1-PaaS* should be connected to the *AutoInc-Req04* network link of AutoInc.

In summary, the VAT is an essential part of the Blueprint Template that specifies the to-be architecture topology of a blueprint. In the further development phases of the blueprint, the resource requirements in the VAT need to be fulfilled by searching and selecting appropriate blueprints from the blueprint repository.

4.6 Invariants Section

Invariants are the end-to-end global constraints that must not be violated by the blueprint and its resource requirements. The blueprint provider can specify the *resource constraints* that prescribe the conditions for all the cloud resources needed for the blueprint, as well as the QoS and policy constraints in separate *QoS Inv Profiles* and *Policy Inv Profiles* respectively.

For example, in Figure 2 the provider of the VM-SaaS prescribes two resource invariant constraints stating that all the network links required for the VM-SaaS must be Ethernet and only asynchronous communications are allowed between the resources. He also constrains his VM-SaaS with further QoS invariants such as the throughput of the service must always be $\geq$ 80req/s and its availability must be $\geq$ 99% on 24/7. Data storage for the VM-SaaS must be only within the Netherlands, according to the policy invariant constraint. Since all these constraints are the global end-to-end invariants specified for the VM-SaaS, the required SMS-Delivery-SMS and CE1-PaaS are also constrained by them.

5   Conclusion and Future Work

In this paper we propose the *Blueprint* concept as the common foundation to address the design, engineering and provision of cross-layered services through the cloud. By using the *Blueprint Template*, cloud service providers can seamlessly participate in the creation of a true business ecosystem where applications, platforms and infrastructures from different providers can be traded, customized and combined. Such a business ecosystem has been exemplified by applying the template for a running scenario throughout the paper. We are currently finalizing a prototype application that allows to design, query and compose cloud-based services using the XML schema of the proposed blueprint template. In the future, we intend to use this application for conducting an empirical study with our industry partners in the 4caasT project such as Ericsson, SAP, and Telefonica.

References

1. Mell, P., Grance, T.: The nist definition of cloud computing. National Institute of Standards and Technology, Information Technology Laboratory (July 2009)
2. Monteiro, A., Pinto, J., Teixeira, C., Batista, T.: Cloud interchangeability - redefining expectations. In: Proceedings of CLOSER 2011 (2011)
3. Keahey, K., Tsugawa, M., Matsunaga, A., Fortes, J.: Sky computing. IEEE Internet Computing 13(5), 43–51 (2009)
4. Galán, F., Sampaio, A., Rodero-Merino, L., Loy, I., Gil, V., Vaquero, L.M.: Service specification in cloud environments based on extensions to open standards. In: Proceedings of the COMSWARE 2009, 19:1–19:12. ACM, New York (2009)
5. Bernstein, D., Ludvigson, E., Sankar, K., Diamond, S., Morrow, M.: Blueprint for the intercloud - protocols and formats for cloud computing interoperability. In: Proceedings of the ICIW 2009. IEEE Computer Society, Los Alamitos (2009)
6. Brunelière, H., Cabot, J., Frédéric, J.: Combining model-driven engineering and cloud computing. In: Proceedings of the MDE4ServiceCloud 2010 (June 2010)
7. Hamdaqa, M., Livogiannis, T., Tahvildari, L.: A reference model for developing cloud applications. In: Proceedings of CLOSER 2011 (2011)
8. Cai, H., Zhang, K., Wang, M., Li, J., Sun, L., Mao, X.: Customer centric cloud service model and a case study on commerce as a service. In: Proceedings of the IEEE International Conference on Cloud Computing (2009)
9. Thrash, R.: Building a cloud computing specification: fundamental engineering for optimizing cloud computing initialtives. CSC Whitepaper (August 2010)
10. Mietzner, R.: A method and implementation to define and provision variable composite applications, and its usage in cloud computing. Dissertation. Universität Stuttgart, Germany (August 2010)
11. Oaks, P., Edmond, D., ter Hofstede, A.: Capabilities: Describing what services can do. In: Orlowska, M.E., Weerawarana, S., Papazoglou, M.P., Yang, J. (eds.) ICSOC 2003. LNCS, vol. 2910, pp. 1–16. Springer, Heidelberg (2003)

Self-management Challenges
for Multi-cloud Architectures
(Invited Paper)

Erik Elmroth, Johan Tordsson, Francisco Hernández,
Ahmed Ali-Eldin, Petter Svärd, Mina Sedaghat, and Wubin Li

Department of Computing Science, Umeå University, SE-901 87 Umeå, Sweden
{elmroth,tordsson,hernandf,ahmeda,petters,mina,wubin}@cs.umu.se
http://www.cloudresearch.se

Abstract. Addressing the management challenges for a multitude of distributed cloud architectures, we focus on the three complementary cloud management problems of predictive elasticity, admission control, and placement (or scheduling) of virtual machines. As these problems are intrinsically intertwined we also propose an approach to optimize the overall system behavior by policy-tuning for the tools handling each of them. Moreover, in order to facilitate the execution of some of the management decisions, we also propose new algorithms for live migration of virtual machines with very high workload and/or over low-bandwidth networks, using techniques such as caching, compression, and prioritization of memory pages.

Keywords: Autonomous cloud management, proactive elasticity control, admission control, cloud governance, scheduling, placement, live virtual machine migration.

1   Introduction

Recent advantages in virtualization combined with multi-tenancy enables cloud infrastructure providers to perform large-scale provisioning of compute or data intensive services. Such a cloud appears to the service (content) provider as a single system always delivering sufficient capacity, where service capacity also can be increased or decreased rapidly to meet workload fluctuations. Despite these recent advances significant research challenges remain in terms of how to achieve e.g., flexibility, robustness, cost-efficiency, and sustainability of cloud infrastructures [2,27,28,29]. Our ongoing efforts combines distributed systems and autonomic computing technologies with the overall aim of creating a self-managed elastic cloud infrastructure. Prominent features of the envisioned infrastructure include seamless integration of local resources and capacity leased from external infrastructure providers, as well as the ability to migrate virtual infrastructures, in parts or as a whole, e.g., for continued provisioning over planned system downtime, fault tolerance, or performance improvements by moving services closer to end-users or service components closer to each other.

W. Abramowicz et al. (Eds.): ServiceWave 2011, LNCS 6994, pp. 38–49, 2011.
© Springer-Verlag Berlin Heidelberg 2011

Our contributions are based on the assumptions that cloud infrastructures will be available as private (for an organization's in-house use) and public (capacity acquired from external providers), that they will be used in isolation or in a variety of conceptually different combinations, and that they will be internal or external to individual organizations or cross-organizational consortia. In particular, following Ferrer et.al. [14], we address *bursted private clouds* (a service provider having a private cloud infrastructured with possibility to expand using external clouds), *federated clouds* (infrastructure providers using partners to ensure the capacity needed to serve the service providers that are their customers), and *multi-clouds* (service providers working directly with multiple external infrastructure providers). The management challenges in focus are not specific to any of the scenarios, but are rather derived from a single cloud deployment abstraction meeting the needs for all three scenarios. For the elastic cloud to be self-managed, challenges lie both in dynamicity of service behavior (with rapid demands for capacity variations and resource mobility) as well as in the scale of resources to manage in future cloud environments.

With the rapidly increasing size of computing systems and the growing complexity of interconnected systems, system management is growing in complexity to a scale necessitating new behavioral abstractions and models for autonomic computing [17]. Due to the nonlinearity of emergent local behavior, it is intrinsically challenging to understand the mappings between local and global behavior and the effects of local and global management actions. New behavioral and managerial abstractions are needed, together with extended methods for distributed or hierarchical control, leveraging learning and optimization theory as well as automated statistical modelling. As a first step, we need to understand the fundamental limits of what global behaviour can be achieved and evaluate autonomic methods for such management challenges.

We are focusing on the three management problems of *admission control* (deciding whether to accept a new service request or not) for safe overbooking of elastic services and long-term capacity planning, *placement (or scheduling)* for optimal mapping of service components in cloud infrastructures comprised of many datacenters, and *proactive elasticity* to rapidly adjust capacity allocation to variations in demand. As these three problems are intrinsically interwined we are also proposing a *governance* approach to optimize the overall system behavior by tuning policies for the management tools handling each of these problems. Due to the complexity of the problems at hand, all of them being affected by several factors and requiring timely decisions under high uncertainty, as well as the large scale of the envisioned cloud infrastructures, our solutions to these four management optimization problems include a wide range of techniques. Moreover, in order to facilitate the rapid enforcement of VM management decisions, we also focus on algorithms for *live migration* of VMs. The aim here is to lower service downtime and reduce network infrastructure overhead, in particular for migration of very high workload VMs and/or over low-bandwidth networks.

Figure 1 outlines a conceptual cloud architecture and illustrates the interactions between admission control, placement, and elasticity. The figure also shows

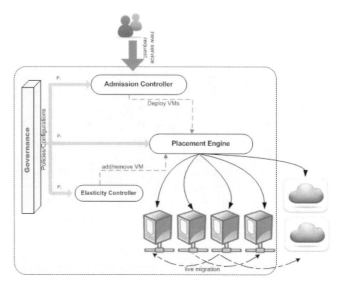

Fig. 1. Conceptual cloud architecture showing interactions between key management functionalities

how governance mechanisms can be used to harmonize the policies and settings for these management operations and how live migration enable re-placement of VMs to continously optimize service and infrastructure operation.

In summary, this contribution identifies and presents partial solutions to a set of fundamental algorithmic challenges that in systems-oriented research [7,9,10,14,19,24,28,29] have been identified as central to cloud infrastructure management. The solutions to these chalenges all to raise the abstraction level in order to substantially optimize cloud resource management, e.g., to enable management of significantly larger systems, to optimize management with respect to obectives expressed to a higher degree in non-functional terms relevant to objective business level objectives, and to provide significantly more optimized lower-level management tools.

2   Predictive Elasticity Control

A key feature of cloud infrastructures is elasticity which is the ability of the cloud to automatically and rapidly scale up or down the resources allocated to a service according to the current demand on the service while enforcing the performance or capacity based Service Level Agreements (SLAs) specified. It should be possible to scale resources either by changing the number of VMs (horizontal elasticity) or by changing the size of the VMs (vertical elasticity) depending on the application's storage, memory, network bandwidth, and computate power requirements. An example is a three-tier application with a bandwidth intensive tier-1, a memory and compute intensive tier-2, and a storage and memory intensive tier-3. Notably, a single service may be associated with more than one type of load, such as compute power, memory requirements, memory bandwidth and network capacity. Scaling decisions might be needed in case of a change either the total capacity required or in a change in the load mix of the service [32].

The elasticity decisions should ideally be able to forecast in advance a change in the load of a service to be able to react to unexpected load changes faster than the rate of change of the load, i.e., in a few seconds. This requires fast and reliable algorithms for usage predictions. We propose a hierarchical control approach with a multi-tier elasticity manager where each tier has a controller composed of separate low-level controllers determining memory, bandwidth, storage and CPU requirements. Using the lower-level controllers' output as input to a higher level decision making component, the controller may issue elasticity decisions for each tier. Currently, there is no available elasticity technique that by far takes into account anything else than very basic parameters. Few current solutions actually go beyond simple reactive (non-predictive) threshold-based allocation adjustment [16,36,39].

We address this problem through the design of a hybrid controller that combine both reactive and proactive components to be used as a lower level controller [1,14]. In our controllers, scale-up is achieved using the reactive component while scale down operations are based on predictive decisions using adaptive proportional control. We have designed two adaptive proportional controllers for scale down that reduce the SLA breakage rate by one tenth compared to a totally reactive controller using thresholds [1,14]. There is a cost incurred though for this reduction which is the percentage of over-provisioned servers.

3   Admission Control for Safe Overbooking

The decision to accept or reject a new elastic service request is one of the key decisions of an infrastructure provider as the services admitted will generate profit at the end or, in case too many or capacity demanding services are admitted, cause loss of profit and bad reputation. Notably, at admission time it is not known how the elasticity requirements will affect future capacity needs. Based on an assumption that not all admitted services will have peaks in demand at the same time, infrastructure providers are expected to perform substantial overbooking w.r.t. the maximum expected capacity per service (e.g., similarly to how airline companies sell more tickets than they have seats and how network providers multiplex datalink bandwidth). Hence, the ability to determine optimal overbooking is crucial for using resources as efficiently as possible while not extensively breaking established SLAs. A unique characteristic of the infrastructure provider admission control problem is that whereas network traffic oscillations are extensively studied and rather well understood [13,15,18,23] much less is known about the elasticity properties of service workloads.

An opportunity for providers, but also a complicating factor is that not only service capacity demand varies over time but also available resources. Cloud federation and cloud bursting may allow an infrastructure provider to aquire additional server resources from other providers. Restrictions for outsourcing of service workloads, economic implications of doing so, as well as policies, ranging from continuous utilization of subcontracted resources to restricting bursting and federation only to SLA violation mitigation in peak load scenarios, all affect the admission control problem. Notably, implications of admission control have rather different time-scales for compute and storage resources, as storage capacity variations are of more long-term character and data is far more costly to migrate.

We propose that this problem is handled with two approaches ideally to be used in combination. The first approach, extending on results from statistical multiplexing of network bandwidth, is to make each admission control decision based on an elasticity analysis for the currently admitted services over a relevant set of time periods, in order to predict the future resource availability. The elasticity analysis includes calculation of probability distributions of load for each service over short to medium time and for the aggregated service workload per cloud over long term. An admission control decision will be made by combining these predictions with very short term ones obtained from elasticity and applying the overall provisioning (governance) policies with respect to risk level. Notably, profiling the new service with respect to elasticity is key for successful admission control.

The second approach is to model the problem as a Markovian decision process and apply reinforcement learning and approximate dynamic programming methods to solve it. Notably, decisions using reinforcement learning for the new service requires historical data for a representative service. Hence, application profiling, e.g., as previously done for overbooking problems in scheduling on time-shared computers is highly relevant also to overbooking in cloud environments [40]. Notably, reinforcement learning is particularly beneficial when comparing short term and long term profits. For related reading, see [8,11,21,22,33].

4   VM Placement (Scheduling)

Given a set of admitted services and the availability of local and possibly remote resources, there are a number of VM placement problems to be solved. For example, VM placement may be subject to minimize cost and achieve certain hardware consolidation levels while complying to SLAs such as providing a certain compute, network, and storage capacity, fulfill requirements for (anti-)affinity (not on the same server, in same datacenter, etc), or even constraints with respect to power consumption [3,11,12,37,41]. Given the dynamic nature of clouds, with significant changes over time both in demand (due to service admission or elasticity actions) and supply (resulting, e.g., from fluctuations in resource availability or off-hours discounts at external partners, etc.), VM placement decisions need to be renewed regularly. Since changes in placement requires migration of already running VMs, migration costs need to be part of the equation, including overhead due to migration downtime, infrastructure capacity loss and monetary loss, etc.

We address the VM placement problem with combinatorial optimization formulations. With a given number of VMs, each VM's instance type (typically the size), current placement, and cost functions for VM provisioning and migration as input, suitable allocation of VMs across local servers and remote datacenters can be determined. For a tradeoff between quality of solution and computation time, we consider a range of methods, from optimal solutions through integer programming solvers, to approximations based on problem relaxations, and heuristic approaches such as greedy formulations. In principle, the constraint solver must enumerate each possible solution, check whether it is viable, and compare the current best one found so far. However in practice, this approach is unnecessarily expensive. To speed up the problem solving process and reduce the computation cost, we also introduce a number of optimizations, e.g., identifying lower and upper bounds that are close to the optimal values to significantly reduce the search space.

For the local (within a datacenter) scenario, VM placement can be formulated as a multi-dimensional (CPU, memory, disk, network requirements) multi-choice (many physical hosts) knapsack problem, taking placement policies into account, e.g., considering load balancing, power saving (server consolidation), and SLA protection. Example SLAs considered include availability guarantees and the algorithms to protect them ensure that, e.g., sufficient resources are allocated to VMs in 95% of all time intervals for a particular service class. Availability SLAs enable some relaxation of various constraints, e.g., that all VMs need to be assigned physical hosts at all time, and thus increases flexibility in management.

For the non-local placement problem, there is a need to handle both the extreme cases (1) where, e.g., a large datacenter needs to subcontract resources from other datacenters for capacity or redundancy reasons and (2) where, e.g., an infrastructure provider for a content delivery network needs to place streaming services close to end users. Typically, the former problem includes only a small number of destinations for placing a large number of VMs whereas the latter involves only a very small number of VMs but the number of destinations (e.g., base stations controlled by a telecommunications infrastructure provider) may be counted in thousands already for a single country. In the second scenario, knowledge of, or even control over, network topology and bandwidth allocations enable more advanced service placement (and replication), minimizing the distance to end-users, but at the same time increasing the complexity of the placement problem. By a hierarchical grouping of VM mappings in scenario (1) and by pruning of distribution networks in (2), we strive for a single approach to manage both scenarios.

Early results using integer programming techniques show how to optimize a utility function for service performance with, e.g., service layout (load balancing), budget, VM configuration requirements as constraints, for a problem reduced (pruned) to a few tens of VMs and a handful of VM types and destinations with feasible solution time constraints for the placement process [20,37]. Our first prototype also takes cost and performance implications for actual VM migration operations into account and allows for modelling of uncertainties, e.g., due to provider's changing conditions or changes in the set of available destinations. Notably, by integrating the placement engine with the VM manager, the whole process of optimization and re-placement of VMs is to be a fully automated process. It is demonstrated that our prototype can support a wide range of dynamic cloud scheduling scenarios, and by proper parametrizations, many interesting characteristics can be obtained.

5 Cloud Governance—High-Level Management

Cloud infrastructures are managed in order to achieve a specific high-level main objective (often referred to as the business-level objective (BLO)), e.g., maximize resource utilization while maintaining fairness among users, or maximize profit without breaking more than a certain fraction of SLAs. In practice, there are a number of low-level management activities that need to be performed to adequately provision resources. These low-level management activities (e.g., admission control, elasticity, and VM placement) can be addressed more or less independently as each one strives to achieve a specific goal related to its own domain. However, without having a global view of the problem, these low-level goals may be in conflict so that the combined effect of low-level managers action fails to optimize the BLO. For example, if too many SLAs are being broken due to lack of capacity for a specific service, it may be that the admission controller is allowing too much overprovisioning, that the elasticity engine is too restrictive, i.e., not requesting additional resources rapidly enough, or that the VM placement engine is packing to many or to few VMs per server. Without a global view, it is in such situations hard for the individual low-level managers to determine appropriate actions to optimize the overall system behavior.

Three approaches have traditionally been used for overall management of cloud infrastructures: (1) enhance low-level actions with features that optimize management with respect to some higher-level objective [25,26], (2) formulate the management problem as an optimization problem [30], and (3) approach cloud management as an autonomic system that is able to adapt itself to real time configuration and changes [5].

Enhancing the low-level managers to act according to higher-level objectives is important, but as an overall solution it is incomplete as the low-level components still operate independently of each other and the overall coordination of the system remains unsolved. Furthermore, optimizing a single low-level activity, e.g., elasticity, is feasible but as more low-level activities are considered it becomes unmanageable to address the overall management as a single optimization problem. Autonomic management offers a more comprehensive approach. However, current solutions typically include all required decision making into the same process, increasing the complexity of optimizing each individual decision making process and of adding additional decision making processes when required.

We propose [31] an autonomic approach based on a *governance model* where a high-level manager dynamically adapt the behaviors of the low-level managers by fine-tuning their policies. The policy adjustments are the results of the high-level manager's optimization towards the BLO, with input of monitoring information about system load and services performance. This approach allows crisp definition of complex BLOs, as this model makes it possible for the high-level manager to optimize some utility function and simultaneously enforce governance policies. Furthermore, it is also possible to tune or modify the BLO (e.g., due to changes in management goals) and automatically adapt the behaviors of the low-level management actions without manual or ad-hoc modifications per component. The governance model can be realized, e.g., through machine learning to allow the system (before training) to be unaware of the effect of individual policies to itself and to service performance [31].

6 Live Migration of Large-Scale Virtual Machines

The ability to efficiently migrate VMs [6], between servers or datacenters, without interrupting the services provisioned inside the VMs, is crucial for the efficient and dynamic resource management presented above. In order to migrate a VM, its state consisting of its memory contents and local file system has to be transferred. Normally, the VM is suspended, it's state is transferred over the network and the VM is resumed on its new host. As the VM is not accessible while it is suspended, services running in the VM will be interrupted for an extended period of time. Live migration addresses this problem by performing migrations in two steps. First, the VM state (all dirty memory pages) is transferred in the background with the VM still running until the estimated time to transfer the remaining dirty pages is below a set threshold. The VM is then suspended, the last few pages are transferred, and the VM is finally resumed on its new host. If the suspension phase, shown in Figure 2 as the *migration downtime*, is short enough, typically less than one second, the migration will be transparent to users of services provisioned on the VM. Despite the widespread support for live migration of VMs in current hypervisors, they have significant shortcomings when it comes to migration of VMs with high workloads and/or migration over low-bandwidth networks [4,38]. In these cases, VM memory pages are often dirtied faster than they can be transferred over the network, which means that a large amount of data needs to be transferred while the VM is suspended, in turn leading to extended migration downtime. This extended downtime causes network time-outs, and as a consequence, interruption and/or failure of the service. In addition, a long total migration time is harmful to the infrastructure, as significant network bandwidth (a scarce resource) is used for the migration.

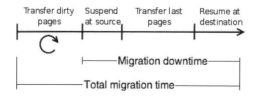

Fig. 2. Overview of a typical live migration process

To overcome these problems, we use a number of complementing techniques, the first being the application of delta compression and caching mechanisms to transfer of memory pages in order to increase migration throughput and thus reduce downtime. A first prototype of this live migration algorithm has recently been implemented as a modification to the KVM hypervisor [34]. Performance results show up to a factor of 100 in reduced migration downtime for a synthetic benchmark, reduction of user-experienced service interruption from eight seconds to zero for live migration of a streaming video server, and successful migration of the large and complex SAP application in environments where the standard approaches fail [34].

However, extended migration downtime is not the only issue with the standard live migration algorithms. As we see it, there are two major challenges, the first being the above described extended migration downtime and the second extended total migration time. The total migration time is measured from when migration is initiated until the VM is running and responding to requests on the destination host as shown in Figure 2. In order to make live migration a useful tool, it is desirable to minimize this time as this allows for faster live migrations and in turn an ability to react more quickly to the varying demands on the services and infrastructure. The total migration time depends on the migration throughput and the amount of data being transferred during migration. Our delta compression approach helps reducing the amount of data being transferred during migration and thus has the ability to reduce total migration time. However, due to its iterative approach, many memory pages are being transferred multiple times as they have been dirtied again between iterations. In order to rectify this problem we propose an approach where a page weight is calculated for each memory page according to how often it is updated. This weight is then used to prioritize the transfer order of memory pages so that the most frequently updated pages are transferred towards the end of the migration. The approach, which we call *dynamic page transfer reordering* shows promising results, especially on VMs running larger, memory intensive applications [35].

7 Concluding Remarks

We have presented a unified approach to key challenges for autonomous cloud management, including results from on-going work on the three topics of elasticity control, admission control, and VM scheduling and the topic of automatic cloud governance for management actions towards high-level management objectives. Moreover, as an enabler, we also show how to facilitate live migration of VMs that are hard ot migrate due to busy memory access patterns. This contribution mainly focus on the overall picture, simultaneously considering these management challenges. For further details about contributions to each individual topic, we refer to recent publications [1,20,31,34,35,37].

Acknowledgement. This work has in part been supported by the European Commissions IST activity of the 7th Framework Program under contract number

257115 (the OPTIMIS project, http://www.optimis-project.eu/). This research has been conducted using the resources of High Performance Computing North.

References

1. Ali-Eldin, A., Tordsson, J., Elmroth, E.: An adaptive hybrid elasticity controller for cloud infrastructures. (2011) (submitted)
2. Armbrust, M., Fox, A., Griffith, R., Joseph, A.D., Katz, R., Konwinski, A., Lee, G., Patterson, D., Rabkin, A., Stoica, I., Zaharia, M.: A view of cloud computing. Communications of the ACM 53(4), 50–58 (2010)
3. Bobroff, N., Kochut, A., Beaty, K.: Dynamic placement of virtual machines for managing SLA violations. In: Proceedings of the 10th IEEE Symposium on Integrated Management, IM (2007)
4. Bradford, R., Kotsovinos, E., Feldmann, A., Schiöberg, H.: Live wide-area migration of virtual machines including local persistent state. In: Proceedings of the 3rd International Conference on Virtual Execution Environments (VEE 2007), pp. 169–179. ACM, New York (2007)
5. Chess, D.M., Segal, A., Whalley, I.: Unity: Experiences with a Prototype Autonomic Computing System. In: ICAC 2004: Proceedings of the First International Conference on Autonomic Computing (ICAC 2004), pp. 140–147. IEEE Computer Society, Washington, DC, USA (2004)
6. Clark, C., Fraser, K., Hand, S., Hansen, J.G., Jul, E., Limpach, C., Pratt, I., Warfield, A.: Live migration of virtual machines. In: Proc. 2nd ACM/USENIX Symposium on Networked Systems Design and Implementation (NSDI), pp. 273–286. ACM, New York (2005)
7. Elmroth, E., Galan, F., Henriksson, D., Perales, D.: Accounting and billing for federated cloud infrastructures. In: Proceedings of the Eighth International Conference on Grid and Cooperative Computing (GCC 2009), pp. 268–275. IEEE Computer Society Press, Los Alamitos (2009)
8. Elmroth, E., Gardfjäll, P.: Design and evaluation of a decentralized system for grid-wide fairshare scheduling. In: Proceedings of the First International Conference on e-Science and Grid Computing (e-Science 2005), pp. 221–229. IEEE Computer Society Press, Los Alamitos (2005)
9. Elmroth, E., Henriksson, D.: Distributed usage logging for federated grids. Future Generations Computer Systems 26(8), 1215–1225 (2010)
10. Elmroth, E., Larsson, L.: Interfaces for placement, migration, and monitoring of virtual machines in federated clouds. In: Proceedings of the Eighth International Conference on Grid and Cooperative Computing (GCC 2009), pp. 253–260. IEEE Computer Society Press, Los Alamitos (2009)
11. Elmroth, E., Tordsson, J.: Grid resource brokering algorithms enabling advance reservations and resource selection based on performance predictions. Future Generation Computer Systems 24(6), 585–593 (2008)
12. Elmroth, E., Tordsson, J.: A standards-based grid resource brokering service supporting advance reservations, coallocation and cross-grid interoperability. Concurrency and Computation: Practice and Experience 25(18), 2298–2335 (2008)
13. Elwalid, A.I., Mitra, D.: Effective bandwidth of general Markovian traffic sources and admission control of high speed networks. IEEE/ACM Transactions on Networking 1(3), 329–343 (1993)

14. Ferrer, A.J., Hernández, F., Tordsson, J., Elmroth, E., Ali-Eldin, A., Zsigri, C., Sirvent, R., Guitart, J., Badia, R.M., Djemame, K., Ziegler, W., Dimitrakos, T., Nair, S.K., Kousiouris, G., Konstanteli, K., Varvarigou, T., Hudzia, B., Kipp, A., Wesner, S., Corrales, M., Forgó, N., Sharif, T., Sheridan, C.: OPTIMIS: a holistic approach to cloud service provisioning. Future Generation Computer Systems (2011) (accepted)
15. Guerin, R., Ahmadi, H., Naghshineh, M.: Equivalent capacity and its application to bandwidth allocation in high-speed networks. IEEE J. on Selected Areas in Communications 9(7), 968–981 (1991)
16. Iqbala, W., Daileya, M.N., Carrerab, D., Janeceka, P.: Adaptive resource provisioning for read intensive multi-tier applications in the cloud. Future Generation Computer Systems 27(6), 871–879 (2010)
17. Kephart, J.O., Chess, D.M.: The vision of autonomic computing. Computer 36(1), 41–50 (2003)
18. Knightly, E.W., Shroff, N.B.: Admission control for statistical QoS: Theory and practice. IEEE Network 13(2), 20–29 (1999)
19. Larsson, L., Henriksson, D., Elmroth, E.: Scheduling and monitoring of internally structure services for federated cloud environments. In: Proceedings of The 16th IEEE Symposium on Computers and Communication (ICCS 2011). IEEE Computer Society, Los Alamitos (2011) (accepted)
20. Li, W., Tordsson, J., Elmroth, E.: Modelling for dynamic cloud scheduling via migration of virtual machines (2011) (submitted)
21. Liu, X., Heo, J., Sha, L., Zhu, X.: Adaptive control of multi-tiered web applications using queueing predictor. In: 10th IEEE/IFIP Network Operations and Management Symposium, pp. 106–114 (2006)
22. Malrait, L., Bouchenak, S., Marchand, N.: Experience with ConSer: A system for server control through fluid modeling. IEEE Transactions on Computers 99 (2010)
23. Massoulié, L., Roberts, J.W.: Bandwidth sharing and admission control for elastic traffic. Telecommunication Systems 15(1-2), 185–201
24. Östberg, P.-O., Elmroth, E.: Increasing flexibility and abstracting complexity in service-based grid and cloud software. In: The 1st International Conference on Cloud Computing and Services Science (CLOSER 2011), pp. 240–249. SciTePress (2011)
25. Perez, J., Germain-Renaud, C., Kégl, B., Loomis, C.: Utility-based reinforcement learning for reactive grids. In: International Conference on Autonomic Computing (ICAC 2008), pp. 205–206. IEEE, Los Alamitos (2008)
26. Pueschel, T., Anandasivam, A., Buschek, S., Neumann, D.: Making Money With Clouds: Revenue Optimization Through Automated Policy Decisions. In: 17th European Conference on Information Systems (ECIS 2009), Verona, Italy, pp. 355–367 (2009)
27. Expert Group Report. The Future of Cloud Computing. European Commission, IST (2010)
28. Rochwerger, B., Breitgand, D., Epstein, A., Hadas, D., Loy, I., Nagin, K., Tordsson, J., Ragusa, C., Clayman, S., Levy, E., Maraschini, A., Massonet, P., Munoz, H., Toffetti, G., Villari, M.: RESERVOIR: When one cloud is not enough. IEEE Computer 44(3), 44–51 (2011)
29. Rochwerger, B., Breitgand, D., Levy, E., Galis, A., Nagin, K., Llorente, I., Montero, R., Wolfsthal, Y., Elmroth, E., Caceres, J., Ben-Yehuda, M., Emmerich, W., Galán, F.: The RESERVOIR model and architecture for open federated cloud computing. IBM J. of Research and Development 53(4) (2009)

30. Salehi, M., Buyya, R.: Adapting Market-Oriented Scheduling Policies for Cloud Computing. In: Hsu, C.-H., Yang, L.T., Park, J.H., Yeo, S.-S. (eds.) ICA3PP 2010. LNCS, vol. 6081, pp. 351–362. Springer, Heidelberg (2010)
31. Sedaghat, M., Hernandez, F., Elmroth, E.: Unifying cloud management: Towards overall governance of business level objectives. In: Proceedings of The 11th IEEE/ACM International Symposium on Cluster, Cloud and Grid Computing (CCGrid 2011), pp. 591–597. IEEE Computer Society, Los Alamitos (2011)
32. Singh, R., Sharma, U., Cecchet, E., Shenoy, P.: Autonomic mix-aware provisioning for non-stationary data center workloads. In: Proceeding of the 7th International Conference on Autonomic Computing, pp. 21–30. ACM, New York (2010)
33. Son, J.D.: Optimal admission and pricing control problem with deterministic service times and sideline profit. Queueing Systems: Theory and Applications 60(1), 71–85 (2008)
34. Svärd, P., Hudzia, B., Tordsson, J., Elmroth, E.: Evaluation of delta compression techniques for efficient live migration of large virtual machines. In: Proceedings of the 7th ACM SIGPLAN/SIGOPS International Conference on Virtual Execution Environments (VEE 2011), pp. 111–120. ACM, New York (2011)
35. Svärd, P., Tordsson, J., Hudzia, B., Elmroth, E.: High performance live migration through dynamic page transfer reordering and compression (2011) (submitted)
36. Toffetti, G., Gambi, A., Pezzè, M., Pautasso, C.: Engineering autonomic controllers for virtualized web applications. In: Benatallah, B., Casati, F., Kappel, G., Rossi, G. (eds.) ICWE 2010. LNCS, vol. 6189, pp. 66–80. Springer, Heidelberg (2010)
37. Tordsson, J., Montero, R.S., Vozmediano, R.M., Llorente, I.M.: Cloud brokering mechanisms for optimized placement of virtual machines across multiple providers (2010) (submitted)
38. Travostino, F.: Seamless live migration of virtual machines over the MAN/WAN. In: Proceedings of the 2006 ACM/IEEE Conference on Supercomputing. ACM, New York (2006)
39. Urgaonkar, B., Shenoy, P., Chandra, A., Goyal, P., Wood, T.: Agile dynamic provisioning of multi-tier Internet applications. ACM Trans. on Autonomous and Adaptive Systems 3(1), 1–39 (2008)
40. Urgaonkar, B., Shenoy, P., Roscoe, T.: Resource overbooking and application profiling in shared hosting platforms. In: 5th Symp. on Operating Systems Design and Implementation, OSDI 2002 (2002)
41. Verma, A., Ahuja, P., Neogi, A.: pMapper: Power and migration cost aware application placement in virtualized systems. In: Issarny, V., Schantz, R. (eds.) Middleware 2008. LNCS, vol. 5346, pp. 243–264. Springer, Heidelberg (2008)

Contrail Virtual Execution Platform Challenges in Being Part of a Cloud Federation*
(Invited Paper)

Piyush Harsh, Yvon Jegou, Roberto G. Cascella, and Christine Morin

INRIA Rennes - Bretagne Atlantique,
Campus Universitaire de Beaulieu, 35042 Rennes, France
{piyush.harsh,yvon.jegou,roberto.cascella,christine.morin}@inria.fr

Abstract. Cloud computing is quickly defining the computing paradigm in the modern networked age. Users can run their large computations online using cloud services at a fraction of the cost compared to setting their own data centers. Clearly cloud computing offers many advantages, and yet many large organizations including governments, financial sector, and health care sector are reluctant in transitioning to cloud computing. Contrail project will address the major concerns behind this reluctance namely mistrust in cloud platforms, lack of Service Level Agreements (SLAs) and Quality of Protection (QoP) of data. Contrail will provide a federation layer support for bringing a multitude of cloud providers, both private and public, together. This will allow multi-tenancy and cloud-bursting capability to end user cloud applications while supporting SLAs and QoP agreements desired by several privacy aware sectors including governments, banks, health care providers to name a few. This paper describes the novel features we are building into the Contrail Virtual Execution Platform (VEP) that will be closely interfaced with the IaaS layer of cloud providers. VEP upgrades the supported cloud providers and brings trust in cloud computing by adding SLAs and QoP features missing at typical IaaS layer. Further this paper outlines challenges faced in being part of a large federation and how VEP will address some of those.

1 Introduction

Cloud offerings are becoming more mature with increasingly sophisticated services available to the consumers. End users and corporations have tools available today that enable them to configure and operate their own private cloud services. These tools are available as commercial products, e.g., VMWare's vCloud [13], as well as open source IaaS alternatives such as OpenNebula [11] and OpenStack [12]. In addition, there are public clouds that operate on pay-as-you-go model such as Amazon's EC2 [1], Microsoft's Azure [5], and Google AppEngine [4] into which consumers can launch their applications and services as needed.

---

* This work is supported by the FP7 257438 Contrail integrated project funded by the European Commission.

W. Abramowicz et al. (Eds.): ServiceWave 2011, LNCS 6994, pp. 50–61, 2011.
© Springer-Verlag Berlin Heidelberg 2011

The above scenario is definitely a huge improvement from traditional data center models of last decade. Even though clouds offer much better price/performance ratio over non-virtualized environments, the true power of cloud computing can only be achieved with seamless federation among different cloud technologies.

A true cloud federation will bring both private and public clouds under the umbrella of one federation where users will have the option to deploy services using resources of multiple providers. The federation will present to the user uniform API/billing/monitoring features regardless of the nature of actual cloud service providers. Moreover, any organization can become part of this federation being both a cloud provider, when its IT infrastructure is not used at its maximal capacity, and a cloud customer in periods of peak activity. Resources that belong to different operators can be integrated into a single homogeneous federated cloud, shown in Figure 1, that users can access seamlessly.

The Contrail project (*www.contrail-project.eu*) aims to achieve these goals by developing an integrated approach to virtualization, offering Infrastructure as a Service (IaaS), services for federating IaaS clouds, and Platform as a Service (PaaS) on top of federated clouds. This calls for the deployment of a transparent, trusted, and reliable *Contrail federation* with operations governed by Service Level Agreements (SLAs) providing support for strong Quality of Protection (QoP) and authentication.

No cloud implementation, commercial or open source, currently implements all features to be supported by Contrail: federation, IaaS as well as PaaS, security, quality of service and protection enforced by service level agreements. Open source cloud platforms such as OpenStack [12], Nimbus [6] or OpenNebula [11] only support the IaaS layer with no quality of service and protection guarantees. However, some of these platforms such as OpenNebula partially support cloud federation.

Full PaaS support is provided by some commercial products such as VMware vCloud^{TM} [13] through the OVF distributed application open format [10]. But these platforms are currently limited to private cloud management only.

A *Contrail federation* integrates both private and public clouds under a common umbrella. User identities, data, and resources are interoperable within the federation, thanks to common supports for authentication and authorization, and to common policy definition, monitoring, and enforcing mechanisms (SLA, QoP, etc.), as well as to a common economic model [14].

The way the Contrail federation is conceived and its open source deployment nature will enable seamless access to provider resources, avoiding potential vendor lock-in for the end users. These users can now deploy their distributed applications on demand on different providers by negotiating resources with the federation, which will choose the best providers based on the application requirements.

In such a scenario, Contrail technology is able to satisfy the user needs for the deployment of elastic and salable applications guaranteeing performance dependability. The run time performance of the application can scale with the number of assigned resources, the user only needs to specify the desired performance level and the Contrail's automatic provisioning system can add resources

on demand during the execution of the application in order to guarantee the
desired performance (thus providing elasticity).

A challenging aspect of Contrail is the management of computing resources
to guarantee this performance dependability and QoS of active virtual execution platforms. Indeed, cloud providers might have different efficiency policies
given that the individual resources being contributed to this federated cloud
will be highly heterogeneous in their hardware configuration and system-level
organization, thus making their interoperability challenging.

The support for efficient cooperation and resource sharing within cloud federation is critical for the Contrail technology. This is achieved through Contrail
Virtual Execution Platform (VEP), an open source technology implementing
standards that exploits resource virtualization to provide virtualized distributed
infrastructures for deployment of end-user applications independently from the
underlying platform. VEP operates above IaaS layer as shown in the figure 1.
In Contrail, each cloud provider will run a copy of VEP software which in turn
will seamlessly integrate its resources with the Contrail federation.

VEP offers reliable application deployment platform that is resilient to operational failures and which supports secure management of user data with a
strong guarantee for QoS. These requirements are critical to make the provider
resources trustworthy so that users can obtain performance guarantees of their
application, bring trust in cloud computing solutions making them suitable to
run the users' businesses safely.

This paper presents the detailed information on VEP, which is one of the
components of Contrail service stack deployed at the cloud resource providers
end in order to seamlessly integrate the resources under Contrail federation.

The remainder of this paper is organized as follows - section 2 outlines the
key challenges inherent in a large cloud federation, section 3 describes the role
of VEP in cloud computing, section 4 describes the components and the design
rationale of the Contrail VEP development effort, and finally section 5 describes
the Contrail progress report, VEP development road map and recap of important
contribution and key points presented in this paper.

2   Challenges of a Large Federation

In a federation many independent members operate together governed by the
agreed upon federation laws. Just like in a society where a federation is successful
only if the individual members operate properly, the same set of challenges and
opportunities exist in a federated cloud. In this section we will list few major
issues that may arise in a federation of clouds. Later on we will see how VEP
helps address some of these concerns.

2.1   Authenticity of Reported Statistics

An end user of a federation of clouds may not know a priori which provider her
application will run on. The user agrees to pay the resources used by her application and in turn may require some form of validation of the reported resource

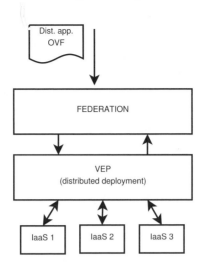

Fig. 1. A simple cloud federation

usage. The provider may fudge the reported statistics in order to fleece the end users. It would be the task of the federation to ensure such a case does not arise. Clear code of conduct and penalties for violation must be defined. Even then, the enforcement could be problematic. Surprise audits of provider logs by federation officials could be one deterrent against frauds by providers. But, the logs themselves may be modified. Fool-proof implementation of anti-fraud measures may be impossible to achieve. Further, for a successful federation, the terms of participation by individual provider must not be too stifling and must not favor large providers against small providers. Finding the correct participation terms and condition balance may prove a key for the success of the federation and yet this may be the most difficult balance to achieve.

2.2   Verification of SLA Adherence

Whenever there is a contract agreed between two parties, the contract enforcement becomes a legally binding obligation. Service Level Agreements (SLAs) in the context of cloud computing could contain agreements on the operating environment and placement restrictions of virtual machines (VMs) at the provider's location. An example SLA object could contain condition that some VMs in an application must not be placed on the same cluster rack as others. There might be CPU load conditions, memory requirements to name a few SLA parameters that could be present.

In a large federation where negotiated SLAs are supported between the user and the provider, the verification of the SLA contract adherence could prove to be challenging. If the user deploys her own VMs as part of the application, the user could embed her own verification code to periodically check if the execution environment is within the negotiated SLA parameters or not. The provider must maintain adequate logs for auditing if need arises.

Typically, initial SLA adherence is not a major issue because the provider checks for locally available resources before accepting an OVF and corresponding SLA object for provisioning. If adequate resources are not available at deployment stage, the SLA contract and OVFs are rejected. Ideally, such rejection should take place at the federation level itself before the deployment request reaches a provider. But the SLA enforcements for dynamic characteristics such as CPU usage should best be done by SLA enforcement agent based on periodic monitored data.

2.3 Scalability of Interface APIs

A single private cloud operator if operating by itself may not have huge customer base, but becoming part of a federation could suddenly change that. The provider APIs throughput that were once sufficient to deal with influx of requests from non-federation customers may prove a serious bottleneck if not properly provisioned for the large federations. As an example, if the provider supports REST interfaces, it would be advisable to stress test the REST APIs and check for scalability and other issues of being part of a large cloud federation. In Contrail, since VEP will be at the interface between the provider and the federation layer, all federation request will first come at VEP and therefore the VEP REST and other APIs will be stress tested for sudden influxes from a large federation customer base.

2.4 Authorization/Authentication Nightmare

Authorization and authentication are required whenever a provider resource needs to be accessed. Primarily it is required to keep track of resource usage for billing and accounting purposes, but also for keeping the compute and storage resources secure from malicious access. Private providers can easily maintain user accounts for authentication/authorization of their users. But once being part of a larger federation, it is not possible to keep account details of all possible users. The provider now must support means to allow resource access to federation users and at the same time keep at bay the malicious users.

One solution is to adopt a two-tier approach and keep the local authentication system intact for the non-federation users, and incorporate a federation authentication module in order to be able to validate the federation users' credentials before allowing access to local resources to federation users.

Other solution could be to elevate all local users as federation users, incorporate local accounts into the federation and provide all local users their new federation account details. But in this approach, the provider risks to loose the business of local users to competing providers under the federation while gaining the simplicity of one unified authentication mechanism.

Regardless of what solution one adopts, there are bound to be headaches in the integration process with respect to users' authentication and authorization with the (likely heterogeneous) providers in a large cloud federation.

2.5   Issue of Trust in the Federation

A federation of cloud providers brings several disparate cloud providers under one umbrella. Every cloud provider has different guiding principles and motives. The issue of trust in the federation is very important for proper operation of the system. The cloud providers must trust the federation. They have certain expectations from the federation, they expect the federation to properly filter out malicious users, they expect the federation to be honest in its accounting and billing practices. In the similar manner, the federation expects the participating cloud providers to adhere to a minimum code of conduct, be truthful in reporting resource usage, properly honor any negotiated SLA contracts, etc. The federation and cloud providers can both maintain some sort of trustworthiness rating system. It need not be uniform across all participating parties, each provider can adopt any suitable rating system (or not).

3   Need for VEP in Cloud Computing

With the growing importance of cloud based services in the computing of tomorrow, it is only a matter of time when there will be a real need for merging disparate IaaS platforms in order to support increasingly complex applications of the future.

The Virtual Execution Platform (VEP) could provide that aggregating glue for bringing different cloud platforms under one umbrella. The standard APIs exported by the VEP software would allow other developers to quickly and easily develop tools for making their own federated platforms tuned for specific tasks that other federations including Contrail may not support.

There are several open source tools already available for accessing public clouds (Amazon EC2), integrating such tools together with VEP would allow quick and easy solution for bringing public and private clouds together. Thus a well designed VEP solution could usher in the next wave of cloud research and open up new vistas for cloud innovations. Keeping this motivation for developing a quality VEP, let us next look at Contrail's VEP design in detail.

4   Contrail Virtual Execution Platform

Virtual Execution Platform (VEP) is a Contrail service that sits just above IaaS layer at the service provider end of the Contrail cloud federation. Some major design goals were kept in mind while designing the VEP architecture. Support for open virtualization standards including Open Virtualization Format (OVF) has been one of the major requirement. Scalability of the API interface in order to support potentially large customer base, interoperability with various open IaaS technologies in order to bring several kinds of cloud providers under the Contrail umbrella, and providing support for elasticity in accordance with the negotiated SLAs have been other major requirements that VEP will satisfy.

It will have selectable built in drivers for various open source IaaS platforms such as OpenNebula and OpenStack. The VEP layer will integrate clouds composed using different technologies under the ambit of Contrail federation. VEP will be very closely integrated with the IaaS layer and will expose uniform APIs to higher layers in the Contrail architecture. It will enable seamless deployment of OVF applications over any underlying supported cloud platform.

In case the federation module suspects that none of the participating Contrail cloud providers can satisfy a user's application resource requirements, it may enable part-deployment of the appliance over public clouds such as Amazon EC2 (cloud-bursting) using user credentials for such public clouds. This capability will be handled by the federation layer and not VEP directly.

Since support for Service Level Agreements (SLAs) and providing Quality of Protection (QoP) to end users is a major feature that Contrail aims to provide, the VEP layer has also been designed keeping the larger Contrail requirements in the picture. The following subsections describe major VEP components and supported features in some detail.

4.1   OVF Deployment Subsystem

Open Virtualization Format (OVF) [10] is an open standard that is used to compose virtual applications. It allows inclusion of multiple VM templates, allows description of interconnect between VMs, individual VM's contextualization to name a few features provided by the OVF standard. It has been developed by the Distributed Management Task Force (DMTF) [3]. It is an up-and-coming standard with increasing vendor support.

VEP will provide full support for OVF v 1.1 standard [15]. The support for OVF in VEP will enable deployment of virtual applications described in OVF XML document over supported IaaS platforms regardless of their native support for OVFs.

OVF deployment subsystem in VEP is responsible for deploying user appliances described within OVF XML document. Figure 2 shows the simplified design of the VEP's OVF deployment module. The user's OVF file is received from the federation layer using REST protocol (refer figure 2 subcomponent a). The user's credentials and authentication parameters are sent as part of HTTP headers in the Contrail REST scheme. Once the request for OVF deployment has been verified, the OVF document along with the corresponding SLA object is sent to the OVF deployment subsystem of VEP stack (refer figure 2 subcomponent b).

Once the OVF document and the corresponding SLA object is received at the VEP layer, the OVF document is validated for correctness against DMTF OVF standard schema document (currently VEP supports OVF v 1.1)(refer figure 2 subcomponent c). If the OVF document fails the validation process, the deployment effort is terminated and a suitable response is reported to the federation layer.

Upon successful validation, the OVF document is parsed (refer figure 2 subcomponent d) and individual elements deconstructed. The deconstructed OVF

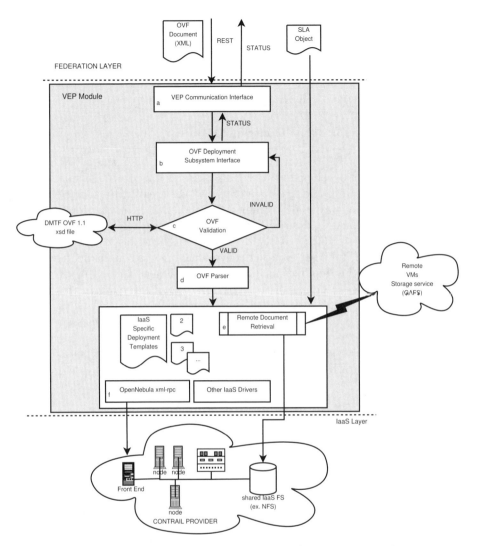

Fig. 2. OVF subsystem in Contrail VEP (simplified version)

components including VM elements, network elements etc. are then linked to their corresponding SLA contracts deconstructed from the SLA object. These linked elements are then used as input in the IaaS translation function which, depending on the type of IaaS environment, generates the template/deployment files for the underlying IaaS platform. For the initial release, VEP aims to provide support for OpenNebula IaaS clouds (refer figure 2 subcomponent f). Later on support for other open source cloud technologies will be developed.

If a virtual machine is stored at a remote location, the OVF deployment subsystem has modules for authenticated remote file transfer (refer figure 2 subcomponent e). The remotely hosted resources (VMs) will be transferred onto the cloud provider's shared file system before the actual virtual appliance deployment takes place at the cloud provider. The Contrail project will incorporate a Global Autonomous File System (GAFS) based on the XtreemOS project. The users' virtual machine image files will be hosted at remote GAFS shares and the OVF subsystem will log on behalf of the user and transfer image files from remote GAFS locations to the cloud provider shared file system.

4.2   REST APIs for other Contrail Modules

REST [16] stands for Representational State Transfer and is a simple yet elegant way to support API development. Using REST, one can provide simple CRUD - Create, Read, Update, and Delete operations over identified resources. REST provides a very clean way of developing APIs and enables quick adoption from cloud developers. Since we desire VEP to be easily integrable in other projects, VEP will provide clear REST APIs for developers. In addition VEP will have clearly defined RESTful APIs for other contrail modules to communicate with it. All requests from other modules including federation layer to VEP layer will be made using REST. The details of the APIs are beyond the scope of this paper. The REST APIs are built over Hyper Text Transfer Protocol (HTTP) protocol messages with support for HTTP GET/PUT/POST/DELETE messages only. Not all methods are available for all users and /or resources. Depending on the nature of the request and the access rights of users' a few or all methods are made available. The VEP REST interface will be stress-tested for scalability.

4.3   OCCI Support

Open Cloud Computing Interface (OCCI) [8] is a set of open standards [7] for managing cloud resources that have been developed through Open Grid Forum (OGF) [9]. The VEP component in the Contrail project will have an extended OCCI support. Again the need to incorporate OCCI in VEP arises from our requirement to be extensible and integrable in other projects. Additionally, as a result of our work and the experiences gained in providing support for OVFs and SLAs, Contrail project will propose an extension to the current OCCI draft for inclusion in the standardization effort within the OCCI community. These extensions will allow the OCCI framework to support OVF deployments along with providing support for SLAs which the standard lacks in its current format. The support for OCCI in VEP will hopefully allow the platform to be integrated in future cloud projects and will allow the open source community to develop feature enhancements and add-ons to the VEP layer in the federation of clouds.

4.4   Application Monitoring and Reporting Module

Application monitoring subsystem is a very integral part of the VEP as it provides support for the proper enforcement of the SLA contracts. Every application that is deployed on provider's IaaS infrastructure is monitored by the VEP module periodically. The collected data is stored in the VEP database for on-demand

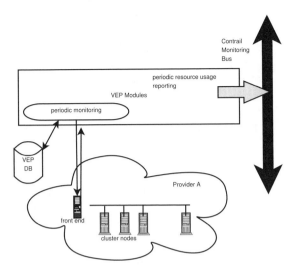

Fig. 3. Reporting subsystem in Contrail VEP (simplified version)

retrieval on user's behalf by the federation, but few statistics are pushed periodically on the monitoring bus to be used by the SLA enforcement module to check for compliance and for making elasticity decisions. Figure 3 shows the simplified schematic of the monitoring subsystem in the VEP module.

Each deployed application is assigned a Universally Unique Identity (UUID) that is assigned by the Contrail federation. The same UUID is included as part of the reported data that helps various modules in the SLA/monitoring system in the federation link the data with the correct application and the negotiated SLA object for verification. The federation monitoring bus over which the periodic data is sent will be a distributed messaging system (example: Apache ActiveMQ [2]) that supports Java Messaging Service (JMS) APIs.

4.5   IaaS Drivers

The VEP software is envisioned for use with multiple open source IaaS clouds. Contrail VEP software eventually plans to support several major IaaS platforms including OpenNebula, OpenStack, Nimbus scientific cloud [6], etc. We will provide appropriate drivers that can be enabled by the cloud providers as desired for interfacing with appropriate IaaS platforms.

4.6   Federation Authentication/Authorization Support

The VEP layer helps a cloud provider become part of the larger Contrail cloud federation. The VEP layer handles all communication to/from the cloud provider and the federation. All requests on behalf of the federation user to the provider comes from the federation layer. Each such request has to be properly authenticated and only authorized requests should be forwarded to the IaaS layer. This check is necessary to prevent resource abuse and is also required for accounting and billing purposes.

Since VEP communicates to federation through REST APIs, each request carries with it the user authorization credentials embedded in the HTTP headers. User certificates and a trusted chain of certificates are used for verification of authorization credentials. The federation maintains the registered user accounts and the resource access rights and other details. The VEP is only interested in finding whether the presented credentials are authentic or not. Once the credentials are verified, the provider's resource access request is forwarded to the proper IaaS cluster.

The VEP also maintains a temporary access control table for active users and their applications that have been deployed through itself. An additional check against this table may also be performed if deemed necessary against the type of access requested.

4.7   Virtual Organization

The Contrail VEP supports the notion of a Virtual Organization (VO). The cloud provider / administrator will have the ability to configure the parameters of the virtual organization including list of hosts, networking connections, storage. The VO users' can submit OVFs for deployment making use of already provisioned VO resources. The billing for such resources will be sent to the VO and not the individual VO users. The VEP will support VOs even if the underlying IaaS platform does not support such a notion of organization. If a supported IaaS platform supports VOs natively (example OpenStack), VEP will make an effort to utilize the supported feature as much as feasible. Thus VEP will provide a uniform notion of VO to end users regardless of the underlying IaaS support of VOs.

5   Concluding Remarks

In this paper, we presented a detailed design of Contrail VEP implementation and rationale for our design. We have discussed the Contrail cloud federation briefly. We have explored the major challenges any cloud provider would face, and must address if they plan to become part of a larger federation. Contrail VEP software proposed support for a broad set of open cloud platforms would help significant number of private cloud operators to seamlessly join Contrail federation. Further, VEP's support of open standards and well defined API set will enable cloud researchers and developers to easily extend its features to suit their future requirements and thus making VEP somewhat future proof.

VEP's full integrated support for Contrail federation authentication and authorization mechanisms, and fully stress tested REST and OCCI interface will address some of the challenges (see 2.3, 2.4) we outlined for being part of a federation. The open source mindset and access to the source code would allow independent verification of monitoring modules and other features and thus would help build some level of trust in VEP and Contrail federation (see 2.5).

The Contrail project road map is well defined, in the initial release the VEP effort will provide complete integration with OpenNebula IaaS platform. Support for other cloud platforms including OpenStack will follow in the subsequent releases. There will be basic scheduling support in the first release, but we plan to provide a full resource scheduling feature in the second release. A full support for OCCI will also be provided in subsequent releases. The first release will also see basic OVF support with more complete support in subsequent releases.

References

1. Amazon Elastic Compute Cloud (Amazon EC2), http://aws.amazon.com/ec2/
2. Apache ActiveMQ, http://activemq.apache.org/
3. Distributed Management Task Force, Inc., http://www.dmtf.org/
4. Google App Engine, http://code.google.com/appengine/
5. Microsoft Azure, http://www.microsoft.com/windowsazure/
6. NIMBUS, http://www.nimbusproject.org/
7. OCCI Specification, http://occi-wg.org/about/specification/
8. Open Cloud Computing Interface, http://occi-wg.org/
9. Open Grid Forum, http://www.ogf.org/
10. Open Virtualization Format (OVF), http://www.dmtf.org/standards/ovf
11. OpenNebula.org - The Open Source Toolkit for Cloud Computing, http://www.opennebula.org/
12. OpenStack.org - Open source software for building private and public clouds, http://www.openstack.org/
13. VMware vCloud, http://www.vmware.com/products/vcloud/overview.html
14. Consortium, C.: Requirements on Federation Management, Identity and Policy Management in Federations, Contrail Deliverable - D2.1 (March 2011)
15. Crosby, S., Doyle, R., Gering, M., et al.: Open Virtualization Format Specification. DMTF, 1.1.0 edn. (January 2010)
16. Fielding, R.T.: Architectural styles and the design of network-based software architectures. Ph.D. thesis, AAI9980887 (2000)

Portability and Interoperability between Clouds: Challenges and Case Study
(Invited Paper)

Dana Petcu

Institute e-Austria Timişoara and West University of Timişoara, Romania
petcu@info.uvt.ro
http://web.info.uvt.ro/~petcu

Abstract. The greatest challenge beyond trust and security for the long-term adoption of cloud computing is the interoperability between clouds. In the context of world-wide tremendous activities against the vendor lock-in and lack of integration of cloud computing services, keeping track of the new concepts and approaches is also a challenge. We considered useful to provide in this paper a snapshot of these concepts and approaches followed by a proposal of their classification. A new approach in providing cloud portability is also revealed.

Keywords: Cloud computing, portability, interoperability.

1 Introduction

Still being in the early stage of developments, cloud computing suffers from the classical problem of too many different approaches. Practically, every new cloud provider comes with its own solution of interfacing with its resources or services. This variety is a reflection not only of different potential angles of approaching the concepts of cloud computing, but it is also a reflection of the variety of underlying offer on the market in what concerns the models of storage, networking, processes licensing or even integration of own resources in a cloud.

The portability and interoperability between clouds are important not only for the protection of the end user investments but also for the cloud ecosystem and market, business applications and data being currently strangled in silos. The main aim of interoperability is to allow the achievement of the full advantage of the cloud properties like elasticity and pay-as-you-go, not of a vendor infrastructure, platform or service. Nowadays, many companies still do not tie their critical applications to specific cloud providers services due to the underlying proprietary technology. Therefore the latest three years have been marked by the development of a considerable number of approaches to tackle with the issues of portability and interoperability. The selection of the appropriate approach to deal with these issues is in danger to become itself a challenge. Therefore we considered useful to present in this paper an overview of the different concepts and approaches undertaken world wide (in Section 2) and thereafter to go deeper into a particular solution currently under development (Section 3).

W. Abramowicz et al. (Eds.): ServiceWave 2011, LNCS 6994, pp. 62–74, 2011.

2   Challenges in Interoperability and Portability

2.1   Defining the Cloud Interoperability

A first challenge in cloud interoperability consists in its definition. As general term, interoperability is a property referring to the ability of diverse systems and organizations to work together (inter-operate). In computer world, this property has the concrete meaning of exchanging information and use of the information that has been exchanged between two or more systems or components. It is a property of a product or system, whose interfaces are completely understood, allowing it to work with other products or systems.

The most simple way to describe the cloud interoperability is by its most used motos like "avoid vendor lock-in", "develop your application one, deploy anywhere", "enable hybrid clouds", or even "one API to rule them all". Browsing the literature, one can found various definitions referring it as the ability to:

- abstract the programmatic differences from one cloud to another;
- translate between the abstractions supported by different clouds;
- flexible run applications locally or in the cloud, or in a combination;
- move applications from one environment to another or run in multiple clouds;
- move services, processes, workloads, and data between clouds;
- use same management tools, server images, software in multiple clouds;
- communicate between providers, port application and data between them;
- federate multiple clouds to support a single application.

2.2   Use Cases of Multiple Clouds

The above enumerated definitions of cloud interoperability are consequences of the different needs of the customers who are dealing with the use of multiple clouds. Use cases of multiple clouds have been reported in numerous papers in the last half decade. In a try to classify them, we can follow the NIST proposal [2] concerning the deployment scenarios in multiple clouds:

Serially, one cloud at a time, with three scenarios: (a) migration between clouds; (b) interface across multiple clouds; (c) work with a selected cloud;
Simultaneously, several clouds at a time, when operate across multiple clouds.

Beyond the well know use cases exposed in the white paper of Cloud Computing Use Cases [1] we draw the attention to the following use cases (after [2,3,4,5]):

Change cloud vendors: migrate some or all of a set of existing services to a new vendor. Customers may will to change providers to make an optimal choice regarding utilization, expenses or earnings. Other reasons to port application or data from one provider to another can be: provider out of business; better options in market than current ones; technology changes; contract termination; legal issues, etc.
Distributed deployment: the application may be distributed across two or more providers and administrative domains simultaneously:

FEDERATED CLOUDS: the providers agree how to mutually enforce policy and governance, establishing a common trust boundary;

- *Scale-out:* in an event occurs unexpectedly or in a peak, the company can still operate its cloud stably by distributing dynamically its load between the resources of its own cloud and a community cloud;
- *Mutual backup and recovery from a disaster:* if an event damages the provider's cloud or causes power outage, cloud resources in other providers are used to restore the services of that provider.

HYBRID CLOUD: applications cross a private-public trust boundary or span multiple clouds (simultaneous use of multiple clouds and both administrative domains and trust boundaries are crossed);

- *Use different cloud services at the same time,* to deploy on-production applications, run tests, or build test environment;
- *Manage selected resources in different clouds,* e.g. e-mail in one cloud, applications in another, and storage in a third one, all of them interacting;
- *Social networks applications* built using multi-tiered web technologies and serving dynamic content to users with unpredictable access and interaction patterns. Each component runs in a separate virtual machine hosted in data centers owned by different providers and must dynamically scale. New plug-ins are created by developers (freedom to choose provider), added to the system and used by others, potentially spiking. An application can have hundreds services in dozens of data centers.

2.3   Types and Targets of Cloud Interoperability

Several criteria for classification of interoperability types can be identified:

AGREEMENT LEVEL
- *syntactic,* when the systems are capable of communicating and exchanging data (using specified data formats, communication protocols).
- *semantic,* as automatically interpretation of the information exchanged, meaningfully and accurately, in order to produce useful results (using a common information exchange reference model);

ADOPTION LEVEL
- *by design* when vendors or individuals use a standard documentation to make products (no specific liability or advantage for any customer for choosing one product over another);
- *post-facto,* result of absolute market dominance of a particular product;

DEPLOYMENT LEVEL
- *horizontal* interoperability of the services at the same deployment level (likely within IaaS, harder to the customized PaaS and SaaS);
- *vertical* interoperability (vertical supply chain) when cloud services can be build on top of other cloud services from other deployment level;

PATTERNS OF INTERACTIONS BETWEEN CLOUDS
- *synchronous:* direct calls, suitable only for very specific real-time applications where the response time is critical;

- *asynchronous:* applications are loosely coupled so that consuming application do not wait for a response (best option in cloud).

The targeted levels for cloud interoperability are the followings (after [6,7,8]):

- *business* level, achieved between different business strategies that are imposed on the services, regulations on the services, and mode of use.;
- *semantic* level, with focus on functions calls and responses for consumers requests as well as message contents;
- *application/service* level when automated, generalized and extensible solutions are provided to use new resources (other than re-compiling, there are no further changes required of the application). Components could be reconfigured while running, or with limited interruption, to respond to changes in usage patterns or resource availability. Application configuration must be resilient to changes in the configuration within each cloud – for example scaling or migration of computational resources. From simple execution-unaware applications using multiple environments, to applications with multiple distributed components, the complexity is non-uniform and depends upon the application A pre-requisite is infrastructure independent programming;
- *management* when a management application coordinate and control components in multiple clouds. Standardized functionality for deployment and migration of VMs is required. Interactions between actors responsible for application management and infrastructure management is needed;
- *technology/infrastructure* level, achieved by agreeing on or accepting particular encoding scheme for requests and response, selection of communication protocol or middleware, language, and the platform for working environment;
- *image/data* looks at VM images, applications, or databases, and how they can be deployed on another host without modification (as pre-deployed, ready to run applications packaged as VMs, namely "work loads").
- *network* seek support to uniform access to individual resources and concatenation/federation (standards for allocation and admission control are needed).

The evolution of interoperability issues has take three stages (after [9]):

Migration: refers to portability of VMs allowing to move VMs between clouds, to create VMs locally and import them, and to share VMs with others (OVF is providing standard packaging, but does not address the problem of different virtual disk formats; further migration/ conversion tools are needed);

Federation: targets networking, portable VMs being moved to the cloud without reconfiguring anything including network settings (transparent migration) or move across multiple clouds and multiple hypervisors;

Burst: targets APIs; as portable VMs and ability to seamlessly integrate deployments are in place, migration and federation "on demand" come in place; interoperability efforts are related to storage (CDMI) and compute (OCCI).

The federation of clouds can be organized in different ways:

HORIZONTAL FEDERATION. Two or more cloud providers join together to create a federated cloud [10]: participants who have excess capacity can share their resources, for an agreed-upon price, with participants needing additional resources (avoiding over provisioning of resources to deal with spikes in capacity demand). Challenges are related to: finding the "best" cloud for a workload by balancing among parameters like QoS and cost; a logical topology is maintained regardless the physical location of the components.

INTERCLOUD. Federation of clouds with common addressing, naming, identity, trust, presence, messaging, multicast, time domain and application messaging [4]. The responsibility for communicating is on the providers' side. The applications are integrating services from multiple clouds and are scaling across multiple clouds. The overall goal is to create a computing environment that supports dynamic expansion or contraction of capabilities for handling variations in demands. Dynamic workload migration is possible.

CROSS-CLOUD. The federation establishment between a cloud needing external resources and a cloud offering resources (not necessarily in agreement), passes through three main phases [11]: discovery, looking for available clouds; match-making, selecting the ones fitting the requirements; authentication, establishing a trust context with the selected clouds.

SKY COMPUTING. Offers a combined use of multiple clouds. Resources, applications and platforms across clouds are used. New services other than those of each individual cloud are provided. Transparency of multiple clouds is provided offering a single-cloud like image. Sky providers are consumers of cloud providers' services offering (virtual datacenter-less) dynamicity [12].

The main supporting actors [2,4] assisting in federation implementation are:

Broker, an entity that manages the use, performance and delivery of cloud services, and negotiates relationships between providers and consumers;

Auditor, a third-party that conducts an independent audit of the operations and determines the security of the cloud implementation;

Coordinator, for exporting cloud services and their management driven by market-based trading and negotiation protocols for optimal QoS delivery;

Exchange, acting as a market maker enabling capability sharing across multiple cloud domains through its match making services.

Orchestrator, for the network of clouds.

2.4 Cloud Portability

While the interoperability is the successful communication between or among systems, portability is the ability to use components or systems lying on multiple hardware or software environments.

The types and solutions for portability are classified (after [8,13]) as follows:

functional portability: ability to define application functionality QoS details in a platform-agnostic manner. OVF provides a basis for portability but does not address complex configuration or interactions with any supporting systems. Domain specific languages are expected to bridge the gap between executable artifacts and high-level semantic models.

data portability: ability for a customer to retrieve application data from one provider and import this into an equivalent application hosted by another provider. Achieving data portability depends on standardization of data import and export functionality between providers. It is necessary to provide a platform-independent data representation, and generate the specific target representations and even the code for the application's data access layer;

services enhancement: use metadata added through annotations. Control APIs allow infrastructure to be added, reconfigured, or removed in real time, either by humans or programmatically based on traffic, outages or other factors.

The requirements of portability at different deployment levels are as follows (after CSA - Cloud Security Alliance documents):

SAAS: the cloud customer is substituting software applications with new ones. The focus is on preserving or enhancing the functionality provided by the application. Portability is evaluated based on open source code base, proprietary or open standard data formats, integration technologies and application server/operating system.

PAAS: some degree of application modification will be necessary to achieve portability. The focus is on minimizing the amount of application rewriting while preserving or enhancing controls, and a successful data migration. Portability is evaluated based on proprietary or open source programming languages for application development, proprietary or open data formats, tight integration or loose coupled services, abstraction layers for queuing and messaging services.

IAAS: the applications and the data migrate and run at a new cloud provider. Portability is evaluate based on ability to port VMs and the underlying configurations across infrastructure providers.

2.5 Interoperability and Portability Requirements

The main requirements for cloud interoperability are (after [4,5,10]):

programming: move from one provider to another without dramatic reimplementation; common set of interfaces; standard API enabling an entity to build something once, then use it to monitor and control a variety of platforms; work with both cloud-based and enterprise-based applications using a single tool set that can function across existing programs and multiple cloud providers; new programming models; ontology of cloud; high level modelling.

application: able to span multiple cloud services; data exchange; data portability; private cloud applications obtain resources from public cloud when excess capacity is needed; location-free applications; workflow management;

monitoring: SLA and performance monitoring; SLAs in support of governance requirements; deliver on demand, reliable, cost-effective, and QoS aware services based on virtualization technologies while ensuring high QoS standards and minimizing service costs; QoS and SLA items to be guaranteed end-to-end; monitoring and management of load balanced applications in an elastic environment; scalable monitoring of system components; service monitoring and audit; publish sets of benchmarks to evaluate performance factors;

deployment: provision resources from multiple cloud services with a single management tool; agreements between providers; service discovery; common platforms to ensure users can navigate between services/applications; enabling a service hosted on one platform to automatically call a service hosted by another; automatically provision services and manage VM instances; virtual organization management; resource discovery and reservation procedure; service setup procedure; interworking between clouds and the network – routing optimization based on monitoring; automatism and scalability – home cloud using discovery mechanisms able to pick out the right foreign clouds; support for multiple hypervisor technologies; application service behavior prediction;

authentication, authorization, security: single sign-on for users accessing multiple cloud; integration of different security technologies (home cloud able to join federation without changing security policies); digital identities; identity federation and management across vendors; standards for security specification, platform components and configuration; authentication procedure when use different domains; cloud trust mechanisms; auditing, security mechanisms for authentication and authorization;

market: economic models driven optimization techniques; market driven resource leasing federation – application service providers host their services based on negotiated SLAs driven by competitive market prices; flexible mapping of services to resources to maximize efficiency, cost-effectiveness, and utilization; accounting; license flexibility.

2.6   Approaches to Cloud Interoperability and Portability

The approaches to interoperability and portability can be classified in building and using: (1) open APIs; (2) open protocols; (3) standards; (4) layers of abstractions; (5) semantic repositories; (6) domain specific languages.

Open APIs are for example jClouds (Java), libcloud (Python), Cloud::Infrastructure (Perl), Simple Cloud (PHP), Dasein Cloud (Java), proprietary APIs being for example Micosoft Azure (.NET) or Fujitsu API. A short list includes (after [14,15]):

JCloud provides a framework for interacting with blob storage, queue storage, and compute resources for a variety of clouds (requires service and location information to access a data item).

Dasein Cloud includes blob storage, compute, and network abstractions (does not include table or queue-based storage, and aiming to interface with all aspects of cloud infrastructures it is quite complex);

CloudLoop provides a filesystem-like interface to blob storage (does not support other abstractions such as tables and queues);

SimpleCloud from IBM, Microsoft, Zend, Nirvanix, Rackspace and GoGrid supports storage management (storage, queues, and databases) and is a PHP API for interacting with blob, table, and queue storage services of several providers (PHP is typically limited to web applications);

OpenNebula provides cloud users and administrators with choice across popular cloud interfaces, hypervisors and clouds, for hybrid cloud computing deployments, and with a flexible software that can be installed (expose most common cloud interfaces, such as vCloud and EC2; use open community specifications, such us OCCI, and open interfaces, such as libcloud and delta-cloud; support the combination of local private infrastructure with EC2 and others through the deltacloud adaptor);

ServerTemplates from RightScale, enables portability, but also lets users take advantage of the unique capabilities of different clouds: it configures servers for a specific cloud, application architecture and operating system;

Appistry, AppZero, and 3Tera created suites providing a layer of abstraction be-tween the programmer and the cloud platforms. Developers create applica-tions for this intermediate layer, which then supports and manages multiple hypervisors or external cloud platforms;

OpenStack has a similar proposal and is a combination of Rackspace cloud ar-chitecture and NASA's Nebula.

The above APIs for multiple clouds can be classified as follows (after [15]):

API WITH MULTIPLE INDEPENDENT IMPLEMENTATIONS (Eucalyptus compati-bility with EC2, AppEngine with AppScale). The shared API is driven by the initial provider and periods of inconsistency between implementations can appear; moreover, two implementations of the same API are not equivalent in terms of scalability, features, maturity, and customer support.

API RUNNABLE ON MULTIPLE CLOUDS not necessarily through multiple inde-pendent implementations (e.g. MapReduce and Hadoop). They focus on par-ticular application model, not necessarily fit for any developers requirements. Significant developer time investment for configuring, deploying, maintaining these services is needed. Implementations are tailored to the specific vendor offering the service (the configuration may differ between vendors).

SEPARATE THE APPLICATION INTO "APP-LOGIC LAYER" AND "CLOUD LAYER" (with code written for each cloud provider). It is the most general option, but requires a time and complexity investment by a developer to initially create the layers and further maintain them over time as the APIs change.

SET OF STANDARDS this is the best solution in terms of cloud interoperability, but it is far from being realized in the commercial space.

Open protocols are for example OCCI (HTTP) or Deltacloud (RedHat), while proprietary protocols are for example Amazon EC2 or VMware vCloud.

vCloud (with TCloud extension) offers the concepts of instance template, storage and network, image element, and vApp (containing one or more VMs).

DeltaCloud by Red Hat, abstract the differences between diverse clouds (sup-ports only computational resources).

OCCI is a specification for remote management of cloud infrastructure, allowing the development of tools for common tasks including deployment, autonomic scaling and monitoring. Its API is based on three concepts: compute, storage and network. It relies on the HTTP protocol.

Many groups are working on cloud computing standards (interoperability ab-initio). The most active groups are (after [16]) CloudAudit, CSA, DMTF, ETSI TC CLOUD, OGF, OMG, OCC, ASIS, SNIA, CCIF, GICTF, ODCA. The OCCI Working Group of OGF, for example, develops mainly a practical specification related to IaaS. DMTFs Open Cloud Standards Incubator (OCSI) focuses on standardizing interactions between cloud environments by developing cloud resource management protocols. Cloud Manifesto is an initiative supported by several companies arguing that cloud should capitalize on standards.

The two widely adopted standards are:

OVF is a DMTF standard that describes virtual appliances for deployment across heterogeneous virtualization platforms (i.e. different hypervisor), allowing the users to deploy their virtual appliances at every cloud provider.

CDMI is a SNIA standard for data management specifying a functional manner on how applications create, retrieve, update, delete data from the cloud.

Technical requirements versus standards were recently discussed in [2]:

Creating, accessing, updating, deleting data in clouds (cross-cloud): standard interfaces to metadata and data objects are needed, current solution is CDMI;

Moving VMs & virtual appliances between clouds (migration, hybrid clouds, recovery, bursting): need a common VM description format – solution: OVF;

Selecting vendor for externally hosted cloud (cost-effective reliable deployment): resource and performance requirements description languages, no solution;

Portable tools for monitoring and managing clouds (simplifies operations as opposed to individual tools per cloud): standard management interfaces to IaaS resources, current solution OCCI;

Moving data between clouds (migration, cross-cloud): standard metadata/data formats for movement; vendor mappings between cloud data and standard formats; standardized query languages – no solution;

Single sign-on access to multiple clouds (simplified access, cross-cloud): federated identity and authorization, solutions from OpenID, OAuth, OASIS, CSA;

Orchestrated processes across clouds and enterprise systems (enhanced applications): standards for APIs/data, solutions from SOA, Intercloud/IEEE;

Discovering cloud resources (selection of clouds): description languages for available resources, catalog interfaces, current solution from DMTF, TM Forum;

Evaluating SLAs and penalties (selection of appropriate cloud resources): SLA description language, no solution;

Auditing clouds (ensure regulatory compliance; verify information assurance): auditing standards, verification check lists, solution from CSA CloudAudit.

There are several barriers in standardization (after [3]): (1) Each vendor likes to put barriers to exit for their customers, unless there is some pressure from their big customers. (2) Each cloud provider offers differentiated services, and want to have special services to attract more customers (a common standard may regulate them). (3) Cloud providers will possibly not agree with an easy and standardized manner to export/import cloud configurations. (4) Standards are nascent and will take years to fully develop. (5) There are numerous standards being developed simultaneously and consensus may be difficult, if not impossible, to attain. (6) As there are a number of different cloud computing models (e.g. SaaS, PaaS, IaaS), this indicates that different standards are needed for each model, rather than one overarching set of standards.

Different layers of abstractions are used for example in the case of:

RESERVOIR: service providers are the mediators between infrastructure providers and end-users (single clients or businesses). Service manifests, formally defining a contract and SLA, play a key role in the whole architecture [10];

SLA@SOI: Framework where cloud services can be traded as economic goods and SLA agreements can be established between customers and service/business providers, service providers and all the way down to infrastructure demands monitoring of the services life-cycle;

CSAL: Abstraction layer, that provides blob, table, and queue abstractions across multiple providers and presents applications with an integrated namespace thereby relieving applications of having to manage storage entity location information and access credentials [15];

RASIC: An open, generic reference architecture for semantically inter-operable clouds introducing an approach for the design, deployment and execution of resource intensive SOA services on top of semantically interlinked clouds [16].

The semantic can be applied to the interface level, the component level, and the data level by utilizing a generic semantic cloud resource data model. Semantics can be also used to annotate the services and the applications deployed by the users on top of the cloud (the challenges to be addressed involve the specifications of the appropriate properties such that the service can be deployed and efficiently executed in the infrastructure). In this context, Unified Cloud Computing [17] is an attempt to create an open and standardized cloud interface for the unification of various cloud APIs; for a unified interface RDF is used to describe a semantic cloud data model (taxonomy and ontology). A functional implementation of UCI is available for on Amazon EC2 or Enomaly ECP.

Domain specific languages provide a cloud neutral application creation strategy. They create a cloud specific application for the platform or interpret it in a cloud specific VM. The complexity of managing heterogenous applications is hidden from the user. Few solutions are available on the market.

3   Case Study: Interoperability in mOSAIC

mOSAIC is a project partially funded by the European Commission in the period 2010-2013 aiming to provide an open source API and platform for supporting applications using multiple clouds. We considered useful to presents its position versus the concepts discussed in the previous section as providing a real snapshot of current activities in the field of cloud portability and interoperability.

mOSAIC approach for interoperability consists in building an open API, offering a layer of abstraction, and applying semantic to interface and component level (see section 2.6). The main targets are hybrid clouds' scenarios and vertical interoperability by design (sections 2.2 and 2.3). The platform best suited applications are the long-time running ones (like in the social network or management of resources scenarios), but entry points in the platform are provided to deploy legacy or scientific applications (using different services at the same time) [18].

In what concerns the API design, mOSAIC team decided to separate the application into application-logic layer and cloud layer (see section 2.6). The application developer do not care about the infrastructure. A descriptor of the application is used to select the proper clouds (it presents the components and their interactions). The code for connecting to a specific cloud is generated at run time using what is named in mOSAIC, interoperability API [19], drivers for a certain category of cloud technologies and connectors to particular cloud services. The applications are decomposed in components runnable of top of different clouds [20]. Cloudlets are the means offered to developer to create components. A cloudlet runs in a container managed by the platform and can have multiple instances. A container hosts a single cloudlet, even if it may host multiple instances of the same cloudlet. Containers can run on multiple clouds. A component is a container and its hosted cloudlet (instances).

Exchanges between clouds are done using cloud based message queues technologies to ensure the syntactic interoperability (see section 2.3), while the high level APIs are ensuring the semantic interoperability. A asynchronous pattern of interaction is expected and an event-driven architecture was adopted.

Based on the current state of the art, mOSAIC is a representative for the "burst" phase in cloud interoperability (see section 2.3). It is build on top of the existing solutions for portable VMs deployment, providing "on demand" federation of cloud services. While it relies upon the current solutions for interoperability at technology–infrastructure, image–data and network level, mOSAIC targets application–service, management and semantic levels of interoperability, supporting applications decoupled from the execution, deploying and controlling the running components [21], and allowing semantic processing based on a particular cloud ontology. The level of deployment targeted by mOSAIC is PaaS (see section 2.4). Being able to combine services from different clouds (without the need establishing a trust context in the selected clouds), to offer transparency of multiple clouds, and to provide new services on top of the existing ones, mOSAIC can be considered a sky computing provider (see section 2.3). As supporting actors the platform uses brokers and coordinators.

4   Final Remarks and Conclusions

Far from being solved, the cloud interoperability and portability problems are treated by various approaches. A deep analysis of these approaches show a limited trace of consensus and worries can be raised about their completeness in the near future. The current paper intended to "draw the line" and to point towards the most successful or promising approaches with the hope to pave the way for further research and development activities in using multiple clouds.

Acknowledgment. This research is partially supported by the grant FP7-ICT-2009-5-256910 (mOSAIC).

References

1. Cloud Computing Use Case Discussion Group. Cloud computing use cases-white paper. Version 2.0 (2009)
2. NIST CCSRWG: Cloud Computing Standards Roadmap (2011)
3. Machado, G.S., Hausheer, D., Stiller, B.: Considerations on the interoperability of and between cloud computing standards. In: Procs. OGF27: G2C-Net (2009)
4. Bernstein, D., Ludvigson, E., Sankar, K., Diamond, S., Morrow, M.: Blueprint for the Intercloud - protocols and formats for cloud computing interoperability. In: Procs. ICIW 2009, pp. 328–336. IEEE Computer Press, Los Alamitos (2009)
5. GICTF: White paper–use cases and functional requirements for inter-cloud computing (2010)
6. Khattak, A.M., Pervez, Z., Sarkar, A.M.J., Lee, Y.-K.: Service level semantic interoperability. In: Procs. IEEE SAINT 2010, pp. 387–390. IEEE CSP, Los Alamitos (2010)
7. Merzky, A., Stamou, K., Jha, S.: Application level interoperability between clouds and grids. In: Procs. GPC Workshops 2009, pp. 143–150. IEEE CSP, Los Alamitos (2009)
8. Oberle, K., Fisher, M.: ETSI CLOUD–initial standardization requirements for cloud services. In: Altmann, J., Rana, O.F. (eds.) GECON 2010. LNCS, vol. 6296, pp. 105–115. Springer, Heidelberg (2010)
9. Williams, J.L.: An implementors perspective on interoperable cloud APIs. Cloud interoperability roadmaps sessions. In: OMG Technical Meeting (2009)
10. Rochwerger, B., Breitgand, D., Epstein, A., Hadas, D., Loy, I., Nagin, K., Tordsson, J., Ragusa, C., Villari, M., Clayman, S., Levy, E., Maraschini, A., Massonet, P., Munoz, H., Tofetti, G.: Reservoir–when one cloud is not enough. Computer 44(3), 44–51 (2011)
11. Celesti, A., Tusa, F., Villari, M., Puliafito, A.: Three-phase cross-cloud federation model: the cloud SSO authentication. In: Procs. AFIN 2010, pp. 94–101. IEEE CSP, Los Alamitos (2010)
12. Keahey, K., Tsugawa, M., Matsunaga, A., Fortes, J.: Sky computing. Internet Computing 13(5), 43–51 (2009)
13. Sheth, A., Ranabahu, A.: Semantic modeling for cloud computing, part 2. IEEE Internet Computing 14(4), 81–84 (2010)
14. Lee, C.A.: An open cloud computing interface status update (and roadmap dartboard) Cloud interoperability roadmaps sessions. In: OMG Technical Meeting (2009)
15. Hill, Z., Humphrey, M.: CSAL: A cloud storage abstraction layer to enable portable cloud applications. In: Procs. CloudCom 2010, pp. 504–511. IEEE CSP, Los Alamitos (2010)
16. Loutas, N., Peristeras, V., Bouras, T., Kamateri, E., Zeginis, D., Tarabanis, K.: Towards a reference architecture for semantically interoperable clouds. In: Procs. CloudCom 2010, pp. 143–150. IEEE CSP, Los Alamitos (2010)
17. Unified Cloud Interface, http://code.google.com/p/unifiedcloud/

18. Di Martino, B., Petcu, D., Cossu, R., Goncalves, P., Máhr, T., Loichate, M.: Building a mosaic of clouds. In: Guarracino, M.R., Vivien, F., Träff, J.L., Cannatoro, M., Danelutto, M., Hast, A., Perla, F., Knüpfer, A., Di Martino, B., Alexander, M. (eds.) Euro-Par-Workshop 2010. LNCS, vol. 6586, pp. 571–578. Springer, Heidelberg (2011)
19. Petcu, D., Craciun, C., Neagul, M., Lazcanotegui, I., Rak, M.: Building an interoperability API for sky computing. In: InterCloud 2011, pp. 405–412. IEEE CSP, Los Alamitos (2011)
20. Petcu, D., Craciun, C., Rak, M.: Towards a cross platform cloud API. Components for cloud federation. In: Procs. CLOSER 2011, pp. 166–169. SciTePress (2011)
21. Petcu, D., Crăciun, C., Neagul, M., Panica, S., Di Martino, B., Venticinque, S., Rak, M., Aversa, R.: Architecturing a sky computing platform. In: Cezon, M. (ed.) ServiceWave 2011 Workshops. LNCS, vol. 6569, pp. 1–13. Springer, Heidelberg (2011)

Enhancing Query Support in HBase
via an Extended Coprocessors Framework

Himanshu Vashishtha and Eleni Stroulia

Department of Computing Science, University of Alberta
{hvashish,stroulia}@cs.ualberta.ca

Abstract. Currently, cloud databases serve as mainstream data storage mechanism for unstructured data, primarily because of their high scalability and ease of availability. However, as yet, they lag behind RDBMs in terms of their support to developers for querying the data. The problem of developing frameworks to support flexible data queries is a very active area of research. In this work we consider HBase, a popular cloud database, inspired by Google's *BigTable*. Relying on the recent *Coprocessor* feature of HBase, we have developed a framework that developers can use to implement aggregate functions like row count, max, min, etc. We further extended the existing Coprocessor framework to support a *Cursor* functionality, so that a client can incrementally consume the Coprocessor generated result. We demonstrate the effectiveness of our extension by comparatively evaluating it against the existing Scanner API with four queries on three different data sets.

Keywords: Hadoop, HDFS, HBase, Coprocessors, Endpoint, Cursor.

1 Introduction

We are witnessing the unprecedented generation of substantial amounts of data. Books are being digitized on a massive scale. Social-networking platforms like twitter, Facebook, YouTube, Flickr, forums, and blogs collect data at mind-boggling rates. Twitter alone produces 15-20 terabytes uncompressed data daily.

This new massive scale of data to be collected, archived and processed makes the traditional model of computing, where an organization invests capital costs in purchasing its own infrastructure and operation costs in maintaining it, impractical and unaffordable. Instead, infrastructure is increasingly provided as a service (IaaS) with specialized providers offering large-scale computational resources (computing power, storage and network bandwidth) at an economical rate. In this new model of computing infrastructure, one can lease storage and virtual machines, configured in a manner that meets the computing task at hand. So affordable are the prices of these offerings that there are more than a few corporations that don't have any infrastructure of their own at all; they store "everything" on the cloud.

The availability of massive and scalable infrastructure brings to the forefront two interesting challenges. One is to develop support for persisting data in a scalable and fault-tolerant manner, assuming infrastructure failures as a norm rather

W. Abramowicz et al. (Eds.): ServiceWave 2011, LNCS 6994, pp. 75–87, 2011.

than as an aberrant behavior. The second challenge involves the development of a software layer that will enable software developers to implement scalable analyses methods, able to process big data with high throughput. These two challenges push the idea of virtualization from the *infrastructure* level to the *platform* level, where the software-engineering challenge is to provide software support to make the manipulation of data on the cloud as easy conceptually as the traditional infrastructures to which most developers are accustomed.

The Apache Hadoop project represents exactly such a platform. Its associated project, Hadoop Distributed File System (HDFS), provides a distributed, scalable and fault-tolerant file system for persisting big data. It is designed for storing and accessing large files (with an assumed upper limit to its size in terabytes). Relying on HDFS, Hadoop supports the map-reduce [6] software-architecture model. This model supports computational tasks, reminiscent of batch processing, where a typical job runs with in the range of few minutes to few hours or more – thus, a less than ideal candidate for on-line query type of workloads, where small subsets of data need to be examined and manipulated.

Google's BigTable [5] was conceived to address exactly this type of computational tasks, providing support for storing data, no longer on a file system, but rather in distributed, sparse, column-oriented, multi-dimensional tables, sorted on a primary key. Apache HBase is an open source Java implementation of BigTable and is widely used in a number of corporations. It stores its data in a data-, called *HTable*. It provides standard APIs for persisting and accessing data from these tables. These APIs work on the principle of "filtering" table rows, and transferring them to the client, putting the onus of their processing on client. In a typical HBase workflow, data is first accessed at the individual nodes, i.e., the *Region servers*, where HTable *Regions* are stored, and is then sent to the client for further processing. A *Region* is an ordered subset of a table. There are some cases where the server could send "locally computed results" to the client. For example, in case of computing row count on a subset of a table, all individual *Regions* could send just the row count.

The new Coprocessors feature of HBase is conceived to address exactly this challenge: developers can now write code to be executed server-side, i.e., at each node where HTable *Regions* are stored, to compute local results that can then be aggregated (relying on the Coprocessor libraries) at the client-side. In our work, we developed six standard aggregate functions, namely (1) row count, (2) max, (3) min, (4) sum, (5) average and (6) standard deviation, using the existing Coprocessor framework. We also extended the Coprocessor framework to support Results streaming, where one can iterate through a Coprocessor generated result at a *Region* across multiple Remote Procedure Calls (RPC).[1]

We organized the remainder of this paper as follows. Section 2 provides background information about HBase and Coprocessors. Section 3 discusses several interesting use cases to motivate and illustrate the relative merits of the original HBase data-access approach vs. the newer Coprocessor approach. Section 4 explains the design of our experiment, including the datasets, the queries and the

---

[1] Part of this work is committed to Apache HBase project and the rest is under review.

infrastructure configurations. Section 5 discusses the results and reflects on the lessons we learned through this experiment. Section 6 reviews research in this area. Finally Sect. 7 summarizes the contributions of this work.

2   Background

This section elaborates about the design of HBase, describes the support it offer to software developers of distributed data-intensive applications.

HBase is a distributed, column-oriented database, built on top of HDFS in order to support low latency random-access patterns on large data. Its design is based on *Google's BigTable*. It is a column oriented, distributed database that stores records sorted by a primary key. Its support for de-normalized schema makes it feasible to store huge tables, spanning across millions of columns to billion of rows. It stores tables across multiple servers by dividing the data set into *Regions*, where each *Region* represents an ordered subset of the table rows. It is designed such that, irrespective of the number of columns in a row, each row is always stored in its entirety, in a single *Region*. These *Regions* store their data in multiple immutable *HFiles*, a HBase-specific file format designed specifically to cater to the requirement of random reads. Each *HFile* has an index block at its end that is used to locate whether or not a particular row is present in the *HFile*. It leverages the benefits of HDFS and also provides the additional benefits of random reads, random writes, and file appends. During a read access, all these *HFiles* from a *Region* are referred to form a unified result for the read. Since these files are immutable, these files are merged on a scheduled basis to form a single, compacted *HFile* to avoid the overhead of reading multiple files. HBase has proven to be an effective solution for storing large datasets as it leverages the benefits of already proven HDFS and also provides faster access to the data.

HBase provides several APIs for accessing data. It is worth mentioning here that there are no datatypes in HBase. It stores all its data as byte arrays.

1. *get(byte[] row)*: fetches a given row;

2. *getScanner(Scan)*: returns a *Scanner* object that is used to iterate on a subset of a table; the argument *Scan* defines the start/stop rows, column families, and other filters to be used while scanning the table;

3. *put(byte[] row)*: inserts a new row; and

4. *delete(byte[] row)*: deletes an existing row.

Given these APIs, the client program requests data through *get* (one row) or *scan* (multiple rows) and proceeds to process the collected rows. It is important to note here that the actual processing occurs at the client-side, after the selected rows have been fetched from their respective *Regions*. HBase originally did not offer any support to developers for deploying code at the nodes where the table *Regions* are stored in order to perform computations local to the data and return results (and not just partial or complete table rows) to the client node. This limitation makes the cost of several computations prohibitive: consider, for example, a row-count process: a developer has to either implement a map-reduce pair of processes over the table, or a sequential scan on the entire data, fetched locally. Data access in HBase is provided by the row key of the table, through a *get*. One can also sequentially *scan* a range of table rows by providing the start and end row keys, through the *scan* API). Developers can subsequently run a map-reduce job, where the data of a single *Region* is provided to a single mapper.

3   Coprocessor Use Cases

HBase Coprocessors, inspired by Google's BigTable Coprocessors [1], is an arbitrary piece of software deployed on a *Region*, addressing a (range of) row(s); the client library resolves these calls to multiple nodes and executes them in parallel. The core *get* and *scan* APIs of HBase simply support the selection of a (sequence of) row(s) and its (their) return to the client-side for further processing. With the original Coprocessor framework, clients cannot request the persistence of intermediate data (or state) at the server; they can only request the invocation of a computation on an entire Region and the return of the complete result set to the client.

Our Coprocessor extension, to which we will refer as *extended endpoint* or simply *endpoints* from now on, is able to perform server-side execution of specific types of BigTable queries in a sequence of steps, and incrementally send the results to the client, by maintaining a pointer (at the server side) recording how much of the Region has been processed. Thus, developers enjoy greater flexibility as they are able to consume the Coprocessors generated results across multiple RPCs.

3.1   Endpoint Queries

As we have already discussed, running map-reduce jobs on a HBase cluster is less than ideal solution for on-line queries. Map-reduce provides high throughput for batch analytical jobs where there is a need to scan the entire table or a large subset of a table. Consider however use cases where (a) one does not need to process the entire table, or (b) one needs to perform a computation on the table in order to produce a single end result for the client. One such example would be "calculating the row count on a sub set of a table with a given property". Currently, the way to implement this query is to invoke a scan of these rows, collect them at the client side, and then count them and compute the result. Clearly, it would be better if one could actually compute the counts at the *Regions'* level, at the server-side, and return them to the client that would still need to aggregate them, i.e., sum the individual counts. In such a scenario, there would be fewer RPCs, less network traffic and simpler client-side computations.

There are several use cases that resemble the type of workload we have described above, such as, for example (a) counting number of rows within a given row range, with the boundary condition being a row count on the entire table; (b) aggregate-statistics functions, such as sum, maximum, minimum, average, standard deviation of a specific column in a given row range; and (c) more generally, a computationally intensive task at the server-side, which would manipulate and substantially transform the table rows. The last use case is necessarily dataset specific, and we emulate it in Sect. 4 using the Bixi dataset.

We now discuss how the above use cases can be implemented with the original HBase *scan* vs. our implementation of scan with Coprocessor endpoints. In the former case, the first step for the client is to get a scanner object from the HTable API. It involves instantiating a *Scan* object that encapsulates query-specific details like start row, stop row, filtering criteria, batch size of the results, etc. This causes the instantiation of a scan object at the *Region* that has the given start row, its registration with the hosting *Region server*, and the return of its identifier to the client. The client incrementally consumes the result from the starting *Region* while iterating over it. When scanning a *Region* is completed, the scanner automatically (from client's perspective) moves to the next *Region*. This process stops upon reaching the stop row.

In case of Coprocessor endpoints, the first step is to define a Coprocessor implementation to be loaded as part of the *Region* instantiation. The next step is to define a pair of *callable* and *callback* objects at the client-side. The callable object is used to envelope method invocations to the server using the Coprocessor RPC framework. The callback object is invoked when results of the above Coprocessor call is available. Its purpose is to perform the client-side aggregation of the results returned from the individual Coprocessor calls from various *Regions*. Note that the calls to the *Regions* are made in parallel and are executed as a batch process. So, if a client happens to call 10 *Regions* via this mechanism, it gets the final result when all the *Regions* have return their local result.

This parallel execution is the key advantage of the Coprocessor framework as compared to the sequential flow in the original *Scan* API. It provides better throughput. In our work we have further improved this feature to produce a cursor infrastructure that streams results from a Coprocessor spanning across multiple RPCs, as opposed to collecting them as a single batch.

3.2 Streaming Results from Coprocessor Endpoints

The original Coprocessor implementation provides the functionality for performing the computation in one RPC. It is assumed that a client exhausts the entire *Region* before returning the local result. This is a stateless call; the server does not maintain any reference to the client request and, therefore, a client has no means to consume the results of individual *Regions* result in an incremental way. Clearly, in many cases the result from a *Region* may be quite large and the client is likely to want to consume it in an *incremental* way. This is the functionality that our extension to the Coprocessor framework provides: namely, enabling a client to consume these endpoint results incrementally. We demonstrate this functionality in our experiment with the NGram dataset (see Sect. 4.2).

We built our extension using the endpoint feature of the Coprocessor framework. An endpoint is a singleton object composed in the *Region* and we need this endpoint object to be stateless to support multiple client-side calls. We cannot store the state of the client as an endpoint attribute. However, each Coprocessor object has an associated *environment* object, which holds the context of the owning Coprocessor, such as the associated *Region* and *Region server*. We utilize the environment object to create a *registry* or map like data structure in it, and use it for temporarily storing client states.

We designed a *Cursor* interface that defines the contract for providing iterative APIs like *next, hasNext* to a Coprocessor result. The concrete implementor of the Cursor interface will define its run-time behaviour such as what processing has to be done on the table rows while doing a *next()* invocation, how are the results per table row to be aggregated, and how the results per RPC call should be sorted (or if they are to rendered in some specific way, for example a group by), etc. The grouping of results per RPC is required because one RPC can return many result rows. This concrete implementation will be a part of the endpoint defined by the client. When a client needs this functionality in its Endpoint, it defines and instantiates a concrete Cursor object as an anonymous object, registers it in the Coprocessor *registry*, and returns a handler to the client. The client can then use this handle in order to use the registered Cursor object.

It is important to note here that the client gets these cursor handlers from all the invoked *Regions*. We define a client-side cursor object, the ClientCursor, that encapsulates these handlers. It maintains a list of all these handlers and exposes iterative methods like *next, hasNext* to the client. For example, invoking the *next* call results in calling all the interested *Regions* in parallel and aggregating their individual results before rendering the aggregation to the client. Whenever a call results in a *null* result from a *Region* in the Endpoint, it is assumed that the respective cursor at the *Region* has exhausted it and that Cursor object is deregistered before it returns. When the *ClientCursor* notices a *null* result from a *Region*, it removes the corresponding handler from its handler list. Thus, no more *next ()* request is sent to this *Region*. Subsequently, it sets its *hasNext* variable to false when the handler list becomes empty, marking the end of results from all *Regions*. To summarize, the ClientCursor takes care of all the parallel calls to the *Regions*. The developer's code is not aware of these cursor handlers that are registered at the server-side. It simply calls *next()* on *ClientCursor* and expects all the *Regions* to return their results.

4 Experiment Setup

To evaluate our work and analyze the relative merits of the two variants of the Coprocessor framework, i.e., the original and our extension, we had to select appropriate datasets and queries. The datasets should be large to be labeled as 'big-data'. And, the selected queries should provide an opportunity of substantial server-side computation and also, to use the results streaming functionality. Query selection and schema design are very much correlated with each other given our prejudice over the type of processing we want to support. Sections 4.1, 4.2 and 4.3 provide a comprehensive picture of our experimental design.

4.1   Datasets

Bixi is a public dataset collected by *Public Bike Systems Inc.* for their Montreal operation in Quebec, Canada. This is a bike renting service, having 404 stations in Montreal. A subscribed user can rent a bike or submit a bike in a station. These stations are equipped with sensors which transmit information in XML format, about their status such as number of available bikes, empty docks, geographical locations etc, at regular intervals. This data is made publicly available at the company website[2]. We used the dataset that was collected on a per minute basis for a period of 70 days, from September 24, 2010 to December 1, 2010. It is a 12 GB dataset that contains 96,842 data-points for all the Montreal stations.

Google NGrams is a collection of N-Grams from the entire google books collection, which the company made available for research work in 2009 [9]. We used the 1-gram dataset for our experiments, which contains 6,641,214 unique words. This dataset is structured in a column separated value (csv) format. The first column is the word in context; the second column is the year in which this word was used; the third, fourth and fifth column represent the word count, unique number of pages and books respectively, containing the word in that year. Thus, for a given word, there is one row for each corresponding year.

4.2   Sample Queries

Evaluation of the result-streaming functionality requires a specific set of queries where one can stream the coprocessor generated results. As mentioned earlier, this poses two conditions: first, there should be some substantial computation that can be transferred to the server and, the result set should be large enough so that the client needs to do more than one RPC to fetch the result from a *Region* (stream results). It is to be noted that the original HBase provides optimizations where one can send a customized number of rows from the server to the client in one RPC. To have a fair evaluation between the original *Scan* and result streaming, we keep this as high as 1000 in most of our experiments, i.e., in each RPC, send 1000 table rows for a *Scan* and similarly, 1000 result rows with Coprocessors from server to client. Therefore, the queries should be able to provide a large number of results. We came up with four different types of queries, based on these datasets we chose.

Our choice of the Bixi dataset was motivated by the fact that it provides opportunities for several interesting *server-side* computations, including general descriptive statistics (sum, min, max, average and standard deviation). In our experiments, we have implemented the following two queries, one invoking a *get* on a given time-stamp and, second invoking a range *scan* over a sequence of time-stamps. **Query 1:** For a given time, central location and radius, get a list of stations with available bikes, sorted by their distance from the given location. **Query 2:** For a given list of stations and a time, get their average bike usage for last 1, 6, 12 and 18hr.

---

[2] https://profil.bixi.ca/data/bikeStations.xml

The NGram dataset has already been the subject of much study. In this work, we wanted to explore it in ways that are not currently supported on the Google's NGram viewer [2]. The current NGram viewer can be used to see the evolution for a specific word or a set of words. It does an exact match of the given word to its dataset. There are some words that share a common prefix up to a good part of their length: for example, there are 424 different words that starts with 'America', spanning across almost 530 years! We use this dataset for the following queries. **Query 3:** For a given word prefix, get the top three count frequencies with their respective years for all the words that share that prefix. **Query 4:** We did the above query for a bag of words in one call, looking at the evolution of words like, 'love', 'blood', 'passion'. We should note that Query 3 involves a range scan with a common prefix, the range for Query 4 was large enough to span multiple *Regions* such that it was executed in parallel across different *Regions* using the Result-Streaming API.

4.3   Schema Design

The performance of HBase is directly correlated to the underlying schema and data-access patterns. While designing the schema one should strive for grouping frequently read columns in one column family. This is because each family is stored as one file (essentially, a *HFile*). This helps in limiting the number of files to be referred in a read call. One more caveat is that HBase tries to open all *HFiles* and read their index blocks in memory for faster lookups. Therefore, having fewer *HFiles* results in a smaller memory footprint. This also means that one should try to have minimum number of column families.

For the Bixi dataset, we chose the time-stamp to be the row key because our access pattern is time-stamp based, and the application is not write heavy; it has only one write per minute (if it were a real time application). We defined one column family and used station ids as column qualifier. We extracted relevant information such as latitude, longitude and other fields from the XML data and persisted it as cell values. Thus, a row size is approximately 90 KB and it has information about all the stations at a given time-stamp.

For the 1-gram dataset, we chose a word as the row key, and years as column qualifiers. All the three frequencies are concatenated with a delimiter and stored as the qualifier value. Thus in order to look for a word we need to read only one row. Accordingly, the row size distribution varies as per the word history, varying from a few bytes to 10s of KB.

4.4   Cluster Setup

We used a 5-node cluster on Amazon EC2 [3] to run our experiments. We used the recommended node configurations, giving more memory to HMaster (HBase Master process) and Namenode (HDFS master process) by running them on *m1.xlarge* instance; and giving more processing power to Region Server (HBase slaves) and Datanodes (HDFS slaves) processes by running them on *c1.xlarge* instances. Since Coprocessors are not yet part of the stable released and we have added/modified HBase source code to add our functionalities, we created our own Amazon machine image (AMI) containing relevant Hadoop and HBase jars.

4.5   Experiment and Results

We uploaded the Bixi and 1gram datasets to Amazon S3 [3]. Because the datasets contain a varying size of rows, in order to have a fair evaluation between the two approaches (reading from cache or from disk), we pre-run each query with the same arguments a number of times, in order to cache the required table rows in the *Region Server*. Thereafter we run the queries and report the average value for the last 3 iterations. Thus, in case we are reading small amount of data and using operating system cache instead of a disk I/O, it should happen for all variations of the experiment. We performed experiments for the queries described in the Sect. 4.2. For all these queries, we set the cache size of scan and the cursor to be 1000 (number of results in one RPC). We now describe the results of these experiments.

Table 1 gives the result for Query 1. This query reads only one row (essentially a *Get* operation) and performs the computation for calculating distances between 404 geographical points. The row size is 90KB, and it makes a negligible difference whether this computation is done at client side or server side.

Table 1. Response time for Query 1, in seconds

Query 1	Get	Coprocessor
response time in sec	1.57	1.61

We used Query 2 for computing the average for the last 1, 6, 12 and 18 hr from a given time value with two variations. In the first condition, we compute these values for 3 stations, and in the other we compute it for all 404 stations. Figure 1 shows the response time of Query 2 for 3 stations. The X and Y axes represents the hour for which the average was computed and the response time of the computation, respectively. In the scanner approach, we only fetch the relevant columns (i.e., the three stations) for the rows that fall in the time range and compute the average value at the client side. Figure 2 shows the response time for all 404 stations. We chose 3 and 404 as the boundary conditions for the query, to realize the effect of processing larger data in this query.

Table 2 shows the response time for Query 3 on the NGram dataset. The target word used was "America" and there are 424 distinct words that start with this prefix. The *scanner* cache size was set to 1000, so all the results were returned in one RPC. In order to test the streaming result from Endpoint functionality, we also executed Query 3 to fetch all words that starts with 'America' with batch size of 100. This is shown in the second row of the Table 2. We also test the result streaming by executing Query 3 to fetch all words that starts with prefix 'A' with a batch size of 1000. There are 219,797 such words spanning across 2 *Regions* and the response times are shown in the third row of the Table 2.

The last row of Table 2 shows the experiment results for Query 4. In this query, a user enters a bag of target words and it returns all the words that match the prefix of either of these words. We used words that start with different letters to evaluate the parallelism provided by the Coprocessor framework.

Table 2. Response time for Query 3 and 4 on NGram dataset (sec)

Prefix	Cache size	Scanner time (in sec)	Coprocessor time (in sec)	Number of unique words
America	1000	1.84	1.66	424
America	100	1.84	1.80	424
A	1000	29.65	**21.15**	219,797
blood, love, change, passion	1000	158.21	**44.7**	NA

5   Evaluation

The four queries described above represent different use cases and we consider them separately. Table 1 reports the response time for Query 1. This query is a *Get* operation as it reads only one row of the table. It involves fetching the row and computing distance between 404 geographical coordinates. Since the row size is only 90 KB, the impact of having the computation at client side or server side is rather insignificant. Thus, we have almost the same response time for *Get* operation and Coprocessor approach.

Query 2 is evaluated under two different scenarios, one with 3 stations and other with all 404 stations, with scan cache size and streaming result batch size equal to 1000. We computed the average number of the available bikes at stations for the last 1, 6, 12 and 18hr from a given time. Since we store the data on a per minute basis, we need to read 60, 360, 720 and 1080 rows respectively. Figure 1 shows response-time results for 3 stations. Note for the Bixi schema, stationIds become the column qualifiers, and one can scan at a granularity of qualifier level. So, we select only those 3 columns for this scenario. The response time for 1 hour computation was better in the case of the scanner and as we move to 18 hr average, the Coprocessor method started to give better response time. This is because in the case of the scanner, all the selected values are sent to the client and as we increased the time window, the number of such rows increased from 60 to 1080. In the case of Coprocessor, the computation was performed at the server-side and only the average value was sent to the client. This difference gets manifested when we increase the number of stations from 3 to 404. Figure 2 shows the result of Query 2 with all 404 stations. In this use case, the Coprocessor gives a better result than the scanner for all the time ranges that we tested. This shows the Endpoint are more effective than normal scanner when it involves computation with a large amount of data.

Queries 3 and 4 were applied on the NGram dataset. We used this dataset to test the streaming-results functionality and tried to build up the case when we can exploit the parallelism that comes inherent with the Coprocessor framework. We tested Query 3 with the prefix as "America". As mentioned in the Sect. 4.2, we are interested in top 3 frequencies of words that share the same prefix. The motivation in designing this query was to ensure that, apart from fetching the

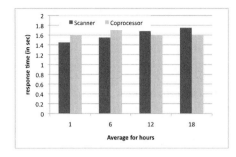   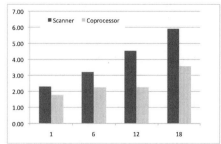

Fig. 1. Response time (in sec) for Query 2 for 3 stations

Fig. 2. Response time (in sec) for Query 2 for all stations

rows, it also entails some processing at server side. For example, the row key "America", which matches the criteria, has more than 500 frequencies for these many years. Table 2 shows the results for this experiment. The difference in response time for *Scanner* and *streaming Endpoint* approach is not large, which is due to the small computation and result size. The overall size of the result was about 630 KB only, which can be termed as an insignificant amount and explains the near same time (rather *Scanner* doing it marginally better). Interestingly, there was almost no effect of changing the cache value from 1000 to 100 in the case of a Scanner, as shown in rows 1 and 2 in the same table. This can be credited to the smaller result size and nuances of virtual environment.

Since we aimed to test the streaming result, we executed a query where the prefix was 'A'; i.e., give the computation for all words starting with the letter 'A'. There are around 0.2 million such words, distributed in 2 *Regions*. The *endpoint* approach finishes the task in 21 seconds as compared to 29 seconds taken by the *Scanner* API. We further expanded this test to consider the query for a bag of words. The aim was to further increase the number of target *Regions* and test the result-streaming functionality. We used a bag of *frequently* used 4 words (good enough to produce large amount of results) and start with different letters to make it more distributed, as shown in the last row of Table 2. Before executing requests to individual *Regions*, the Coprocessor framework first sorts the argument row keys to define a range of "interesting" *Regions*. Then it executes requests across all such *Regions*. It may happen that some interleaving *Regions* do not have any of the target word, in that case they return a *null* result. The *ClientCursor* makes sure that these *Regions* are not called in the next invocation (as explained in Sect. 3.2). In case of the scanner, the call starts at the *Region* having the start key, and flows sequentially to the *Region* containing the stop key. The inherent parallel execution of Endpoint approach makes it finish the task in 44 sec as compared to 158 sec taken by *Scanner* API.

In case where an interleaving *Region* does not have any result rows, the entire *Region* has to be scanned before sending a *null* result. This scanning of the entire Region in *one* RPC may take a while in case when there are many such *Regions*. Therefore, in the first call to fetch result, these *null* resulting *Regions* behave as bottleneck because the ClientCursor needs to aggregate results from all *Regions* before rendering result to client. We plan to improve this feature as our immediate future work.

6   Related Work

Cloud databases, irrespective of their high scalability, lack the strong query semantics present in relational database systems; they are designed in a fundamentally different architecture than traditional RDBMs, they lack secondary join support and query languages. The primary reason for their relatively sparse functionalities is their relative immaturity as a technology, as compared to RDBMs which have been around for past 35-40 years. Thus, this field opens up number of research directions for optimizing both at software and hardware level.

Konstantinou et al [7] used HBase for storing document indexes for a real-time application. They used the existing APIs and commented that their application has to make client-side merging two queries before rendering the complete solution. It required two server trips before producing the end result. In a similar work of creating and storing document index, N. Li et al [8] defined HIndex, that gets persisted on top of HBase and supports parallel lookup of target indexes. These indexes are fetched and results are merge at the client-side.

A Coprocessor Endpoint supporting result streaming will help such use cases as it permits filtering and merging at server-side. Our claim is supported by the results in Figure 2, which shows that its performance is better than normal scan operation for a substantially large ngram dataset.

7   Conclusion

We are seeing an unprecedented growth of data in the last decade, primarily unstructured. This has led people to look for alternatives storage solutions, other than traditional RDBMs. Cloud databases seem to solve the scalability issues, as they have been running on cluster size in the order of 100s of nodes. The current tradeoff is that they lack support of structure query language, database objects like trigger, stored procedures which are present in RDBMs. This provides an active field of research to explore novel ways to improve it. We focused on HBase and used its newly developed Coprocessor framework to improve the current query execution mechanism. The main contributions of this work are as follows.

1. We designed and implemented standard aggregate functions using Coprocessors infrastructure. This work has been committed to the Apache HBase.

2. We designed a cursor framework that provides support for streaming results from the Coprocessor endpoints. It adds on to the existing Coprocessor framework where one can *incrementally* access the results set generated by Coprocessors at a given *Region*. This work is under review by the HBase team.

3. The cursor framework can also be used to create a parallel scanner infrastructure. The idea is it can use the parallelism inherently provided by the Coprocessor framework, and one can stream in results in parallel.

Acknowledgment. We thank Gary Helmling of the HBase team for his constant support and guidance, particularly for effective design and implementation suggestions. We also thank Fabrice [4] for providing us the Bixi dataset. Our work is supported by IBM, NSERC, iCORE, and Alberta Advanced Education and Technology.

References

1. (2011), `http://www.odbms.org/download/dean-keynote-ladis2009.pdf`
2. (2011), `http://ngrams.googlelabs.com/datasets`
3. (2011), `http://aws.amazon.com/`
4. (2011), `http://www.linkedin.com/pub/fabrice-veniard/4/389/153`
5. Chang, F., Dean, J., Ghemawat, S., Hsieh, W., Wallach, D., Burrows, M., Chandra, T., Fikes, A., Gruber, R.: Bigtable: A distributed storage system for structured data. ACM Transactions on Computer Systems (TOCS) 26(2), 1–26 (2008)
6. Dean, J., Ghemawat, S.: Mapreduce: Simplified data processing on large clusters. Communications of the ACM 51(1), 107–113 (2008)
7. Konstantinou, I., Angelou, E., Tsoumakos, D., Koziris, N.: Distributed indexing of web scale datasets for the cloud. In: Proceedings of the 2010 Workshop on Massive Data Analytics on the Cloud, pp. 1–6. ACM, New York (2010)
8. Li, N., Rao, J., Shekita, E., Tata, S.: Leveraging a scalable row store to build a distributed text index. In: Proceeding of the First International Workshop on Cloud Data Management, pp. 29–36. ACM, New York (2009)
9. Michel, J., Shen, Y., Aiden, A., Veres, A., Gray, M., Pickett, J., Hoiberg, D., Clancy, D., Norvig, P., Orwant, J., et al.: Quantitative analysis of culture using millions of digitized books. Science 331(6014), 176 (2011)

Complex Service Provisioning
in Collaborative Cloud Markets

Melanie Siebenhaar*, Ulrich Lampe, Tim Lehrig,
Sebastian Zöller, Stefan Schulte, and Ralf Steinmetz

Multimedia Communications Lab (KOM)
Technische Universität Darmstadt, Germany
melanie.siebenhaar@KOM.tu-darmstadt.de

Abstract. Today's cloud consumers gain a high level of flexibility by using externally provided cloud-based services. However, they have no means
for requesting combined services from different clouds or for enforcing an
individual quality level. Laying the foundation for market-based cloud collaborations including the negotiation of individual quality parameters is
an important aspect for future cloud computing. Cloud consumers, especially enterprises are then able to request complex services with consumer-
driven quality guarantees according to their individual needs and are not
concerned with the problem on how to make the different components
work together. In this paper, we present an approach for collaborative
complex service provisioning in cloud computing and an evaluation of selected mechanisms for the negotiation of quality parameters in such a collaborative market-based scenario.

1   Introduction

Cloud computing has recently attracted a lot of attention with respect to IT
architectures and aims to provide computing resources in a highly dynamic and
flexible manner. In 2010, the cloud computing market reached a large market
volume and its size will grow further in the next years [11]. Nevertheless, cloud
computing is still in a very early stage concerning open standards and interfaces [13], so that consumers cannot change selected cloud providers very easily.
A vision aiming at these issues is a global cloud marketplace [1], which does not
depend on the specifics of a certain vendor offering standardized interfaces. Such
a cloud marketplace would also facilitate the combination of different services
from various cloud providers and enable cloud federation scenarios [8]. Hence, it
can be considered as a first step towards the Future Internet [7]. To realize the
vision of a global cloud marketplace, several requirements have to be fulfilled.
Quality parameters, such as reliability or availability, are especially crucial in a
business environment. In order to retain control of the service quality, so-called
Service Level Agreements (SLAs) can be negotiated between the service consumer and the cloud provider to ensure a level of quality consumers can rely
on. Basically, an SLA represents a contract between two parties and defines

---

* Corresponding author.

W. Abramowicz et al. (Eds.): ServiceWave 2011, LNCS 6994, pp. 88–99, 2011.

the objectives (e.g., quality parameters) the cloud provider has to fulfill and the penalties in case the provider violates the agreement. At present, cloud providers offer no or only limited support for the negotiation of individual quality parameters [1]. Thus, consumers, especially enterprises are not able to obtain Quality of Service (QoS) guarantees according to their specific business constraints. But enabling consumer-driven QoS guarantees would increase the flexibility and efficiency when using cloud-based services. Furthermore, consumers wish to dynamically combine services from different cloud providers without further effort for the interconnection of the different components. This requires the collaboration between multiple cloud providers. Hence, an automated mechanism is required to negotiate individual QoS guarantees and to dynamically select collaboration partners from a set of multiple cloud providers.

In this paper, we present a collaborative cloud market model for complex service provisioning. The collaboration allows cloud providers to share their resources and to offer complex services on the cloud computing marketplace. Besides the selection of collaboration partners, negotiating individual QoS parameters is also a major issue that we address in the paper. The remainder of the paper is structured as follows. Section 2 describes the requirements for collaborative complex service provisioning, Section 3 introduces our collaborative market model and Section 4 presents initial experimental results of our approach. The paper closes with a discussion of related approaches in Section 5 and with a conclusion and future directions in Section 6.

2   Problem Statement

Our work focuses on a mechanism for collaborative complex service provisioning, in which services from different cloud providers can be combined to a bundle.

Definition 1 (Bundle). *A bundle B is a set S of m different functional services. Each component c in the bundle has communication relationships with a subset of $S \setminus \{c\}$, i.e., with some of the other components in the bundle.*

For example, an enterprise could request a set of services from multiple cloud providers to fulfill internal business activities, e.g., a Customer Relationship Management solution, data storage, virtual machines for data processing, and a database [8]. In this scenario, multiple providers offer heterogeneous services on the envisioned global cloud marketplace, where the following assumptions hold:

- **Specialization:** Each provider has specialized in providing specific service types. The providers participate in the market, because they are unable to provide all the required services on their own [9].
- **Comparability:** We assume that the services can be classified according to their functionality. Hence, all providers in a single category are competing with the other providers in the same category.
- **Standardized Interfaces:** There are no consumer switching costs due to specific service properties when changing cloud providers. The development of cloud standards is currently addressed by several activities[1].

---

[1] An overview can be obtained from http://cloud-standards.org/

- **Scalability:** In our basic model, we further neglect resource constraints in the first instance. Thus, we assume that each provider has unlimited resource capacities concerning the provider's specific service types.
- **Collaboration:** After the determination of the collaboration partners, the providers are responsible for providing the bundle. Since the several components in the bundle must be able to directly communicate with each other according to their communication relationships, the providers must establish connections between the components coming from multiple clouds. Such a so-called sky computing scenario [5] typically requires to lay a virtual site over the distributed resources among the different administrative domains.
- **Adaptability:** Finally, we assume that the cloud providers can vary the QoS levels that they provide according to their cost functions. Since they have private information, e.g., concerning their cost factors, a negotiation of QoS parameters is necessary.
- **Relationships:** Although cloud providers are located worldwide, they cannot establish data centers everywhere. Thus, they may have difficulties in fulfilling all QoS requirements, e.g., due to network delays. Hence, the relationships between the different components must be taken into account since they have a direct impact on the QoS parameters.

Two major issues that have to be addressed arise in such a collaborative cloud market scenario: How to negotiate the QoS parameters of a bundle with multiple cloud providers and how to select the collaborating parties? Cloud consumers must specify their requirements (e.g., upper or lower bounds) for the whole bundle and for each service that is part of the bundle. A market model is required to maximize the consumer's utility and the cloud providers' utility (in terms of cost), while considering the boundaries for the different parameters.

3   Approach

3.1   System Model and Notation

Our model consists of three main actors: service consumers, cloud providers and a market platform. Service consumers SC can request a bundle of services at the market platform and specify their requirements concerning the non-functional properties of the bundle, i.e., QoS parameters and price. These requirements are used by the market platform to compose the bundle. The composition is structured into two phases: the negotiation between the market platform and the cloud providers and the selection of the collaboration partners for the provision of the bundle. The two phases are described in the following.

To perform a first analysis, we assume a sequential order of the m services within the bundle B. The consideration of more complex communication relationships will be part of our future work. Furthermore, the services can be grouped into functional categories Cat_i with $i \in (1, \ldots, m)$. Each category consists of a set of cloud providers CP with p elements, where each element represents a cloud provider offering a service with the same functionality. The cloud

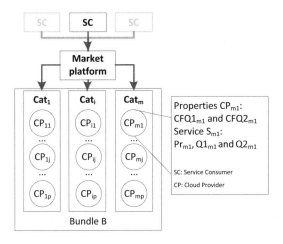

Fig. 1. Market system

providers are denoted with $CP_{i,j}$ and the service a cloud provider $CP_{i,j}$ delivers with $S_{i,j}$, where $i \in (1, \ldots, m)$ and $j \in (1, \ldots, p)$. We assume that a service $S_{i,j}$ is, besides its functionality, described with three properties: price $Pr_{i,j}$ and two QoS parameters $Q1_{i,j}$ and $Q2_{i,j}$, which are generic representations of possible QoS parameters (e.g., availability). From the service consumers' point of view, price is a negative attribute and QoS parameters are positive attributes. Service consumers specify their requirements with two elements: thresholds and utility functions. Both are provided for the functional category level as well as for the whole bundle. The thresholds on category level are $ThCatPr_i$, $ThCatQ2_i$ and $ThCatQ2_i$ for price and QoS parameters. In addition, the service consumer uses a utility function $UCat_i(S_{i,j})$, which shows the consumer's utility dependent on the non-functional properties of a service. The utility function is described in Section 3.2. During the negotiation, the goal of the market platform is to maximize the utility of the service consumer for each functional category while keeping the provided thresholds. Analogously, the cloud providers have a cost function, which specifies what effort is required to provide the QoS properties at a certain quality level for a given service. Therefore, each cloud provider $CP_{i,j}$ has two cost factors $CFQ1_{i,j}$ and $CFQ2_{i,j}$ for the two QoS parameters. The cost function $UCP_{i,j}(S_{i,j})$ reflecting the utility of a cloud provider is described further in Section 3.2. The overall model with its actors is shown in Figure 1.

It is not sufficient to specify only the requirements of single services of the bundle, but also the overall bundle must fulfill certain requirements. Therefore, the thresholds and an additional utility function for the service consumer are specified at bundle level. This information comprises the three thresholds $ThBuPr$, $ThBuQ1$ and $ThBuQ2$ and the utility function of the service consumer for the bundle $UBu(B)$. The goal of the market platform for the composition of the overall bundle is to fulfill the thresholds and to maximize the consumer's utility for the bundle. This problem is based on the previous negotiations in the functional categories and deals with the optimal selection among the resulting offers of the negotiation process.

3.2   Negotiation of Quality of Service

Negotiation takes place between the cloud providers and the market platform. The market platform uses the utility function of the service consumer and the provided thresholds for the negotiation. A service $S_{i,j}$ fulfills all thresholds if:

$$ThCatPr_i \geq Pr_{i,j} \text{ and } ThCatQ1_i \leq Q1_{i,j} \text{ and } ThCatQ2_i \leq Q2_{i,j} \quad (1)$$

The utility function is assumed to be additive and has a decreasing marginal utility (shown by the square roots) for both QoS parameters [2]. Each non-functional property of a service has an individual weight. The weight of the price is negative, whereas the weights of the QoS parameters are positive to express the utility for the service consumer. The weights are denoted with $wCatPr_i$, $wCatQ1_i$ and $wCatQ2_i$. The utility function of the service consumer is as follows:

$$UCat_i(S_{i,j}) = wCatPr_i * Pr_{i,j} + wCatQ1_i * \sqrt{Q1_{i,j}} + wCatQ2_i * \sqrt{Q2_{i,j}} \quad (2)$$

As already stated, each cloud provider has a cost function. In this function, every provider makes use of other cost factors to enforce certain QoS parameters, which are both negative, since the cloud providers have higher costs for providing better (higher) QoS values. Hence, the cost function represents the utility of the cloud providers. The utility function for the cloud provider $CP_{i,j}$ is as follows:

$$UCP_{i,j}(S_{i,j}) = Pr_{i,j} + CFQ1_{i,j} * Q1_{i,j} + CFQ2_{i,j} * Q2_{i,j} \quad (3)$$

The two parties fulfill the requirements for a negotiation, since they have different preferences for the given properties and want to maximize their utility. For the negotiation, a mechanism is required that specifies the protocol and the strategy of the parties on both sides. The given scenario with the market platform on the one side and p cloud providers in a functional category on the other side and three negotiation domains (price and QoS parameters) requires support for one-to-many negotiations and multiple attributes.

After an analysis of different negotiation protocols based on [12], which can be used in automated negotiations, we decided to use the contract net protocol [15] and the English auction [2] for an initial evaluation of the negotiation in the model. The contract net protocol is a simple protocol originally used for distributing tasks in computer systems. The tasks are specified by a central manager and sent to providers. The providers return an offer for the specification with the smallest price they can provide. After one round, the central manager assigns a task to the provider with the best offer. Using the contract net protocol, the price of the offer is calculated as follows:

$$Pr_{i,j}^{CNP} = -CFQ1_{i,j} * ThCatQ1_i - CFQ2_{i,j} * ThCatQ2_i \qquad (4)$$

The cloud providers make a bid, if the QoS parameters they can provide meet the desired thresholds, i.e., an offer is valid, if $Pr_{i,j}^{CNP} \leq ThCatPr_i$. Since the utility function of the service consumer is private, the cloud providers only optimize the price of their offers according to the given thresholds. The assumption is that they are willing to make a bid until they gain no utility from the offer anymore. Hence, the value of the utility function is minimized in order to maximize the probability for a bid to get accepted.

In the English auction, bidders may bid for a particular good during several rounds, until no bids can be made anymore. A bid is valid, if it exceeds the currently highest ranked bid. Finally, the highest bid wins the auction. We use the English auction as a reversed auction (i.e., the cloud providers making offers which can be accepted by the marketplace) with a multi-attribute extension that enables the consideration of all requirements. In the original version of the English auction, cloud providers can be outbid during a single round. In our scenario, the market platform chooses the best offer after each single round and sets it as lowest bid for the next round. The dominant strategy for the cloud providers is to increase their offers in each round by a minimal difference $DiffOff$ between two offers. The increase does not refer to the price, but to the utility of the service consumer. This enables to consider not only the price, but all non-functional attributes for the auction. The calculation of the values for the increase and the prices is adapted from [2]. The QoS parameters are calculated as follows:

$$Q1_{i,j}^{EA} = \left(\frac{\frac{wCatQ1_i}{wCatPr_i}}{2 * CFQ1_{i,j}} \right)^2 \quad \text{and} \quad Q2_{i,j}^{EA} = \left(\frac{\frac{wCatQ2_i}{wCatPr_i}}{2 * CFQ2_{i,j}} \right)^2 \qquad (5)$$

Based on these values and the utility of the current best offer $S_i^{BestOffer}$, the price is calculated as follows:

$$Pr_{i,j}^{EA} = \frac{\frac{wCatQ1_i^2}{|wCatPr_i|}}{2*|CFQ1_i|} + \frac{\frac{wCatQ2_i^2}{|wCatPr_i|}}{2*|CFQ2_i|} - UCat_i(S_i^{BestOffer}) - DiffOff}{-wCatPr_i} \qquad (6)$$

However, there is a major difference between a standard English auction and the scenario in this work: the thresholds for the non-functional properties. These thresholds limit the properties and can lead to invalid solutions. Therefore, the approach used in this work adjusts the QoS parameters, if the calculated values are below the thresholds, and uses the new values for the calculation of the price.

Both negotiation protocols lead to a number of offers in each functional category. These offers must be composed to a bundle in the next step, which is described in the next section.

3.3   Partner Selection for Collaboration

The second part of the collaboration process is the selection of collaboration partners from the set of valid offers S_i^{Val} for each Cat_i after the negotiation.

The size of S_i^{Val} is less or equal p, because not every cloud provider must make an offer. The selection of the collaboration partners is designed as optimization problem, which selects one service from each functional category. Each valid service $S_{i,j}$ has a binary decision variable $x_{i,j}$, which is 1 if the service is part of the optimal solution and 0 if not. The selection is based on the properties of the services as well as the connections between the services. Connections between services only exist if the services are neighbors in the sequential order of the bundle. A connection between services $S_{i,j}$ and $S_{i+1,k}$ is denoted with $Con_{i,j,i+1,k}$ and has the non-functional properties $CPr_{i,j,i+1,k}$, $CQ1_{i,j,i+1,k}$ and $CQ2_{i,j,i+1,k}$. The connections have an additional decision variable $y_{i,j,i+1,k}$, which is 1 if each variable $x_{i,j}$ and $x_{i+1,k}$ is 1. The aggregation operators of the non-functional properties are assumed to be summations. The second QoS parameter uses two additive functions to separate between services and connections. Other aggregation operators like multiplication or min-operators are also possible and can be considered in future research. The utility function of the service consumer for the bundle is as well additive and uses different weights to increase the flexibility just as the utility function of the service consumer for the functional categories. The weights $wBuPr(\leq 0)$, $wBuQ1(\geq 0)$ and $wBuQ2(\geq 0)$ are used for both, services and connections. The weighted utility and objective function and constraints are defined in Model 1, which is a linear optimization problem that can be solved optimally with a branch-and-bound approach [4].

4   Experimental Results

For the evaluation, the previously described model has been implemented. The implementation is agent-based and describes the behavior of the market platform and the cloud providers during the negotiation and solution of the optimization problem. The evaluation is a proof-of-concept for the developed model and, at the same time, analyzes the influence of the amount of cloud providers on the negotiation. The tests have been performed on a laptop with a 64bit dual core 2.53 GHz processor with 4 GB RAM and Windows 7 as operating system. For the simulation of the agents, Repast Simphony[2] has been used and the optimization problem has been modeled and solved with LPSolve[3]. The number of cloud providers within a category is varied between 2, 4, 6, 8, and 10 cloud providers. For each variation, 20 test cases have been generated. The scenario has been tested exemplary for 5 functional categories. The values for the parameters of the following evaluation are shown in Table 1. The table shows the ranges of the random numbers or if no range is given the fixed values of the parameters. Besides these parameters, the English auction uses a minimal difference between offers of 0.5 utility units.

The median run times of the two negotiation protocols are shown in Figure 2. They are distributed from 1.9 to 13.6 ms. For both protocols, the run time increases with a growing number of cloud providers. The contract net protocol

---

[2] http://repast.sourceforge.net/
[3] http://lpsolve.sourceforge.net/5.5/

Model 1. Collaboration Partner Selection Problem

Objective Function (Maximize):

$$\sum_{i=1}^{m} \sum_{j \in S_i^{Val}} x_{i,j}(wBuPr * Pr_{i,j} + wBuQ1 * Q1_{i,j} + wBuQ2 * Q2_{i,j}) + \sum_{i=1}^{m-1} \sum_{j \in S_i^{Val}} \sum_{k \in S_{i+1}^{Val}}$$

$$y_{i,j,i+1,k}(wBuPr * CPr_{i,j,i+1,k} + wBuQ1 * CQ1_{i,j,i+1,k} + wBuQ2 * CQ2_{i,j,i+1,k}) \quad (7)$$

Constraints:

$$ThBuPr \geq \sum_{i=1}^{m} \sum_{j \in S_i^{Val}} x_{i,j} * Pr_{i,j} + \sum_{i=1}^{m-1} \sum_{j \in S_i^{Val}} \sum_{k \in S_{i+1}^{Val}} y_{i,j,i+1,k} * CPr_{i,j,i+1,k} \quad (8)$$

$$ThBuQ1 \leq \sum_{i=1}^{m} \sum_{j \in S_i^{Val}} x_{i,j} * Q1_{i,j} + \sum_{i=1}^{m-1} \sum_{j \in S_i^{Val}} \sum_{k \in S_{i+1}^{Val}} y_{i,j,i+1,k} * CQ1_{i,j,i+1,k} \quad (9)$$

$$ThBuQ2 \leq \sum_{i=1}^{m} \sum_{j \in S_i^{Val}} x_{i,j} * Q2_{i,j} \quad (10)$$

$$ThBuQ2 \leq \sum_{i=1}^{m-1} \sum_{j \in S_i^{Val}} \sum_{k \in S_{i+1}^{Val}} y_{i,j,i+1,k} * CQ2_{i,j,i+1,k} \quad (11)$$

$$\sum_{j \in S_i^{Val}} x_{i,j} = 1 \forall i \in (1,\ldots,m) \quad (12)$$

$$\sum_{j \in S_i^{Val}} \sum_{k \in S_{i+1}^{Val}} y_{i,j,i+1,k} = 1 \forall i \in (1,\ldots,m-1) \quad (13)$$

$$x_{i,j} + x_{i+1,k} - y_{i,j,i+1,k} \leq 1 \forall i \in (1,\ldots,m-1) \wedge \forall j \in S_i^{Val} \wedge \forall k \in S_{i+1}^{Val} \quad (14)$$

shows slightly higher run times than the English auction. The reason for this is that the contract net protocol produces a larger set of valid services than the English auction, which increases the time to solve the optimization problem.

The service consumer's utility considered in the problem is measured on two levels: for each category and for the overall bundle. For the former, the absolute and the relative utility of the consumer is measured and for the latter, we only measure the absolute utility, since the relative utility is 100% for all the offers. The relative utility is calculated by using the Lagrange method [4] to evaluate the maximal possible utility a cloud provider can provide without given boundaries and without achieving an own utility. The result is set as maximum and the achieved utility is set in relation to it. The results for the relative utility are shown in Figure 3(a). They show that the contract net protocol reaches a relative utility of 60% and remains on the same level for all scenarios. The English auction achieves a similar level, but the relative utility decreases for a higher number of

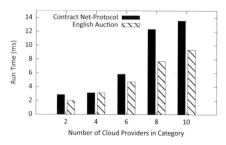

Fig. 2. Run time of negotiation protocols

cloud providers within the categories. The reason for this decrease is that more providers lead to a higher probability that one provider cannot reach the optimal values for the non-functional properties. Thus, this provider increases the utility faster, which leads to earlier discards of other providers and lowers the value. Another result, the best absolute utility within a category, is shown in Figure 3(b). Concerning the utility, the contract net protocol does not depend on the number of cloud providers and remains on the same level. In contrast, the English auction shows a positive correlation between the number of cloud providers and the best achieved utility. The reason for this is, that more providers lead to a higher competition and, therefore, a higher utility value. The probability that the two best providers have similar cost factors and increase their offers to the maximum is higher in scenarios with many providers.

The evaluation of the service consumer's utility for the bundle is shown in Figure 4. The median utility achieved with the English auction is much higher for the chosen weights than the utility achieved with the contract net protocol. This can be explained with the low values for the two QoS parameters resulting from the contract net protocol in contrast to the high values resulting from the English auction. Low values lead to a low utility, since the achieved price cannot compensate them.

It can be observed from the evaluation that both negotiation protocols show small median run times and thus, are applicable in a dynamic collaborative environment. Concerning the utility of the bundle, the English auction achieves higher median utility values than the contract net protocol. However, the

Table 1. Values of the parameters for the evaluation

Category		**Bundle**	
Parameter	Values	Parameter	Values
$CFQ1_{i,j}$ and $CFQ2_{i,j}$	$[0;1]$		
$wCatPr_i$	-1	$wBuPr$	-1
$wCatQ1_i$ and $wCatQ2_i$	2	$wBuQ1$ and $wBuQ2$	0.5
$ThCatPr_i$	$[15;20]$	$ThBuPr$	$[15;20]*m$
$ThCatQ1_i$	$[0;5]$	$ThBuQ1$	$[0;3]*m$
$ThCatQ2_i$	$[0;5]$	$ThBuQ2$	$[0;1]$

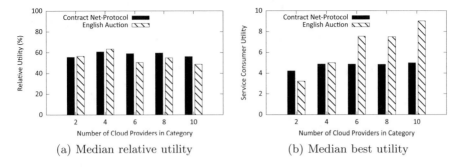

(a) Median relative utility   (b) Median best utility

Fig. 3. Service consumer median utility of negotiation protocols for categories

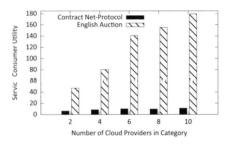

Fig. 4. Service consumer median utility of negotiation protocols for bundle

English auction depends on the amount of the providers. In summary, the contract net protocol is preferable in scenarios, where the services must only satisfy minimal requirements and the price is considered as the most important criteria. In contrast, the English auction should be applied in case of a large number of providers in order to achieve a high utility. Nevertheless, no negotiation mechanism outperforms the other in all settings.

5 Related Work

A lot of research has been done in cloud computing. Yet, only a few approaches focus on market-based scenarios. To the best of our knowledge, this is the first work that combines the negotiation of individual consumer-driven QoS guarantees and the selection of collaboration partners from sets of competing cloud providers in a market-based cloud computing scenario. In contrast, Buyya et al. [1] present a vision of a cloud market for trading resources in order to establish a balance between supply and demand. The authors also consider the negotiation of QoS parameters between a consumer and a provider. However, collaborations are not considered in their work. Based on the market model of Buyya et al., Sim [14] focuses on QoS negotiations to allow for flexible pricing. He divides his scenario into two disjunct markets for cloud services and cloud infrastructure resources interconnected via brokers. Again, collaborations are not part of his work. Concerning the selection of collaboration partners, Hassan et al. [3] propose a multi-objective optimization model with multiple target functions that depend on each other. The authors' goal is to minimize the price and to maximize the service quality and the performance of collaborative past relationships. The collaborations are initiated by primary cloud providers, who identify a specific business opportunity and search for appropriate partners. In the second step, the resulting groups of collaborating cloud providers use the market to offer a set of services to consumers, who can bid a price for the set of services. Negotiating individual consumer-driven QoS guarantees is not considered in their approach. In their work in [6], Briscoe and Marinos describe a community cloud market model, where community members provide and manage the resources. The authors also discuss the enforcement of certain QoS levels with the help of a community currency serving as a means for admission control. However, collaborative resource provisioning is in the focus of their work, disregarding the negotiation of individual QoS guarantees.

6   Conclusion

In this paper, we have presented an approach for collaborative complex service provisioning in cloud computing and introduced a corresponding market model. The model provides a good solution for market-based collaborations in cloud computing and considers individual consumer-driven QoS guarantees. Furthermore, the model can be adapted to different negotiation mechanisms and consumer and/or provider requirements. Hence, it serves as a foundation for future investigations concerning collaborative cloud markets. In addition, we have explored the applicability of different QoS negotiation mechanisms in the designed market model. The results revealed that both investigated negotiation mechanisms are applicable in a dynamic collaborative setting. Although each strategy offers advantages in some situations, no single negotiation mechanism outperforms the other in all settings. Thus, further negotiation mechanisms (e.g., Vickrey auction[4]) will be explored in future work. Also, smaller cloud providers will not be able to offer an unlimited amount of resources. Hence, a small amount of resources could also be considered as an incentive for collaborations. Therefore, further directions for future work are the consideration of restricted resource capacities of the providers as well as time constraints, which evolve through parallel consumer requests for the same resources and the temporary allocation of the resources.

Acknowledgments. The work presented in this paper was performed in the context of the Software-Cluster project SWINNG (www.software-cluster.org). It was partially funded by the German Federal Ministry of Education and Research (BMBF) under grant no. "01|C10S05". In addition, this work is supported in part by E-Finance Lab Frankfurt am Main e.V. (http://www.efinancelab.com). The authors assume responsibility for the content.

---

[4] The Vickrey auction is a sealed-price sealed-bid auction, where the best strategy is to bid the best estimate value of a good [10].

References

1. Buyya, R., Yeo, C.S., Venugopal, S., Broberg, J., Brandic, I.: Cloud Computing and Emerging IT Platforms: Vision, Hype, and Reality for Delivering Computing as the 5th Utility. Future Generation Computer Systems 25(6), 599–616 (2009)
2. David, E., Azoulay-Schwartz, R., Kraus, S.: An English Auction Protocol for Multi-attribute Items. In: Padget, J., Shehory, O., Parkes, D.C., Sadeh, N.M., Walsh, W.E. (eds.) AMEC 2002. LNCS (LNAI), vol. 2531, pp. 52–68. Springer, Heidelberg (2002)
3. Hassan, M.M., Song, B., Yoon, C., Lee, H.W., Huh, E.N.: A Novel Market Oriented Dynamic Collaborative Cloud Service Infrastructure. In: 2009 World Conference on Services - II (SERVICES-2 2009), pp. 9–16 (2009)
4. Hillier, F., Lieberman, G.: Introduction to Operations Research, 8th edn. McGraw-Hill, New York (2005)
5. Keahey, K., Tsugawa, M., Matsunaga, A., Fortes, J.: Sky Computing. IEEE Internet Computing 13(5), 43–51 (2009)
6. Marinos, A., Briscoe, G.: Community Cloud Computing. In: Jaatun, M.G., Zhao, G., Rong, C. (eds.) Cloud Computing. LNCS, vol. 5931, pp. 472–484. Springer, Heidelberg (2009)
7. Müller, P., Reuther, B.: Future Internet Architecture – A Service-oriented Approach. it–Information Technology 50(6), 383–389 (2008)
8. Nair, S.K., Porwal, S., Dimitrakos, T., Ferrer, A.J., Tordsson, J., Sharif, T., Sheridan, C., Rajarajan, M., Khan, A.U.: Towards Secure Cloud Bursting, Brokerage and Aggregation. In: 8th IEEE European Conference on Web Services (ECOWS 2010), pp. 189–196 (2010)
9. Paletta, M., Herrero, P.: A MAS-Based Negotiation Mechanism to Deal with Service Collaboration in Cloud Computing. In: 2009 International Conference on Intelligent Networking and Collaborative Systems (INCOS 2009), pp. 147–153 (2009)
10. Parsons, S., Rodriguez-Aguilar, J.A., Klein, M.: Auctions and Bidding: A Guide for Computer Scientists. ACM Computing Surveys 43(2), 1–59 (2011)
11. Pettey, C., Tudor, B.: Gartner Says Worldwide Cloud Services Market to Surpass $ 68 Billion in 2010 (June 2010), http://www.gartner.com/it/page.jsp?id=1389313 (last access: May 07, 2011)
12. Sandholm, T.: Distributed Rational Decision Making. In: Weiß, G. (ed.) Multiagent Systems: A Modern Introduction to Distributed Artificial Intelligence, ch. 5, pp. 201–258. MIT Press, Cambridge (1999)
13. Schneidermann, R.: For Cloud Computing, the Sky is the Limit. Signal Processing Magazine 28(1), 15–144 (2011)
14. Sim, K.M.: Towards Complex Negotiation for Cloud Economy. In: Bellavista, P., Chang, R.-S., Chao, H.-C., Lin, S.-F., Sloot, P.M.A. (eds.) GPC 2010. LNCS, vol. 6104, pp. 395–406. Springer, Heidelberg (2010)
15. Smith, R.G.: The Contract Net Protocol: High-Level Communication and Control in a Distributed Problem Solver. IEEE Transactions on Computers 29(12), 1104–1113 (1980)

Network Events Correlation for Federated Networks Protection System

Michał Choraś[1,2], Rafał Kozik[1,2], Rafał Piotrowski[3],
Juliusz Brzostek[4], and Witold Hołubowicz[1,5]

[1] ITTI Ltd., Poznań, Poland
mchoras@itti.com.pl
[2] Institute of Telecommunications, UT&LS Bydgoszcz, Poland
[3] Military Communication Institute, Zegrze, Poland
[4] NASK, Warsaw, Poland
[5] Adam Mickiewicz University, Poznań
holubowicz@amu.edu.pl

Abstract. In this paper a concept and an architecture of the Federated Networks Protection System (FNPS) is proposed. The system components are described and, particularly, the Decision Module (FNPS-DM) is discussed. The major contributions of the paper are: concept of federated networks security, the proposition of the network events correlation approach and semantic notations aimed at detecting complex cyber attacks and 0-day exploits. Moreover P2P based communication between federated networks is proposed.

1 Introduction

Nowadays, especially after successful cyber attacks on Estonia, Georgia, Iran and on companies like Google and Sony, cyber attacks are considered a major threat for critical infrastructures (e.g. power grids) and homeland security (e.g. financing system)[1]. For example, in 2008 successful DDoS (Distributed Denial of Service) attacks were targeted at Georgian government sites, Georgian president site and servers of National Bank of Georgia [1]. Cyber attacks are also considered a threat for military networks and public administration computer systems. The goal of the Federated Networks Protection System developed in the SOPAS project is to protect public administration and military networks which are often connected into Federations of Systems (FoS). While adopting the concept of federation of networks, the synergy effect for security can be achieved.

In our approach, we use the capability of the federated networks and systems to share and exchange information about events in the network, detected attacks and proposed countermeasures. Such approach to share information about network security (between trusted entities and networks) follows the Federation of Systems (FoS) idea. Also in our case, FoS concept refers to a set of different systems, which are not centrally managed, but cooperate in order to share knowledge and increase their security. Such approach has recently gotten much

W. Abramowicz et al. (Eds.): ServiceWave 2011, LNCS 6994, pp. 100–111, 2011.
© Springer-Verlag Berlin Heidelberg 2011

attention and may replace inefficient approach of "closed security" [2]. The concept of federated networks and systems has gained much attention also in the context of critical systems, military networks and NNEC [3][4][5].

The major contribution of this paper is the proposition of the networks protection system based on the concept of federated networks security. Moreover, original design of Federated Networks Protection System (FNPS) architecture, Decision Module (FNPS-DM) and network events correlation approach enhanced with semantic notations are presented.

This paper is structured as follows: in Section 2 the general architecture of the Federated Networks Protection System (FNPS) is presented. The components of the Decision Module (FNPS-DM), the correlation mechanism, semantic approach and ontology, rules distribution, P2P enabled communications between domains and graphical user interface are described in detail in Section 3. Section 4 presents sample scenario showing capabilities of our approach. Conclusions are given thereafter.

2   General Architecture of Federated Networks Protection System (FNPS)

The general architecture of the Federated Networks Protection System (FNPS) is presented in Fig. 1. It consists of several interconnected domains, which exchange information in order to increase their security level and the security of the whole federation.

Different subnetworks are arranged in domains, according to the purpose they serve (e.g. WWW, FTP or SQL servers) or according to their logical proximity (two networks closely cooperating with each other). In each of the domains, a Decision Module (FNPS-DM) is deployed. Each DM is responsible for acquiring and processing network events coming from sensors distributed over the domain.

If the attack or its symptoms are detected in one domain, the relevant information are disseminated to other cooperating domains so that appropriate countermeasures can be applied.

In our approach, the basic idea is to re-use the already available and existing sensors deployed in particular domains. Additionally, we will also use the following sensors distributed in the networks and used in Federated Networks Protection System (FNPS):

- Dedicated application layer sensors (e.g. log parsers),
- Dedicated IDS and IPS systems (e.g. we will use SNORT [7]),
- Dedicated Anomaly Detection Systems [8],
- ARAKIS system [9],
- HoneySpider Network (HSN) system [10].

Following FoS concept and information sharing paradigm, those systems do not have to be deployed in each domain.

Currently, IDS or IPS systems are installed in networks as typical means of cyber defense. In FNPS we will use SNORT system, also with additional FNPS

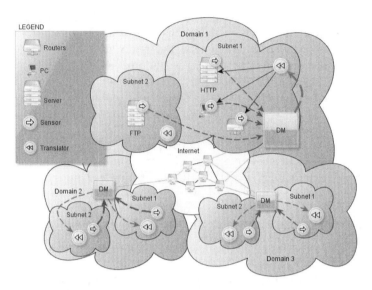

Fig. 1. General Architecture of Federated Networks Protection System (FNPS)

preprocessors. Anomaly Detection Systems rely on the existence of a reliable characterization of what is normal and what is not, in a particular networking scenario. More precisely, anomaly detection techniques base their evaluations on a model of what is normal, and classify as anomalous all the events that fall outside such a model.

ARAKIS and HSN are existing commercial systems developed by NASK (SOPAS project partner). These systems, if available in the network, will be used as sensors in FNPS. However, there is no need to install these systems in each domain. The important idea is to use and share important information from the domain in which ARAKIS and/or HSN are installed with other members of the federation.

ARAKIS is early warning system detecting novel network threats. ARAKIS-GOV, a version dedicated for protecting public administration networks, is widely installed in polish public networks.

ARAKIS system uses low interaction server side honeypots. Each honeypot acts as a server exposing most popular services and passively waits to be attacked. The system uses cutting edge technologies to detect anomalies and generate on-the-fly accurate attacks signatures. The public dashboard of the project shows a snapshot of network activity observed by the system ([9]). Additionally, ARAKIS can correlate events detected by its components and finds cross-domains infections and misconfigurations of network devices.

The HoneySpider Network (HSN) is a system focused primarily on attacks against, or involving the use of, web browsers. The HoneySpider Network is a system based on the client-side honeypots. Basically, HSN actively interacts with servers and processes malicious data. It engages a client honeypot solutions and a novel crawler application specially tailored for the bulk processing of URLs [10].

Each Decision Module can react to network events and attacks by sending information to the Translator element. The output information from DMs is the General Reaction Rule describing attack symptoms (information about network events) and particular reaction rule to be applied by reaction elements. Translator has the knowledge about its subnet capabilities and can access the necessary reaction elements (e.g. firewalls, filters or IDS). Reaction elements can be reconfigured by Translator in order to apply commands sent by the Decision Module.

All Decision Modules within the federation can also interact with each other and exchange security information. Particularly information about network incidents, like attack in one domain, may be sent to different Decisions Modules in order to block the attacker before the consequent attack takes place on another domain. Communication between domains and Decision Modules is based on P2P (Peer-to-Peer) in order to increase communication resiliency and enable data replication.

3   Decision Module

Decision module in FNPS federated system is responsible for correlating network events in order to detect and recognize malicious events in the network. FNPS-DM consists of the following components (see Fig.2):

- Correlation Engine (e.g. based on the Borealis system),
- CLIPS rule engine,
- Ontology (in OWL format),
- Graphical User Interface.

Borealis is a distributed stream processing engine and is responsible for gathering information generated by the network sensors [11]. Correlation engine has mechanism that allows the Decision Module to efficiently execute multiple queries

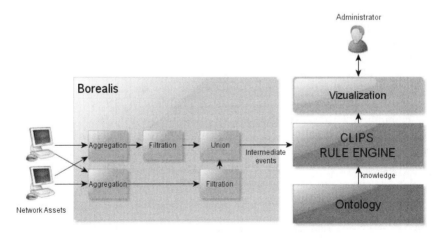

Fig. 2. Decision Module architecture and components

over the data streams in order to perform event correlation. The result of a correlation process is an intermediate event that is further processed by CLIPS rule engine [12].

CLIPS uses ontology that describes broad range of network security aspects (we use "SOPAS ontology" developed in our project). CLIPS engine identifies whenever some attacks or malicious network events have been discovered. The information describing the network incident and reconfiguration procedures are sent to Translator (see Fig. 1). Moreover, detailed information in human readable format are generated and visualized to network administrators via FNPS-DM GUI.

3.1   Event Correlation Mechanism

Data received from network sensors is arranged in streams. Each stream is built of multiple tuples (events). Each tuple, depending on sensor type, may have different schema. Borealis allows to process streams in order to correlate information coming from different sources and to detect network incidents more efficiently.

The query that is executed over the multiple streams consists of operators. There are different kinds of operators provided by the Borealis engine that allow for aggregation, filtering and joining data coming from different streams.

3.2   Ontology

In both computer science and information science, an ontology is a form of representing a data model of a specific domain and it can be used to e.g.: reason about the objects in that domain and the relations between them. Ontology defines basic terms and relations comprising the vocabulary of a topic area as well as the rules for combining terms and relations to define extensions to the vocabulary [13].

In the proposed Federated Networks Protection System, we use network security domain ontology developed in this project (SOPAS Ontology). The knowledge about various security aspects is modeled and formalized in the OWL format [14]. Moreover, semantic rules are developed in SWRL language [15].

The ontology describes security aspects and provides common language that increases interoperability between domains. It allows the DMs to communicate using common abstract layers and to reason about security facts using common language. However, different sensors have different data formats, therefore some effort has to be made by administrators to inform the system what particular parameters and values stand for (especially when new sensors are added).

The main classes and relations of the proposed ontology are shown in Fig. 3. These describes following aspects:

- Attacks, symptoms, attack impact and reactions to attack,
- IM - Intermediate events (schemas, types and relations such as IM-Sensor or IM-Asset),

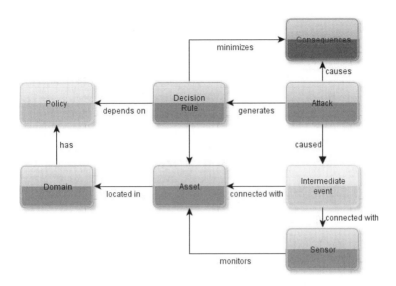

Fig. 3. Main classes of the SOPAS ontology

- Asset description and their relations - details are stored in CMDB (Configuration Management Database) format,
- Policy (what reactions are recommended/allowed in the particular domain),
- Decision Rules (how to react to attack).

According to Fig.2 only intermediate events are matched with the knowledge stored in the ontology. The intermediate events are obtained via the Borealis query that is executed over the streams of a network events. Their names, types and schemas are maintained in the ontology.

Some examples of intermediate events are: multiple login failed action, multiple request generated to several IPs by particular IP, multiple request generated to one IPs by particular IP to multiple services, multiple request generated by one IP to particular service, established connection to suspicious URL and suspicious SQL query.

3.3   Decisions Enhanced with Semantic Reasoning

Each intermediate event received by CLIPS rule engine is considered as attack symptom and as such is matched with knowledge in the ontology in order infer the most probable attack.

The example of symptom matching is graphically presented in Fig.4. When the symptoms are received by CLIPS rule engine the most probable attacks are inferred. However one symptom could match several attacks, therefore CLIPS is responsible for computing the probability score and alerting about these attacks, for which the calculated score exceeds the detection threshold.

In other words CLIPS is used to estimate the probability $p(A|o_1, o_2, \ldots, o_n)$ of particular attack A given the observations $o_1, o_2, \ldots, o_n$. For all the known

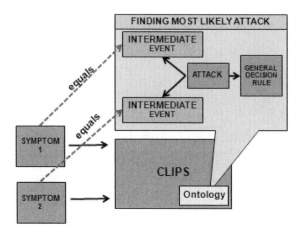

Fig. 4. Matching sensor events (symptoms) with knowledge in ontology

attacks (maintained in ontology) and known symptoms the problem of finding the most probable attack becomes a MAP (Maximum A-Posteriori) problem (1).

$$A^* = \arg\max_A p(A|o_1, o_2, \ldots, o_n) \tag{1}$$

We have assumed that observations (intermediate events) are mutually independent. Such approach allows us to apply Bayes theorem to estimate the probability of the attack (see equation 2). Z indicates scaling factor.

$$p(A|o_1, o_2, \ldots, o_n) = \frac{1}{Z} p(A) \prod_{i=1}^{N} p(o_i|A) \tag{2}$$

The probability of particular attack is established in two steps. In the first step, CLIPS engine calculates the product of probabilities $p(o_i|A)$ (this information is maintained in ontology and describes how efficiently the observation o_i indicates the attack A). In the second step, CLIPS decides if attack occurred (if the score exceeds the system threshold).

The prior probability ($p(A)$) is a uniform one at the system startup and it is updated dynamically as attacks are detected. This allows the system to adapt differently in different domains.

If the attack is detected it may have accompanying (described in ontology) general decision rule that will minimize consequences. There are several pre-defined general reactions such as blocking, traffic redirection (e.g. to a trap or back to the attacker), administrator notification or service disabling.

The ontology defines different security policies (what reactions are recommended/allowed in the particular domain) for different domains, therefore CLIPS additionally matches this knowledge with appropriate general reaction rule to avoid policy violation.

3.4   General Decision Rules Distribution

In order to provide high system flexibility, the Translator element is introduced in the proposed system. Translators are distributed over the domains and are responsible for interacting with the reaction elements inside the subnetworks. Translators have knowledge about the particular subnet capabilities and its topology. Particularly they have access (ssh, telnet, ldap) to the reaction elements. The decision rules sent by Decision Modules have a general format (e.g. Block particular IP). The translator is responsible for translating it to appropriate format (e.g IPTABLES) and applying it to appropriate asset (e.g. gateway).

The General Decision Rule is sent to Translator module using SOAP protocol. The SOAP method has two arguments: gdrType and gdrParam:

bool trExecute(GDRType gdrType, Map gdrParam)

The grdType defines types of reaction. These can be (depending on particular domain policy encoded in the ontology):

- Block/Drop
- Echo
- Forward to trap
- Admin notification

The Block/Drop reaction allows the Translator to drop the traffic coming from the particular IP address. Echo indicates to redirect traffic back to the attacker. This reaction forces the remote bot/worm to hack itself or other bot machine. Similar reaction is "Forward to trap", which allows to redirect traffic to the trap for further analysis. The "Admin notification" produces text message (warning) for the system administrator. The grdParam argument defines additional (specific for particular reaction) parameters such as trap address, IP address of the attacker, time the rule is valid, etc.

In order to provide security information exchange the DM in the federation can also share the General Decision Rules applied in the domains. In example if the user inside one domain is infected with malicious code, the DM can share that information and decide if the access for that user should be blocked to particular domain.

3.5   P2P-Enabled Communication between Domains

In order to provide a robust, self path-replicated and resilient communication between different domains in federation (between Decision Modules), P2P technology is used. This approach allows the proposed system to overcome IP addressing issues and minimize the configuration cost.

The proposed P2P overlay network is dedicated only for a communication between domains in federation in order to minimize the impact on network traffic. Each Decision Module is a peer hosting and requesting data concerning federation security aspects. It is assumed that federation may have several public IP addresses where lightweight P2P application can be installed. This allows to multiply a number of routing points in a P2P overlay network. Moreover, it is possible that other machines (not only DMs) may also act as peers in FNPS overlay network.

The proposed approach allows the system to have redundant communication channels between Decision Modules. Particularly, when a physical connection is under attack or is congested, the communication packets still have a opportunity to reach the destination DM using a different path.

The used communication channels are encrypted using the SSL algorithm. This allows to protect the communication against the packet sniffing (by third persons). Additionally, payload is encrypted with different keys and it can be only decrypted by domains that belong to the same distribution group (nodes relaying the message can not read the payload).

3.6   Graphical User Interface and Visualization

The visualization methods and Decision Module GUI will allow the administrator of the proposed FNPS system to increase the situational awareness.

Current operation tools for monitoring computer networks are not designed to provide the operator with good situational awareness. Typically, these tools are mainly experience-based solutions with a raw or tabular data presentation user interface.

The goal of the Decision Module GUI is to visualize the network status and provide information about historical and current network events and security incidents. DM will use data about historical network performance, information from the underlying online FNPS system and reported network events. The tool will analyze and present the threats, provide support and guidance to the

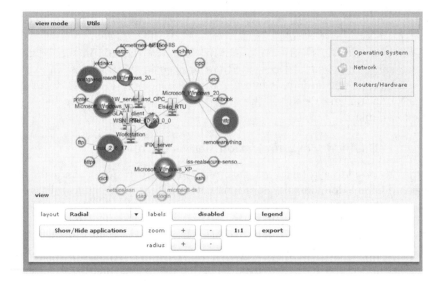

Fig. 5. Visualization of security incidents

operator and will evaluate potential actions to be taken as well as decisions made by the administrator.

One of the visualization examples is shown in Fig. 5. This screen aims at visualizing the topology and network incident (in one of the domains of the federation) in the same time.

Furthermore, GUI allows the administrator to visualize the network events currently processed by the Decision Module, manage the communication between different DMs and decide what types of decisions rules can be distributed and shared with other domains.

4   SQLIA Attack Detection Scenario

SOPAS is not yet a finished project with final products developed, but we can show some preliminary results and application scenarios.

The SQLIA (SQL Injection Attack) scenario demonstrates how weakly protected domains can benefit from federation and sharing the information in order to increase their security level. SQLIA is ranked #1 in The Ten Most Critical Web Application Security Risks released by Open Web Application Security Project (OWASP) [16].

Simplified topology of the federation is presented in Fig. 6. It consists of 4 domains. Decision Modules (orange boxes) are deployed in each domain. There are also different services (green boxes) and sensors responsible for detecting particular type of attacks (blue boxes).

We assume that domains trust each other and cooperate in process of sharing the security information.

Firstly, the attacker scans the federation to find HTTP services. Particularly attacker aims at finding unsecured services running on unusual ports. The sensors in domain 2 and 3 detect port scanning and report this fact to their Decision Modules. This information is forwarded to domain 1 and 4. The source address of attacker is stored by Decision Modules as suspicious one.

The HTTP services discovered by attacker are further penetrated in order to find application flaws. The unusual traffic in HTTP service logs is spotted by sensors, but only in the domain 1. Moreover, the sensors in the domain 2 report an increasing number of failed and an untypical SQL queries to the database. Also the sensors in the domain 4 report an unusual and huge traffic (typically this domain is rarely visited). The Decision Modules exchange this information using P2P enabled communication.

Now, thanks to information sharing in federation, all the domains are able to analyze the complete set of information.

The ontology is engaged and the problem is inferred as the SQL Injection Attack (SQLIA).

Each Decision Module works out a reaction appropriate to its policy stored in the ontology (each domain may have a different policy). The Decision Modules in the domains 1, 3 and 4 decide to inform the administrator about the attack, while the DM in domain 4 decides both to block the traffic (there are already some

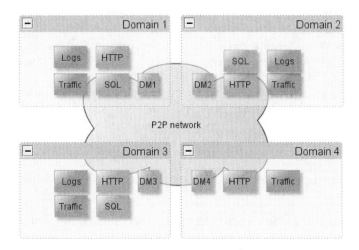

Fig. 6. Simplified topology diagram of the federation (orange box - decision module, green box - hosted services, blue box - installed sensors)

failed queries to database, suggesting that the flaw was spotted by the attacker) and to inform the administrator. The DM in domain 4 sends the request to the Translator to block the traffic coming from the attacker. Then the Translator sends an appropriate command to one of the Reaction Modules to block the attacker.

5   Conclusions

This paper presents preliminary results of the national project SOPAS funded by Ministry of Science and Higher Education of Poland in the theme of homeland security.

The major contribution of this paper is the concept of Federated Networks Protection System that is being developed in the SOPAS national research project. In particular, we focused on the Decision Module, the correlation mechanism and the semantic reasoning based on the ontology used to detect cyber attacks. The presented system is dedicated for federated networks and systems used by the public administration and military sector. Such systems can increase their overall security and resiliency by sharing and exchanging security related information and general reaction rules. We also presented a sample scenario (SQLIA attack detection) to show how the proposed system can detect complex attacks and benefit from information sharing between federated domains.

Acknowledgement. This work was partially supported by Polish Ministry of Science and Higher Education funds allocated for the years 2010-2012 (Research Project number OR00012511).

References

1. Enabling and managing end-to-end resilience, ENISA (European Network and Information Security Agency) Report (January 2011)
2. Choraś, M., D'Antonio, S., Kozik, R., Holubowicz, W.: INTERSECTION Approach to Vulnerability Handling. In: Proc. of WEBIST 2010, vol.1, 171–174. INSTICC Press, Valencia (2010)
3. NATO Network Enabled Feasibility Study Volume II: Detailed Report Covering a Strategy and Roadmap for Realizing an NNEC Networking and Information Infrastructure (NII), version 2.0
4. El-Damhougy, H., Yousefizadeh, H., Lofquist, D., Sackman, R., Crowley, J.: Hierarchical and federated network management for tactical environments. In: Proc. of IEEE Military Communications Conference MILCOM, vol. 4, pp. 2062–2067 (2005)
5. Calo, S., Wood, D., Zerfos, P., Vyvyan, D., Dantressangle, P., Bent, G.: Technologies for Federation and Interoperation of Coalition Networks. In: Proc. of 12th International Conference on Information Fusion, Seattle (2009)
6. Coppolino, L., D'Antonio, L., Esposito, M., Romano, L.: Exploiting diversity and correlation to improve the performance of intrusion detection systems. In: Proc. of IFIP/IEEE International Conference on Network and Service (2009)
7. SNORT project homepage: http://www.snort.org/
8. Choraś, M., Saganowski, L., Renk, R., Holubowicz, W.: Statistical and signal-based network traffic recognition for anomaly detection. Expert Systems (Early View) (2011), doi: 10.1111/j.1468-0394.2010.00576.x
9. ARAKIS project homepage: http://www.arakis.pl
10. HSN project homepage: http://www.honeyspider.net/
11. Borealis project homepage:
    http://www.cs.brown.edu/research/borealis/public/
12. CLIPS project homepage: http://clipsrules.sourceforge.net/
13. Neches, R., Fikes, R., Finin, T., Gruber, T., Patil, R., Senator, T., Swartout, W.R.: Enabling Technology for Knowledge Sharing. AI Magazine 2(3), s.36–s.56 (1991)
14. OWL Web Ontology Language Semantics and Abstract Syntax (June 2006),
    http://www.w3.org/TR/owl-features/
15. SWRL: A Semantic Web Rule Language Combning OWL and RuleML, W3C Member Submission, http://www.w3.org/Submission/SWRL/
16. OWASP Top Ten -2010. The Ten Most Critical Web Application Security Risks. Published by Open Web Application Security Project, OWASP (2010)

An Autonomic Security Monitor
for Distributed Operating Systems
(Invited Paper)

Alvaro E. Arenas, Benjamin Aziz, Szymon Maj, and Brian Matthews

[1] Department of Information Systems, Instituto de Empresa Business School,
Madrid, Spain
`alvaro.arenas@ie.edu`
[2] School of Computing, University of Portsmouth, Portsmouth, U.K.
`benjamin.aziz@port.ac.uk`
[3] AGH University of Science and Technology, Krakow, Poland
`smaj@student.agh.edu.pl`
[4] e-Science Centre, STFC Rutherford Appleton Laboratory, Oxfordshire, U.K.
`brian.matthews@stfc.ac.uk`

Abstract. This paper presents an autonomic system for the monitoring of security-relevant information in a Grid-based operating system. Our approach is multi-layered. The first layer is security-agnostic, monitoring the states of processes and jobs. The second layer is security-aware, monitoring pre-defined security events and co-relating then using rule-based policies. Policies are capable of controlling the system environment based on changes in levels of CPU/memory usage, accesses to system resources, detection of abnormal behaviour such as DDos attacks.

1 Introduction

Monitoring is the act of collecting information concerning the characteristics and status of resources of interest. Monitoring open distributed systems is an active research area, and monitoring security properties is still considered a challenge. The aims of this paper is to present the monitoring of security-relevant information in the distributed operating system XtreemOS [3], a Grid-based operating system (OS) based on Linux.

The main contributions of the paper are the following. First, describing an abstract architecture for monitoring security properties in a distributed operating systems. Second, presenting an autonomic system that triggers corrective actions on monitored events. Finally, showing the implementation of the architecture and its integration into the XtreemOS operating system

The structure of the paper is as follows. Next section acts as background section, introducing the main concepts related to monitoring distributed systems. Section 3 focuses on the XtreemOS systems, describing its general monitoring subsystem. Then, Section 4 explains how the general XtreemOS monitor was customised for monitoring security properties. Section 5 describes an autonomic

W. Abramowicz et al. (Eds.): ServiceWave 2011, LNCS 6994, pp. 112–121, 2011.

rule-based system that exploits monitored data in order to take some actions. Section 6 shows the implementation of the secure monitoring subsystem. Then, Section 7 compares our work with others. Finally, Section 8 concludes the paper and highlights future work.

2 Background

We start by revising the main concepts and terminology related to monitoring, following the terminology defined in [7].

- An *entity* is any networked resource, which can be unique, having a considerable lifetime and general use. Typical entities are processors, memories, storage media, network links, applications and processes.
- An *event* is a collection of timestamped, typed data, associated with an entity, and represented in a specific structure.
- An *event schema* defines the typed structure and semantics of an event.
- A *sensor* is a process monitoring an entity and generating events.

Our interest is in monitoring distributed operating systems, and in particular Grid-based operating systems. Hence, our starting point is the Grid Monitoring Architecture (GMA) [5] proposed by the Open Grid Forum. The main components of the GMA are the following.

- A *producer* is a process providing events.
- A *consumer* is any process that receives events
- A *registry* is a lookup service that allows producers to publish the event types they generate, and consumers to find out the events they are interested in.

After discovering each other through the registry, producers and consumers communicate directly. GMA defines three types of interactions between producers and consumers. Publish/subscribe refers to a three-phase interaction consisting of a subscription for a specific event type, a stream of events from a producer to a consumer, and a termination of the subscription. Both the establishment and the termination of a subscription can be initiated by any of the two parties. A *query/response* is an one-off interaction initiated by a consumer and followed by a single producer response containing one or more events. Lastly, a *notification* can be sent by a producer to a consumer without any further interactions.

3 Monitoring in a Distributed Operating System

This section first presents a brief description of the XtreemOS distributed operating system and then gives a general overview of its monitoring component. The XtreemOS Grid OS is based on the Linux OS, extended as needed for enabling and facilitating Grid computing [3]. XtreemOS Grid spans multiple administrative domains on different sites, comprising heterogeneous resources that can be shared by the participating organisations. As illustrated in Figure 1, XtreemOS is composed of two subsystems:

- The XtreemOS foundation, called *XtreemOS-F*, is a modified Linux kernel embedding Virtual Organization (VO) support mechanisms and providing kernel level process checkpoint/restart functionalities.
- The high-level Grid services, called *XtreemOS-G*, which comprises several Grid OS distributed services to deal with resource and application management in VOs, and it is implemented on top of XtreemOS-F at user level. The three main subsystems of XtreemOS-G comprises: Data Management, which federates multiple data stores located in different adminitrative domains; VO Management, which manage the life-cycle of VO, including the management and enforcement of VO security policies; finally, the Application Execution Management (AEM) subsystem is in charge of discovering, selecting and allocating resources for job execution, as well as starting, controlling and *monitoring* jobs. XtreemOS also includes a set of services facilitating scalability, including a scalabe publish/subscribe subsystem.

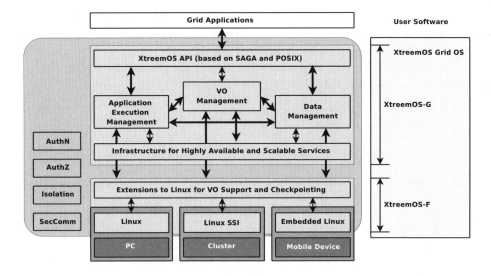

Fig. 1. The XtreemOS Software Architecture (taken from [3])

XtreemOS follows the philosophy of associating a job with multiple processes running on several nodes, similar to the Linux process-thread paradigm. To this end, XtreemOS defines a hierarchy of entities composed of the job, job unit and process. In order to check the status of jobs and processes, XtreemOS AEM includes a monitoring infrastructure [4], which allows one to monitor the system with user-defined events at the abstraction levels of jobs, processes and threads.

Figure 2 shows an abstraction of the XtreemOS monitoring infrastructure. XtreemOS AEM includes two main components: the *Job Manager*, which provides job management features such as scheduling and storing job-related information; and the *Execution Manager*, which manages execution of jobs at the

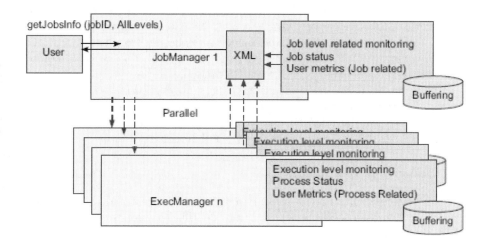

Fig. 2. The XtreemOS Monitoring Infrastructure (taken from [4])

process level. Monitoring is performed at each of these levels, based on events defined by the user or by the system. XtreemOS events, called metrics in [4], have an event schema including a value type (Boolean, integer, timestamp, ⋯) and a scope. A scope (JOB, JOBUNIT or PROCESS) indicates the source of monitoring information.

The monitoring service in XtreemOS is a general one used by AEM services as well as other XtreemOS services including the security monitoring service described in the following section.

4   Monitoring Security in XtreemOS

Our main objective is to exploit the XtreemOS monitoring infrastructure in order to assess the security status of the distributed system. This section describes an instantiation of the XtreemOS monitor subsystem to monitor security events. First we describe the architectural distribution of the XtreemOS monitor; then, we introduce the main use cases exploiting the security-monitoring capabilities; and finally, outline the security events defined.

4.1   Security Monitoring and Auditing

XtreemOS defines two types of sites (organisations) participating in a distributed system: A *core site* is a site hosting and executing XtreemOS services and is considered essential; usually it includes services such as VO membership management, VO security policy management and auditing services. Generally, there is only one core site per XtreemOS Grid. Any other site participating in a Grid is considered a *resource site*, usually providing resources to that Grid.

We define two types of monitors. First, the *resource monitor* is responsible for monitoring resource-related events such as CPU utilizations, memory usage, network traffic, job status and job exit codes. There is one resource monitor for each site participating in a Grid. Second, the *core monitor* monitors events related to the Grid and VOs, and information collected from core XtreemOS services such as VO Management. There is one instance of the core monitor executing in the core site of the XtreemOS system.

In addition, we define an auditing service responsible for managing the monitored information. It uses the monitors as a source of information, which is stored in historical database for later analysis. There is one instance of the auditing service executing in the core site of the XtreemOS system.

4.2   Security Requirements

In order to define what type of information should be monitored, we analysed a portfolio of fourteen Grid applications and identified the following use cases in which the monitoring of security-related information is required:

- *CPU/Memory Usage Restrictions.* In this requirement, the system should be able to register the amount of computational resources used by a user's total number of jobs. As soon as the user's jobs use more than the specified quota, the system takes an action; for instance, to forbid submitting any more jobs by that user. A variation of this requirement would be to allow the quota to be dynamically calculated based on the status of the distributed resources, rather than presetting it statically during the initialization of the system. The restriction on user actions may have expiration time, which may also be based on predictions.

- *Defense Against DDos Attacks.* The aim of this case is to make the system more resistant to Distributed Denial of Service (DDOS) attacks. A resource analyzes incoming packets locally and exchanges aggregated meta information with other resources, hence monitoring the traffic data. Accumulated knowledge enables detection and prevention of such attacks.

- *Dynamic Access Control.* Cases like this aim at restricting potentially harmful accesses to resources dynamically. An access to a resource is governed by dynamically changing attributes, which could be managed and controlled according to either a Separation of Duty model or a Chinese wall policy model.

- *VO Usage Policy Enforcement.* This case restricts available actions in a VO. Users actions in the VO are monitored and possibly stopped and/or logged if they do not match the predefined policies. These may forbid usage of certain actions or restrict the frequency of such actions. Monitoring repeated unreasonable requests or failed attempts to use the resource in a short amount of time may lead to the suspicion that the user is attempting to misuse the resource with ominous intent.

- *Malicious Behaviour Detection.* Another important requirement of Grid systems is to detect possible misbehavior of jobs in a Grid environment and warn users in time to minimise the risk of damage from malicious behaviour. If the monitoring system detects certain characteristic patterns in events over some period of time during job executions, then this may imply execution of malware, therefore, requiring further the release of a warning to the affected users.

– *Peak Hours Detection.* This requirement is related to determining time periods during which the resources are scarce and times when resources are abundant. The system monitors resource availability in time and determines trends, presenting useful statistical information.

4.3   Monitoring and Auditing Capabilities

Based on the requirements, the XtreemOS system has defined the following monitoring and auditing capabilities.

Monitoring Capabilities. These are related to the monitoring of various information related to resource metrics, jobs, events, nodes and policy violations.

– *Monitoring Resource Metrics.* This capability allows the administrators to obtain notifications when particular values for resource metrics change or reach certain levels. For example, these include CPU utilization levels, memory usage levels and the amount of network traffic.
– *Monitoring Jobs.* This use case allows the administrators to monitor job-related information. Different job metrics can be monitored, for example, job status, job submission time and job exit status, as well as higher-level information such as the number of jobs currently running on a node or over several nodes.
– *Monitoring Nodes.* This includes the monitoring of various nodes in the Grid. Example of what can be monitored on a node includes its state and the state of the containers running on the node.
– *VO Policy Violation Monitoring.* This capability generates notifications about any policy violations in the system. In an autonomic policy system, this is very important as it may trigger the evolution process for new rules and policies. For example, if a user continuously violate their CPU usage quota on a particular node, it may trigger a new rule that blocks the specific user from submitting future jobs to the node.

Auditing Capabilities. Auditing capabilities include any functionality that is based on the information gathered from the monitoring capabilities. These include archiving and securing monitored data, querying historical database and the generation of the various VO, node and user behaviour reports.

– *Archiving and Securing Monitored Data.* This capability simply allows any monitored data to be archived in a historical database. In most cases, monitored data is sensitive information that needs protection for future references. Hence, this capability includes functionalities to protect monitored data by using encryption or access control mechanisms.
– *Querying Historical Database.* This use case allows the querying of the historical database in order to retrieve information about past events at different level of granularity: process, jobs, VOs.

– *Report Generation.* This capabilities allows generation of detailed reports about either the VO state, the state of a particular node in the Grid, or a specific user's behaviour over a period of time.

5   Autonomic Management of Security Events

The monitoring and auditing capabilities described previously allows one to monitor events, store them in a database, and query for particular events. In order to achieve more autonomous behaviour, we have extended the monitoring capabilities with a rule-based system able to analyse monitored information in real-time and take corrective actions accordingly, which themselves could lead to new rules.

The rule-based system consists of four elements: *Event Feeder*, which provides the stream of external events generated by the monitors into the autonomic system; *Rule Engine*, the logic of the system; *Rule Base*, which contains the collection of rule defined in the system; and *Action Executor*, which takes action to affect external environment. In addition, there is a *Working Memory* that is built dynamically from incoming facts and events during the life of system. These main components of the architecture are shown in Figure 3.

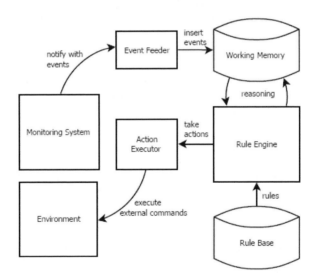

Fig. 3. Architecture of the XtreemOS Autonomic Monitoring Sub-System

Next, we describe in more detail each of these components.

– *Event Feeder* is the part of architecture responsible for communicating with the monitoring system. Its implementations gather events either by subscribing to notifications from the monitoring system or by reading event objects from external streams, like files. Events are then inserted directly into the working memory, where the rule engine should react to them immediately. Different implementations of this subsystem can handle different monitoring systems and varying event formats, converting events into a suitable type if necessary.

- *Rule Engine* works in stream mode, which means it can analyze events in real-time, immediately firing any applicable rules. When a rule activated by some incoming event fires, the result may call the action executor as well as add new facts into the working memory. The newly added facts may lead to other rules being fired and this potentially-recursive process is called *reasoning* or *inferring*.

- *Rule Base* contains all of the system's logic except for the relation to the external environment. It is loaded into the system and compiled during initialisation, therefore it is not possible to modify it during runtime. Rules however can be modified before loading the system, but also may be configurable while being loaded into the system.

- *Action Executor* is responsible for the manipulation of external environment. Consequences of some rules may affect external environment like restricting user's accesses, as opposed to rules only affecting the working memory.

6 Implementation

The general XtreemOS monitoring component is part of the Application Execution Management (AEM) component [4]. XtreemOS monitoring includes events and metrics. Examples of events include "job failed", "VO created" or "user certificate not valid". By contrast, metrics are user-defined and has associated a value. Examples of metrics include "cpu utilization - 80%", "free disk - 100.5 GB" or "jobs running - 5".

Information for Process Monitoring is obtained from a daemon reading the /proc/pid file in the nodes. The Job Monitoring implementation provides interfaces to get the information associated to jobs (*getJobsInfo*, *getJobMetrics*); mechanisms to add new information to the generated by the system - user metrics (*addJobMetric*, *setMetricValue*, *removeJobMetric*); and mechanisms to be notified when certain monitoring events fire (*addMonitoringCallback*).

The Monitoring Manager collects monitoring data from various sources and stores it for a period of time. Interested parties define monitoring rules which describe what to monitor. When conditions of the monitoring rule are met, a notification is issued. A particular monitoring rule is identified by monitoring rule name to which interested parties subscribe to receive notifications. The Monitoring Manager implementation provides interfaces for saving events and metrics (*saveEvent*, *saveMetric*); mechanisms for setting monitoring rules and subscribing to monitoring notifications (*addNotification*, *subscribe*, *unsubscribe*); and functionalities for defining aggregated metrics.

The Auditing Manager permanently stores monitoring data received from the Monitoring Manager. Data is archived in a history database that can be later analyzed and used for generating reports. The Auditing Management implementation provides interfaces for defining archiving rules (*addArchiveRule*, *cancelArchiveRule*); and querying the database (*query*). Hibernate is used as query language.

The implementation of the Autonomic Manager of Security Events was carried out using the Java Drools technology, a platform for developing writing rules and performing event processing. We have defined a Manager class that encapsulates and hides Java Drools interface in order to simplify starting and stopping of the system. The Drools rule engine itself is not thread-safe, but Manager synchronizes all necessary methods, thus the whole system may be used by multiple threads, as its methods are non-blocking. The Manager implements the *EventEntryPoint* interface, which is passed on as an argument to the EventFeeder when it starts. In addition, we have defined a Configuration call that sets the initial parameters of the system. Objects representing parameters are inserted into the working memory when starting the system, therefore any subsequent additions will not affect execution.

7 Discussion

The approach we followed in this work on monitoring security information is multi-layered. The first layer is security agnostic, i.e. low-level information is detected using the XtreemOS AEM infrastructure [4], monitoring the states of various processes and jobs. Second, based on the information collected by the AEM, a security-aware monitoring and auditing service [6] is implemented, whose monitored events could be queried directly from a database. Finally, an autonomic security monitoring service is also implemented based on the information collected from the AEM monitor; the service is dynamic in the sense that is able to evolve the various rules depending on the status of resources, the jobs running within, and the environment.

This is not the first attempt at achieving comprehensive monitoring in Grid systems. In [5], the authors define a full Grid monitoring architecture, though the architecture is designed with performance of Grid systems in mind, rather than security. There are many systems that have been developed to support real-time monitoring in Grids; for instance, Ganglia [2] is used within the Globus community as a result of its integration with the Globus Meta Directory Service (MDS). The main advantage of XtreemOS monitoring approach in comparison with Ganglia is the tight integration of XtreemOS with low-level OS features, enabling good performance and lowering the system load [4]. On the other hand, Ganglia has been widely used over various platforms including Cluster platforms. In [1], a Grid monitoring infrastructure is defined, called OCM-G, which can be used to support the development of various Grid monitors. However, OCM-G is rather more complicated to use than the case of XtreemOS monitoring as it requires monitored applications to include special "probes" to be inserted in their source code and then re-compiled before becoming suitable for monitoring.

8 Conclusion and Future Work

This paper describes the monitoring of security properties in the XtreemOS operating system. Monitoring security is seen as a particular case of XtreemOS monitoring, where relevant events and user metrics are monitored and aggregated in order to determine potential security problems. In addition, we presented a Java-Drools-based autonomic monitoring system, which further extends the functionality of the standard security monitoring service in XtreemOS with capabilities for the evolution of rules and policies based on the dynamic information collected from the resources, jobs and VOs.

There are many directions for future work. Mainly, we would like to exploit the XtreemOS autonomic monitoring service for the enforcement of more complex autonomic security policies, in particular, focusing on the runtime detection of malicious job signatures that could imply viral behaviour. The autonomic monitoring service itself is somehow independant of the XtreemOS system in that it only relies on the information collected by the AEM, therefore, another main direction for future work will involve integrating the service with other Grid middleware systems, in particular Globus and gLite.

References

1. Baliś, B., Bubak, M., Funika, W., Szepieniec, T., Wismüller, R., Radecki, M.: Monitoring grid applications with grid-enabled OMIS monitor. In: Fernández Rivera, F., Bubak, M., Gómez Tato, A., Doallo, R. (eds.) Across Grids 2003. LNCS, vol. 2970, pp. 230–239. Springer, Heidelberg (2004)
2. Massie, M.L., Chun, B.N., Culler, D.E.: The Ganglia Distributed Monitoring System: Design, Implementation, and Experience. Parallel Computing 30(7), 817–840 (2004)
3. Morin, C., Jégou, Y., Gallard, J., Riteau, P.: Clouds: a new playground for the xtreemos grid operating system. Parallel Processing Letters 19(3), 435–449 (2009)
4. Nou, R., Giralt, J., Corbalan, J., Tejedor, E., Fito, J.O., Perez, J.M., Cortes, T.: XtreemOS Application Execution Management: A Scalable Approach. In: 11th ACM/IEEE International Conference on Grid Computing (2010)
5. Tierney, B., Aydt, R., Gunter, D., Smith, W., Swany, M., Taylor, V., Wolski, R.: A Grid Monitoring Architecture (2002)
6. XtreemOS Consortium: Fourth specification, design and architecture of the security and vo management services. In: XtreemOS Public Deliverables-D3.5.13. Work Package 3.5 (December 2009),
   http://www.xtreemos.org/publications/public-deliverables/
7. Zanikolas, S., Sakellariou, R.: A Taxonomy of Grid Monitoring Systems. Future Generation Comp. Syst. 21(1), 163–188 (2005)

A Novel Systemic Taxonomy of Trust in the Online Environment

(Invited Paper)

Tanja Ažderska and Borka Jerman Blažič

Laboratory for Open Systems and Networks, Jozef Stefan Institute, Jomova 39,
1000 Ljubljana, Slovenia
{atanja,borka}@e5.ijs.si

Abstract. Trust and reputation comprise a wide research area in social sciences, but are also pillars of many social phenomena that shape the Internet socio-economic scene. The blossoming of virtual communities largely changed the way trust is formed and propagated. The few existing taxonomies provide only initial insights into the ways trust-benefits can be felt; they are neither complete nor elaborated in a systemic manner to provide a proper framework guided by real system-principles. In this paper, we propose a multidimensional framework for guiding the design-process, and assessing the completeness and consistency of reputation systems. Our framework is based on System theory principles; it identifies reputation system components, and more importantly, defines their interrelations. It considers the interaction-centric, dynamic and environment-dependent trust-establishment and detects five major factors that guide reputation mechanisms design. The presented framework is applied to BarterCast reputation mechanism deployed in the BitTorrent-client Tribler.

Keywords: trust, taxonomy, reputation mechanisms, system theory, context.

1 Introduction

The Internet is an environment of ubiquitous devices, entities and interactions among them, where the inherent uncertainty and risk require new tools to support decision making. Apart from Internet's commercial expansion, traditional social networking relies on unwritten protocols, like gossiping and rumors, to judge about one's trustworthiness and reliability. A global consensus on person's reputation has neither been required nor needed, yet the social model has been successfully supporting legitimate interactions, identifying untrustworthy individuals. The advent of Social networking and computational semantics opens up a myriad of opportunities for merging the human-centric and dynamic character of trust with the technical possibilities of Information and Communication Technologies. The growth of user-generated content, the vast offer of service providers, and the wealth of collaborative and market-based platforms, have added new levels of complexity in the processes of information filtering and decision making. They require systemic approaches for treating trust and reputation (T&R). Hence, the success of online trust-based methods

W. Abramowicz et al. (Eds.): ServiceWave 2011, LNCS 6994, pp. 122–133, 2011.

depends largely: a) on the research aimed at identifying where these methods offer the most benefit and b) on the quality of the frameworks where the system design principles reside. Our work is a contribution in both the aspects. The framework defined here is guided by the principles of System theory and taxonomic organization. It defines five major factors that influence the reputation mechanisms design and provides a multidimensional map of the interdependencies among the system components based on those factors. Such approach would also testify that trust awareness is as needed online as it is offline.

To develop the outlined topics, the paper is organized as follows: the next section briefly examines related work, defines the notions of T&R and the progress towards their formalization. Succeeding sections outline the methodology used and introduce the proposed framework based on the principles of General Systems Taxonomy. Practical observations from other trust taxonomies and models are elaborated through the framework enabling addition of a new level of granularity to the existing research map on T&R. Sec.5 illustrates the application of the newly designed approach for the specific case of distributed environments, mapping the BarterCast reputation mechanism across the dimensions of the framework. The paper concludes with a review of the presented topics, outlining our future research plans.

2   Short Survey of the State of the Art in Trust and Reputation

The Notion of Trust and Reputation. *Trust* is a social manifestation we face on a daily basis. However, its definition is hard to grasp. One reason for this is its strong context-dependence. As a social conformity, trust gives researchers a hard time when it comes to defining its computational analog. Therefore, incorporating it into online scenarios has not been very fruitful. The literature on T&R in social sciences is exhaustive [1], [2]. The common attitude supports the aspect of relying on others' willingness to perform beneficial actions. Based on Gambetta's attitude on trust [3]:

Definition 1. Trust is the belief, i.e., the subjective probability that an entity will perform in a way likely to bring the expected benefit, or not to do unexpected harm.

Despite the interchangeable use of the concepts of T&R, reputation deserves its own and more specific definition that would stress how it differs from trust.

Definition 2. Reputation is the empirical memory about an entity's past behavior, performance, or quality of service, in a specific context, i.e., domain of interest.

Hence, reputation is a quantitative representation of trustworthiness bounded by the domain of interest. It results from calculation and assessment and is based on facts rather than mere opinion and belief (e.g., I trust you because of your good reputation), unlike trust, which is a more subjective evaluation of someone's performance (e.g., I trust you despite your bad reputation). However, considering trust only as a *subjective probability* leaves out an extremely important concept related to trust, that of *risk*. This fact has been the catalyst of a vigorous debate between social psychologists and economists [2]. Thus, Josang defines two types of trust, *Reliability* and *Decision trust* [4]. The former covers the aspect of trust as stated by Definition 1. The latter considers the risk brought about by the uncertainty of transactional outcomes and is used to extend the first definition, which now gains the following structure:

Definition 3. Trust is the extent to which one entity is willing to depend on others' decisions, accepting the unpredictable risk of a negative (undesired) outcome.

Formalization of Trust and Reputation. Much of the research on trust evaluation has its roots in Game Theory, where concepts like quality, cost and utility are more formally defined [5]. The most fundamental trust problems there are captured by the Prisoner's Dilemma [6]. It demonstrates the tradeoffs in people's decisions to maximize either their own profit or the overall outcome of the game, and is also used in strategies for fostering online cooperation in technical implementations, such as in BitTorrent's tit-for-tat policy [7]. However, it is often people's sense of community contributing to outcomes that improve community welfare [8]. Moreover, if members are held responsible for their actions, there is a greater pressure to adhere to the rules. Fehr has shown that, given the opportunity, individuals vigorously punish selfishness, even if punishment is costly to induce [9]. Despite this early work on trust relations and conflict resolution in, the notion of computational trust appears significantly later, when Marsh formalized trust in distributed artificial intelligence [10]. Although distinguished by its simplicity, this work brings the substantial finding about agents' tendency to group together into clusters with similar trustworthiness and interests. However, it considers groups as encountering and equally resolving trust choices like the individual agents, omitting scenarios where trust may be undesirable to nourish (like adverse collusion). A work that relates quality and uncertainty within the framework of reputation is the Akerlof's study on the *lemon markets* [11]. Analyzing the effect of social and trading reputation on transaction outcome and market maintenance, the study shows how low-quality goods can squeeze out those of high quality because of the information asymmetry in the buyers' and sellers' knowledge. Reputation mechanisms (RMs) would balance this asymmetry by incentivizing sellers to exchange high-quality goods and helping buyers make informed decisions. Akerlof makes an instructive distinction between the *signaling* and *sanctioning* role of RMs, which is only recently considered in computer science [12]. The formal modeling of T&R is mainly done by the use of a mathematical and formal logics apparatus. We omit that body of work here, as this paper is part of the *identification*, rather than the *modeling* phase of a RM.

Trust Taxonomies. Several taxonomies of trust have been designed in the past decade [4], [13-15]. As a categorization of system entities, components and connections, taxonomy is hardly a useful systemic approach if it only identifies the RM entities. Cohesive factor for all systems, which has not been tackled by any of the known approaches, is identification of connections between the RM components. The framework presented in this paper not only specifies that, but it also provides analysis in several dimensions across the factors influencing RM's design. To entitle this work a systemic approach, we turn to the principles of General Systems Taxonomy and determine the RM's position in the general systems space. Our taxonomy differs from the existing in the field in a few crucial aspects: 1) It follows a systemic approach of revealing the design issues in building RMs and relies on System Theory principles; 2) It relates the RM subsystems in a way that not only allows understanding of their interrelations, but also of their connection to the environment where the overall system evolves; 3) It sets a common ground for the vast, but scattered research on computational T&R; 4) Most importantly, it determines the 'system' concept applicability of the defined taxonomy and detects the factors required for its completeness. The following sections outline the main content of the framework.

3   Reputation Systems through the General Systems Taxonomy

One of the most prominent works in General Systems Taxonomy is that of Nehemiah Jordan [16]. According to him, a system's taxonomy has three organizing principles: 1) Rate of change, 2) Purpose, and 3) Connectivity. Each principle defines two antitheses, resulting in the three pairs of properties shown in Table 1.

Table 1. Organizing principles of Jordan's Systems Taxonomy (the categories to which we assign RMs are bolded and italicized)

Rate-of-change	Purpose	Connectivity
Structural (static)	Purposive (system-directed)	Mechanistic (non-densely connected)
Functional (dynamic)- D	*non-purposive (environment-directed) - E*	*Organismic (densely connected) - C*

Dynamicity (D). Static systems exhibit no change in a defined time-span. RMs should provide long-term incentives and support decision-making in a dynamic manner. To do that, they consider the quality of experiences of the system entities and the history of transactions among them. RMs are directly tackled by the requirement of good information convergence (for proper signaling), as well as timely response (for proper sanctioning), which makes them very dynamic with a high *rate of change*.

*Environmental-orientation (E).*The principle of purpose determines the direction of energy/information flow, inside or outside the system. The two possibilities are a system-directed or an environment-oriented flow. The former maintains stable conditions inside the system, whereas the latter modifies it to obtain a desired state or bypass certain disturbances. Although man-made systems are usually purposive, those with state and output depending on social factors tend not to be. RMs are human-centric, utility-driven and are expected to perform well in conditions of high risk and uncertainty. This classifies them as non-purposive, i.e., environment-directed.

Dense connectivity (C). The principle of *connectivity* states two possibilities: systems are a) *mechanistic*, i.e., not densely connected and the removal of parts or connections produces no change in the remaining components; or b) *organismic*, i.e., densely connected and the change of a single connection affects all the others. RMs depend heavily on the interactions among system entities. They are of inherently non-linear nature, implying that the outcome of each interaction has no predictable impact on the overall RM. This does not imply that a result obtained by some kind of superposition method cannot be produced with satisfying success-rate. It merely questions the relevance of the score obtained in such a way. Although many proposed models rely on the ability to determine general reputation score for an entity, there has been no evaluation in the literature of the success-rate in terms of impact. This is no surprise, as RMs are non-linear complex and densely connected.

The significance of considering General Systems Taxonomy is in the clarification and simplification of the often-misused concept of *a system*. Our work establishes RMs as real systems, and by using sufficient generality and simplicity, categorizes them as *dynamic (D), densely connected(C) and environment-oriented (E)*. In the next section we move to identification of the RM components, and determine their interrelations. Moreover, we identify which of the design factors recognized so far by the research community do not consider the complete D-C-E nature of RMs.

4   A Novel Taxonomical Framework for Reputation Mechanisms

The contribution of our proposal is part of the work on both trust taxonomies and RM design: 1) It categorizes common and important concepts in the research on RMs, establishing a common systemic vocabulary; 2) It represents a novel approach to multi-dimensional mapping and assessment of the completeness and consistency of a RM; 3) It introduces additional granularity in the current taxonomic map of RMs, considering the notion of reputation and its application to the RM components; 4) It employs the D-C-E nature of RMs to detect additional factors that influence RMs design, providing better completeness of the taxonomy.

As a skeleton, we take Stanford's taxonomy [13], whose categorization of components is given in Table 2. In addition to the subsystems and factors outlined in [13], the framework resulting from our work (presented in Fig. 1) will allow a direct mapping of the models across the factors-dimension and subsystems-dimension in a consistent manner. This enables an immediate establishment of the interdependence between: a) the various RM subsystems; b) the subsystems and the RM as a whole; c) the RM and the general system where the RM is deployed; d) the RM and the environment where the overall system resides.

Table 2. Breakdown of Reputation System Components (Marti *et al.*)

Reputation Systems		
Information Gathering	*Scoring and Ranking*	*Response*
Identity Scheme	Good vs. Bad Behavior	Incentives
Information Sources	Quantity vs. Quality	Punishments
Information Aggregation	Time-dependence	
Stranger-Policy	Selection Threshold	
	Peer Selection	

4.1   Redefining the Factors of Impact

To specify the requirements and implications of designing an efficient RM, [13] considered the following factors of impact: a) The limitations and opportunities imposed by the *system architecture* where the RM is deployed; b) The expected *user behavior*; c) The goals of *adversaries*. As stated in Section 3, RMs are of a *D-C-E* nature. Here, we claim that the *user-architecture-adversaries* trinity (the details of which can be found in [13]) is insufficient for capturing the complete set of factors that influence RM design, as trust is context dependent and established in a highly dynamic environment. Table 3 contains an assessment of the factors of impact on a D-C-E scale. It demonstrates which of them do not consider one or more system properties (D, C or E). The analysis show that the C-nature of RMs is not considered at all. Moreover, the dynamicity of the system environment is a crucial element that must be accounted for in the design of human-centric systems, as they operate in a dynamic way within a dynamic environment. Finally, the interactions and relations between entities and the environment are not captured by any of the known trust taxonomies, and consequently, by none of the computational trust models.

Table 3. Evaluating the factors of impact on a D-C-E scale (Y ="Yes" – *does consider*, N = "No" – *does not consider*)

Factor / Property	User behavior	System Architecture	Goals of adversaries
Dynamic (D)	Y: through churn	*N:needed to capture environment evolution*	Y: by adversarial strategies
Densely connected (C)	*N: very small number of users can have a large impact on the system*	*N: the RM has a huge impact as subsystem of the overall system*	*N: necessary to consider for the system resilience*
Environment-oriented (E)	*N: environment influence on entity behavior (so far considered only as system-oriented)*	Y: by considering the various properties of a centralized, distributed, hybrid architecture	Y: few attacks (Sybil attack, collusion) resemble this nature of the RM

The *system architecture* was extensively elaborated as an influencing factor in [13]. Our work acknowledges it as such in completeness, and adds five new factors. The detected lack of considering the dynamicity and environment-orientation by the *system architecture* will be covered by the five new factors. As a first distinctive element from Stanford's taxonomy, we introduce the more general concept of *reputation entity* and recognize *users* as only one type of these entities. *Entity* refers to a party who participates in the process of reputation evaluation, either as an evaluator or as an evaluated side. We distinguish two types of reputation entities, *active* and *passive*. The former is enrolled actively in the reputation process: aggregating and disseminating information, acting upon certain triggers, and evaluating each other's and the trustworthiness of the passive entities. Examples are agents, users, peers, etc. In contrast, passive entities are those whose trustworthiness is evaluated by the active entities; they do not provide any feedback, and do not participate in the aggregation of reputation scores. Examples are items, comments, video/audio content, etc.

4.2 Active Entity Behavior (AEB): Considers the D and E Nature of RMs

Some technical aspects of RMs attributed to AEB are mainly challenges in coping with the network dynamics. This implies considering the *availability* of entities in the network, as they are online for unknown periods of time and do not smoothly join and leave the system. Furthermore, forbidden communication among unreachable entities makes *connectivity* an additional design consideration. The importance of anticipating AEB in a human-centric system goes beyond mere understanding of the technical implications on human-computer interaction. A system burdening its users with unreasonable conditions for enrollment and continuous participation, or with inflexible access to its resources, will encumber its users and edge them out. RMs must exhibit a high adaptive capability to address these issues. An important part of the solution is both the hard-technical and the soft-usability aspects. The former may include availability and connectivity checking to form an overlay of reliable entities, while the latter will require bootstrapping techniques for the new-coming entities, and incentive policies for those who have already established some history of experiences.

4.3   Resilience and Evolutionism: Considers the D, C and E Nature of RMs

The circular, interlocking and time-relationships among RM components are also important in determining entities' behavior. There are often properties of the overall solution that might not be found among the properties of its subcomponents, making the behavior of the whole system impossible to explain in terms of the behavior of its parts. In fact, this is a common property of complex systems that depend on social dynamics. Most of the known approaches use the MAS (Multi-Agent Systems) model, which is based on the assumption of the existence of multiple interacting agents as active entities. From the D-C-E nature of RMs, it follows that the MAS model is somehow restricted, as issues like insufficient adaptive capacity (in terms of communication, cooperation, context specialization, spatial/temporal organization), and complexity are not considered. Yet, the system as a whole is expected to have a higher resilience, even when some of its reputation components are exposed to malicious exploitation, or system entities exhibit sudden change in behavior. Systems that satisfy these requirements are classified as CAS (Complex Adaptive Systems), where any element in the system can be affected and may affect several other systems. The idea to use CAS-approach in the design of RMs has not been investigated in any depth so far. It is an evolutionary approach to tackling resilience and dynamics issues in complex, socio-technical environments.

4.4   Context: Considers the D and E Nature of RMs

Reputation information is significant only if put into a relevant *context. Context is the set* of circumstances or facts that surround a particular event or situation.[1] Despite the various types of trust defined in the literature, very few definitions consider its context-dependency. The most prominent approaches in this direction incorporate semantics into reputation information, mainly in the form of ontology [17]. However, most of the current proposals employ context for content-filtering purpose and none of them considers its impact of on the separate RM components. By considering context in the reputation evaluation, not only can the level of the entities' expertise be determined, but also the domain of its relevance. One way to address this issue is by implementing a method for assessing context similarity according to some given criterion. This would enable having a weighting scheme for assigning different levels of importance to the reputation information according to the similarity of contexts in which the entities reside. Such result could be used both as a measure of the impact in a reputation assessment, and as an interoperability enabler between different systems.

---

[1] http://dictionary.reference.com

4.5 Time: Considers the D and C Nature of RMs

Some relations between reputation and *time* have been studied extensively; however, many important time-properties have not received the expected attention. Each RM subsystem is influenced by the choice for: the permanency of IDs, the recentness of information, the time-stamp of feedback actions, convergence of the reputation value, synchronization of time- driven actions, or reputation updates. A proper time-policy would allow incorporating the traditional analogs for *forgiveness* and *forgetting* into

Subsystem	Factor	Context	Time	Privacy	RE	AEB
Information gathering	ID Scheme	Non-linkable; Minimal; Verifiable	Traceability; Accountability	Anonymity; Pseudonyms; Real identity	Identity independent of users and machines	Whitewashing; Sybil attack: Spoofing; Forging
	Information Sources	Role-based (raters; recommenders; Privilege-based (moderators, reviewers)	Persistency of behavior information	Gathering sensitive information	Self-organizing; Adaptable	Transitivity rate; Spread of trust-chain (# of hops); Small-world concept; Imitating established norms
	Information aggregation	Transitivity	Optimized dissemination process; Information convergence	Storage of certain information	Non-linear interactions; Collective intelligence	False positive/negative; Collusion vs. Exploitation
	Integrity check	Witnesses; Credibility	Sudden change in behavior	Data, Entity, System, Institutional Integrity	Considering that small causes can have large results	Reputation-weighted witnessing;
Scoring and ranking	Inputs	QoS, Quantity	Time-stamp of certain action	Tacit system knowledge	Interaction pattern: Dynamic type of strategy; Considers both physical and conceptual space	History of transactions; Behavioral trends;
	Computation engine	Deterministic; Probabilistic; Fuzzy; Flow; Semantic; Axiomatic	Time-driven inputs and events	Privacy as a metric	Possibility for recurrence	Learning requirements; Optimization criteria; Depends on system vulnerabilities
	Outputs	Single-value; Trust interval	Time-driven response and actions; Information propagation	Availability of information according to privileges	Success criteria; Performance measure	Single-value; Graphical representation; Vector of values;
Response	Threshold	Requirement for strangers; Inducing transaction; Entity selection	Sliding time-window; Time-to-Live (TTL) actions	Similarity of preference	Dynamic; adaptive; Multiple flexible thresholds	Rare service by one or few malicious entities
Response (Incentives)	Reward	Money; Service; Forgiveness	Forgetting factor; Preventing multiple	Personalized services depending on the level of privacy	Cooperation-driven; Supports a great diversity of entity types; Repairing trust; utility/risk-dependant	Monetary rewards vs. Social altruism; Context and entity-dependant
Response (Incentives)	Punish	Regret; Banning	Recentness of contribution	Regulation-by-law	Evolution selection principles	Malicious vs. exploited entity
Stranger policy	Stranger policy	Pessimistic; Optimistic; Adaptive	Adaptive	Optimistic	Essentially adaptive	Bootstrapping; Dynamics;

Fig. 1. Taxonomy framework of system entities, design factors, and their interrelations

the result. In addition to the trustworthiness with respect to some expertise, insights into entities' experience with regard to the claimed quality can also be obtained. Clearly, the time-issues in RMs depend on the subsystem observed. Some ways to address the issues include: introducing a sliding window when the reputation gains certain importance; time-discounting of the various (meta) results obtained at certain instants or a combined weighing with an entities' reputation in a given context.

4.6 Privacy: Considers the D, C and E Nature of RMs

The interest in information is accompanied by *privacy* requirements. Many RM design choices face privacy challenges; RMs are expected to keep balance between the heterogeneity of users and their interest in information, enable inferring fragile trust information from less sensitive sources and restrict certain functions to be exploitable by everyone. As their main purpose is the embodiment of trust on the Internet, it would be useful to investigate where the offline forms of regulation-by-law fit in the online world and whether they can be used to help the trust establishment. Online, people acknowledge lower competences, tolerate worse experiences, exhibit lower privacy requirements, accept greater risks and act under higher uncertainty. The fast convergence of the reputation effects degrades reputation as soon as the information propagates the network. By limiting this to the relevant context, RMs will be more adaptable and flexible to user demands. The novel systemic framework is summarized in Fig. 1. It is multidimensional as it is based on the factors identified to capture the RM's D-C-E nature and defines their relation to the RM subsystems.

5 The BarterCast Use-Case through the Taxonomy Framework

BarterCast (BC) [18] is a distributed RM deployed in the BitTorrent-client Tribler [19]. It is led by the premise that social phenomena affect positively system usability and performance. We briefly introduce BC, and then map it across the framework dimensions. For more extensive description of BC, we refer the reader to [18-20].

For peers (client software), BC uses permanent IDs (*PermIDs*) based on a public key scheme, validated by a challenge-response mechanism to prevent spoofing. Users are referred to by *pseudonyms*. The social network creation is facilitated by the ability to import contacts from other networks (MSN, Gmail). For privacy-preserving, there is an *erase from profile* option. Context information is stored in *MegaCaches* to support trust-based social groups. For content discovery, a *semantic overlay* of *taste buddies* (peers with similar taste) is maintained and discovered by a *gossiping protocol* [20]. Exchanging data is done by 1) *exploitation*, with the buddies, or 2) *exploration*, with a random new peer. Only *direct experience* (for aggregated amount of service) is exchanged during the gossip. Peers maintain *private* (based on an entity's interactions with a single entity) and *shared history* (about interactions with all entities) and *subjectively* calculate the reputation. BC considers paths of two hops, due to the small-world effect in P2P file-sharing networks [21]. To obtain initial lists of neighbors, new peers use either pre-known super-peers or an *overlay swarm* to bootstrap into the network. The network is represented as a graph, with the peers as nodes and directed edges denoting aggregated amount of service. The scoring algorithm takes as inputs the *quantity* (MBs upload) and the *quality* (contribution) of service, finds the highest reputation that a *source node* can assign to a *target node,* and gives a value in [-1,1]. BC has few types of incentives. A *cooperative download* improves the download performance of group members. Despite tit-for-tat, there are *rank* and *ban policy*, allowing initial cooperation in the order of peers' reputation, if it is above a negative threshold (to differ strangers from disreputable peers). Costly procedures for using system resources additionally discourage malice.

Fig. 2 maps BC to the framework, suggesting a space for substantial improvement. BC performs no integrity check of reputation entities and subsystems across any of the factors. This can be achieved by introducing witnessing scheme, similar to that in [22]. Coping with dynamics is tackled on network level (availability and connectivity check), not considering many time-properties. Although information is validated upon the 10 most recent transactions, this choice is fixed rather than based on system or interaction dynamics. One way to give time-meaning of information is by time-discounting that will weigh information according to its recentness. Furthermore, BC lacks a penalizing policy. In an open, anonymous and dynamic environment, providing mechanisms that hold community members responsible for their actions is of crucial importance. Despite accounting for *taste similarity*, *taste* is much more

Subsystem \ Factor	Context	Time	Privacy	RE	AEB
Information gathering					
ID Scheme	Non-linkable; Verifiable	permanent ID (PermID)	pseudonyms	N (machine-dependent ID)	challenge-response; combats free-riding; Sybil-dependent ID
Info. Sources	taste-buddies; subj. reputations	10 most recent interactions	N	semantic overlay	considers 2 hops; employs small-world concept
Info. Aggregation	MegaCaches for context-info; private and shared history	N	gossiping only about direct experience	exploitation & exploration	exploitation & false feedback restricted by the information capacity of edges; collusion possible
Integrity check	N	N	N	N	N
Scoring and ranking					
Inputs	Quantity (Upload in MB); Only positive contribution;	N	Privacy as a metric	cooperative downloading protocol	History of transactions
Comp. engine; algorithm based on *arctan* function	Maximum-flow algorithm based on *arctan* function	N	N	N	No learning; Depends on system vulnerability
Outputs	Single value in the interval [-1,1]	N	N	optimistic unchoking	GUI for browsing peers
Response					
Threshold	negative reputation threshold	Sliding window over 10 transactions	Preference similarity	Cooperation driven	Reputation-based peer selection
Incentives — Reward	Improved service; Rank policy; tit-for-tat	N	*Erase from profile option*	N	relies on social altruism of taste-buddies; does not take risk into account
Incentives — Punish	N	N	N	N	N
Stranger policy	N	N	N	N	bootstrapping; connectivity & availability check

Fig. 2. Mapping BarterCast onto the multidimensional framework

subtle than preference. Results from Behavioral Economy show that users are often unaware of their taste, even for experiences from previously felt outcomes [23]. Importing contacts from other social networks requires well-defined privacy policies, system interoperability and context-switching awareness. None of those is elaborated enough to justify such design choice. BC is led by the fact that, although non-resistant to cheating, real-world communities work well with millions of users. However, this does not speak about the impact these entities can have on the overall system welfare. A small percentage of peers in a file-sharing community contribute the largest amount of resources. Freeriding or collusion can have an impact that largely outweighs the benefit of RM design and maintenance. Finally, the small-world idea is not an organizational aspect of BC nodes, and the system performance and accuracy might benefit largely from a full gossip, instead of two-hop message exchange.

6   Concluding Remarks and the Way Forward

Handling numerous online experiences in a short time-span requires highly scalable solutions for trust establishment. In such a dynamic environment, having no RM to capture interaction trends is equal to being equipped for a world that no longer exists. The presented taxonomy is a systemic approach to designing dynamic, densely connected and environment-oriented RMs. It improves the existing work on trust taxonomies, but is flexible for improvement. As major factors that influence RM design we included *context, time, privacy, active entity behavior, resilience and evolutionism*, in addition to *system architecture*. The insights were incorporated into a multidimensional framework, together with the RM subsystems, to establish their connections. The result is a more granular categorization of design choices/decisions. Finally, we mapped BC as a representative distributed socially inspired RM onto our framework, revealing some weaknesses and proposing improvements of its design.

Our future work will be a system-modeling approach to resolving the design issues for a novel RM. According to the outlined principles, the model will consider the system dynamicity and evolutionism. It will employ System theory methods, allowing the use of sophisticated tools for evaluation and verification. Moreover, it is a step towards the standardization of RMs design. A multidisciplinary approach is thus essential for preserving practicality, but adding innovation as well.

References

1. Fowler, J.H., Christakis, N.A.: Cooperative behavior cascades in human social networks. Proceedings of the National Academy of Sciences 107(12), 5334–5338 (2010)
2. Castelfranchi, C., Falcone, R.: Trust is much more than subjective probability: Mental components and sources of trust. In: 32nd Hawaii International Conference on System Sciences - Mini-Track on Software Agents, Maui, vol. 6 (2000)
3. Gambetta, D.: Can We Trust Trust? In: Trust: Making and Breaking Cooperative Relations, pp. 213–237 (1988)
4. Josang, A., Ismail, R., Boyd, C.: A survey of trust and reputation systems for online service provision. Decision Support Systems 43(2), 618–644 (2007)

5. Chin, S.H.: On application of game theory for understanding trust in networks. In: International Symposium on Collaborative Technologies and Systems, Baltimore, MD, USA, pp. 106–110 (2009)
6. Fudenberg, D., Tirole, J.: Game Theory. The MIT Press, Cambridge (1991)
7. Cohen, B.: Incentives Build Robustness in BitTorrent (2003)
8. Ba, S.: Establishing online trust through a community responsibility system. Decision Support Systems 31(3), 323–336 (2001)
9. Fehr, E., Gächter, S.: Fairness and Retaliation: The Economics of Reciprocity (2000)
10. Marsh, S.P.: Formalising trust as a computational concept (1994)
11. Akerlof, G.A.: The Market for 'Lemons': Quality Uncertainty and the Market Mechanism. The Quarterly Journal of Economics 84(3), 488–500 (1970)
12. Dellarocas, C.: The Digitization of Word of Mouth: Promise and Challenges of Online Feedback Mechanisms. Management Science 49(10), 1407–1424 (2003)
13. Marti, S., Garciamolina, H.: Taxonomy of trust: Categorizing P2P reputation systems. Computer Networks 50(4), 472–484 (2006)
14. Huynh, T.D.: Trust and Reputation in Open Multi-Agent Systems (2006)
15. Alani, H., Kalfoglou, Y., Shadbolt, N.: Trust strategies for the semantic web. In: McIlraith, S.A., Plexousakis, D., van Harmelen, F. (eds.) ISWC 2004. LNCS, vol. 3298, pp. 78–85. Springer, Heidelberg (2004)
16. Jordan, N.: Themes in Speculative Psychology. Routledge, New York (2003)
17. Golbeck, J., Parsia, B., Hendler, J.: Trust Networks on the Semantic Web. In: Proceedings of Cooperative Intelligent Agents, pp. 238–249 (2003)
18. Meulpolder, M., Pouwelse, J.A., Epema, D.H.J., Sips, H.J.: BarterCast: A Practical Approach to Prevent Lazy Freeriding in P2P Networks
19. Pouwelse, J.A., et al.: TRIBLER: a social-based peer-to-peer system. Concurrency and Computation: Practice and Experience 20(2), 127–138 (2008)
20. Pouwelse, J.A., et al.: Buddycast: An Operational Peer-To-Peer Epidemic Protocol Stack
21. Newman, M.E.J.: Models of the Small World - A Review
22. Kamvar, S.D., Schlosser, M.T., Garcia-Molina, H.: The Eigentrust algorithm for reputation management in P2P networks. In: Proceedings of the Twelfth International Conference on World Wide Web - WWW 2003, Budapest, Hungary, p. 640 (2003)
23. Ariely, D., Loewenstein, G., Prelec, D.: Tom Sawyer and the construction of value. Journal of Economic Behavior & Organization 60(1), 1–10 (2006)

Orchestrating Security and System Engineering for Evolving Systems

(Invited Paper)

Fabio Massacci[1], Fabrice Bouquet[2], Elizabeta Fourneret[2], Jan Jurjens[3],
Mass S. Lund[4], Sébastien Madelénat[5], JanTobias Muehlberg[6], Federica Paci[1],
Stéphane Paul[5], Frank Piessens[6], Bjornar Solhaug[4], and Sven Wenzel[3]

[1] Univ. of Trento, IT, [2] Lab. d'Inform. de Franche-Comté, FR, [3] TU. Dortmund, DE,
[4] SINTEF ICT, NO, [5] Thales Research & Tech., FR, [6] Katholieke Univ. Leuven, BE
{name.surname}@{disi.unitn.it,lifc.univ-fcomte.fr,
cs.tu-dortmund.de,sintef.no,thalesgroup.com,cs.kuleuven.be}

Abstract. How to design a security engineering process that can cope with the dynamic evolution of Future Internet scenarios and the rigidity of existing system engineering processes? The SecureChange approach is to orchestrate (as opposed to integrate) security and system engineering concerns by two types of relations between engineering processes: (i) vertical relations between successive security-related processes; and (ii) horizontal relations between mainstream system engineering processes and concurrent security-related processes. This approach can be extended to cover the complete system/ software lifecycle, from early security requirement elicitation to runtime configuration and monitoring, via high-level architecting, detailed design, development, integration and design-time testing. In this paper we illustrate the high-level scientific principles of the approach.

Keywords: We would like to encourage you to list your keywords in this section.

1 Introduction

It is taken for granted that Future Internet scenarios, being them on content, services or things will be characterized by a quick pace of evolution: it should be possible to quickly design new services, or swiftly quickly integrate new devices providing new and interesting contents to the end users. This quick pace of evolution should be supported at all times by maintaining security and trust properties.

This assumption is somehow at odds with strong opposing forces that are currently shaping the engineering process in industry. In order to cope with complexity and quality control the system, software, and service engineering process in industry has been (is, and will likely be) subject to strong push towards rigidity, especially when strong security requirements are at stake. The need to show compliance with standards e.g. ISO 15288 [18] and ISO 12207 [17], respectively for system and software

W. Abramowicz et al. (Eds.): ServiceWave 2011, LNCS 6994, pp. 134–143, 2011.

engineering makes often the engineering process rigid. On one hand stakeholders demand flexibility to accommodate changes; on the other hand they demand compliance to standards in process and product. Process rigidity is further increased when security aspects standards are further taken into account. The use of ISO 2700x, EBIOS, CRAMM, BSIMM or SDLC might be mandated by customers or regulations and the design process must also be compliant with those standards.

For complex systems the engineering process is often supported by artifacts (UML models of the system to be, DOORS format for requirements, UML risk profiles in CORAS etc), and companies tend to adapt and customize these artifacts to fit their needs and application domains (e.g. by using Eclipse GMF), in order to decompose and compartmentalize the work. Some parts of the processes might also be outsourced so that a shared artifact may no longer exist.

In this scenario, integrating security and trust concerns which address simultaneously the calls for fast changes and hard compliance is difficult. While it is widely recognized that security considerations must be considered from the start, most research proposals have focused on new fully integrated security-system engineering processes (eg [34,13,14]). This is the "default solution" in many European Projects: yet another integrated process for security (service, content, things) engineering.

Yet, all integrated processes have significant difficulties in adoption. The main reason behind these difficulties is that security-related activities (e.g. assessment, engineering and assurance [5,30]) must comply with the constraints and pace of the legacy mainstream engineering processes, methods and tools (e.g. [18,17]). The rigidity factors that we have mentioned above makes each step of engineering process highly customized and de facto unchangeable, as the switching cost would be too high. So there is no chance to adopt an entirely new security engineering process that can cope with the dynamicity and evolution challenges of the Future Internet.

So what happens when a security requirement or a threat model changes? Changes must percolate through each step, with its own specific security artifacts and security processes and many errors might be introduced in this endeavor.
Is there another way?

1.1   The Contribution of This Paper

The gist of the SecureChange project is to propose a security engineering process that can be deployed in practice without requiring a practically impossible integration of all its parts. Our idea is to deal with evolution and to accommodate proprietary steps by using *orchestration* instead of integration [10]. In order to orchestrate the various steps in the process we consider two types of relations: (i) vertical relations between successive security-related processes; and (ii) horizontal relations between mainstream system engineering processes and concurrent security-related processes.

The orchestrated process is based on the *separation of concern principle*. An important advantage of separation of concern is that in-depth expertise in the respective domains is not a prerequisite. The orchestrated process allows the separate domains to leverage on each other without the need of full integration. However consistency of concerns must still ensured. For example security risk managers, requirement managers, and system designers share a minimal set of concepts which is the interface between their own processes: each process is conducted separately and only when a change affects a concept of the interface, the change is propagated to the other domain following the ideas behind conceptual mappings [4] and relations [15].

In the next section we present the overall Security Engineering process and then discuss the specification (Sec.3) and design (Sec.5) steps of the lifecycle with their interplay with risk assessment (Sec.4). Then we focus on validation (Sec.6) and verification (Sec.7) steps and conclude the paper (Sec.8).

2   The Security and System Engineering Orchestrated Process

A system lifecycle typically has eight phases as illustrated in Figure 1: (i) architecting, (ii) specification, (iii) design, (iv) realisation or acquisition, (v) integration and verification, (vi) validation and deployment, (vii) operation and maintenance, and (viii) disposal. During the evolution process, a system may occupy several of these phases at the same time: earlier specs might be going already through security testing while new requirements might still be at the architectural phase. Security risk management activities can be conducted regardless of the system lifecycle phase although the pursued goals may differ.

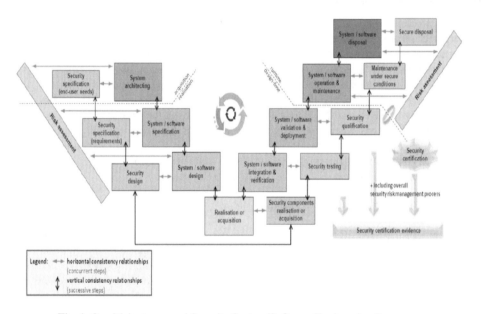

Fig. 1. One Mainstream and Security System/Software Engineering Processes

The first phase is classically performed by the customer, using architectural frameworks (AF) such the NATO AF. It produces end-user requirements as documented in a call-for-tender. During this phase, the main goal of the security activities is to elicit security needs, possibly consolidated by a threat assessment.

The following phases, except operation, are mainly performed by the system provider.

During the specification phase, the main goal of the security activities is to define the system requirements, and thus gain early assurance that the proposed architectural solution is sound with respect to security concerns. This step encompasses a high-level risk assessment [24] backing-up the specification of security requirements.

During this phase it is important to be able to quickly update models and bring them in synch [29,1]. The end customer might be involved in the loop and must be able to do some form of what-if scenarios [31]. For example it must be possible to identify possible evolutions and discuss possible tactical solutions in the choice of the components (e.g. the residual risk that a particular component might become useless depending on the outcome of a standardization body).

In contrast, during the design phase, the system degrees of freedom slowly freeze. As time goes by, any major change in design has increasingly significant costs, may require going back to the customer and could lead to unacceptable delays. Changes must be managed differently. The main goal is to make sure that the security properties are preserved across evolution. We accept the change because we know that security properties won't change. Technically this is an obvious observation. We could just re-verify the design after the change and see if the properties still hold. The challenge is to just specify the "delta" and use patterns or stereotype to capture only the "delta" of the change and specify the conditions on the delta that preserve security properties [22]. Proven security design patterns may be used. Security risk assessment is performed in parallel, re-defining security objectives until residual risks are acceptable. Some early validation techniques [23] may be applied in order to gain early assurance that the system design is sound.

The main goal of the security activities during the realisation or acquisition phase is to implement or acquire the countermeasures. In some cases, when the proposed security controls are elementary or available off-the-shelf, this activity may be carried out as part of the mainstream engineering process. When SOA technology is the targeted platform, security-as-a-service might be the right solution [16].

During the integration & verification phase, the main goal of the security-related activities is to integrate and test the countermeasures. As for realisation or acquisition, the integration of the security countermeasures may be carried out as part of the mainstream engineering process; however testing represents a security-specific task, aiming at proving that the information system protects data and maintains functionality as intended.

During the validation/quality check phase, the main goal of the security-related activities is the security qualification of the system, which will potentially lead to certification. The qualification of a product gives evidence of the robustness of the security services of the product. It is based on: (i) the verification of the conformity of the product with the security characteristics specified in the target, on the basis of an evaluation realized by a laboratory approved by a certification authority, e.g. ANSSI in France; (ii) the approval, by the certification authority, of the relevance of the security target with respect to the planned use and the requested level of qualification. This qualification allows: a) to separate the purely technical assessment of the system from a wider assessment of its ability to protect sensitive information in given conditions; b) to recognize that the same system can allow for the protection of information of different levels, and thus can obtain various levels of approval, according to the conditions of use.

During the operation & maintenance phase, the main goal of security risk management is to monitor the effectiveness of the countermeasures to determine the extent to which the controls are implemented correctly, operating as intended, and producing the desired outcome with respect to meeting the security requirements for the system or enterprise. In case security is found to be flawed, the previous activities may be performed anew to ensure an acceptable level of risk.

3 Secure Specification and Design

This section focuses on the early steps of the system development lifecycle, i.e. security requirement specification, security design and security risk assessment, which are carried out concurrently to system specification and design. We explain here the intuition behind the orchestration aspects (see [10] for details).

The security analysis during the requirement phase is based on an iterative security methodology for evolving requirements (SeCMER for short, see [6] for details). It supports: (i) requirements elicitation, (ii) automatic detection of requirement changes that cause the violation of security properties and (iii) argumentation analysis to check that security properties are preserved and to identify new security properties that should be taken into account.

These steps are present in almost all "traditional" integrated security engineering methodologies (see e.g. [13,14,8]). The distinguishing feature here is that we do not envisage the existence of a single integrated model. Every iteration of the SeCMER process starts with the requirements elicitation phase, which processes a change request as a set of incremental changes on a requirement model. Different aspects of security requirements can be modelled with different state-of-the-art requirement languages such as SI* [27] or Problem Frames (PFs) [31] or use traditional text-based description such as DOORS [7]. An underlying conceptual models maps the notions SI* to the other models such as PFs or other target security domain specific languages [26]. In this way an analyst can use its favourite (or mandatory) model to capture some requirements and use another model for validation purposes. For example, by using the propositions in the requirements model, argumentation analysis [33] determines whether the design has exploitable vulnerabilities that might expose valuable assets to malicious attacks.

For this approach to work we need an automatic orchestration process which uses event-condition-action rules called evolution rules [2,1]. Whenever a change to the requirement model matches some evolution rule(s), the change is automatically detected, and the transformation engine applies specified actions on the requirement model and checks whether the existing security goals are still satisfied after the change. If this is not the case, the change is passed onto the argumentation process, in order to consider whether the security goal can be restored. When even that is not possible, the security goal will be passed back to the elicitation process where the goal will have to be renegotiated and/or reformulated. The same technology can then be used across all vertical and horizontal relations.

4   The Mutual Evolution of Risk and Requirement Analysis

The risk assessment process must be as well adapted as well: a static risk methodology cannot cope with system evolution and the very dynamic process for managing security requirements that we have just discussed. In this section we exemplify the process by using the CORAS approach [24] which is a model-driven approach to risk assessment that is closely based on the ISO 31000 [19] standard. An alternative using Thales's risk assessment modelling language is described in [10].

The CORAS method consists of a risk assessment method, a language for risk modelling, as well as a tool to support the activities of the method. For changing and evolving systems the challenge is that previous security risk assessment results may become invalid and obsolete after the occurrence of a change. SecureChange addresses this challenge by generalising the CORAS approach [24] to the setting of evolving systems [25]. The generalised approach incorporates techniques for tracing changes from the target system to the risk model. For the secure specification and design, this is depicted in Figure 1 by the horizontal relations from risk assessment to the system specification and design, respectively. A change that is proposed for the latter can be traced to affected parts of the risk model that in turn are reassessed and updated. The risk assessment will document how the security risks evolve, and moreover identify options for risk treatment that can be taken into account during specification and design so as to keep the security risks acceptable under change. Moreover, risks that change should explicitly be analysed and documented as such.

A key principle is that only the parts of the risk picture that are affected by system changes should be analysed anew. The same principles of orchestration and separation of concerns are applied in this setting. The key concepts in the requirements models (loosely speaking the requirements APIs) are mapped into the concepts of the risk assessment model (the risk's APIs). Then the evolution rules orchestrate the process by keeping the models in synch. For example, a change request during the specification phase may lead to changes in the requirement model, such as the identification of new assets. As part of the interface between the requirement and risk model, this model artefact can be passed to the security risk assessment. By separation of concern, the risk assessment proceeds with this change separately until eventually the interface is invoked again and treatments are passed back and included in the requirement model as security goals.

5   Managing Evolution during the Design Step

As we have already mentioned the analysis of changes during the design process must change focus and try to identify as much as possible the changes that preserve the security properties established during the earlier phases.

In the SecureChange project we have used the UMLsec profile [23] to perform the security design and its early validation. The UMLsec profile is based on the mainstream software engineering modelling language UML and defines stereotypes which are used together with tags to formulate the security requirements and assumptions of a system at design time. These corresponds to the links in the horizontal relations in Figure 1 between the mainstream system engineering process and the security engineering process.

The profile has been extended to the UMLseCh profile for specifying one or more evolutions on a model [22]. The stereotypes «add», «del», and «substitute» can be used to precisely define which model elements are to be added, deleted, and substituted in a model, and together with constraints in first-order predicate logic that allow to coordinate and define more than one evolution path. Constraints give criteria that determine whether the requirements are met by the system design by referring to a precise semantics of the used fragment of UML.

Based on the UMLseCh stereotypes used in the diagrams we can compute all possible "delta"s of a model and check whether an evolution of the design will preserve the security properties of the system. Besides the ability to analyse the security properties of all possible evolutions, we have an efficiency gain, since the analysis of the delta performs better than the re-evaluation of the complete design models.

Once the security properties have been confirmed to hold we can use the model to propagate the security-preserving changes to the later phases, thus moving the process along the vertical relations in Figure 1. During the realization phase one can use the code generation tools generally available for UML. In the testing phase we can use model-based testing tools such as the one presented later in this paper. A further possibility, once we have the horizontal traceability link between security properties and system properties is to generate security monitors from the UMLsec specification to monitor the secure execution of the system.

6 Security Testing of Evolving Systems

With the overall goal to provide means of security verification and validation for evolving systems, Secure Change has a strong focus on verification techniques and test generation that can be applied to implementation artefacts during the development and deployment phases of the software life-cycle.

Following the vertical relations in Figure 1 on the design models one can automatically generate the test models [11] where the traceability to the security requirements (the horizontal relations) is preserved.

We can classify tests [12] with respect to requirements evolution: only the first time ever all tests are *new*; as the system evolves and requirements and design models are orchestrated together we can progressively divide tests in eight different groups: *new*, *un-impacted* (by evolution), *re-executed* (i.e. impacted by evolution but the test values are not changed), *outdated* (i.e. deleted by evolution), *failed* (i.e. animation of test failed, e.g. due to a modification of the system behaviour), *updated* (i.e. same as previous test, but oracle values changed), *adapted* (i.e. new version of test to cover a previous requirement) and *removed* (by the user).

These eight status of the test are used to structure the test repository into four sets of test suites: *evolution* (contains new, adapted and updated tests exercising the novelties of the system), *regression* (contains un-impacted and re-executed tests exercising the unmodified parts of the system), *stagnation* (contains outdated and failed tests, which are invalid w.r.t. the current version of the system), *deletion* (contains removed tests).

The advantage of our approach is to keep track of test cases through evolution. This allows a better stability and transparency of the test suite which is an important industrial criterion and is a key factor to help the validation team to prioritise test execution. From the test models we can now use an efficient test generation process that takes into account changes in requirements and previous test status.

7 Security Verification of Evolving Systems

In many security critical applications it is also important to achieve stronger guarantees than those achievable with testing. For example embedded Java applet codes for smart card technology supporting identity, banking or health services must be certified with respect to Common Criteria security certification on assurance levels EAL4+ and EAL7. This means formally proving that the embedded software on the smart card device ensures a set of properties related to confidentiality, integrity, availability and authenticity of its assets.

These formal verification steps must be deployed during the realisation and verification phases of the system engineering process illustrated in Figure 1 and therefore must be able to implement automatic rely guarantee reasoning for programs written in Java and C (as opposed to formal assurance about model specifications used in Section 5). For example, in SecureChange we used the VeriFast prover [21] to verify the absence of memory safety errors, data races, and to prove functional correctness. Applying VeriFast requires the source code of the program under verification to be annotated with method contracts in terms of separation logic [35]. The key strengths of VeriFast are its support for specifying and verifying deep data structure properties, reasoning about concurrent programs and its predictably short verification times, thereby providing immediate feedback to developers and testers.

In order to support evolution a key aspect of verification technologies is to explore possibilities to reuse verification artefacts, such as code annotations, to leverage re-certification of the card when change occurs. In the scenario considered in the project two non-trivial Java Card applets have been annotated and verified with respect to the absence of transaction errors, out-of-bounds operations, invalid casts and null-pointer de-references [29]. Furthermore, the full functional correctness has been proven for one applet. Using VeriFast, we were able to identify a total of thirteen bugs in one of the applets, with a relatively low annotation overhead of about one line of annotations per three lines of code. Ongoing work on VeriFast focuses on further reducing the annotation overhead [29,35] and providing support for highly concurrent usage of data structures [20].

Run-time verification techniques can then be used at load-time to complement the assurance guarantees obtained by development time verification techniques. For example one can use the Security-by-Contract approach to check that the updates of applets on the platforms maintain it security properties [8].

8 Conclusions

In this paper, we have proposed an overview of model-based security engineering activities performed in symbiosis with mainstream system engineering activities. The baseline approach ensures the consistency of the different models, and allows for change management throughout the complete system lifecycle. The key idea of the project is to automatically orchestrate the changes by providing suitable mapping and traceability link across different artefacts and processes. These features should make industrial adoption easier.

The project's approach has been validated on a large IT system, namely an Air Traffic Management (ATM) in the setting of the introduction of the Arrival Manager (AMAN) for traffic management while the later phases have been validated by considering the evolution of the smart-card systems based on GlobalPlatform. The application to a Service Oriented Architecture has also being validated in the scenario of the security of a multimedia home gateway and this is reported elsewhere [15, 3].

Acknowledgments. This work has been partly funded by the EU FP7 FET IP Secure Change project. We would like to thank other members of the SecureChange consortium and notably G. Bergmann, R. Breu, F. Innerhofer-Oberperfler, A. Tedeschi, and T. T. Thun for many useful suggestions.

References

1. Bergmann, G., et al.: Change-Driven Model Transformations. Change (in) the Rule to Rule the Change. In: Software and System Modeling (to appear, 2011)
2. Bergmann, G., Horváth, Á., Ráth, I., Varró, D., Balogh, A., Balogh, Z., Ökrös, A.: Incremental evaluation of model queries over EMF models. In: Petriu, D.C., Rouquette, N., Haugen, Ø. (eds.) MODELS 2010. LNCS, vol. 6394, pp. 76–90. Springer, Heidelberg (2010)
3. Breu, M., Breu, R., Löw, S.: Living on the MoVE: Towards an Architecture for a Living Models Infrastructure. International Journal on Advances in Software, 290–295 (2010)
4. Chechik, M., et al.: Relationship-based change propagation: A case study. In: Proc. of the ICSE Workshop on Modeling in Software Engineering (MISE 2009), pp. 7–12. IEEE, Los Alamitos (2009)
5. De Win, B., et al.: On the secure software development process: CLASP, SDL and Touchpoints compared. Information and Software Technology 51(7), 1152–1171 (2009)
6. Deliverable 3.2 "A Methodology for Evolutionary Requirements", http://www.securechange.eu
7. DOORS, http://www-01.ibm.com/software/awdtools/doors/
8. Dragoni, N., et al.: A Load Time Policy Checker for Open Multi-Application Smart Cards. In: Proc. of IEEE Policy 2011. IEEE, Los Alamitos (2011)
9. Elahi, G., Yu, E., Zannone, N.: A vulnerability-centric requirements engineering framework: analyzing security attacks, countermeasures, and requirements based on vulnerabilities. Requirements Engineering 15, 41–62 (2010)
10. Félix, E., Delande, O., Massacci, F., Paci, F.: Managing Changes with Legacy Security Engineering Processes. In: Proc. of IEEE Int. Conf. on Intelligence and Security Informatics (2011)
11. Fourneret, E., et al.: Selective Test Generation Method for Evolving Critical Systems. In: Proc. of 1st Int. Workshop on Regression Testing. IEEE, Los Alamitos (2011)
12. Fourneret, E., et al.: Model-Based Security Verification and Testing for Smart-cards. In: Proc. of ARES 2011. IEEE, Los Alamitos (2011)
13. Giorgini, P., Massacci, F., Mylopoulos, J., Zannone, N.: Requirements engineering for trust management: model, methodology, and reasoning. Internat. Journal of Information Security 5(4), 257–274 (2006)

14. Haley, C., Laney, R., Moffett, J., Nuseibeh, B.: Security requirements engineering: A framework for representation and analysis. IEEE Trans. Softw. Eng. 34, 133–153 (2008)
15. Hassine, J., Rilling, J., Hewitt, J.: Change impact analysis for requirement evolution using use case maps. In: Proc. of the 8th Intl. Workshop on Principles of Software Evolution, pp. 81–90. IEEE, Los Alamitos (2005)
16. Innerhofer-Oberperfler, F., Hafner, M., Breu, R.: Living Security – Collaborative Security Management in a Changing World. In: Proc. of IASTED Int. Conf. on Soft. Eng. (2011)
17. ISO 12207, Systems and software engineering — Software life cycle processes, ISO (2008)
18. ISO 15288, Systems and software engineering — System life cycle processes, ISO (2008)
19. ISO 31000, Risk management – Principles and guidelines, ISO (2009)
20. Jacobs, B., Piessens, F.: Expressive modular fine-grained concurrency specification. In: Proc. of POPL 2011, pp. 271–282. ACM, New York (2011)
21. Jacobs, B., Smans, J., Piessens, F.: A quick tour of the VeriFast program verifier. In: Ueda, K. (ed.) APLAS 2010. LNCS, vol. 6461, pp. 304–311. Springer, Heidelberg (2010)
22. Jürjens, J., Marchal, L., Ochoa, M., Schmidt, H.: Incremental security verification for evolving uMLsec models. In: France, R.B., Kuester, J.M., Bordbar, B., Paige, R.F. (eds.) ECMFA 2011. LNCS, vol. 6698, pp. 52–68. Springer, Heidelberg (2011)
23. Jürjens, J.: Secure Systems Development with UML. Springer, Heidelberg (2005)
24. Lund, M.S., Solhaug, B., Stølen, K.: Model-Driven Risk Analysis – The CORAS Approach. Springer, Heidelberg (2011)
25. Lund, M.S., Solhaug, B., Stølen, K.: Risk Analysis of Changing and Evolving Systems Using CORAS. In: Aldini, A., Gorrieri, R. (eds.) FOSAD 2011. LNCS, vol. 6858, pp. 231–274. Springer, Heidelberg (2011)
26. Massacci, F., Mylopolous, J., Paci, F., Tun, T.T., Yu, Y.: An Extended Ontology for Security Requirements. In: 1st Internat. Workshop on Information Systems Security Engineering (WISSE 2011), London (2011)
27. Massacci, F., Mylopoulos, J., Zannone, N.: Computer-aided support for Secure Tropos. Automated Software Eng. 14, 341–364 (2007)
28. Normand, V., Félix, E.: Toward model-based security engineering: developing a security analysis DSML. In: Proc. of ECMDA-FA (2009)
29. Philippaerts, P., et al.: The Belgian Electronic Identity Card: A Verification Case Study. In: Proc. AVOCS 2011 (2011) (submitted)
30. System Security Eng. Capability Maturity Model, http://www.sse-cmm.org/index.html
31. Tran, M.S., Massacci, F.: Dealing with Known Unknowns: Towards a Game-Theoretic Foundation for Software Requirement Evolution. In: Mouratidis, H., Rolland, C. (eds.) CAiSE 2011. LNCS, vol. 6741, pp. 62–76. Springer, Heidelberg (2011)
32. Tun, T.T., Yu, Y., Laney, R., Nuseibeh, B.: Early identification of problem interactions: A tool-supported approach. In: Glinz, M., Heymans, P. (eds.) REFSQ 2009 Amsterdam. LNCS, vol. 5512, pp. 74–88. Springer, Heidelberg (2009)
33. Tun, T.T., et al.: Model-based argument analysis for evolving security requirements. In: Proc. of the IEEE SSIRI 2010, pp. 88–97. IEEE, Los Alamitos (2010)
34. van Lamsweerde, A.: Elaborating security requirements by construction of intentional anti-models. In: Proc. of ICSE 2004, pp. 148–157. ACM, New York (2004)
35. Vogels, F., Jacobs, B., Piessens, F., Smans, J.: Annotation inference for separation logic based verifiers. In: Bruni, R., Dingel, J. (eds.) FORTE 2011 and FMOODS 2011. LNCS, vol. 6722, pp. 319–333. Springer, Heidelberg (2011)

FI-WARE Security: Future Internet Security Core
(Invited Paper)

Antonio GarcíaVázquez[1], Pedro Soria-Rodriguez[1], Pascal Bisson[2],
Daniel Gidoin[2], Slim Trabelsi[3], and Gabriel Serme[3]

[1]Atos, Albarracín 25, 28037 Madrid, Spain
{antonio.garcia,pedro.soria}@atos.net
[2]THALES SERVICES, Campus Polytechnique
1, avenue Augustin Fresnel, 91767 Palaiseau France
{pascal.bisson,daniel.gidoin}@thalesgroup.com
[3]SAP Labs France,
805, Avenue du Docteur Maurice Donat BP 1216, 06254 Mougins Cedex, France
{slim.trabelsi,gabriel.serme}@sap.com

Abstract. Security is becoming a major issue in the development of new environments. Within the European Commission Programs oriented to define the Future Internet; the challenge taken on by FI-WARE project has been the design of server oriented architecture inspired by *Secure by Design* principles.

Security in FI-WARE is defined as context adaptive architecture that guarantees protection against external attacks; privacy in communications & personal data sharing; and secure & trustworthy services as the default operation mode of the Future Internet.

Keywords: Future Internet, Context based security, Dynamic Security and compliance. Run-time adaptive services.

1 Introduction

In the context of FI-PPP programs (*Future Internet Public Private Partnership*) [1] the goal of the FI-WARE [3] project is to advance the global competitiveness of the EU economy by introducing an innovative infrastructure for cost-effective creation and delivery of services, providing high quality of service and security guarantees.

The key deliverables of FI-WARE will be an open architecture and a reference implementation of a novel service infrastructure, building upon generic and reusable building blocks developed in earlier projects.

The security mechanisms will ensure that the delivery and usage of services is trustworthy.

The security layer of FI-WARE should be context-aware and should deal with highly dynamic and unpredictable context changes.

This *Context Based Security* architecture inherits from *Secure by Design* and Privacy *by Design* [2] the concept that the future of secure & privacy cannot be assured solely by compliance with regulatory frameworks or by the use of privacy enhancing technologies; rather, secure & privacy assurance must become an organization's default mode of operation and must be taken into account in the early stages of the design of the system architecture because it has a fundamental impact on it.

W. Abramowicz et al. (Eds.): ServiceWave 2011, LNCS 6994, pp. 144–152, 2011.

In our approach Future Internet's security core architecture offers to the other services of FI-WARE a solid and trustworthy enough structure allowing service providers to focus on security requirements but delegate their implementation to the core Future Internet platform, as it will provide the needed security solutions.

On reaching these objectives it becomes essential to have means to:

- Develop an efficient security monitoring system which not only is able to quickly respond against attacks but is intelligent enough to perform early attack detection and offers support capabilities for decisions and actions to be taken.

- Offer a security market place where both *Basic* an *Additional* security services are offered to applications and services to dynamically configure their required security level and where any provider could contribute with new solutions.

- Provide a Context-based security and compliance framework to support the dynamic supervision and adaptation of the security of systems in the context of a changing environment. This framework helps searching and browsing thought the marketplace catalogue, in order to find the most appropriate service to fulfill the Security and Compliance requirements from the end-user environments, and to deploy into the target system.

2   The FI-WARE Approach

This paper presents the architecture that will support the run-time and context-aware provision and monitorization of security and dependability (S&D) solutions. The

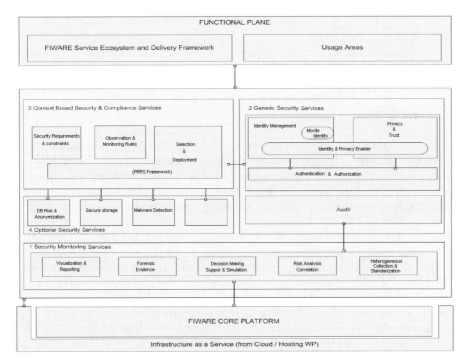

Fig. 1. Overall FI-WARE security architecture

overall ambition of the Security Architecture of FI-WARE is to demonstrate that the Vision of an Internet that offers *context based secure* services is becoming a reality.

FI-WARE security architecture will focus on key security functionalities such as identity management or security monitoring to be delivered as so-called *generic security enablers* that will be integrated with the design and implementation of the FI-WARE itself.

This architecture is designed to be extensible to meet additional security requirements coming from user applications in run-time mode by deploying the appropriate so-called *optional security enabler*.

2.1 Generic Security Enablers

In **FI-WARE** a **Generic Enabler (GE)** is defined as: A functional building block of FI-WARE. Any implementation of a Generic Enabler (GE) is made up of a set of components which together supports a concrete set of Functions and provides a concrete set of APIs and interoperable interfaces that are in compliance with open specifications published for that GE.

The *Generic Security Enablers* will define the general core security mechanisms of the Future Internet.

These *Generic Security Enablers* will be present by default in any FI-WARE instance to assure that trust, security, privacy and resilience are its default mode of operation.

The Core *Generic Security Enablers* will provide these baseline services in FI-WARE instances:

- Security monitoring
- Context base security & compliance
- Other Generic Services such as: Identity and Access Management, Privacy and Trust, Authentication & Authorization services

2.2 Security Monitoring

The advanced Security Monitoring system will covers the whole spectrum from acquisition of events up to visualization and reporting, going through normalization of heterogeneous events and correlation, risk analysis and business impact evaluation, but also going beyond thanks to a digital forensic for evidence tool and assisted decision making support in case of cyber attacks that helps in the selection of adequate countermeasures.

We propose a security monitoring enabler composed of a number of industrial and academics security components. Some of them cooperate, and it is extremely challenging, to collect heterogeneous information coming from security sensors, security and privacy events, anti-malwares alerts, user privilege change tracking, objects access (with success or failure) and security compliance violations. Others components in an innovative approach allow to draw up a topology of vulnerability, to identify the potential cyber attacks and give a original business vision of risk. This enabler will also provide comprehensive situational views, context adapted (Instant mobility, safe city, smartagrifood, etc) and stakeholder oriented (business managers, security operators, service providers, cloud computing managers, etc) so that corresponding proactive actions can be taken in a timely and effective manner.

The Digital forensic framework will allow establishing the proof of a malicious action observing the European legislations that stands that the collection and exploitation of evidence should not change the proof elements, and a second opinion will always allow finding the same results.

The volumes of data to be processed, the diversity of technologies used in the context of use cases, the dispersion of information with massive cloud computing technologies usage, are some of the challenges that face the FI-WARE Security Monitoring GE.

2.3 Context-Based Security and Compliance (PRRS Framework)

The Platform for Run-time Reconfigurability of Security (PRRS) is a *Security enabler* in the Future Internet core architecture that allows an end-user application or service, to direct a request to the *PRRS* framework describing its particular security requirements.

Then the framework will search into the "security market" of *Security Enablers* in order to find the most appropriate solution to fulfill both the requirements received and any applicable regulation from Private or Public sources.

Finally it will deploy into the end-user environment the selected security solution.

Furthermore the framework will also instantiate a runtime monitor with the responsibility of detect anomalous behavior or non-conformance.

In case of a non-conformance detected the framework will take compensation actions for the automated adaptation of the deployed security mechanism to the changing context conditions.

2.4 Optional Security Services

Specific end-user applications will require optional security services to fulfill their requirements which although they are potentially applicable across a number of end-user applications, unlike generic services, it is not expected that all of them will make use of any particular one.

The architecture is able not only to support the instantiation of the *Security Enablers* which supports these services (thanks to Dynamic security management service), but define and maintain a standard security market where any security developer could integrate its technology into the Future Internet security platform, after proper validation and certification.

Sample *Optional Enablers* that could be often included are:

- Database risk evaluation services
- Data anonymization services
- Secure storage services
- Malware detection service

3   Context-Based Security and Compliance

The key component of these service is the PRRS [5] Framework defined taking into account previous software models and experiences [6].

The PRRS framework provides run-time support to applications, by managing S&D solutions and monitoring the systems' context.

The communication between the different components of the architecture and the end-user applications that will require its services will be performed by a new standard language (USDL-SEC) to be defined.

This business service oriented language will be able to describe & register security services or capabilities.

In a nutshell, the USDL-SEC language will support the following characteristics:

- Describe functional security services provided by the platform and needed by applications
- Describe the interface offered by the security enablers to the applications
- Provide mechanisms to cover both high level description of the service and detail functionalities & implementations.
- Provide event management capabilities to allow monitors get the context event information from the security enablers they overseen.
- Describe requirements and compliance rules to be fulfilled in an specific end-user environment

3.1   PRRS Framework

PRRS is implemented as a service running in a device, on top of the operating system, and listening to end-user applications requests.

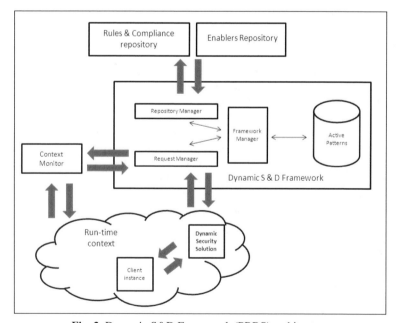

Fig. 2. Dynamic S&D Framework (PRRS) architecture

End-user applications send requests in order to fulfill their security requirements to the framework; these requests, once processed by the PRRS, are translated into S&D Solutions to be deployed as executable components in the context of the end-user application which is running.

The communication between end-user applications, the deployed executable components the framework is supported by the *USDL-SEC* language as we describe above.

PRRS framework also provides another two *USDL-SEC* interfaces in order to communicate not only with end-user applications, but with monitoring components and Rules and enablers repositories

The PRRS Framework also provides external monitoring components with the rules that the end-user applications context must fulfil.

The monitoring components then get context and status events from the end user and the S&D security solution, and will trigger the PRRS Framework in case of a non-compliance detection.

On the other hand framework offers an interface to get access to both Rules and Enablers repositories.

From the rules repository it will get, as USDL-SEC patterns, the description of public laws and private agreements that should be applied in many scenarios; furthermore end-user applications will have the possibility to refer to some of this existing rules instead of describe their requirements in detail.

Finally PRRS framework will get access to the Enablers repository where, mainly optional security enablers created by any secure aware developer will be registered.

From the service and interface description provided by this enablers, the PRRS framework will select the most suitable solution to fulfill the end-user applications requirements.

The architecture of the PRRS has been designed taking into account the wide variety of target devices where the system will run. The main elements of the architecture have been split into separate components.

This makes possible the implementation of each component by a separate way; for example implement each component for a specific platform, in the cases where this is necessary.

The Framework manager is the core of the system. It controls the rest of the components of the system. It processes requests from end-user applications orchestrating the instantiation of the *Security Enabler* selected.

It also sends monitoring rules to monitoring services that monitor the proper operation of Enablers, and also takes the necessary recovery actions when it is informed by monitoring services of a monitoring rule violation by the reactivation, reconfiguration, deactivation and/or substitution of the *Enabler*.

Framework Manager delegates some of its more complex duties into two components, the *Request Manager* and the *Repository Manager*.

Request Manager is in charge of:

- Managing the different service request form the end-user applications
- Getting the notification from the monitoring systems
- Sending monitors rules must overseen and update them in case of their change
- Getting status information from the deployed Enables

Repository Manager is in charge of implementing the communication between repositories and PRRS framework.

3.2 USDL-SEC

The language will extend existing standard USDL 3.0 (we call it *USDL-SEC*) [4] by implementing a new module security oriented. USDL 3.0 aims to describe a service along with functional and non-functional properties in single and complete description file. It provides means to compare and select services according to consumer needs. A service description is first made by a service provider, which then exposes it to a service broker. Once a service consumer selects a specific service, the service provider deploys its service and runs it.

Any Security model is fully defined by its associated properties file allowing consumers and providers to agree on a security protocol, through expressions of concrete mechanisms and links to existing standard such as WS-SecurityPolicy, XACML, P3P, *etc...*

This properties file also describes actions operated by the service provider on a declarative-basis. That is the provider claims to undertake actions to achieve a higher level of security.

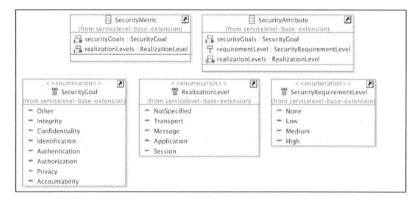

Fig. 3. Meta-Model for the USDL-SEC Module

The Figure 3 depict the associated meta-model of the USDL-SEC module. The module expresses metrics on the quality of security concerns for different realization levels.

A level is a distinction that can be referred to the OSI model which specifies if a security description applies to the *Transport* level, the *Application* level or another level mentioned in Figure 3.

The security expressiveness is defined by a set of property, such as *Authentication, Confidentiality, Privacy, etc...* Those properties relate to both the aforementioned *Generic Security Enablers* and undermentioned *Optional* ones.

The current version of the USDL-SEC specification is not sufficient to depict the security functionalities defined by FI-WARE Security. For this reason one of our next tasks will be the enhancement of this description to cover as much as possible these security functionalities. Security patterns should then be attached to the descriptions in order to facilitate the deployment and the consumption of the generic security services.

4 Optional Security Enablers

The optional security service enabler is used to customize the security service description within USDL-SEC when the security functionality is not covered by the specification described before. This extension targets directly the application domain usage. For example, if we want to describe and publish a malware scanning service the basic version of USDL-SEC is not sufficient. The goal here is to make easily extendible the security service description for customized usage. This functionality will help developers to define and describe their own services through the USDL standard by adding new functionalities and new capabilities.

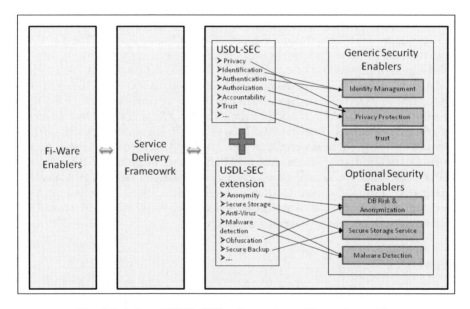

Fig. 4. Relation of USDL-SEC and extensions with security enables

In FI-WARE we want to overcome the limitations of the traditional service description languages that usually do not take into account the extensions wanted by the users. Most of the time the user has to add manually new elements and modify the delivery framework in order to take into account the new functionalities. Such approach is not feasible for any user.

This optional security service will provide all the technical support to let users use and extend the USDL-SEC service description easily.

The USDL registry entity in charge of publishing and discovering the services must be able to understand the meaning of the optional security services in order to provide an efficient search engine.

5 Future Works

FI-WARE will provide a Core Platform architecture based upon services called *Generic Enablers.*

A so-called *"FI-WARE Testbed"* instance will be generated to allow third parties run and test Future Internet Applications based on FI-WARE Generic Enablers.

As the architecture is designed to be secure aware any subsequently service should also fulfill these requirements.

End-user applications and services can trust the security of their transactions under the default operation mode of the Future Internet architecture, without reliance on individual security add-ons and disparate security solutions and configurations that represent potential security risks themselves.

Furthermore, thanks to the application of a context base security philosophy, Future Internet itself will have enough mechanisms both to face external attacks and adapt its security level to the changing application context.

Acknowledgments. The work published in this article has partially received funding from the European Commission's Framework Programs 6 and 7. The FI-WARE project started in May 2011 led by Telefónica Investigación y Desarrollo with the collaboration of Atos among other partners (THALES Communications SA, SAP AG, IBM Israel – Science and Technology LTD, IBM Research GMBH, Telecom Italia S.P.A., France Telecom SA, Nokia Siemens Networks GMBH & CO. KG, Nokia Siemens Networks Telekommunikacios Kereskedelmi ES Szolgaltato, Nokia Siemens Networks OY, Deutsche Telekom AG, Technicolor R&D France SNC, Ericsson AB, Engineering - Ingegneria Informatica SPA, Alcatel-Lucent Italia S.P.A., Alcatel-Lucent Deutschland AG, Siemens AG, Intel Performance Learning Solutions Limited, NEC Europe LTD, Fraunhofer-Gesellschaft Zur Foerderung Der Angewandten Forschung E.V., Institut National De Recherche En Informatique Et En Automatique, Universidad Politecnica De Madrid, Universitaet Duisburg-Essen, Universita Degli Studi Di Roma La Spienza, University Of Surrey).

References

1. Future internet PPP: http://www.fi-ppp.eu/
2. Privacy by Design Principles:
   http://www.ipc.on.ca/images/Resources/
   7foundationalprinciples.pdf
3. FI-Ware project. Funded by European Commission. Under grant FP7 – 285248,
   http://www.fi-ware.eu/
4. USDL - Internet of services:
   http://www.internet-of-services.com/index.php?id=288&L=0
5. PRRS framework: Atos Origin product based in the results of Serenity project[6]
6. Serenity project. Funded by European Commission. Under grant IST-027587,
   http://www.serenity-project.org

A General Method for Assessment of Security in Complex Services[*]

Leanid Krautsevich[1], Fabio Martinelli[2], and Artsiom Yautsiukhin[2]

[1] Department of Computer Science, University of Pisa, Pisa, Italy
krautsev@di.unipi.it
[2] Istituto di Informatica e Telematica, Consiglio Nazionale delle Ricerche, Pisa, Italy
{fabio.martinelli,artsiom.yautsiukhin}@iit.cnr.it

Abstract. We focus on the assessment of the security of business processes. We assume that a business process is composed of abstract services, each of which has several concrete instantiations. Essential peculiarity of our method is that we express security metrics used for the evaluation of security properties as semirings. First, we consider primitive decomposition of the business process into a weighted graph which describes possible implementations of the business process. Second, we evaluate the security using semiring-based methods for graph analysis. Finally, we exploit semirings to describe the mapping between security metrics which is useful when different metrics are used for the evaluation of security properties of services.

Keywords: business processes, services, semirings, risk, security metrics, design graph.

1 Introduction

Rapidly changing world requires rapidly changing solutions. This is one of the reasons why service oriented technologies (Grid, Web Services, Cloud) become so popular. The idea behind such technologies is to be agile, easily reconfigurable and provide different alternatives to fulfil the same goal. Thus, service consumer is able to select the alternative she likes the most, i.e., the service which has the most suitable qualities, expressed as Service Level Agreement (SLA).

Security requirements also must be included in the agreement, in order to protect valuable assets not only during data transmission, but also during data usage [12,13]. Naturally, selection of the most suitable business process must take into account security requirements. Usually, requirements, or policies (we use terms requirements and policies interchangeably) are precisely expressed with help of metrics, which indicate the quantity of some parameter. We assume that metrics may be evaluated using statistical methods, intrusion detection systems, using questionnaires, or simply assigned by security specialists [14,15].

---

[*] This work was partly supported by EU-FP7-ICT NESSoS and EU-FP7-ICT ANIKE-TOS projects.

W. Abramowicz et al. (Eds.): ServiceWave 2011, LNCS 6994, pp. 153–164, 2011.

Service consumer is able to select the service which has the best metric values. The problem appears as soon as we have a complex service, *a business process*, which is composed of several simple services. A way to aggregate the values of simple services is required for the evaluation of the complex service. Moreover, existing alternatives of the implementation of a business process should be compared and the optimal alternative should be selected. Such analysis is useful not only for service consumers, but also for the service orchestrator which provides the complex service hiding the implementation details. For example, instead of selection of the most secure implementation, the orchestrator may find the level of protection it is able to guarantee even in case of problems with some simple services. Finally, the method for the analysis should be independent from the metric used for the evaluation, since simple services may be evaluated using different security metrics[1].

1.1   Contributions

The main contributions of this paper are the following.

- Provide a general method for aggregation of security metrics and selection the most secure implementation of a business process. This goal is achieved using a special mathematical structure "semirings".
- We have shown how similar metrics could be combined to conduct a general analysis. This goal is achieved by considering relations between metrics using mapping between semirings.

The paper is structured as follows. Section 2 presents a primitive transformation of a business process described in Business Process Modelling Notation into a graph. In Section 3, we evaluate overall security of a business process analysing the graph with help of semiring-based methods. Section 4 shows how the relation between security metrics may be described. Section 5 is devoted to the related work. Section 6 presents directions for future work and a conclusion.

2   Decomposition of a Business Process into a Design Graph

We consider a general business process (complex service) composed of simple abstract services. An abstract service describes a single job that should be done during the execution of the business process. Many notations for description of the business processes could be used as a starting point for the analysis. For example, Business Process Execution Language (BPEL) [1] is one of the most well-known and wide-spread notations. The main disadvantage of using BPEL for our purpose is that this language requires too much low-level details, which are not used for the analysis. On the other hand, the process can be described with Business Process Modelling Notation (BPMN) [2]. BPMN is a

---

[1] We admit, that security is not the only quality which must be taken into account during selection of the best alternative, but in this article we focus only on security.

high-level notation and, thus, is suitable for the analysis of high-level security properties. On the other hand, it is also only a graphical notation and an ad-hoc formalisation is required for automatic transformation of the model.

We follow BMPN for the description of a business processes. We consider a business process which is composed using the four basic structured activities: sequence, choice, flow, and loop. *Sequence* describes a situation when the services or structured activities are executed sequentially. *Choice* allows selecting a service on the basis of attributes of the business process or events external to the business process. *Flow* is used to denote two or more services or activities run in parallel. *Loop* supports the iterative execution of services and activities.

We extend this set with one more structured activity called *design choice* similarly to Massacci and Yautsiukhin [17,16], which denotes a design alternative for a business process. Design alternatives denote sub-processes which fulfil the same functional goal, but in different ways (i.e., these are different sub-processes). The alternatives provide different qualities in general, and security properties in particular. Semantics of the design choice is similar to a regular choice, but the design choices are solved during the implementation of the business process, while the regular choice is solved during the execution. We exploit a gateway with letter "X" inside to denote the regular choice and a gateway with letter "D" inside to denote the design choice in a business process diagram.

Each abstract service has several real instantiations, *concrete services*. Concrete services are run by different service providers. For instance, an on-line trading platform may be provided by Amazon or eBay, off-the-shelf e-mail solution by Gmail or Hotmail. We suppose that an orchestrator of a business process signs a contract with each service providers that deliver concrete services for the implementation of the business process. The contract is based on a service level agreement proposed by a service provider and accepted by a service consumer. The orchestrator determines the security level of each concrete service analysing the policies. The security level is computed as a security metric which the orchestrator exploits for the future security evaluation and selection of the business process implementations. An essential goal of the orchestrator is to solve all design choices and select instantiations for the abstract services in a way to obtain the most secure implementation of the business process.

Example 1. We consider an on-line shop as an example of the business process (see Figure 1). First, a customer uses an on-line engine for searching and selecting items for buying. The owner of the shop would like to choose the way to implement the on-line engine. She considers two alternatives: to buy an on-line trading platform or to rent a server and install a content management system (CMS) there. Second, selected items are paid using a payment service. Third, items are shipped to the customer. Finally, the customer gets information about the payment and conditions of shipping by e-mail or VoIP service. The owner considers two opportunities to organise an e-mail service: to run an off-the-shelf e-mail solution or to organise her own e-mail server buying a hosting and installing an e-mail server software. We numerate abstract services for further convenience.

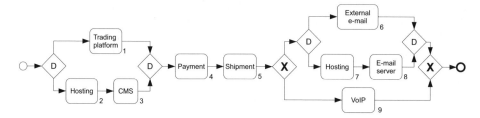

Fig. 1. Example of a business process in BPMN: an on-line shop

2.1   A Mathematical Model

We make a mathematical model of a business process in order to use it later for our analysis. A high level business process can be easily transformed into a graph in several ways (e.g., [17,16]). We propose first to make the transformation into a process algebra. We use a notation similar to Calculus of Communicating Systems (CCS) [19]. Then we build the graph according to the execution flow.

In the process algebra there are several operators, which are useful for formalising a process. Let a_i be an abstract service, S^A be the set of all jobs (abstract services) in a business process such that $a_i \in S^A$. P and Q are two processes consisting of actions combined with basic operators and terminated with $\mathbf{0}$. *Sequence* activity can be formalised as $a_i.P$, i.e., first action a_i is executed and then process P. Parallel activity *Flow* is coded as $P|Q$. *Non-deterministic choice* is formalised as $P + Q$, i.e., process P or process Q is executed.

In the current work we simplify the transformation assuming that an orchestrator has information about usual execution of business process in advance. Thus, all *choices* except design choices are known in advance and we can consider only a part of the initial business process containing design choices only. *Loop* activity is considered as a number of the same executions in a raw. We assume that the orchestrator knows exact number of loops or uses the average number. The following technique is used to obtain a graph after the transformation of the business process into the process algebra.

We call a *Design Graph* a graph composed of concrete services connected with edges representing message flow in a business process. The root node of the graph is an empty node representing the beginning of the business process. For the sequential composition, the child of a node is the next executed service in a process algebra description. In case of parallel composition we select any activity first and then another one, hence, the parallel composition is a sequence of nodes in the graph. Intuition behind such transformation is that we consider the security of the business process and all parallel branches should be successfully executed for the successful execution of the business process. Regular choices are solved according to assumption above. A node has several outgoing edges if corresponding service is followed by a design choice. We call such node an "or-node". Outgoing edges lead to nodes corresponding to the first services in design alternatives grouped by the design choice. In addition, "or-node" is used to represent a choice between concrete services. Finally, an empty node is used to conclude the graph. The direction of connections is the same as the direction of message flow in the business process diagram. Moreover, each node is assigned with a weight according to the value of a metric expressing service security. Source node and final nodes have zero weights. Now, we are able to formalise the Design Graph we receive after transformation of a business process description.

Definition 1. *Let $S^A = \{a_i\}$ be a set of abstract services. Let also $S^C = \{c_{ij}\}$ be a set of concrete services and any $c_{ij} \in S^C$ is a j-th concrete service for an abstract service a_i. Then, we define Design Graph as a tuple $\langle N, E, L \rangle$. Where*

- *$N = \{n_{ij}\} \cup \{n_0\} \cup \{n_\infty\}$ is a set of nodes, where nodes n_{ij} correspond to the concrete services c_{ij}, n_0 and n_∞ are initial and final nodes corresponding to the start and the end of the business process;*
- *E is a set of edges between nodes which correspond to the message flow in the business process;*
- *$L : N \mapsto D$ is a labelling function which assigns to every node a number from the domain D of a security metric, the source node and the final node are always assigned with zero value of the metric.*

Example 2. We continue Example 1. Consider transformation from a business process in Figure 1 into a Design Graph. Suppose the owner of the on-line shop knows that most of her customers prefer to be contacted via e-mail. This information helps an orchestrator of the business process to remove the exclusive choice between a VoIP service and implementation of e-mail service on the final step of the business process.

The design graph starts with the initial node n_0 which has three children n_{11}, n_{12}, and n_{21}. Nodes n_{11} and n_{12} describes the selection between concrete services instantiating a trading platform in Figure 1 (e.g., n_{11} is for Amazon and n_{12} is for eBay). The alternative implementation of the on-line engine is presented by node n_{21} which stands for a hosting service and two its children n_{31} and n_{32} denoting CMSs. Nodes n_{41} and n_{42} represent payment services, n_{51} stands for shipping service, n_{61} and n_{62} denote external mailing services, n_{71} and n_{72} represent hosting for an e-mail server, n_{81} and n_{82} are the e-mail server software. The graph ends with the node n_∞ which stands for the end of the business process. We display the resulted Design Graph produced from the business process in Figure 2.

Now if we follow the mathematical model every implementation of the business process is represented as a path in the Design Graph.

Definition 2. *Let $\langle N, E, L \rangle$ be a Design Graph and $n, n', n'' \in N \land N' \subseteq N \land E' \subseteq E$. A path from n to n' is a sub-graph $\pi_{\langle n, n' \rangle} = \langle N', E', L' \rangle$ such that*

1. *$N' = \{n\}$ and $E' = \emptyset$ if $n' = n$;*
2. *$N' = \{n'\} \cup N''$ and $E' = \{\langle n', n'' \rangle\} \cup E''$, where $\langle N'', E'', L'' \rangle$ is a path $\pi_{\langle n, n'' \rangle}$;*
3. *$L' \equiv L$.*

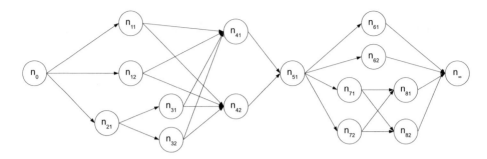

Fig. 2. A design graph representing an on-line shop

Any path $\pi_{\langle n_0, n_\infty \rangle}$ represents implementation of the business process, where n_0 is the initial node and n_∞ is the final node.

In addition we define set $P(n_0, n_\infty) = \{\pi_{\langle n_0, n_\infty \rangle}\}$ representing all the possible paths between n_0 and n_∞. Each path has its own weight obtained by aggregating weights of nodes belonging to the path. The weight of the path is representing the security metric for an implementation of a business process. Aggregating of weights corresponds to aggregating of metric values. The problem of the selection of the most suitable implementation of the business process can be seen as *to find such path in a Design Graph that the weight of the whole path is the best one (e.g., maximal or minimal) among all possible.* We call the path with optimal value of metric the *shortest path* and denote it as $\pi_{\langle n_0, n_\infty \rangle}^{S} \in P(n_0, n_\infty)$. Implementation of the business process corresponding to the shortest path has the best value of the security metric. This implementation is the most secure one.

3   Security-Aware Selection of a Business Process Implementation

As soon as the Design Graph is built we can start analysing it in order to select the implementation of a business process which satisfies the desirable customer's policies. First, we simplify the task and select the most secure business process implementation among other alternatives. Naturally, if this selection does not satisfies the desirable customer's policies then no other implementation does.

We aim at the assessment of the security of a business process using different security metrics. However, in this section, we assume that the security of all concrete services is assessed using the same security metric. This assumption will be relaxed in Section 4. Each node n_{ij} in a Design Graph is assigned with weight $w_{ij} = L(n_{ij})$. The initial n_0 and the final node n_∞ are assigned with a zero value. We look for a method that allows abstracting the security metrics and using universal algorithms for the computation of the shortest path in graphs.

Mehryar Mohri [20] proposed a framework that contains algorithms for searching for the shortest path in a weighted graph, extending the work of Edsger

Dijkstra [9]. The framework exploits the notion of *semiring* for the abstraction of weights and operators over weights. A semiring consists of a set of values D (e.g., natural or real numbers), and two types of operators: aggregation ($\otimes$) and comparison ($\oplus$) values and constraints. Formally, the semiring is defined as follows [4]:

Definition 3. Semiring T *is a tuple* $\langle D, \oplus, \otimes, \mathbf{0}, \mathbf{1} \rangle$:

- D *is a set of elements and* $\mathbf{0}, \mathbf{1} \in D$;
- $\oplus$, *is an additive operator defined over (possibly infinite) set of elements D, for $d_1, d_2, d_3 \in T$, it is communicative ($d_1 \oplus d_2 = d_2 \oplus d_1$) and associative ($d_1 \oplus (d_2 \oplus d_3) = (d_1 \oplus d_2) \oplus d_3$), and $\mathbf{0}$ is a unit element of the additive operator ($d_1 \oplus \mathbf{0} = d_1 = \mathbf{0} \oplus d_1$).*
- $\otimes$ *is a binary multiplicative operator, it is associative and commutative, $\mathbf{1}$ is its unit element ($d_1 \otimes \mathbf{1} = d_1 = \mathbf{1} \otimes d_1$), and $\mathbf{0}$ is its absorbing element ($d_1 \otimes \mathbf{0} = \mathbf{0} = \mathbf{0} \otimes d_1$);*
- $\otimes$ *is distributive over additive operator ($d_1 \otimes (d_2 \oplus d_3) = (d_1 \otimes d_2) \oplus (d_1 \otimes d_3)$);*
- $\leq_T$ *is a partial order over the set D, which enables comparing different elements of the semiring, the partial order is defined using the additive operator $d_1 \leq_T d_2$ (d_2 is better than d_1) iff $d_1 \oplus d_2 = d_2$.*

The weight $\delta^S(\pi^S_{\langle n_0, n_\infty \rangle})$ of the shortest path $\pi^S_{\langle n_0, n_\infty \rangle}$ is computed using additive operator $\oplus$:

$$\delta^S(\pi^S_{\langle n_0, n_\infty \rangle}) = \bigoplus_{\forall \pi_{\langle n_0, n_\infty \rangle} \in P(n_\infty, n_0)} \delta(\pi_{\langle n_0, n_\infty \rangle}) \tag{1}$$

Here $P(n_0, n_\infty)$ is the set of all paths from the initial node n_0 to the final one n_∞. The cost $\delta(\pi_{\langle n_0, n_\infty \rangle})$ of the path $\pi_{\langle n_0, n_\infty \rangle}$ is computed using multiplicative operator:

$$\delta(\pi_{\langle n_0, n_\infty \rangle}) = \bigotimes_{\forall n_{ij} \in \pi_{\langle n_0, n_\infty \rangle}} w_{ij} \tag{2}$$

We need to express security metrics as *semirings* for exploitation of universal algorithms for the search of the shortest path in a weighted graph.

3.1 Semirings for Expressing Security Metrics

Security of the business process and concrete services is assessed using security metrics. Different semirings must be used to express different metrics. In the following list we display several semirings and describe metrics expressed using these semirings.

- Weighted semiring $\langle R^+, min, +, \infty, \mathbf{0} \rangle$ represent the *risk of a successful attack* on a business process. A path in a tree computed under preferences using weighted semiring will minimize the overall sum of risks of successful attacks on services composing the business process. We assume that the business process is compromised if a successful attack compromises at least one service included in the business process.

- Probability semiring $\langle [0,1], max, \times, \mathbf{0}, \mathbf{1} \rangle$ expresses the *probability of a successful operation* of the business process (a resistance to all attack). In case we know the probability p_i of compromising the ith service, then $(1 - p_i) \in [0,1]$ is the probability to tolerate all attacks.
- Semiring $\langle N^+, min, +, \infty, \mathbf{0} \rangle$ serves for identification of a path with the *minimal number of attacks*.

This is not a complete list of metrics and semirings that can be used for the search of a way for the optimal execution of a business process. Other semirings can be defined for other metrics if necessary. Note, that semirings serve also for the assessment of non-security properties of the business process. For instance, semiring $\langle N^+, min, +, \infty, \mathbf{0} \rangle$ is used for identification of the minimal number of steps to reach the end goal of the business process. Semiring $\langle R^+, max, min, \mathbf{0}, \infty \rangle$ allows evaluating the *latency* of the business process if we assume that only one delay may occur during the execution of the business process. Probability semiring $\langle [0,1], max, \times, \mathbf{0}, \mathbf{1} \rangle$ may be used to express users *trust* to the business process.

We are able to apply any semiring-based algorithm (e.g., Generic Single Source Shortest Distance [20]) for searching of the shortest path after a semiring was chosen and the problem is defined by Equations 1 and 2. Note, that the algorithm uses the weights on the edges while we use the weights on the nodes. The algorithm can still be applied if we use the weights for the node as the weight of every incoming edge leading to this node.

Example 3. Suppose each concrete service is assessed with the quantitative risk value. Weighted semiring $\langle R^+, min, +, \infty, \mathbf{0} \rangle$ is used to represent the risk. There are 48 possible paths in the graph presented in Figure 2. Without loss of generality, we consider just two paths for shorter explanation. Let weights of nodes be $w_{11} = 100$, $w_{41} = 120$, $w_{51} = 150, w_{61} = 90$, $w_{62} = 110$, $w_0 = w_\infty = 0$. First, we find the weights for paths $\pi^1_{\langle n_0, n_\infty \rangle} = n_0 n_{11} n_{41} n_{51} n_{61} n_\infty$ and $\pi^2_{\langle n_0, n_\infty \rangle} = n_0 n_{11} n_{41} n_{51} n_{62} n_\infty$. The weights $\delta^1(\pi^1_{\langle n_0, n_\infty \rangle}) = 480$ and $\delta^2(\pi^2_{\langle n_0, n_\infty \rangle}) = 500$ are computed using multiplicative operator $\oplus$ of weighted semiring. Second, the best weight is selected using additive operator min: $\delta^S = min(\delta^1, \delta^2) = 480$. The shortest path is $\pi^S_{\langle n_0, n_\infty \rangle} = \pi^1_{\langle n_0, n_\infty \rangle}$. Note, that here we used a simplified computation for this example, when the mentioned algorithms (e.g., [20]) are much more efficient.

The idea of exploitation of semirings has several advantages. The first advantage is that it allows re-evaluating of security of a business process and choose an alternative implementation of the business process. The need of the alternative implementation may be caused by the change of the security level of current implementation or by the change preferences of an orchestrator. The second advantage is that the orchestrator can evaluate the business process using different security criteria and select several implementations corresponding to different security metrics. The orchestrator can exploit an implementation satisfying the major part of criteria.

4   Interoperability of Services

Our idea requires services being assessed using the same metric. However in the real world a situation when security of all services is evaluated using the same metric is not always possible. Also a service consumer may express her security requirements using metric different than service provider's one. For instance, consider a situation when the security of the first part of services is assessed using minimal number of attacks and the security of the second part is assessed using risk. One more example is a situation when the service provider assesses risk level using quantitative risk while service customer uses qualitative risk scale. There is a need for a method that can evaluate the security in case of several metrics. We propose to tackle the issue by mapping between security metrics. The metrics used for an evaluations of services may be mapped to the most general one (e.g., risk) on the basis of formal relations between metrics considered in [14,15]. The relations may be expressed using mappings between semirings presented by Bistarelli et al. [3]. The analysis described in Sections 2 and 3 should be applied after the mapping is done.

Suppose there are two semirings $T = \langle D, +, \times, 0, 1 \rangle$ and $\widehat{T} = \langle \widehat{D}, \widehat{+}, \widehat{\times}, \widehat{0}, \widehat{1} \rangle$. Our goal is to map the first semiring onto the second one. A Galois insertion $\langle \alpha, \gamma \rangle : \langle D, \leq_T \rangle \rightleftharpoons \langle \widehat{D}, \leq_{\widehat{T}} \rangle$ is used for the mapping. Here α and γ are two mappings such that

- α and γ are monotonic,
- $\forall d \in D, d \leq_T \gamma(\alpha(d))$,
- $\forall \widehat{d} \in \widehat{D}, \alpha(\gamma(\widehat{d})) \leq_{\widehat{T}} \widehat{d}$.

If there is a constraint satisfaction problem (CSPs, [4]) H over semiring T we get a problem $\widehat{H} = \alpha(H)$ over semiring $\widehat{T}$ applying α. Similarly, we obtain the problem $H' = \gamma(\widehat{H})$ over semiring T applying the mapping γ to the problem $\widehat{H}$ over semiring $\widehat{T}$.

The mapping has several useful applications. First, the mapping allows evaluating bounds for the solution of H if the solution of the problem $\alpha(H)$ is known. If there is the problem H over T, and $\widehat{h}$ is an optimal solution of problem $\alpha(H)$ with semiring value $\widehat{d}$ in $\alpha(H)$ and d in H, then there is an optimal solution h of H with semiring value $\overline{d}$ such that $d \leq \overline{d} \leq \gamma(\widehat{d})$. Second, a mapping is called *order preserving* if $\bigotimes_{d \in I_1} \alpha(d) \leq_{\widehat{T}} \bigotimes_{d \in I_2} \alpha(d) \Rightarrow \bigotimes_{d \in I_1} d \leq_T \bigotimes_{d \in I_2} d$, where I_1 and I_2 are two sets of elements from D. If the mapping is order preserving then the set of all optimal solutions of the problem H over T is the subset of optimal solutions of the problem $\alpha(H)$ over $\widehat{T}$.

A problem of searching the shortest path in a graph is a CSPs problem [20]. Thus, we are able to find bounds for a weight of the shortest path in a Design Graph if we do mapping between metrics using semirings. The bounds may be used as an approximated value of the security of business process. The bounds also may be used as a starting point for searching a precise value. If the mapping is order preserving, the set of shortest paths in the graph after the mapping contains all shortest paths for the graph before the mapping. Thus, we can also use this set as a starting point for searching a precise value of a security for the business process.

5 Related Work

The process of selection the optimal business process must also be based on the quality of protection as one of the essential criteria. Such claim has been recently raised by various authors [11,12].

The first problem here is to find a method of security assessment suitable for services. Henning [10] proposed to evaluate a service against 15 security domains each of which is evaluated separately and a level (from 1 to 4) is assigned to it. Casola et al. [6] proposed a method for selection of the best alternative based on the distance between two lists of security levels using the assessment results provided by the method of Henning. In another work Casola et al. [5] proposed a more generic method for aggregation of different appraisals common for security and quality of service. Another approach to security assessment of a service is to use risk for aggregation. For example, Krautsevich et al. [13] proposed to assess risk of satisfaction of every security policy and then find the overall risk. The overall risk is then used to select the most secure service.

The second problem in assessment of services is to find the quality of protection for a complex service, i.e., service which consists of other services. Cheng et al. [7] proposed a framework for aggregation of downtime of a BP. The authors consider the BP as a set of services, rather then as a structured sequence of steps. Derwi et al. [8] analysed security in pervasive computing using multi-objective optimisation. The aim of the analysis was to analyse the workflow in order to select a set of security solutions. Our goal is slightly different, we focus on selection the best alternative. Moreover, we consider a more complex scenario, when nodes have some complex value, in contrast to the work of Derwi et al., where 0-1 metrics were considered.

The closest approach to our work is the work of Massacci and Yautsiukhin [17,16]. The authors proposed an approach which transforms a business process to a tree and selects the most secure alternative according to the defined aggregation functions. In our work, we proposed a different way of graph construction and, more important, generalised the problem using semirings. Although, the method proposed by Massacci and Yautsiukhin is able to solve wider range of problems, our current proposal is based on a well-developed mathematical structure (semirings) and, thus, automatically allows applying different existing algorithms for analysis. Moreover, semirings allow considering interoperability of services assessed using different security metrics.

Similar problems have been considered in a non-security domains. For example, Jeager et al. [18] provided several aggregation functions for such criteria as minimal execution time, cost, etc. Yu et al. [21] proposed a method for selection of alternative business processes using the graph theory. These works do not consider security assessment. Moreover, our goal is to propose a generic framework which can be applied to different metrics (satisfying the required conditions).

6   Conclusion

This paper is the first attempt to assess the security of business processes using semirings. We described a simplified decomposition of a business process into a design graph. We considered computing security metric values for implementations of business process and selecting of the best implementation on the basis of semiring-based methods for weighted graphs analysis. We provided the idea for mapping between security metrics for the case when security properties are expressed using different metrics.

We would like to notice that this paper is just an initial step towards the assessment of the security using semirings. We are going extend the method in several ways. First, we are going to relax the assumptions on the transformation of a business process into the a design graph, since orchestrator often does not have an information to avoid choices and loops. Second, we will aim at expressing more metrics as semirings. Third, we will try to determine explicitly mappings between security metrics on the basis of their formal relation. Fourth, we are going to focus on the case when parameters of the business process are dynamic. In particular, we are going to consider the cases when the security level of concrete services may change or a monitoring system returns different values, rather than the ones declared in SLAs. Another example could be a new concrete services added to the business process on-the-fly or, vice versa, become unavailable. These cases require re-evaluation of the affected part of the process and may result in selection of another composition. Finally, we would like to implement the method as a software prototype and evaluate its performance.

References

1. Business process execution language for web services version 1.1 (2003),
   http://public.dhe.ibm.com/software/dw/specs/ws-bpel/ws-bpel.pdf
   (April 13, 2011)
2. Business process model and notation (bpmn) version 2.0 (January 2011),
   http://www.omg.org/spec/BPMN/2.0 (May 19, 2011)
3. Bistarelli, S., Codognet, P., Rossi, F.: Abstracting soft constraints: Framework, properties, examples. Artificial Intelligence 139, 175–211 (2002)
4. Bistarelli, S., Montanari, U., Rossi, F.: Semiring-based constraint satisfaction and optimizatio. Journal of ACM 44(2), 201–236 (1997)
5. Casola, V., Fasolino, A.R., Mazzocca, N., Tramontana, P.: An ahp-based framework for quality and security evaluation. In: Proceedings of 12th IEEE International Conference on Computational Science and Engineering. IEEE, Los Alamitos (2009)
6. Casola, V., Mazzeo, A., Mazzocca, N., Rak, M.: A SLA evaluation methodology in Service Oriented Architectures. In: Quality of Protection, Part 3. Advances in Information Security, vol. 23, pp. 119–130. Springer, Heidelberg (2005)
7. Cheng, F., Gamarnik, D., Jengte, N., Min, W., Ramachandran, B.: Modelling operational risks in business process. Technical Report RC23872, IBM (July 2005)
8. Dewri, R., Ray, I., Ray, I., Whitley, D.: Security provisioning in pervasive environments using multi-objective optimization. In: Jajodia, S., Lopez, J. (eds.) ESORICS 2008. LNCS, vol. 5283, pp. 349–363. Springer, Heidelberg (2008)

9. Dijkstra, E.W.: A note on two problems in connexion with graphs. Numerische Mathematik 1(1), 269–271 (1959)
10. Henning, R.: Security service level agreements: quantifiable security for the enterprise? In: Proceedings of 1999 Workshop on New Security Paradigms. ACM, New York (2000)
11. Irvine, C., Levin, T.: Quality of security service. In: Proceedings of the 2000 Workshop on New Security Paradigms. ACM, New York (2000)
12. Karabulut, Y., Kerschbaum, F., Robinson, P., Massacci, F., Yautsiukhin, A.: Security and trust in it business outsourcing: a manifesto. Electronic Notes in Theoretical Computer Science 179, 47–58 (2006)
13. Krautsevich, L., Lazouski, A., Martinelli, F., Yautsiukhin, A.: Risk-based usage control for service oriented architecture. In: Proceedings of the 18th Euromicro Conference on Parallel, Distributed and Network-Based Processing. IEEE, Los Alamitos (2010)
14. Krautsevich, L., Martinelli, F., Yautsiukhin, A.: Formal approach to security metrics.: what does "more secure" mean for you? In: Proceedings of the Fourth European Conference on Software Architecture: Companion Volume. ACM, New York (2010)
15. Krautsevich, L., Martinelli, F., Yautsiukhin, A.: Formal analysis of security metrics and risk. In: Ardagna, C.A., Zhou, J. (eds.) WISTP 2011. LNCS, vol. 6633, pp. 304–319. Springer, Heidelberg (2011)
16. Massacci, F., Yautsiukhin, A.: An algorithm for the appraisal of assurance indicators for complex business processes. In: Proceedings of the 3rd Workshop on Quality of Protection. ACM, New York (2007)
17. Massacci, F., Yautsiukhin, A.: Modelling of quality of protection in outsourced business processes. In: Proceedings of the The Third International Symposium on Information Assurance and Security. IEEE, Los Alamitos (2007)
18. Jaeger, G.R.-G.M.C., Mühl, G.: QoS aggregation in web service compositions. In: Proceedings of the IEEE International Conference on e-Technology, e-Commerce and e-Service, EEE 2005 (2005)
19. Milner, R.: Communicating and Mobile Systems: the pi-Calculus. Cambridge University Press, Cambridge (1999)
20. Mohri, M.: Semiring frameworks and algorithms for shortest-distance problems. Journal of Automata, Languages and Combinatorics 7(3), 321–350 (2002)
21. Yu, T., Lin, K.-J.: A broker-based framework for qos-aware web service composition. In: Proceedings of the IEEE International Conference on e-Technology, e-Commerce and e-Service. IEEE, Los Alamitos (2005)

Adaptive Services and Energy Efficiency

(Invited Paper)

Barbara Pernici*

Politecnico di Milano,
Piazza Leonardo da Vinci 32, 20133 Milano, Italy
http://www.dei.polimi.it/people/pernici

Abstract. In general, the use of adaptive services and adaptation frameworks for services is justified by the need of providing a flexible environment for service execution in changing environments, due to changes of context or changes in requirements. Such flexibility allows providing services in ways that are most suited to the current situation of invocation of the service. A parameter that is commonly used to assess the fitness of services in changing situations is quality of service, that commonly includes parameters such as, for instance, response time, availability, trust. Adaptivity can also be the basis for building dynamic service compositions driven by other types of goals, and in this talk the focus is on building adaptive services with the goal of improving energy efficiency. Energy efficiency is defined as the ability of a system to make an efficient use of the available resources. In variable and changing contexts the use of resources might be overprovisioned, in order to be able to cope with situations of system overload, maintaining the quality of service guarantees associated with a given service. As a result, in general we see a tradeoff between requirements imposed by quality of service and energy efficiency requirements. Adaptivity can help smoothing this tradeoff, since the services can be configured dynamically to exploit the available resources in a better way.

We analyze energy efficiency in service compositions from two different perspectives. The first case is the execution of services in large service centers, in which services are executed dynamically sharing computing resources and storage systems. Such a case is studied in the GAMES (Green Active Management of IT Services) European project, in which IT resources are managed dynamically according to the context of execution and the characteristics of the services, which are driving adaptation policies. A second perspective is the use of dynamic services as enablers of energy efficiency strategies in given application domains, such as services in smart environments, e.g. in homes or buildings. In this case adaptive services can help reducing CO_2 emissions since the energy consuming resources can be controlled by adaptive services, based on the context which is providing information about the environment and behavior of inhabitants.

---

* This work has been partially supported by the EU GAMES FP7 Project
http://www.green-datacenters.eu/

W. Abramowicz et al. (Eds.): ServiceWave 2011, LNCS 6994, pp. 165–166, 2011.

Research directions in both perspectives require the ability to manage monitoring information dynamically, to ensure an adequate level of granularity of the information, and to model and control the components of the environment in order to provide adaptivity to support energy efficiency on one hand, and on the other hand to guarantee the quality of service required by the applications.

A Performance Comparison
of QoS-Driven Service Selection Approaches

Valeria Cardellini, Valerio Di Valerio, Vincenzo Grassi,
Stefano Iannucci, and Francesco Lo Presti

DISP, Università di Roma "Tor Vergata", Italy
{cardellini,di.valerio,iannucci}@ing.uniroma2.it,
{vgrassi,lopresti}@info.uniroma2.it

Abstract. Service selection has been widely investigated as an effective
adaptation mechanism that allows a service broker, offering a composite
service, to bind each task of the abstract composition to a corresponding implementation, selecting it from a set of candidates. The selection
aims typically to fulfill the Quality of Service (QoS) requirements of the
composite service, considering several QoS parameters in the decision.
We compare the performance of two representative examples of the per-
request and per-flow approaches that address the service selection issue
at a different granularity level. We present experimental results obtained
with a prototype implementation of a service broker. Our results show
the ability of the per-flow approach in sustaining an increasing traffic of
requests, while the per-request approach appears more suitable to offer
a finer customizable service selection in a lightly loaded system.

1 Introduction

A major trend to tackle the increasing complexity of service-oriented systems
(SOSs) is to design them as runtime self-adaptable systems, so that they can
operate in highly changing and evolving environments. The introduction of self-
adaptation allows a system offering a composite service to meet both functional
requirements, concerning the overall logic to be implemented, and non functional requirements, concerning the quality of service (QoS) levels that should
be guaranteed to its user. The adaptation in a SOS may take place at two different levels. At the *horizontal* level, the adaptation involves mainly the *service
selection*, that determines the binding of each task in the composite service to
actual implementations, leaving unchanged the composition logic, while at the
vertical level the composition logic can be altered [7].

In this paper, we focus on the adaptation at the horizontal level and consider
the granularity level at which the adaptation can be performed. With the *per-
request* grain, the adaptation concerns a single request addressed to a composite
service, and aims at making the system able to fulfill the QoS requirements of
that request, independently of the concurrent requests that may be addressed to
the system. With the *per-flow* grain, the adaptation concerns an overall flow of

W. Abramowicz et al. (Eds.): ServiceWave 2011, LNCS 6994, pp. 167–178, 2011.
© Springer-Verlag Berlin Heidelberg 2011

requests, and aims at fulfilling QoS requirements concerning the global properties of that flow.

In this paper, we compare the performance of the per-flow and per-request approaches considering a service broker that offers a composite service to prospective users having differentiated QoS requirements. To this end, we consider two representative methodologies that tackle the service selection at the per-request and per-flow grains and incorporate them into the MOSES (MOdel-based SElf-adaptation of SOA systems) prototype [4], a runtime adaptation framework for a SOS architected as a service broker. We compare the performance of the two methodologies under two workload scenarios characterized by different workload patterns, considering as main performance metric the fulfillment of the composite service's response time agreed by the broker with its users.

Most of the proposed methodologies for service selection focus on the *per-request* case (*e.g.*, [1,2,5,8,9,11,12]) and have been formalized as optimization problems. Zeng et al. [12] present a global planning approach based on integer programming. Ardagna and Pernici [2] model the service composition as a mixed integer linear problem and their technique is particularly efficient for large process instances. Alrifai and Risse [1] combine global optimization with local selection techniques to reduce the optimization complexity. Canfora et al. [5] follow a quite different strategy based on genetic algorithms. Since the per-request service selection problem is NP-hard, heuristic algorithms have been proposed, e.g., [8,9,11]. For the per-request approach we focus on the methodology in [2], which is one of the top performing state-of-the-art approaches.

A few works have focused on the per-flow granularity. Beside the proposal in [6], that we use as representative case of the per-flow approach and takes the form of a linear problem, a per-flow methodology is in [3], where service selection is based on a constrained non-linear optimization problem. The work in [3] is also, until now, the only comparison between the per-flow technique therein presented and the per-request proposals in [1,2]; however, the performance comparison in [3] concerns only the optimization time reduction due to the different problem formulations and is conducted through simulation. On the other hand, in this paper we compare the per-flow and per-request approaches plugging them into the MOSES prototype, thus analyzing their impact on the overall performance of a real service-oriented system.

The paper is organized as follows. In Sect. 2 we analyze the per-request and per-flow service selection approaches. In Sect. 3 we provide an overview of the MOSES system. In Sect. 4 we present the MOSES-based experiments to compare the performance and effectiveness of the two approaches. We conclude in Sect. 5.

2   QoS-Driven Service Selection Approaches

We consider a service broker, which offers to prospective users a composite service with a range of different service classes, which imply different QoS levels and monetary prices, exploiting for this purpose a set of existing concrete services. The broker acts as a full intermediary between users and concrete services, performing a role of service provider towards the users and being in turn a requestor to the concrete services used to implement the composite service. Its main task is to drive the adaptation of the service it manages to fulfill the Service Level Agreements (SLAs) negotiated with its users, given the SLAs it has negotiated with the concrete services while optimizing a suitable broker utility function, *i.e.*, response time or cost. Within this framework, one of the main broker tasks is to determine a service selection that fulfills the SLAs it negotiates with its requestors, given the SLAs it has negotiated with the providers. The selection criteria correspond to the optimization of a given utility goal of the broker.

In this section we present the per-request and the per-flow approaches to service selection, following the formulations presented in [2] and [6], respectively.

Let us denote by $\mathcal{S}$ the set of abstract tasks that compose the composite process P offered by the broker, where $S_i \in \mathcal{S}$, $i = 1, \ldots, m$, represents a single task, being m the number of tasks composing P. Figure 1(a) shows an example of business process workflow. For each task S_i, we assume that the broker has identified a pool $\Im_i = \{cs_{ij}\}$ of candidate concrete services implementing it.

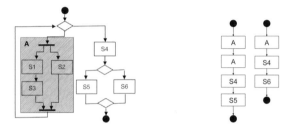

Fig. 1. Example of workflow (left) and execution paths (right)

For each candidate service, the broker negotiates a SLA with its provider, establishing the values of the QoS attributes provided by each concrete service in correspondence with a mean volume of requests generated by the broker for that service. Then, the broker may negotiate a SLA with each requestor, establishing the offered QoS level of the composite service. We consider the following subset of representative QoS attributes:

- *response time*: the interval of time elapsed from the service invocation to its completion;

- *availability*: the probability that the service is accessible when invoked;

- *cost*: the price charged for the service invocation.

Our general model for the SLA between the composite service users and the service broker (acting the provider role) consists of a tuple $\langle R_{max}, A_{min}, C_{max}, L \rangle$, where: R_{max} is the upper bound on the service response time, A_{min} is the lower bound on the service availability, C_{max} is the upper bound on the service cost per invocation. The provider can also specify the additional parameter L, that indicates that performance thresholds R_{max} and A_{min} will hold provided that the request rate generated by the users does not exceed the load threshold L.

The broker (acting the user role) negotiates and defines SLAs with the providers of the concrete services. For each $cs_{ij} \in \Im_i$, we denote with the tuple $\langle r_{ij}, a_{ij}, c_{ij}, l_{ij} \rangle$ the corresponding SLA, whose parameters have the same meaning of the SLAs negotiated by the broker with the composite service users.

The SLAs stipulated in the per-request and per-flow approaches differ in two aspects. The first one regards the granularity level at which the SLAs with the composite service users are managed by the service broker. In the per-request approach, the broker tries to meet the QoS constraints for *each individual request* submitted to the composite service, irrespective of whether it belongs to some flow generated by one or more users, and taking into account the *worst case* (*i.e.*, the maximum number of iterations in a loop and different branches). On the other hand, in the per-flow approach the service level objectives stated in the SLA concern the average value of the QoS attributes calculated over all the requests pertaining to the *flow of requests* generated by a given user. In the per-flow formulation in [6] the analysis focused on the *average case* rather than the worst one. To compare the two approaches, in this paper we modify the original formulation in [6], so that the per-flow approach takes the worst case into consideration (specifically, the maximum number of invocations to each abstract task rather than the average number). The second difference about the SLAs in the two approaches regards the load threshold, which is not contemplated by the per-request approach. As we will see in Sec. 4, this limits the applicability of the per-request approach, which hardly scales with workload increases.

2.1 Per-request Approach

In the per-request approach we need to identify the concrete service to be bound to each abstract service for all execution paths [2]. The per-request optimization problem is formulated as a Mixed Integer Linear Programming (MILP) problem. We denote with the vector $\boldsymbol{x} = [\boldsymbol{x}_1, \ldots, \boldsymbol{x}_m]$ the optimal policy for a request to the composite service, where each entry $\boldsymbol{x}_i = [x_{ij}]$, $x_{ij} \in \{0, 1\}$, $i \in \mathcal{S}$, $j \in \Im_i$, denotes the adaptation policy for task S_i and the constraint $\sum_{j \in \Im_i} x_{ij} = 1$ holds. That is, x_{ij} is the decision variable equal to 1 if task S_i is implemented by concrete service cs_{ij}, 0 otherwise. Assume that the per-request policy $\boldsymbol{x}$ determines that for a given request $\boldsymbol{x}_i = [0, 0, 1, 0]$. According to this policy, for S_i the broker binds the request to cs_{i3}.

Following the per-request strategy in [2], we need to consider all the possible *execution paths* derived from the workflow. An *execution path* ep_n is a set of tasks $ep_n = \{S_1, S_2, \ldots, S_I\} \subseteq \mathcal{S}$, such that S_1 and S_I are respectively the initial and final tasks of the path and no pair $S_i, S_j \in ep_n$ belongs to alternative branches. An execution path may also contain parallel sequences but it does not contain loops, which are *peeled* (see Fig. 1(b) for two execution paths derived from the workflow of Fig. 1(a)). A probability of execution $freq_n$ is associated with every execution path and can be evaluated as the product of the probabilities of executing the branch conditions included in the path. Branch conditions that arise from loop peeling produce other execution paths. Therefore, the set of all the execution paths identifies all the possible execution scenarios of the process.

The general goal of the optimization problem is to maximize the aggregated QoS value, considering all of the possible execution scenarios, *i.e.*, all the execution paths arising from the business process. For simplicity's sake, in the formulation below we consider that the service broker's goal is to minimize for each request the response time of the composite service it offers.

$$\text{Problem \textbf{per-request: min}} \sum_{ep_n} freq_n * R_n(\boldsymbol{x})$$

$$\text{subject to: } R_n(\boldsymbol{x}) \leq R_{max} \quad \forall ep_n \tag{1}$$

$$\log A_n(\boldsymbol{x}) \geq \log A_{min} \quad \forall ep_n \tag{2}$$

$$C_n(\boldsymbol{x}) \leq C_{max} \quad \forall ep_n \tag{3}$$

$$x_{ij} \in \{0,1\} \; \forall j \in \Im_i, \sum_{j \in \Im_i} x_{ij} = 1 \quad \forall i \in \mathcal{S} \tag{4}$$

$R_n(\boldsymbol{x})$, $A_n(\boldsymbol{x})$ and $C_n(\boldsymbol{x})$ denote the response time, availability, and cost of the execution path ep_n. We note that the minimization of the response time is only one of the possible objective functions that can be used, depending on the utility goal of the broker. An alternative expression can be found in [2], where the objective function is formulated using the weighted z-scores of QoS attributes.

2.2 Per-flow Approach

While in the per-request approach the optimization problem atomically considers a single request, in the per-flow it is assumed to have a set K of service classes, with $k \in K \subseteq \mathbb{N}$, for each business process P. Hence, the SLA with each user u of a class $k \in K$ is defined as a tuple $\langle R_{max}^k, A_{min}^k, C_{max}^k, L_u^k \rangle$. The optimization problem takes simultaneously into account the overall flow of requests belonging to the service classes. Anyway, the granularity level of the service classes may be arbitrarly fine, so that each user could have its own service class.

In the per-flow approach we need to identify the concrete service to be bound to each abstract service for all the service class. For each class k, we denote with the vector $\boldsymbol{x}^k = [\boldsymbol{x}_1^k, \ldots, \boldsymbol{x}_m^k]$ the optimal policy, where each entry $\boldsymbol{x}_i^k = [x_{ij}^k]$, $0 \leq x_{ij} \leq 1$, $i \in \mathcal{S}$, $j \in \Im_i$, denotes the adaptation policy for task S_i and the constraint $\sum_{j \in \Im_i} x_{ij}^k = 1$ holds. That is, the policy define a probabilistic binding between S_i and its implementation in $\Im_i$, whereby each entry x_{ij}^k of $\boldsymbol{x}_i^k$ denotes the probability that the class-k request will be bound to concrete service cs_{ij}. As an example, consider the case $\Im_i = \{cs_{i1}, cs_{i2}, cs_{i3}, cs_{i4}\}$ for task S_i. Assume that the per-flow policy $\boldsymbol{x}$ determines that for a given class k $\boldsymbol{x}_i^k = [0, 0.2, 0.5, 0.3]$. According to this policy, given a class-k request for S_i, the broker binds the request: with probability 0.2 to cs_{i2}, 0.5 to cs_{i3}, and 0.3 to cs_{i4}.

The per-flow approach is formulated as a Linear Programming (LP) problem, and therefore its computational cost is lower than the alternative approach. As in the per-request formulation, we consider the minimization of the response time, but in this case the latter regards the aggregated flow of requests.

$$\text{Problem } \textbf{per-flow: min} \sum_{k \in K} L^k R^k(L, \boldsymbol{x})$$

$$\textbf{subject to: } R^k(L, \boldsymbol{x}) \leq R^k_{max} \quad \forall k \in K \tag{5}$$

$$\log A^k(L, \boldsymbol{x}) \geq \log A^k_{min} \quad \forall k \in K \tag{6}$$

$$C^k(L, \boldsymbol{x}) \leq C^k_{max} \quad \forall k \in K \tag{7}$$

$$\sum_{k \in K} x^k_{ij} V^k_{\alpha,i} L^k \leq l_{ij} \quad \forall j \in \Im_i, \forall i \in \mathcal{S} \tag{8}$$

$$x^k_{ij} \geq 0 \quad \forall j \in \Im_i, \sum_{j \in \Im_i} x^k_{ij} = 1 \quad \forall i \in \mathcal{S} \tag{9}$$

where: $L = [L^k]_{k \in K}$ and $L^k = \sum_u L^k_u$ is the aggregated class-k users service request rate (being u a user); $R^k(L, \boldsymbol{x})$, $A^k(L, \boldsymbol{x})$, and $C^k(L, \boldsymbol{x})$ the class-k response time, availability, and cost, respectively, under the adaptation policy $\boldsymbol{x} = [\boldsymbol{x}^k]_{k \in K}$. Their expression requires knowledge of $V^k_{\alpha,i}$, which is the α-quantile of the number of times S_i is invoked by class-k requests: for further details we refer the reader to [6]. Here (8) represents the request load assigned to each concrete service and ensures that the load does not exceed the volume of invocations l_{ij} agreed with the service providers. As in the per-request approach, the minimization of the response time is just a possible utility goal of the broker.

3   MOSES System

MOSES is a QoS-driven runtime adaptation framework for service-oriented systems, intended to act as a *service broker* and designed with a flexible and modular system architecture. In the following, we provide an overview of the MOSES system; a detailed description of the per-flow methodology (for whom MOSES has been originally designed) and prototype can be found in [6] and [4], respectively.

We first describe the core MOSES modules and then the remaining ones that enrich the basic functionalities. The *Optimization Engine* computes the optimal solution that drives the runtime binding according to the two alternative approaches in Sect. 2. To achieve a flexible implementation, the Optimization Engine exposes the same interface to the other MOSES modules irrespectively of the specific approach. The *BPEL Engine* executes the business process, described in BPEL, that defines the user-relevant business logic. Finally, the *Adaptation Manager* is the actuator of the adaptation actions determined by the Optimization Engine: it is actually a proxy interposed between the BPEL Engine and any external service provider. Its functionality is to dynamically bind each abstract task's invocation to the real endpoint identified by the Optimization Engine.

The main execution sequence for a composite service request managed by MOSES differs according to the service selection approach. With the per-request one, every core module is involved in the execution, as depicted in Fig. 2(a): the user issues a process invocation to the BPEL Engine which, in turn, requests to the Optimization Engine the optimization problem solution, considering the specific SLA parameters agreed with the user for that request. The optimal solution, that encompasses all the abstract tasks that will be invoked during the request execution, is kept in the Storage layer, so that it can be retrieved for each abstract task to concrete implementation binding that occurs during the processing of that request. When the BPEL Engine reaches an `invoke` activity, it contacts the Adaptation Manager, which retrieves the needed runtime binding information from the Storage and invokes the selected concrete service.

The per-flow approach follows a different pattern: the optimization problem solution is not computed synchronously at the receipt of every request for the composite service, but rather only for the flow to whom that request belongs and only when some monitoring module determines its need to react to some change occurred in the MOSES environment. The corresponding sequence diagram is thus simplified, because it does not include the gray shaded box in Fig. 2(a).

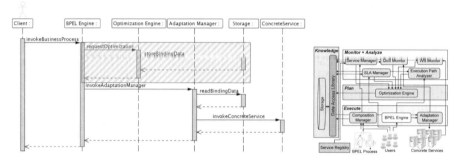

Fig. 2. MOSES system: request execution flow (left) and high-level architecture (right)

In a system subject to a quite sustained request rate, performing a per-request solution of the optimization problem could cause an excessive computational load, especially for a large-scale optimization problem, being the problem formulated as MILP. To mitigate this issue, we have improved the per-request execution sequence by introducing the caching of each calculated solution of the optimization problem corresponding to a given instance of the system model. Therefore, if a request matches with a cached solution (in terms of SLA and system parameters), similarly to the per-flow approach, the binding is retrieved from the Storage layer without involving the Optimization Engine.

MOSES is architected as a self-adaptive system based on the MAPE-K (Monitor, Analyze, Plan, Execute, and Knowledge) reference model for autonomic systems [10]. Figure 2(b) shows how the MOSES modules implement each MAPE-K macro-component, together with the system inputs (*i.e.*, the business process and the set of concrete services). This input is used to build a model (Execute), which is kept up-to-date at runtime (Monitor). The monitored parameters are analyzed (Analyze) in order to know if adaptation actions have to be taken; if needed, a new adaptation policy is calculated (Plan).

The modules in the Monitor+Analyze macro-component capture changes in the MOSES environment and, if they are relevant, modify at runtime the stored system model and trigger the Optimization Engine. The *Service Manager* and *WS Monitor* detect the addition or removal of concrete services, respectively. The *QoS Monitor* detects violations of the service level objectives stated in the SLAs between MOSES and the service providers. The *Execution Path Analyzer* tracks variations in the usage profile of the abstract tasks. The *SLA Manager* manages the arrival/departure of a user with the associated SLA, eventually performing a contract admission control.

4   Experimental Comparison

In this section, we present the experimental analysis we have conducted using the MOSES prototype to compare the per-flow and per-request approaches.

4.1   Experimental Setup

The MOSES prototype is based on the Java Business Integration (JBI) implementation called OpenESB and the relational database MySQL. We use Sun BPEL Service Engine for the business process logic, and MATLAB and CPLEX to solve respectively the per-flow and per-request optimization problems. We refer to [4] for a detailed description of the MOSES prototype.

The testing environment consists of 3 Intel Xeon quad-core servers (2 Ghz/core) with 8 GB RAM each (nodes 1, 2, and 3), and 1 KVM virtual machine with 1 CPU and 1 GB RAM (node 4); a Gb Ethernet connects all the machines. The MOSES prototype is deployed as follows: node 1 hosted all the MOSES modules in the Execute macro-component, node 2 the storage layer together with the candidate concrete services, and node 3 the modules in the Monitor+Analyze and Plan macro-components. Finally, node 4 hosted the workload generator. We consider the workflow of Fig. 1(a), composed of 6 stateless tasks, and assume that 4 concrete services (with their respective SLAs) have been identified for each task, except for tasks S_1 and S_3 for which 5 implementations have been identified. The respective SLA parameters, shown in Tab. 1(left), differ in terms of cost c_{ij}, availability a_{ij}, and response time r_{ij} (in sec). The concrete services

Table 1. SLA parameters for concrete services (left) and service classes (right)

cs	r_{ij}	a_{ij}	c_{ij}	cs	r_{ij}	a_{ij}	c_{ij}	cs	r_{ij}	a_{ij}	c_{ij}
cs_{11}	2	0.995	6	cs_{31}	1	0.995	5	cs_{51}	1	0.995	3
cs_{12}	1.8	0.99	6	cs_{32}	1	0.99	4.5	cs_{52}	2	0.99	2
cs_{13}	2	0.99	5.5	cs_{33}	2	0.99	4	cs_{53}	3	0.99	1.5
cs_{14}	3	0.995	4.5	cs_{34}	4	0.95	2	cs_{54}	4	0.95	1
cs_{15}	4	0.99	3	cs_{35}	5	0.95	1				
cs_{21}	1	0.995	2	cs_{41}	0.5	0.995	1	cs_{61}	1.8	0.99	1
cs_{22}	2	0.995	1.8	cs_{42}	0.5	0.99	0.8	cs_{62}	2	0.995	0.8
cs_{23}	1.8	0.99	1.8	cs_{43}	1	0.995	0.8	cs_{63}	3	0.99	0.6
cs_{24}	3	0.99	1	cs_{44}	1	0.95	0.6	cs_{64}	4	0.95	0.4

Class k	R_{max}^k	A_{min}^k	C_{max}^k
1	14	0.9	39
2	17	0.88	35
3	19	0.86	32
4	22	0.84	29

are simple stubs; however, their non-functional behavior conforms to the guaranteed levels expressed in their SLA. The perceived response time is obtained by modeling each service as a M/G/1/PS queue implemented inside the Web service deployed in the Tomcat container. For all concrete services the load threshold l_{ij} is equal to 10 req/sec and the response time knee is beyond it.

On the user side, we assume a scenario with four classes of the composite service managed by MOSES. The SLAs negotiated by the users are characterized by a range of QoS requirements as listed in Tab. 1(right), with users in class 1 having the most stringent performance requirements (being willing to pay the highest cost) and users in class 4 the least stringent ones (being willing to save money). The usage profile of the service classes is given by the following values for the maximum number of service invocations: $V_{\alpha,1}^k = V_{\alpha,2}^k = V_{\alpha,3}^k = 3$, $V_{\alpha,4}^k = 1$, $k \in K$; $V_{\alpha,5}^k = 0.7$, $V_{\alpha,6}^k = 0.3$, $k \in \{1,3,4\}$; $V_{\alpha,5}^2 = V_{\alpha,6}^2 = 0.5$, being $\alpha = 0.96$.

To issue requests to the composite service managed by MOSES we have developed a workload generator in C language using the Pthreads library. It mimics the behavior of users that establish SLA contracts before accessing the composite service. For the per-flow approach, upon the arrival of a new contract there is a preliminary invocation to the SLA Manager for the admission control: a new contract is accepted if the **per-flow** problem can be solved given the SLA requested by the new user and the SLAs agreed by MOSES with its currently admitted users. On the other hand, for the per-request approach there is no admission control, because each request is treated independently of other concurrent requests. Once its SLA contract has been accepted, the user u starts issuing requests to the composite service at a rate L_u^k until the contract ends.

4.2   Experimental Results

To compare the per-flow and per-request service selection approaches, we consider two different workload scenarios. In the *first scenario*, we consider each service class per time (*i.e.*, in a specific experiment the requests pertain only to one of the service classes in Table 1(right)) and we stress the MOSES system by progressively increasing the request rate. To this end, we set for all the contracts a fixed duration equal to 100 sec and $L_u^k=1$ req/sec, while the contract interarrival rate ranges from 0.01 to 0.3 contr/sec for each step of the overall experiment: this setting corresponds to an overall request arrival rate L^k from 1 to 30 req/sec. Each single step (corresponding to a given request rate) lasts 15 minutes. At each step, to avoid overwhelming a just started GlassFish instance, which has a significant setup time, the workload generator does not immediately issue requests at the required request rate but within a ramp (set to 100 sec), during which the request rate is linearly incremented until it reaches the desired value.

For space reasons we focus our analysis on the most sensitive SLA parameter to the workload increase, *i.e.*, the response time, obtained by the requests of class 1, which has the most stringent SLA requirements. Figure 3(a) shows the response time of the composite service achieved by the two alternative approaches for an increasing request rate and with the MOSES monitoring modules disabled

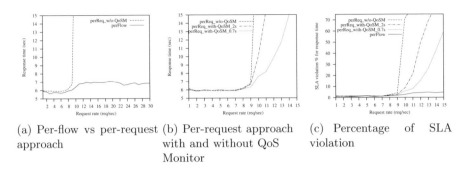

(a) Per-flow vs per-request approach

(b) Per-request approach with and without QoS Monitor

(c) Percentage of SLA violation

Fig. 3. Scenario 1: response time of the composite service for class 1

(except the SLA Manager). We observe that while the per-flow response time remains well below the agreed SLA value (equal to 14 sec), for the per-request approach (denoted by perReq_w/o-QoSM) the response time increases exponentially approximately at the concrete services' load threshold (set to 10 req/sec). In a lightly loaded system, the per-request approach is effective to address the adaptation to each single request. However, when the workload increases, it incurs in stability and management problems, since it takes adaptation actions just for a single request, independently of the other concurrent requests. Therefore, the concrete services identified as the best ones by the per-request deterministic policy are overwhelmed by the requests. On the other hand, the probabilistic per-flow policy chooses the best implementations only until their load threshold is not exceeded (see (8) of the **per-flow** problem); at that point, it distributes the requests among a subset of (possibly all) the available concrete services. This behavior is evident in Fig. 3(a), where the response time increases from around 6 to 7 sec at the concrete services' load threshold. The stable behavior of the per-flow approach is counterbalanced by an amount of dropped SLA contracts; the rejection percentage ranges from 7% (for 12 req/sec) to 59% (for 30 req/sec).

To improve the performance of the per-request approach, we activate the QoS Monitor, so that after a SLA violation the agreed values of the concrete services' parameters are updated in the system model with the measured values and the triggered Optimization Engine calculates a new solution of the **per-request** problem. The SLA violation is detected when the data monitored during one time window exceed by 20% the SLA agreed by MOSES with the service providers. We can see in Fig. 3(b) that the monitoring activity and the subsequent reaction improve the per-request behavior: when the best implementation for a given task becomes overloaded, the requests are shifted towards another concrete service determined by the new adaptation policy. However, the improvement is achieved at a cost of having a very reactive system, characterized by a quite frequent monitoring activity because the monitored data are analyzed either to 2 or even 0.7 sec, denoted by perReq_withQoSM_2s and perReq_withQoSM_0.7s in Fig. 3(b).

Let us now consider how in the first scenario the SLA is satisfied: Fig 3(c) shows the percentage of violations for the response time agreed with the users.

While under the per-flow approach only few requests suffer from a SLA violation, the percentage dramatically increases for the per-request service selection, even with a frequent monitoring activity.

In the *second scenario* we consider a mixed workload in which MOSES offers simultaneously the composite service to all the service classes in Table 1(right). We assume exponential distributions of parameters λ_k and $1/d_k$ for the contract inter-arrival time and duration and a Gaussian distribution of parameters (μ_k, σ_k) for the request inter-arrival L_u^k. Each user u generates its requests to the composite service according to an exponential distribution with parameter L_u^k. The values of the workload model parameters are $d_k = 100$ and $(\mu_k, \sigma_k) = (3, 1)$ $\forall k$; λ_k, d_k, and μ_k values have been set so that for Little's formula $L_k = \lambda_k \mu_k d_k$ and therefore on average $L = (L^k) = (1.5, 1, 1)$. For space reason, we analyze only how the response time of the composite service varies over time for the most demanding class 1, as shown in Figs. 4(a)-4(c) (the horizontal line is the agreed response time, as reported in Tab. 1). Although in the second scenario the system is only subject to a moderate workload intensity (the average overall request rate is 6,37 req/sec, being 20,4 req/sec the peak and 4,29 req/sec the standard deviation), we find that the response time level achieved by the per-flow approach has a much more stable trend and does not suffer from the SLA violations of the per-request service selection. The percentage of dropped contracts by the per-flow approach is 12%.

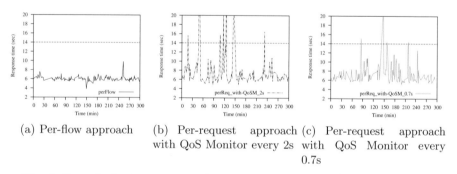

(a) Per-flow approach   (b) Per-request approach (c) Per-request approach with QoS Monitor every 2s with QoS Monitor every 0.7s

Fig. 4. Scenario 2: response time of the composite service over time for class 1

5   Conclusions

In this paper, we have compared the per-flow and per-request approaches to address the service selection issue for a service broker which offers a composite service with different QoS levels. Our results show that in a lightly loaded system, it is effective to tailor the service selection to each single request, independently of other concurrent requests, to customize the system with respect to that single request. On the other hand, in a system subject to a quite sustained flow of requests, performing a per-request selection could incur in stability problems, since the "local" decisions could conflict with the decisions independently determined for other concurrent requests. Furthermore, the solution of the per-request problem at a frequent rate could cause an excessive computational load due to its MILP formulation. In the latter scenario, the per-flow approach is likely to be more effective, even if it loses the potentially finer customization features of the per-request approach and can drop SLA contracts when there are not enough system resources. We plan to extend the performance comparison to other representative proposals for service selection and to address the lack of a "global" system view that currently affects the per-request approach.

References

1. Alrifai, M., Risse, T.: Combining global optimization with local selection for efficient qos-aware service composition. In: Proc. WWW 2009, pp. 881–890 (2009)
2. Ardagna, D., Pernici, B.: Adaptive service composition in flexible processes. IEEE Trans. Softw. Eng. 33(6), 369–384 (2007)
3. Ardagna, D., Mirandola, R.: Per-flow optimal service selection for web services based processes. J. Syst. Softw. 83(8) (2010)
4. Bellucci, A., Cardellini, V., Di Valerio, V., Iannucci, S.: A scalable and highly available brokering service for SLA-based composite services. In: Maglio, P.P., Weske, M., Yang, J., Fantinato, M. (eds.) ICSOC 2010. LNCS, vol. 6470, pp. 527–541. Springer, Heidelberg (2010)
5. Canfora, G., Di Penta, M., Esposito, R., Villani, M.: A framework for QoS-aware binding and re-binding of composite web services. J. Syst. Softw. 81(10) (2008)
6. Cardellini, V., Casalicchio, E., Grassi, V., Lo Presti, F., Mirandola, R.: Flow-based service selection for web service composition supporting multiple qos classes. In: Proc. IEEE ICWS 2007, pp. 743–750 (2007)
7. Hassine, A.B., Matsubara, S., Ishida, T.: A constraint-based approach to horizontal web service composition. In: Cruz, I., Decker, S., Allemang, D., Preist, C., Schwabe, D., Mika, P., Uschold, M., Aroyo, L.M. (eds.) ISWC 2006. LNCS, vol. 4273, pp. 130–143. Springer, Heidelberg (2006)
8. Liang, Q., Wu, X., Lau, H.C.: Optimizing service systems based on application-level QoS. IEEE Trans. Serv. Comput. 2, 108–121 (2009)
9. Menascé, D.A., Casalicchio, E., Dubey, V.: On optimal service selection in service oriented architectures. Perform. Eval. 67, 659–675 (2010)
10. Salehie, M., Tahvildari, L.: Self-adaptive software: Landscape and research challenges. ACM Trans. Auton. Adapt. Syst. 4(2), 1–42 (2009)
11. Yu, T., Zhang, Y., Lin, K.J.: Efficient algorithms for web services selection with end-to-end qos constraints. ACM Trans. Web 1(1), 1–26 (2007)
12. Zeng, L., Benatallah, B., Dumas, M., Kalagnamam, J., Chang, H.: QoS-aware middleware for web services composition. IEEE Trans. Softw. Eng. 30(5) (2004)

Optimal Admission Control
for a QoS-Aware Service-Oriented System

Marco Abundo, Valeria Cardellini, and Francesco Lo Presti

DISP, Università di Roma "Tor Vergata", Italy
marco.abundo@gmail.com, cardellini@ing.uniroma2.it,
lopresti@info.uniroma2.it

Abstract. In the service computing paradigm, a service broker can build new applications by composing network-accessible services offered by loosely coupled independent providers. In this paper, we address the admission control problem for a a service broker which offers to prospective users a composite service with a range of different Quality of Service (QoS) classes. We formulate the problem as a Markov Decision Process (MDP) problem with the goal of maximizing the broker revenue while guaranteeing non-functional QoS requirements to its already admitted users. To assess the effectiveness of the MDP-based admission control, we present experimental results where we compare the optimal decisions obtained by the analytical solution of the MDP with other policies.

1   Introduction

In the Service Oriented Architecture (SOA) paradigm, the design of complex software is facilitated by the possibility to build new applications by composing loosely-coupled services. The so built composite service is offered by a *service broker* to different classes of users characterized by diverse Quality of Service (QoS) requirements. To this end, the broker and its users generally engage in a negotiation process, which culminates in the definition of a *Service Level Agreement* (SLA) about their respective duties and QoS expectations.

In the upcoming Internet service marketplace, multiple service providers may offer similar competing services corresponding to a functional description but at differentiated levels of QoS and cost. Therefore, in undertaking the management of the SOA-based system that offers the composite service, the broker has to select at runtime the best set of component services implementing the needed functionalities (with which we assume the service broker has contracted a SLA specifying the QoS the component service will provide to the broker) in order to maximize some utility goal (e.g., its revenue) while guaranteeing the QoS levels to the composite service users.

A significant number of research efforts have been devoted to service selection issues, e.g., [1, 6, 7]. The common aim of these works is to identify for each abstract functionality in the composite service a pool (eventually a singleton) of corresponding concrete services, selecting them from a set of candidates. All these efforts implicitily assume that a user is admitted to the service as long

W. Abramowicz et al. (Eds.): ServiceWave 2011, LNCS 6994, pp. 179–190, 2011.

as enough resources are available to serve its requests at the required QoS level without violating existing users' QoS. Nevertheless, it is not surprising that such a simple policy, which we will call hereafter *blind*, might not turn to be optimal with respect to maximizing the broker utility.

In this paper, to overcome the limitations of the aforementioned results we study the admission problem for the *MOdel-based SElf-adaptation of SOA systems* (MOSES) service broker we proposed in [4, 7], which manages a composite service offering differentiated QoS service classes. We formulate the optimal admission control problem as a Markov Decision Process (MDP) problem with the goal to maximise the broker discounted expected infinite horizon reward while guaranteeing non-functional QoS requirements to its users. Our results show the MDP-based admission control always guarantees significantly higher average rewards than the *blind* policy. We also considered finite horizon policies which are computationally more efficient than the infinite horizon counterpart and that allow us to tradeoff optimality with computational complexity/time-horizon length. Our findings show that even with the simple 1-step horizon policy it is possible to achieve better results with respect to the *blind* policy, quite close to the infinite horizon optimum, but at a fraction of the computational cost.

A considerable number of research efforts have focused on the application of MDP-based models and stochastic programming to SOA systems and, more generally, to software systems [2, 3, 5, 8–10, 12, 14]. Some of these works have proposed self-healing approaches in order to support the reconfiguration of running services, e.g., [3, 8], considering also proactive solutions for SOA systems [12]. Some recent approaches [9, 10, 14] have used MDPs to model service composition with the aim to create automatically an abstract workflow of the service composition that satisfies functional and non-functional requirements, and also to allow the composite service to adapt dynamically to a varying environment [14]. Some of the aforementioned works have proposed MDP-based admission control in service-oriented systems [2, 5] and are therefore most closely related to ours. In [2] Bannazadeh and Leon-Garcia have proposed an admission control for service-oriented systems which uses an online optimization approach for maximizing the system revenue, while in [5] Bichler and Setzer have applied an MDP-based formulation to tackle admission control for media on demand services. However, both these works do not consider composite services organized according to some business logic, while our approach is able to manage the admission control for a composite service whose workflow entails the composition patterns typical of orchestration languages such as BPEL [11], which is the de-facto standard. To the best of our knowledge, the approach we propose in this paper is the first admission control policy based on MDPs for QoS-aware composite services.

The rest of the paper is organized as follows. In Section 2 we present the SOA system managed by the service broker. In Section 3 we present our MDP problem. Then, in Section 4 we sketch out the implementation of our admission policies and present the simulation experiments to assess the effectiveness of the proposed MDP-based approach. Section 5 concludes the paper.

2   MOSES System

MOSES is a QoS-driven runtime adaptation framework for SOA-based systems, designed as a service broker. In this section, we provide an overview on the MOSES system for which we propose in this paper MDP-based admission control policies. A detailed description of the MOSES methodology, architecture and implementing prototype can be found in [7] and [4], respectively.

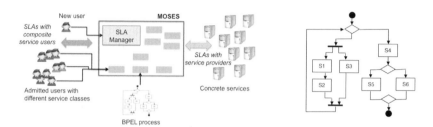

Fig. 1. MOSES operating evenironment (left); MOSES-compliant workflow (right)

MOSES acts as a third-party intermediary between service users and providers, performing a role of provider towards the users and being in turn a requestor to the providers of the concrete services. It advertises and offers the composite service with a range of service classes which imply different QoS levels and monetary prices. Figure 1 (left) shows a high-level view of the MOSES environment, where we have highlighted the MOSES component on which we focus in this paper, i.e., the *SLA Manager*. The workflow that defines the composition logic of the service managed by MOSES can include all the different types of BPEL structured activities: `sequence`, `switch`, `while`, `pick`, and `flow` [11]. Figure 1 (right) shows an example of BPEL workflow, described as a UML2 activity diagram, that can be managed by MOSES. The figure also shows the functionalities (named *tasks* and represented by $S_1, \ldots, S_6$) needed to compose the new added value service.

MOSES performs a two-fold role of service provider towards its users, and of service user with respect to the providers of the concrete services it uses to implement the composite service it is managing. Hence, it is involved in two types of SLAs, corresponding to these two roles. MOSES presently considers the average value of the following attributes:

- *response time*: the interval of time elapsed from the service invocation to its completion;
- *reliability*: the probability that the service completes its task when invoked;
- *cost*: the price charged for the service invocation.

Our general model for the SLA between the provider and the user of a service consists of a tuple $\langle T, C, R, L \rangle$, where: T is the upper bound on the average service response time, C is the service cost per invocation, R is the lower bound on the service reliability. The provider guarantees that thresholds T and R will hold on average provided that the user request rate does not exceed L.

In the case of the SLAs between the composite service users and MOSES (acting the provider role), we assume that MOSES offers a set K of service classes. Hence, the SLA for each user u of a class $k \in K$ is defined as a tuple $\langle T_{\max}^k, C^k, R_{\min}^k, L_u^k, P_\tau^k, P_\rho^k \rangle$. The two additional parameters P_τ^k and P_ρ^k represent the penalty rates MOSES will refund its users with for possible violations of the service class response time and reliability, respectively. All these coexisting SLAs (for each u and k) define the QoS objectives that MOSES must meet. We observe that MOSES considers SLAs stating conditions that should hold globally for a *flow* of requests generated by a user. To meet these objectives, we assume that MOSES (acting the user role) has already identified for each task $S_i \in \mathcal{F}$ in the composite service a pool of corresponding concrete services implementing it. The SLA contracted between MOSES and the provider of the concrete service $i.j \in I_i$ is defined as a tuple $\langle t_{ij}, c_{ij}, r_{ij}, l_{ij} \rangle$. These SLAs define the constraints within which MOSES should try to meet its QoS objectives.

New users requesting the composite service managed by MOSES are subject to an accept/deny decision, with which MOSES determines whether or not it is convenient to admit the user in the system according to the user SLA and the system state. We will present in Section 3 the MDP-based formulation of the admission control carried out by the SLA Manager component. Once a user requesting a SLA has been admitted by the SLA Manager, it starts generating requests to the composite service managed by MOSES until its contract ends. Each user request involves the invocations of the tasks according to the logic specified by the composite service workflow. For each task invocation, MOSES binds dynamically the task of the abstract composition to an actual implementation (i.e., concrete service), selecting it from the pool of network accessible service providers that offer it. We model this selection by associating with each task S_i a vector $\boldsymbol{x}_i = (\boldsymbol{x}_i^1, ..., \boldsymbol{x}_i^{|K|})$, where $\boldsymbol{x}_i^k = [x_{ij}^k]$ and $i.j \in I_i$. Each entry x_{ij}^k of $\boldsymbol{x}_i^k$ denotes the probability that the class-k request will be bound to concrete service $i.j$. MOSES determines the service selection strategy $\boldsymbol{x}$ by solving the following revenue maximization problem **MAXRW**:

$$\mathbf{max} \; C(\Lambda, \boldsymbol{x}) = \sum_{k \in K} \Lambda^k \left[C^k - \left(C^k(\Lambda, \boldsymbol{x}) + P_\tau^k \tau^k + P_\rho^k \rho^k \right) \right]$$

$$\textbf{subject to:} \; T^k(\Lambda, \boldsymbol{x}) \leq T_{\max}^k + \tau^k, \quad k \in K \tag{1}$$

$$R^k(\Lambda, \boldsymbol{x}) \geq R_{\min}^k - \rho^k, \quad k \in K \tag{2}$$

$$C^k(\Lambda, \boldsymbol{x}) \leq C^k, \quad k \in K \tag{3}$$

$$l_{ij}(\Lambda, \boldsymbol{x}) \leq l_{ij}, \quad j \in I_i, \; i \in \mathcal{F} \tag{4}$$

$$r_{ij}^k \geq 0, j \in I_i, \sum_{j \in I_i} r_{ij}^k = 1, \quad i \in \mathcal{F}, \; k \in K \tag{5}$$

$$\tau^k \geq 0, \rho^k \geq 0, \quad k \in K \tag{6}$$

where: $\Lambda = (\Lambda^k)_{k \in K}$ and $\Lambda^k = \sum_u L_u^k$ is the aggregate class-k users service request rate; $T^k(\Lambda, \boldsymbol{x})$, $R^k(\Lambda, \boldsymbol{x})$, and $C^k(\Lambda, \boldsymbol{x})$ the class-k response time, reliability and implementation cost, respectively, under the service selection strategy $\boldsymbol{x}$. The objective function $C(\Lambda, \boldsymbol{x})$ is the broker per unit of time reward. It is the sum over all service classes of the service class-k invocation rate Λ^k times the per invocation reward, that is C^k minus the cost $C^k(\Lambda, \boldsymbol{x})$ (which is increased by the penalty $P_\tau^k \tau^k + P_\rho^k \rho^k$ for service violation). For space limitations we omit the details on inequalities (1)-(6), which can be found in [7].

Since the proposed optimization problem is a Linear Programming problem it can be efficiently solved via standard techniques. We will denote by $\boldsymbol{x}^*(\Lambda)$ the optimal service selection policy.

3   An MDP Formulation for MOSES Admission Control

In this section we formulate the MOSES admission control problem as a Continuous-time Markov Decision Process (CTMDP). We first present our broker model and define the user state space model. Then, we define the broker actions/decisions and present the state transition dynamics. Finally, we present our performance criterion and how to compute the optimal policy.

3.1   Model

We consider a broker that has a fixed set of candidate concrete services (and associated SLAs) with which offers the composite service to prospective users. Prospective users contact the broker to establish a SLA for a given class of service k and for a given period of length. We model the arrival process for service class k and contract duration of expected length $1/\mu_d$ as a Poisson process with rate λ_d^k. We assume that the contract durations are exponentially distributed with finite mean $1/\mu_d > 0$, $d \in D = \{1, \ldots, d_{\max}\}$ (which we assume for the sake of simplicity to not depend on the service class k). Upon a user arrival, the broker has to decide whether to admit a user or not. If a user is admitted, the user will generate a flow of requests at rate L^k for the duration of the contract. When a user contract expires, the user simply leaves the system. The broker set of actions is then just the pair $\mathcal{A} = \{a_a, a_r\}$, with a_a denoting the accepting decision and a_r the refusal decision.

We model the state of our system as in [15]. The state s consists of the following two components:

- the broker users matrix $n = (n_d^k)_{k \in K, d \in D}$, where n_d^k denotes the number of users for each service class k and expected contract duration $1/\mu_d$ before the last random event occurred;
- the last random event ω.

n takes values in the set $\mathcal{N}$ of all possible broker user matrices for which the optimization problem **MAXRW** introduced in Section 2 has a feasible solution.

ω represents the last random event, *i.e.*, a user arrival or departure, occurred in the system. We will denote it by a matrix $\omega = (\omega_d^k)_{k \in K, d \in D}$, where $\omega_d^k = 1$ if a new user makes an admission request for service class k and for a contract duration with mean $1/\mu_d$, $\omega_d^k = -1$ if an existing user of class k and contract duration of mean $1/\mu_d$ terminates his contract, and $\omega_d^k = 0$ otherwise. We will denote by Ω the set of all possible events.

The state space $\mathcal{S}$ consists of all possible user configuration-next event combinations, *i.e.*, $\mathcal{S} = \{ s = (n, \omega) | n \in \mathcal{N}, \omega \in \Omega, \omega_d^k \geq 0 \text{ if } n_d^k = 0 \}$. It is important to observe that, following [15], there is a subtle relationship between a state $s = (n, \omega)$ value and the associated user configuration n. Indeed, if the current state is $s = (n, \omega)$ it means that the user configuration *was* n before the last occurred event ω. The actual current user configuration is instead n', which depends on both the event ω and the decision a taken by the broker as discussed below.

For each state $s = (n, \omega)$, the set of available broker actions/decisions $A(s)$ depends on the event ω. If ω denotes an arrival, the broker has to determine whether to accept it or not; thus $A(s) = \{a_a, a_r\}$. If, instead, ω denotes a contract termination, there is no decision to take and $A(s) = \emptyset$.

System transitions are caused by users arrivals or departures. Given the current state $s = (n, \omega)$, the new state $s' = (n', \omega')$ is determined as follows:

- ω' is the event occurred;
- n' is the user configuration *after* the event ω (the previous event) and the decision $a \in A(s)$ taken by the broker upon ω. n' differs from n upon a user departure or a user arrival provided it is accepted. In compact form we can write $n' = n + \omega \mathbf{1}_{\{a \neq a_r\}}$, where $\mathbf{1}_{\{.\}}$ is the indicator function.

Table 1. System transitions

Event ω	Decision	Next state $s' = (n', \omega')$
arrival	admitted ($a = a_a$)	$(n + \omega, \omega')$
	refused ($a = a_r$)	(n, ω')
departure	-	$(n + \omega, \omega')$

Observe that while the system is in state s the actual user configuration is n', which will characterize the next state s'. Table 1 summarizes all the possible transitions. The associated transition rates are then readily obtained:

$$q_{ss'} = \begin{cases} \lambda_d^k & \omega_d'^k = 1 \\ \mu_d n_d'^k & \omega_d'^k = -1 \end{cases} \tag{7}$$

An admission control policy π for the service broker is a function $\pi : \mathcal{S} \to \mathcal{A}$ which defines for each state $s \in \mathcal{S}$ whether the broker should admit or refuse a new user. We are interested in determining the admission control policy which maximizes the broker discounted expected reward/profit with discounting rate $\alpha > 0$. For a given policy π let $v_\alpha^\pi(s)$ be the expected infinite-horizon discounted reward given s as initial state, defined as

$v_\alpha^\pi(s) = E_s^\pi \left\{ \sum_{i=1}^\infty \int_{\sigma_n}^{\sigma_{n+1}} e^{-\alpha u} c(s_i, a_i) du \right\}$ where $\sigma_1, \sigma_2, \ldots$ represents the time of the successive system decision epochs which, in our model, coincide with user arrivals and departures. $c(s_i, a_i)$ is the broker reward between decision epochs i and $i+1$, that is MOSES reward under the optimal service selection strategy x^* between the two decision epochs. To compute its value, let us denote by $\Lambda^k(s,a)$ the aggregate class-k users service request rate when the state is s and the broker action was a and let $\Lambda(s,a) = (\Lambda^k(s,a))_{k \in K}$. Then, $\Lambda^k(s,a) = n'^k L^k$ where $n' = n + \omega \mathbf{1}_{\{a \neq a_r\}}$ is the next state configuration, given the actual state is $s = (n, \omega)$ and decision a was taken, and $n'^k = \sum_{d \in D} n_d'^k$ is the number of users in service class k. We thus have

$$c(s, a) = C(\Lambda(s,a), x^*(\Lambda(s,a)) \tag{8}$$

The optimal policy π^* satisfies the optimality equation (see 11.5.4 in [13]):

$$v_\alpha^{\pi^*}(s) = \sup_{a \in A(s)} \left\{ \frac{c(s,a)}{\alpha + \beta(s,a)} + \sum_{s' \in S} \frac{q_{ss'}}{\alpha + \beta(s,a)} v_\alpha^{\pi^*}(s') \right\}, \forall s \in S \tag{9}$$

where $\beta(s,a)$ is the rate out of state s if action a is chosen, i.e., $\beta(s,a) = \sum_{k \in K} \sum_{d \in D} (\lambda_d^k + n_d'^k \mu_d)$. In (9), the first term $\frac{c(s,a)}{\alpha + \beta(s,a)}$ represents the expected total discounted reward between the first two decision epochs given the system initially occupied state s and taken decision a. The second term represents the expected discounted reward after the second decision epoch under the optimal policy. The optimal policy π^* can be obtained by solving the optimality equation (9) via standard techniques, e.g., value iteration, LP formulation [13].

A potential limitation of the infinite-horizon approach we presented above arises from the curse of dimensionality which gives rise to state explosion. As shown in the next section, in our setting, even for small problem instances, we incurred high computational costs because of the large state space. As a consequence, this approach might not be feasible for online operation where a new policy must be recomputed as user statistics or the set of concrete services vary over time unless we resort to heuristics. In alternative, we also consider finite horizon policies which not only are amenable to efficient implementations, and allow to trade-off complexity vs horizon length, but also take into account the fact that in a time varying system it might not be appropriate to consider a stationary, infinite horizon policy. In a finite-horizon setting, our aim is to optimize the expected N step finite-horizon discounted reward given s as initial state, $v_\alpha^{\pi N}(s)$, which is defined as (3.1) with ∞ replaced by N in the summation, where N defines the number of decision epochs over which the reward is computed.

For finite horizon problem, the optimal policy π_N^* satisfies the following optimality equation:

$$v_{i,\alpha}^{\pi_N^*}(s) = \sup_{a \in A(s)} \left\{ \frac{c(s,a)}{\alpha + \beta(s,a)} + \sum_{s' \in S} \frac{q_{ss'}}{\alpha + \beta(s,a)} v_{i+1,\alpha}^{\pi_N^*}(s') \right\}, \forall s \in S \tag{10}$$

where $v_{i,\alpha}^{\pi_N}(s)$ is the expected discounted reward under policy π from decision epoch i up to N and $v_\alpha^{\pi_N}(s) = v_{1,\alpha}^{\pi_N}(s)$. The optimal policy π_N^* can be computed directly from (10) via backward induction by exploiting the recursive nature of the optimality equation [13].

4   Experimental Analysis

In this section, we present the experimental analysis we have conducted through simulation to assess the effectiveness of the MDP-based admission control. We first describe the simulation model and then present the simulation results.

4.1   Simulation Model

Following the broker model in Section 3, we consider an open system model, where new users belonging to a given service class $k \in K$ and expected contract duration $1/\mu_d$ arrive according to a Poisson process of rate λ_d^k. We also assume exponential distributed contract duration. Once a user is admitted, it starts generating requests to the composite service according to an exponential inter-arrival time with rate L_u^k until its contract expires.

The discrete-event simulator has been implemented in C language using the CSIM 20 tool. Multiple independent random number streams have been used for each stochastic model component. The experiments involved a minimum of 10,000 completed requests to the composite service; for each measured mean value the 95% confidence interval has been obtained using the run length control of CSIM. The admission control policies have been implemented in MATLAB.

4.2   Experimental Results

We illustrate the dynamic behavior of our admission control policies assuming that MOSES provides the composite service whose workflow is shown in Figure 1 (right). For the sake of simplicity, we assume that two candidate concrete services (with their respective SLAs) have been identified for each task, except for S_2 for which four concrete services have been identified. The respective SLAs differ in terms of cost c, reliability r, and response time t (being the latter measured in sec.); the corresponding values are reported in Table 2 (left) (where $i.j$ denotes the concrete service). For all concrete services, $l_{ij} = 10$ invocations per second.

On the user side, we assume a scenario with four classes (i.e., $1 \le k \le 4$) of the composite service managed by MOSES. The SLAs negotiated by the users are characterized by a wide range of QoS requirements as listed in Table 2 (right), with users in class 1 having the most stringent performance requirements and highest cost paid to the broker, and users in class 4 the least stringent performance requirements and lowest cost. The penalty rates P_τ^k and P_ρ^k are equal to the reciprocal of the corresponding SLA parameter. Furthermore, for each service class we consider two possible contract durations (i.e., $d_{\max} = 2$),

Table 2. Concrete service (left) and service class (right) SLA parameters

$i.j$	c_{ij}	r_{ij}	t_{ij}	$i.j$	c_{ij}	r_{ij}	t_{ij}	$i.j$	c_{ij}	r_{ij}	t_{ij}
1.1	6	0.995	2	2.4	1	0.95	5	5.1	2	0.99	2
1.2	3	0.99	4	3.1	2	0.995	1	5.2	1.4	0.95	4
2.1	4.5	0.99	1	3.2	1.8	0.995	2	6.1	0.5	0.99	1.8
2.2	4	0.99	2	4.1	1	0.995	0.5	6.2	0.4	0.95	4
2.3	2	0.95	4	4.2	0.8	0.99	1				

Class k	C^k	$R^k_{\min}$	$T^k_{\max}$
1	25	0.95	7
2	18	0.9	11
3	15	0.9	15
4	12	0.85	18

which can be either *short* or *long*. Therefore, the system state $s = (n, \omega)$ is characterized by a 4×2 broker users matrix n, as defined in Section 3.1.

We compare the results of the following admission control policies for MOSES. Under the **infinite horizon** policy, the admission control decisions are based on the optimal policy π^*, which is obtained by solving the optimality equation (9) via the value iteration method setting the discount rate $\alpha = -\ln(0.9) = 0.1054$. With the **1-step horizon** policy, the admission control decisions are based on the optimal policy π^*_N with a local 1-step reasoning, *i.e.*, $N = 1$. In this case, as explained in Section 3, we obtain π^*_N by solving (10). Finally, with the **blind** policy, no reasoning about future rewards is considered, because MOSES accepts a new contract request if the service selection optimization problem **MAXRW** described in Section 2 can be solved given the SLA requested by the new user and the SLAs agreed by MOSES with its currently admitted users.

We consider three different scenarios, where we vary the arrival rate of the contract requests. In all the scenarios the amount of request generated by an admitted user is $L^k_u = 1$ req/sec and the contract duration is fixed to $(1/\mu_d)_{d \in D} = (50, 200)$, where the first component corresponds to short contracts and the latter to longer contracts. In the following, we will denote short and long contracts with s and l, respectively.

In the *first scenario*, we set the matrix $(\lambda^k_d)_{k \in K, d \in D} = \begin{pmatrix} 0.02 & 0.02 \\ 0.02 & 0.02 \\ 0.02 & 0.02 \\ 0.02 & 0.02 \end{pmatrix}$, that is all the contract requests arrive at the same rate, irrespectively of the service class.

In the *second scenario*, $(\lambda^k_d)_{k \in K, d \in D} = \begin{pmatrix} 0.02 & 0.02 \\ 0.02 & 0.02 \\ 0.04 & 0.04 \\ 0.08 & 0.08 \end{pmatrix}$, that is contract requests for service classes 3 and 4 arrive at a double (class 3) or quadruple (class 4) rate with respect to requests for service classes 1 and 2. In the *third scenario*, $(\lambda^k_d)_{k \in K, d \in D} = \begin{pmatrix} 0.08 & 0.08 \\ 0.04 & 0.04 \\ 0.02 & 0.02 \\ 0.02 & 0.02 \end{pmatrix}$, that is contract requests for service classes 1 and 2 arrive at a quadruple (class 1) or double (class 2) rate with respect to requests for service classes 3 and 4. To compare the performance of the different admission control policies, we consider as main metrics the average reward per second of the service broker over the simulation period and the percentage of rejected contract requests. Furthermore, for the MDP-based admission control policies we analyze also the mean execution time. For space reason, we do not show the QoS satisfaction levels achieved by the users for the response time, reliability, and cost SLA parameters. Anyway, we found that once a contract request has been accepted, the QoS levels specified in the SLAs are quite largely met by MOSES for each flow of service class, independently on the admission policy.

Table 3. Average reward per second

Admission policy	Scenario 1	Scenario 2	Scenario 3
Blind	40.536	25.012	58.801
1-step horizon	59.607	63.865	75.751
Infinite horizon	66.737	65.553	76.116

Table 3 shows the average reward per second earned by the service broker for the various admission control policies and under the different considered scenarios. As expected, the infinite horizon policy maximizes the broker reward, achieving significant improvements over the blind policy under all scenarios. In these scenarios, the 1-step horizon policy yields results close to the optimum.

We now separately analyze the performance metrics for each scenario. From Table 3 we can see that in the first scenario the 1-step horizon policy let the broker earn 47% more than the blind policy, while the improvement achieved by infinite horizon policy over blind is even higher, being equal to almost 65%.

Figure 2 (left) shows the percentage of rejected SLA contracts for all the service classes, distinguishing further between short and long contract durations, achieved by the different admission control policies (for each policy, the first four bars regard the short-term contracts for the various service classes, while the latter four the long-term ones).

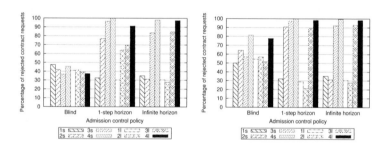

Fig. 2. Rejected contract requests under scenario 1 (left) and 2 (right)

While the blind policy is not able to differentiate among the service classes from the admission control point of view, the MDP-based policies tend to accept the more profitable classes 1 and 2, which pay more for the composite service, and to reject the less profitable ones.

For the second scenario, which is characterized by a higher contract request arrival rate for classes 3 and 4, Figure 2 (right) shows that, as expected, all the admission control policies reject a higher percentage of contract requests for these classes with respect to the first scenario. However, MDP-based admission control, independently on the horizon width, prefers clearly service classes 1 and 2 with respect to 3 and 4, since the former ones yield higher rewards than the latter which instead experienced high refusal percentages. We also observe that the infinite horizon policy slightly differentiates within classes 1 and 2 according to the contract duration: long-term contracts are preferred to short-term ones (a reduction in the rejection decisions equal to 16% and 11% for long-term classes 1 and 2, respectively). Analyzing the average reward reported in Table 3, we can see that under the second scenario the MDP-based policies allow the broker to more than double its revenue: the 1-step horizon and infinite horizon policies let the broker earn 155% and 162% respectively more than the blind policy. In

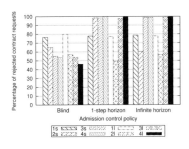

Fig. 3. Rejected contract requests under scenario 3

the third scenario, where classes 1 and 2 experience higher arrivals rates the MDP-based admission control policies still allow to achieve a good improvement in the reward gained by the broker, as reported in Table 3 (29% and 29.5% for 1-step horizon and infinite horizon policies, respectively, when compared to the blind one). Figure 3 shows the corresponding rejection percentage.

Under all the considered scenarios, the 1-step horizon policy allows the service broker to make a profit comparable, although slightly reduced, to the infinite horizon policy. However, a strong argument in favor of the 1-step horizon policy regards the execution time needed to achieve the optimal decision. We have measured the mean execution time on a machine with Intel Core 2 Duo T7250 2 GHz and 2 GB RAM. The 1-step horizon policy requires only 0.0021 sec, while the infinite horizon one requires 233 sec. for the state space generation, 5502 sec. for the matrix generation, and 800 sec. for the value iteration method. This long execution time is also due to the computation of $c(s, a)$, which requires to solve the service selection optimization problem (see (8)). Therefore, the reduced computational cost of the 1-step horizon policy makes it amenable to take online admission control decisions.

5 Conclusions

In this paper, we have studied the admission control problem for a service broker, MOSES, which offers to prospective users a composite service with different QoS levels. We have formulated the admission control problem as a Markov Decision Process with the goal to maximize the broker discounted reward, while guaranteeing non-functional QoS requirements to its users. We have considered both infinite-horizon and the less computational demanding finite-horizon cost functions. We have compared the different solutions through simulation experiments. Our results show that the MDP-based policies guarantee much higher profit to the broker while guaranteeing the users QoS levels with respect to a simple myopic policy which accepts users as long as the broker has sufficient resources to serve them. In particular, the simple 1-step horizon policy achieves near to optimal performance at a fraction of the computational cost which makes it amenable to online implementation.

In our future work we plan to implement the MDP-based admission control in the existing MOSES prototype and run experiments in realistic scenarios.

References

1. Ardagna, D., Pernici, B.: Adaptive service composition in flexible processes. IEEE Trans. Softw. Eng. 33(6), 369–384 (2007)
2. Bannazadeh, H., Leon-Garcia, A.: Online optimization in application admission control for service oriented systems. In: Proc. IEEE APSCC 2008 (2008)
3. Beckmann, M., Subramanian, R.: Optimal replacement policy for a redundant system. OR Spectrum 6(1), 47–51 (1984)
4. Bellucci, A., Cardellini, V., Di Valerio, V., Iannucci, S.: A scalable and highly available brokering service for SLA-based composite services. In: Maglio, P.P., Weske, M., Yang, J., Fantinato, M. (eds.) ICSOC 2010. LNCS, vol. 6470, pp. 527–541. Springer, Heidelberg (2010)
5. Bichler, M., Setzer, T.: Admission control for media on demand services. Service Oriented Computing and Applications 1(1), 65–73 (2007)
6. Canfora, G., Di Penta, M., Esposito, R., Villani, M.: A framework for QoS-aware binding and re-binding of composite web services. J. Syst. Softw. 81 (2008)
7. Cardellini, V., Casalicchio, E., Grassi, V., Lo Presti, F.: Flow-based service selection for web service composition supporting multiple QoS classes. In: Proc. IEEE ICWS 2007, pp. 743–750 (2007)
8. Chen, M., Feldman, R.: Optimal replacement policies with minimal repair and age-dependent costs. Eur. J. Oper. Res. 98(1), 75–84 (1997)
9. Doshi, P., Goodwin, R., Akkiraju, R., Verma, K.: Dynamic workflow composition: using Markov decision processes. Int'l J. Web Service Res. 2(1) (2005)
10. Gao, A., Yang, D.q., Tang, S.w., Zhang, M.: Web Service Composition Using Markov Decision Processes. In: Fan, W., Wu, Z., Yang, J. (eds.) WAIM 2005. LNCS, vol. 3739, pp. 308–319. Springer, Heidelberg (2005)
11. OASIS: Web Services Business Process Execution Language Version 2.0 (January 2007)
12. Pillai, S., Narendra, N.: Optimal replacement policy of services based on Markov decision process. In: Proc. IEEE SCC 2009, pp. 176–183 (2009)
13. Puterman, M.L.: Markov Decision Processes: Discrete Stochastic, Dynamic Programming. Wiley, Chichester (1994)
14. Wang, H., Zhou, X., Zhou, X., Liu, W., Li, W., Bouguettaya, A.: Adaptive service composition based on reinforcement learning. In: Maglio, P.P., Weske, M., Yang, J., Fantinato, M. (eds.) ICSOC 2010. LNCS, vol. 6470, pp. 92–107. Springer, Heidelberg (2010)
15. Wu, C., Bertsekas, D.: Admission control for wireless networks. Tech. Rep. LIDS-P-2466, Lab. for Information and Decision Systems, MIT (1999)

Cloud Service Engineering: A Service-Oriented Perspective on Cloud Computing
(Invited Paper)

Stefan Tai

Karlsruhe Institute of Technology (KIT), Karlsruhe, Germany
tai@kit.edu

Abstract. We study cloud computing from the perspective of service engineering: the development of service-oriented application architectures that use cloud services, and the development of cloud services for use in service-oriented application architectures. We discuss the inter-relationship between cloud computing and service engineering and argue for a *cloud service engineering* research agenda to advance research and practice of engineering cloud-based applications.

1 Introduction

Cloud computing is receiving enormous attention in both industry and academia. Among the benefits associated with cloud computing are supply side, demand-side, and multi-tenancy economies of scale. *Cloud services* are a fundamental component in cloud computing: infrastructure and platforms are provided and consumed as on-demand services [1].

Cloud services are unlike application Web services of traditional service-oriented architectures. Cloud services are middleware services to host applications. Using and composing cloud services hence is more like using and composing middleware. Existing (Web) service-oriented computing standards and specifications, however, target the description, interoperability, and composition of applications. Corresponding standards and specifications for cloud services are missing to-date.

In this paper, we take a service-oriented perspective on cloud computing. We discuss the inter-relationship between cloud services and (service-oriented) application architecture. We argue for a *cloud service engineering* research agenda to advance research and practice of engineering applications that use cloud services.

2 A Motivating Example

Consider a Web application that needs to manage very large amounts of data. The main requirements on a storage solution for the Web application are cost-efficiency and Internet-level scalability. Cloud storage services (such as Amazon's S3) have been designed with exactly these demands in-mind. They offer a simple, cost-efficient interface to read and write data objects. Scalability and availability of storage are

W. Abramowicz et al. (Eds.): ServiceWave 2011, LNCS 6994, pp. 191–193, 2011.

typically achieved behind the curtains through replication schemes; multiple replicas of the data are distributed within the same or across different geographic availability zones.

While the use of such cloud storage may seem like a natural fit to the application, the use of a cloud storage service has implications on the qualities of the application. In order to understand these implications, understanding important internals of the underlying cloud infrastructure is beneficial, if not critical.

Let us assume that the cloud storage service under consideration internally uses a ring-based replication scheme and an (N,R,W) quorum, such as Amazon's Dynamo storage architecture [2]. Optimistic write and read requests are performed: among N replica nodes, W nodes are required for a successful write operation, and R nodes are needed for a successful read operation. A typical (N,R,W) configuration is (3,2,2).

Lowering R or W in such a system will increase read availability or write availability, respectively, and improve performance in terms of client latency. Strong data consistency, however, cannot be ensured once the propagation of updates is handled asynchronously in the background – in cloud computing and cloud storage services, *eventual consistency* [3] correspondingly has to be carefully considered and responsibilities previously on the database layer (such as conflict resolution) are now shifted to the application layer. Pessimistic read and write operations that aim at strong consistency can be configured by increasing R and W to equal N, but this would significantly impact availability and client latency.

3   Cloud Service Engineering: Research Challenges

The motivating example above illustrates how configurations of internals of a cloud service can have a significant impact on qualities (and responsibilities) of the application, and, how application requirements on availability or data consistency may drive the configuration of cloud service internals, provided that there are corresponding "tuning-knobs" such as those for setting an (N,R,W) configuration. We also see that different qualities may be in conflict to each other, such as the well-known trade-off between consistency and availability in distributed data storage.

In traditional (Web) service-oriented computing, the implementation of services is hidden and middleware and infrastructure details are not exposed in (WSDL) service descriptions and (BPEL) service compositions. Hiding implementation details is a long-hailed software engineering principle. With the WS-* platform architecture, one can argue, some middleware and implementation aspects may be exposed by means of declarative policies that find its way into (SOAP) message headers for interoperability purposes [4]. Current (WS-* and Web) standards, however, do not differentiate between application services and cloud services as the middleware to host applications, but treat all services in a uniform manner.

We argue that cloud services require dedicated abstractions in (Web) service engineering. In particular, we believe that special attention should be paid to the non-functional qualities of application architectures and their inter-relationship with cloud services. To this end, we identify the following initial set of research challenges of *cloud service engineering*:

a. Modeling the (non-functional) qualities of applications and the trade-offs between qualities;
b. Modeling cloud services with respect to the application qualities that they have an impact on;
c. Providing sophisticated monitoring support to observe select qualities and trade-offs at runtime;
d. Providing (runtime) "tuning-knobs" for cloud services for quality management (in addition to traditional service interfaces);
e. Integrating the above in a multi-criteria decision support system and method for using and configuring cloud services in application architecture;
f. Integrating the above in novel (application architecture and business process) service composition models that differentiate application services and cloud (middleware) services.

4 Next Steps

The above identified research challenges require further elaboration and concrete solutions. Here, we simply aim to motivate the need for a *cloud service engineering* research agenda. In our ongoing research related to the above challenges some first ideas are suggested ([5], [6]).

In summary, we argue to reconsider some of the established principles of traditional service-oriented computing, such as uniform service abstractions and hiding of all service implementation details. We believe that dedicated cloud service abstractions in the engineering of (service-oriented) application architectures, along with appropriate "tuning-knobs" for cloud service internals, will prove to be very advantageous, especially for understanding and managing application qualities and application quality trade-offs.

References

1. Baun, C., Kunze, M., Nimis, J., Tai, S.: Cloud Computing: Web-based, dynamic IT services. Springer, Heidelberg (2011)
2. DeCandia, G., et al.: Dynamo: Amazon's highly available key-value store. In: Proc. SOSP 2007. ACM, New York (2007)
3. Vogels, W.: Eventually consistent. Communications of the ACM 52(1) (2009)
4. Curbera, F., Khalaf, R., Mukhi, N., Tai, S., Weerawarana, S.: The next step in Web services. Communications of the ACM 46(10) (2003)
5. Klems, M., Menzel, M., Fischer, R.: Consistency Benchmarking: Evaluating the Consistency Behavior of Middleware Services in the Cloud. In: Maglio, P.P., Weske, M., Yang, J., Fantinato, M. (eds.) ICSOC 2010. LNCS, vol. 6470, pp. 627–634. Springer, Heidelberg (2010)
6. Menzel, M., Schönherr, M., Tai, S.: (MC2)2: Criteria, Requirements and a Software Prototype for Cloud Infrastructure Decisions. Software: Practice & Experience (2011)

Preventing Performance Violations of Service Compositions Using Assumption-Based Run-Time Verification

Eric Schmieders and Andreas Metzger

Paluno (The Ruhr Institute for Software Technology)
University of Duisburg-Essen, Essen, Germany
{eric.schmieders,andreas.metzger}@paluno.uni-due.de

Abstract. Service-based Applications (SBAs) will increasingly be deployed in highly distributed and dynamic settings. To a large extent this dynamicity is caused by the trend to increasingly compose SBAs using third-party services. Those services are provided by external organizations and are thus not under the control of the SBA provider. For critical application domains (such as emergency or financial) and important customers (such as key accounts), the SBA developer needs to ensure that each individual SBA instance will live up to its expected requirements even though its constituent, third-party services might fail. To prevent such requirements violations, SBAs should be equipped with monitoring, prediction and adaptation capabilities which are able to foresee and avert menacing violations. Several approaches exploiting preventive adaptations have been presented in the literature, but they rely on the existence of cost models or comprehensive training data that limit their applicability in practice. In this paper we present SPADE, an automated technique that addresses those limitations. Based on assumptions about the SBA's constituent services (derived from SLAs), SPADE formally verifies the SBA against its requirements during run-time. The experimental evaluation of SPADE, using data collected for six real services, demonstrates its practical applicability in predicting violations of performance requirements.

1 Introduction

Service-orientation is increasingly adopted as a paradigm to build highly dynamic, distributed applications from individual software entities, offered as services. In this paper we refer to such applications as Service-based Applications, or SBAs for short. There is a clear trend that future SBAs will be increasingly composed from third-party services that are accessible over the Internet [15]. As a consequence, SBAs will increasingly depend on the functionality and quality offered by those third parties [5].

If the services that are provided by third parties do not deliver the expected (or contractually agreed) functionality or quality, failures of the running SBA can happen if no countermeasures are taken. As an example, if a service fails

W. Abramowicz et al. (Eds.): ServiceWave 2011, LNCS 6994, pp. 194–205, 2011.
© Springer-Verlag Berlin Heidelberg 2011

to respond within the contractually agreed 500ms and there is no compensation for this fault, this may lead to a violation of the performance requirements of the overall SBA. Thus, researchers have proposed to equip SBAs with self-adaptation capabilities which enable them to autonomously adapt to the faults of third-party services during run-time [14].

Especially in application scenarios where the provider of an SBA needs to ensure that each running SBA instance provides the guaranteed end-to-end quality properties, there is a strong need to monitor and adapt individual SBA instances. One example are SBAs offered to "key accounts" or "premium" applications, i.e., SBAs for which the provider agreed to pay severe contractual penalties in case of a violation of the promised quality. Another example are applications which might pose financial risks, e.g. caused by fire damage, or endanger human lives. Imagine a fire emergency scenario, in which human beings are endangered if the distributed, service-oriented emergency control system does not react as expected (e.g., does not dispatch ambulances in time).

Current approaches for self-adaptive SBAs follow either reactive or preventive strategies. Reactive strategies propose the execution of monitoring rules (cf. [8] and [16]) to identify deviations during run-time, e.g. using Complex Event Processing. Adaptations are triggered, based on monitored deviations. Monitoring rules cover QoS-properties of a single service, parts of the workflow or an end-to-end requirement. These approaches react on a requirements deviation and are hence not suitable to prevent the deviation itself (cf. further explanations in [6] and [5]). As motivated above, in an emergency situation such a reactive response can lead to critical situations, as it might delay the timely dispatch of operational forces, for example fire engines or ambulances.

To address these problems, researchers have proposed to employ preventive adaptation, which enables SBAs to predict future failures and to perform preventive actions. Although several approaches for preventive adaptation have been presented in the literature (see Section 2), they pose certain limitations, such as the need for cost models or comprehensive training data. In this paper, we aim to address these limitations. Specifically, we will describe and validate the SPADE technique (*SPecification- and Assumption-based DEtection of adaptation needs*).

SPADE equips SBAs with adaptation capabilities, empowering them to adapt themselves preventively. To achieve this, SPADE uses run-time verification techniques, execution data of the monitored instances and assumptions concerning the SBAs' context, derived from Service Level Agreements (SLAs) of third-party services. Together, these mechanisms are used for performance prediction, which is able to detect menacing performance requirements violations of running SBAs. SPADE can thus be used in settings where no cost models or training data are available.

The remainder of this paper is structured as follows. Section 2 provides further insight into the limitations of current approaches for preventive adaptation. In Section 3, we introduce a more complex scenario and example to illustrate the key concepts of SPADE. In Section 4, we describe the SPADE approach in detail. The applicability and effectiveness of SPADE are experimentally evaluated in

Section 5. The experiments were performed on the basis of the example SBA from Section 3 and a monitoring data from six real-world services. Section 6 concludes and provides an outlook on future work.

2   Related Work

Existing approaches related to preventing SLA violations of SBAs can be grouped into two major classes: (1) approaches that aim to predict the SLA violation of an *individual* SBA instance and to prevent the violation by adapting that SBA instance; (2) approaches that reason about failures of SBAs at the *model* level (and not at the level of running SBA instances) and which aim to prevent SLA violations of future SBA instances by modifying the specification (model) of the SBA.

Instance Level prevention (1): Various approaches which aim at preventing SLA violations of running SBA instances, have been presented in the literature. Ivanovic et al. propose a combination of computational cost analysis and simulations taking the load of allocated resources into account (i.e. invoked services) in order to predict the QoS characteristics of a service composition (see [10] and [9]). This approach has two critical shortcomings. First, the approach requires a cost function offered by the service providers involved in the SBA. This severely impacts on the practical applicability of the approach, as such cost functions are currently not available. Second, the sketched application only has a restricted access to the load of third party services, as the SBA provider can only meter the load produced by its own applications. Thus, the prediction could lack preciseness and reliability. Still, the approach can be considered complementary to SPADE, as, once available, a cost function and assumptions concerning the resource load would provide a good means to refine the present assumption concept used by SPADE.

Several approaches propose machine learning techniques, such as neuronal and Bayesian networks, to predict a menacing SLA violation (e.g. [12], [11], [17], and [13]). The effectiveness of these approaches strongly relies on historical data, which is required as training data. As observed by the authors, several hundreds, or in some cases, even thousands of executions are necessary to ensure the expected precision for the SLA violation prediction. This means that these approaches will exhibit severe limitations as for the applicability if only a small amount of historical data is available. Also, the prediction component usually has to be re-trained after each adaptation of the SBA. Still, those approaches can be employed complementary to SPADE. While SPADE provides reliable results independent of the amount of historical data, it might well be that, as soon as sufficient data is available, the precision of the prediction using machine learning is superior to those of SPADE.

Model Level prevention (2): Complementary to the approaches presented above, approaches which aim at preventing SLA violations of potential future SBA instances have been presented in the literature. The approach presented by Ghezzi et al. in [7] suggests to adapt the workflow specification to meet the

SBA's requirements. The solutions focus on reliability as a quality attribute. To predict the reliability of an SBA the historical data of past SBA instances is fed into a probabilistic model checker. The monitored data of past faulty instances is extrapolated and compared with the reliability values stipulated in the SLA. In case the predicted value violates the SLA, the workflow specification is adapted. As the prediction relies on past faulty instances, the approach cannot be used directly to avoid an SLA violation of an individual instance, which is the aim of approaches of class (1) and SPADE especially.

3   Example SBA

To illustrate and evaluate SPADE in the remainder of this paper, we will use an abstract example of a service-based application, which is depicted in Fig. 1. In the middle of the figure, the workflow is depicted as an activity diagram. On the right hand side of the figure, the third-party services that are invoked by the SBA (i.e., by the actions of the workflow) are shown. Finally, on the left hand side, the service response times for one actual execution of the SBA are given.

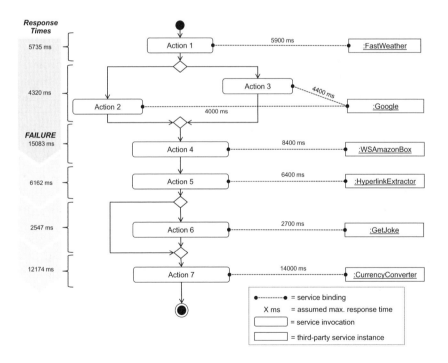

Fig. 1. Example SBA

4   The SPADE Approach

In this section we present the SPADE approach. For that reason, we structure the design time and run-time activities along the phases of the SBA life-cycle model as elaborated by the S-Cube Network of Excellence (see Fig. 2). To illustrate the approach, each life-cycle description comprises an *example* paragraph explaining SPADE by means of the example SBA introduced in Section 3.

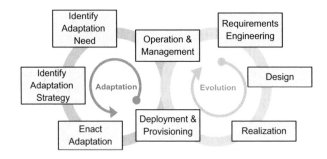

Fig. 2. S-Cube SBA Life-Cycle Model [14]

Requirements Engineering: In the requirements engineering phase, the functional and quality requirements for the SBA are elicited and documented.

In order to assess automatically whether the application deviates from its requirements during operation, functional and non-functional requirements are formally expressed as input to SPADE. We propose to already perform this formalization during the requirements engineering phase, as this facilitates an early validation of the requirements, e.g., by means of formal consistency checks (cf. [1]), and hence reduces the risk of expensive corrections in later phases.

To formalize the SBA requirements, SPADE uses the specification language ALBERT (cf. [2]). We choose ALBERT because of its capability to express logical and temporal dependencies of monitoring data along an executed path.

Example: For the example SBA from Section 3, we formalize the required response time $r_{per} \in R_{ASC}$, which demands an end-to-end response time of at most 55 seconds. In ALBERT r_{per} can be formalized as $r_{per} := onEvent$ $(start, "Action1") \rightarrow Within(onEvent(end, "Action7"), 55000)$. The *onEvent* operator evaluates to true if the activity specified in its second argument performs the state change denoted in its first argument. The *Within* operator evaluates to true if its first argument evaluates to true within the amount of milliseconds specified in its second argument.

Design: During the design phase, the activities and the control flow of the application are specified (e.g. in BPEL or YAWL). Together with the definition of the workflow, candidate services are identified that can provide the functionality and quality to fulfill the requirements of the SBA [4].

Following the same reasoning as in the requirements engineering phase, we suggest to formalize the workflow during the design phase already in order to reduce the risk of later corrections. We extend the idea presented by Bianculli et al. [2] and propose using the BOGOR model checker during run-time. ALBERT expressions can be executed by BOGOR. We formalize the workflow using BIR, the BOGOR Input Representation.

Example: In order to use the BOGOR Model Checker, we specify the workflow of the example SBA by using BIR. The resulting specification S_{ASC} can then be executed and analyzed by BOGOR.

Realization: To achieve the desired end-to-end quality of SBAs, contracts between service providers and service consumers on quality aspects of services are established. Following [4], this means that for each candidate service, the best quality level for the available budget is negotiated and stipulated in an SLA. In SPADE, the quality levels that have been negotiated and agreed upon with the service providers are formalized. We treat quality levels as assumptions (A) about the SBA's context. We formalize A using ALBERT again.

During design time, a service repository must be established, e.g. based on UDDI. This serves as a pool for alternative services. These services can be converted during run-time.

Example: For our example we use the assumed response time given in the example SBA (see Fig. 1). The assumption for the $a_{FastWeather}$ service bound to *Action 1* is formalized as follows[1]: $a_{FastWeather} := onEvent\ (start\ ,"Action\ 1")$ $\rightarrow Within(\ onEvent(end, "Action\ 1"\ ), 5900)$

Deployment: The deployment and provisioning phase comprises all the activities needed to make the SBA available to its users. During the deployment phase, SPADE uses BOGOR to check whether the workflow specification (S), under the given assumptions (A), satisfies the requirements (R), i.e. whether S, $A \models R$. In case the requirements are not satisfied, the phases of the evolution loop (cf. Fig. 2) are re-executed, e.g., in order to bind faster services. If the SBA is successfully verified, the SBA is deployed on the run-time environment. In the case of SPADE, we use the GlassFish application server[2].

Example: The specification of the abstract service composition evaluates to true, i.e. S_{ASC} and A_{ASC} satisfy R_{ASC}. Thus, the SBA is deployed.

Operation and Management: This phase comprises the execution of the SBA and the monitoring of its constituent services using service monitoring techniques.

To identify assumption violations during the operation of the SBA, monitoring mechanisms are employed. SPADE uses the monitoring facilities of the GlassFish application server to check, whether the monitoring data $m_i \in M$ of service i satisfies the related formalized assumptions $a_i \in A$, i.e. whether $m_i \models a_i$.

---

[1] The complete set of formalizations is available from
http://www.s-cube-network.eu/SPADE
[2] http://glassfish.java.net/

Example: During the execution of the abstract service composition let us assume that the monitoring data $m_{FastWeather}$ and m_{Google} satisfy their related assumptions, leading to an cumulative run-time of 10055 ms. Let us further assume that the subsequent service $WSAmazonBox$ responds too late. Instead of the assumed 8400 milliseconds, the invocation lasts 23083 ms, i.e. $m_{Google} \not\models a_{Google}$. Due to this deviation, the current instance is suspended and the next phase is entered immediately, as a performance violation could be indicated.

Identify Adaptation Needs: If an assumption violation has been identified, SPADE checks whether the requirements are still satisfied. For all services that have been invoked, SPADE replaces the assumption values by concrete monitoring data. This means that only for the services not invoked, the assumptions are used during run-time verification. SPADE thus uses a subset $A' \subseteq A$ together with the set of monitored data M to check whether $S, M, A' \models R$.

Similar to the deployment phase, SPADE utilizes BOGOR to perform this verification during run-time. If the check reveals that R is still satisfied, the workflow execution is continued. Otherwise, an adaptation must be triggered.

Example: To determine whether the requirement in the example is still met, the workflow specification (S_{ASC}), the monitoring data $(m_{FastWeather}, m_{Google}$ and $m_{WSAmazonBox})$ together with the assumptions of the to be invoked services $(a_{HylinkExtractor}, a_{CurrencyConverter}, a_{GetJoke})$ are checked against the requirement r_{per}. The predicted end-to-end duration is 56238 ms, which exceeds the 55 seconds demanded by r_{per}. In consequence, the workflow actually have to be adapted, as otherwise a performance violation seems to be in all probability.

Identify Adaptation Strategy: Subsequent to an identified adaptation need, the next step is to create an appropriate adaptation strategy such that the menacing SLA violation can successfully be averted.

SPADE is equipped with service substitution capabilities, as this is one of the few adaptation techniques that can be used to compensate for lost time. Furthermore, SPADE exploits the CHOCO constraint solver[3] to determine which not-yet-invoked services have to be substituted. We consider the workflow as a graph $G = (V, E)$, composed from a set of vertices V, representing the workflow actions, and a set of edges E, representing the transitions between these actions. We consider $p = (v_i, ..., v_j)$ as path in G. Path p includes all v, which are executed until the occured deviation, i.e. $p = \{(v_n, ..., v_m) | v \in V \wedge invoked(v)\}$. G' is a subgraph of G containing all $v_1...v_n$ which are not yet executed, i.e. $G' = \{(v_n, ..., v_m) | v \in V \wedge \neg invoked(v)\}$.

We now define a set of paths $P' = \{p' \in G'\}$ to formalize our constraint as $p_{per} + p'_{per} \leq r_{per}$, where p_{per} is the already consumed end-to-end execution time, p'_{per} is the cumulative response time of a possible workflow path in G' and r_{per} is the performance requirement of the monitored service composition. CHOCO has to solve this constraint with respect to the response times of the available alternative services (available from the service repository) for each $p' \in P'$. CHOCO also has to consider the remaining possible paths of the workflow. Right after the

---

[3] http://www.emn.fr/z-info/choco-solver/

invocation of the deviating service we do not know which path will be followed during the further execution of the workflow instance. Thus, we scrutinize a subset of P', i.e. P''. P'' contains paths for which performance violations are predicted. The constraint solver calculates a combination of services invoked along each $p'' \in P''$, based on the response time of alternative services. The necessary adaptation actions are easily derived from the results, as each identified combination exposes the services, which need to be substituted as well as their substitution. The required substitutions are summarized (where double entries are avoided) in the adaptation strategy which is propagated to the mechanisms of the next phase.

Example: In our abstract service composition example we are facing two paths in G'_{ASC}, i.e. $p1 = (Action5, Action7)$ and $p2 = (Action5, Action6, Action7)$. Both paths will violate r_{per} and therefore have to be adapted. Based on the output of the constraint solver, services for $Action5$ and $Action6$ are chosen to be substituted by faster services, thus satisfying r_{per}.

Enact Adaptation: During this last adaptation phase the adaptation strategy is executed. For this purpose, the instructions comprised in the adaptation strategy are dispatched. The dispatching usually utilizes the facilities provided by the chosen run-time environment or involves additional adaptation mechanisms.

In SPADE we use the interception-mechanisms provided by the GlassFish application server. We exploit the built-in Enterprise Service Bus to manipulate the target of a message. These messages are generated by the workflow engine, when a service has to be invoked. We switch the target service of the invocation to the service identified during the previous phase.

Example: In our example, the two service invocations $Action5$ and $Action6$ are redirected to the substituting services. For this purpose the message routing table comprising the message destinations is manipulated. Consequently, the execution of the instance is resumed.

5   Experimental Evaluation

This section presents the experiments we performed to assess the efficiency of SPADE in detecting adaptation needs. Experimental validations of comprehensive approaches like SPADE must be accurate and comprehensive as well. To reduce this complexity, we focus on SPADE's ability in identifying adaptation needs in our first set of experiments.

Our measurement of SPADE's efficiency is twofold. First, we examined unnecessary adaptations, i.e. false positives, as such adaptations could lead to avoidable costs, e.g., when replacing a free service with a commercial service to compensate for faults. Secondly, we count the amount of situations in which SPADE cannot perform an adaptation. It can happen that a service invocation leads to a violation of an SLA, such that the end-to-end requirement is already violated. In those situations, the SBA instance obviously cannot be adapted preventively in order to avert that requirements violation, as the requirement has already been violated. Both values are expected to be low, as a low value implies a high number of cases where SPADE was successfully applied.

Experimental Design: The performed experiments are based on a simulated execution of the example SBA's and its services. This enables the reproducibility of the test results for the exact same "input" data, thus allowing other researchers to reproduces the performed tests. We simulate the example SBA, introduced in Section 3. Specifically, we simulate the execution of the workflow and retrieve the response times for its constituent services from a large set of monitoring data [3]. This dataset comprises real monitoring data, which was crucial for our experimental design. By using realistic monitoring data, we show the applicability of SPADE in realistic settings. The number of SBA instances that can be experimentally assessed is limited by the size of the used dataset. To each service invocation within an SBA instance we assign one single data point from the dataset of the respective service. In the example SBA, this allows for the execution of 5884 different SBA instances[4].

Determining the Degree of False Positives: In our experiments, one single SBA instance is represented by one path through the example SBA together with the concrete monitoring data. As part of the simulation, we calculate the end-to-end response time for each SBA instance execution by adding the monitored response times of the invoked services along the SBA instance's path. Based on this *calculated SBA instance response time*, we can determine false positive adaptation triggers. Once SPADE has triggered an adaptation, it is checked whether the calculated SBA instance response time violates the SBAs end-to-end requirements. For example, the check indicate that the assumed instance response time exceeds the upper bound of $r_{per} \leq 55$ (seconds) as in our example, thus an adaptation is triggered. However, if the calculated instance response time reveals that the requirement would not have been violated in case the SBA execution continues without adaptation, we consider this workflow instance as a false positive. To take the duration of the three phases into account, in which SPADE suspends the execution of the workflow instance, we measured this duration (i.e. ca. 170 ms) and added it to the calculated SBA instance response time.[5]

Determining the Degree of Impossible Adaptations: There were situations in which service invocations deviated from their stipulated response time, such that the performance requirement is violated. In these situations, it is too late to apply SPADE as the performance requirement is already violated. To determine the percentage of these situations we put the number of the service invocations which lead to these SLA violations in relation to the amount of all service invocations.

---

[4] Please note that in the example SBA, the Google service is bound twice. There are 2943 data points in the Google dataset. In order to provide data for each binding, we split the dataset in half and assigned an interleaved subset to each of the two service invocations. Each subset comprises 1471 datasets. As the workflow of the example SBA allows four different paths, this leads to a total number of 5884 SBA instances.

[5] The measuring has been carried out on an Intel Core i5-760 platform with a 2.80 GHz CPU and 4 GB RAM.

Data Analysis and Interpretation: The SPADE approach has been applied to 5884 SBA instances (cf. row (a) in Table 1). 629 of those SBA instances have been executed without any assumption violations (b). During the execution of the complementary 5255 SBA instances assumptions have been violated (c). This number is explained in the discussion on threats to validity. For those SBA instances, SPADE has identified 604 preventive adaptation triggers (d)[6].

Table 1. False Positives in Relation to Executed SBA Instances

Description		%	SPADE
SBA Instances Executed (a)			5884
SBA Instances without Assumption Violation (b)	b/a	629	10.7%
SBA Instances with Assumption Violation (c)	c/a	5255	89.3%
SBA Instances with Adaptations (d)	d/a	604	10.3%
False Positive Adaptations (e)	e/a	**72**	**1.2%**

72 of the adaptation triggers were false positives (e). Thus, 1.2% of the work-flow instances would have been unnecessarily adapted. With respect to the challenging time constraint of 55 seconds, motivated by the introductory emergency scenario, we consider the percentage of false positives extremely promising, especially, as an unnecessary adaptation does not imply an SLA violation. Furthermore, the amount of situations in which SPADE cannot adapt is very low as well. As depicted in row (c) of Table 2, a total of 825 out of 28624 service invocations, i.e. 2.5%, lead to situations where an adaptation is not possible. Nevertheless, this could still mean a threat in an emergency setting. We will discuss this shortcoming in our future work section (cf. Section 6).

Table 2. Invocations leading to Performance Violation

Description		%	SPADE
Service Invocations in Executed SBA Instances (a)			32362
Actual Service Invocations until Adaptation Trigger (b)	b/a	30784	95.1%
Assumption Viol., where Adaptation is not Possible (c)	c/b	825	2.5%

Discussing Threats to Validity: First exploratory checks indicate that the efficiency of SPADE depends on the concrete values for assumptions and requirements. This can pose a threat to internal validity, as it might be the case that the values used in the example SBA are not realistic. We address this issue by referring to failure rates of service invocations observed in a case study, in which 150 different services have been examined [18]. In our experiments we approximate the observed service failure rate of 95% by adjusting the monitoring rules (which use the assumption values) accordingly, thus aligning the experimental

---

[6] Please note that only those situations have been counted as triggers, in which adaptations were still possible (cf. below and Table 2).

design to the observed, realistic values. In order to learn more about the effect of assumptions and requirements values on SPADE's efficiency, we are planning several series of experiments during which we vary both values.

The example SBA does not cover all possible control constructs available to build SBAs (such as loops and forks), which might pose threats to external validity. We thus will extend our SPADE prototype with a full-fledged model checker to handle more complex workflows and will perform further experiments based on this update to improve the applicability of the SPADE approach.

6   Conclusions and Future Work

This paper described the SPADE approach, which is an automated technique to determine adaptation needs to trigger preventive adaptations of SBAs. As SPADE does not rely on historical data, SPADE overcomes some of the shortcomings of the existing solutions. The applicability of SPADE has been supported by experimental results, using monitoring data of real services.

We plan to continue our work on preventive adaptation in two directions. First, we will combine SPADE with our PROSA approach. The PROSA approach is capable of predicting quality violations of individual services. The combined approach is expected to act in situations in which SPADE is not able to prevent requirements violations as intended.

Secondly, we plan to apply SPADE in a cross-layer adaptation setting. In this setting, SPADE is expected to exploit the adaptation mechanisms of two different layers: the service composition and the service infrastructure layer. We expect that harmonizing the adaptation on both layers will increase the number of situations in which SPADE is able to compensate for deviations, which thus may increase SPADE's success in avoiding requirements violations.

Acknowledgments. We cordially thank Benedikt Liegener for contributing to the set up of the experiments, as well as Marian Benner, Mark Rzepka and Osama Sammodi for helpful comments on earlier drafts of the paper. The research leading to these results has received funding from the European Community's 7th Framework Programme FP7/2007-2013 under grant agreement 215483 (S-Cube).

References

1. Bauer, F.L., Berghammer, et al.: The Munich Project CIP: Volume I: the wide spectrum language CIP-L. Springer, London (1985)
2. Bianculli, D., Ghezzi, C., Spoletini, P., Baresi, L., Guinea, S.: A guided tour through SAVVY-WS: A methodology for specifying and validating web service compositions. In: Börger, E., Cisternino, A. (eds.) Advances in Software Engineering. LNCS, vol. 5316, pp. 131–160. Springer, Heidelberg (2008)
3. Cavallo, B., Di Penta, M., Canfora, G.: An empirical comparison of methods to support QoS-aware service selection. In: 2nd International Workshop on Principles of Engineering Service-Oriented Systems, PESOS 2010 (co-located with ICSE 2010, Cape Town), pp. 64–70 (2010)

4. Comuzzi, M., Pernici, B.: A framework for qos-based web service contracting. ACM Transactions on Web 3(3) (2009)
5. Di Nitto, E., Ghezzi, C., Metzger, A., Papazoglou, M., Pohl, K.: A journey to highly dynamic, self-adaptive service-based applications. Automated Software Engineering (2008)
6. Gehlert, A., Bucchiarone, A., Kazhamiakin, R., Metzger, A., Pistore, M., Pohl, K.: Exploiting assumption-based verification for the adaptation of service-based applications. In: Symposium on Applied Computing (SAC), Sierre, Switzerland, March 22-26. ACM, New York (2010)
7. Ghezzi, C., Tamburrelli, G.: Reasoning on non-functional requirements for integrated services. In: Proceedings of the 2009 17th IEEE International Requirements Engineering Conference. RE 2009, pp. 69–78 (2009)
8. Hermosillo, G., Seinturier, L., Duchien, L.: Using complex event processing for dynamic business process adaptation. In: Proceedings of the 2010 IEEE International Conference on Services Computing, SCC 2010 (2010)
9. Ivanović, D., Treiber, M., Carro, M., Dustdar, S.: Building dynamic models of service compositions with simulation of provision resources. In: Parsons, J., Saeki, M., Shoval, P., Woo, C., Wand, Y. (eds.) ER 2010. LNCS, vol. 6412, pp. 288–301. Springer, Heidelberg (2010)
10. Ivanovic, D., Carro, M., Hermenegildo, M.: Towards data aware qos-driven adaptation for service orchestrations. In: Proceedings of the 2010 IEEE International Conference on Web Services, ICWS 2010, pp. 107–114 (2010)
11. Leitner, P., Wetzstein, B., Karastoyanova, D., Hummer, W., Dustdar, S., Leymann, F.: Preventing SLA violations in service compositions using aspect-based fragment substitution. In: Maglio, P.P., Weske, M., Yang, J., Fantinato, M. (eds.) ICSOC 2010. LNCS, vol. 6470, pp. 365–380. Springer, Heidelberg (2010)
12. Leitner, P., Wetzstein, B., Rosenberg, F., Michlmayr, A., Dustdar, S., Leymann, F.: Runtime prediction of service level agreement violations for composite services. In: Dan, A., Gittler, F., Toumani, F. (eds.) ICSOC/ServiceWave 2009. LNCS, vol. 6275, pp. 176–186. Springer, Heidelberg (2010)
13. Lin, K.J., Panahi, M., Zhang, Y., Zhang, J., Chang, S.H.: Building accountability middleware to support dependable soa. IEEE Internet Computing 13, 16–25 (2009)
14. Papazoglou, M., Pohl, K., Parkin, M., Metzger, A. (eds.): Service Research Challenges and Solutions for the Future Internet: Towards Mechanisms and Methods for Engineering, Managing, and Adapting Service-Based Systems. Springer, Heidelberg (2010)
15. Tselentis, G., Domingue, J., Galis, A., Gavras, A., Hausheer, D.: Towards the Future Internet: A European Research Perspective. IOS Press, Amsterdam (2009)
16. Wang, H., Zhou, X., Zhou, X., Liu, W., Li, W., Bouguettaya, A.: Adaptive service composition based on reinforcement learning. In: Maglio, P.P., Weske, M., Yang, J., Fantinato, M. (eds.) ICSOC 2010. LNCS, vol. 6470, pp. 92–107. Springer, Heidelberg (2010)
17. Zeng, L., Lingenfelder, C., Lei, H., Chang, H.: Event-driven quality of service prediction. In: Bouguettaya, A., Krueger, I., Margaria, T. (eds.) ICSOC 2008. LNCS, vol. 5364, pp. 147–161. Springer, Heidelberg (2008)
18. Zheng, Z., Zhang, Y., Lyu, M.R.: Distributed qos evaluation for real-world web services. In: Proceedings of the 2010 IEEE International Conference on Web Services, ICWS 2010, pp. 83–90. IEEE Computer Society, Washington, DC, USA (2010)

A Taxonomy of Service Engineering Stakeholder Types

Qing Gu[1], Michael Parkin[2], and Patricia Lago[1]

[1] Department of Computer Science, VU University Amsterdam, The Netherlands
[2] European Research Institute for Service Science, Tilburg University,
The Netherlands

Abstract. The support of stakeholders is critical to the success of any project, and is equally important in SOA-related projects. Traditional software development methodologies no longer meet the requirements for developing service-based applications, or SBAs, due to the shift away from monolithic application development to service provision and composition. This shift introduces more types of stakeholders, each of which can take multiple roles within the lifecycle of the SBA, and who have an interest in or are influenced by the service-oriented software process.

To understand these stakeholder types and roles, this paper presents an initial set of stakeholder types and roles solicited from within the EC's Network of Excellence in Software Services and Systems (S-Cube). By describing these stakeholder types in the context of the S-Cube service engineering lifecycle, we demonstrate the lifecycle phases each stakeholder and role is involved in during the development and operation of SBAs. The stakeholder roles and types found and the methodology we describe for their discovery aids the identification of the requirements for these stakeholders and contributes to research in service engineering methodologies.

Keywords: SOA, Service-Oriented Software Engineering, Stakeholders.

1 Introduction

A stakeholder can be defined as "any group or individual who can affect or is affected by the achievement of the organization's objectives" [5]. In the field of software engineering, the identification of stakeholders and how to address their concerns has been of significance in the areas of requirements engineering and architectural design [3,25]. In this paper, we take the stakeholder concept and apply it to service-oriented software engineering (SOSE) with the aim of identifying groups or individuals who can effect or who are effected by the engineering of Service-Based Applications (SBAs).

SBAs are composed of one or more software services each realizing an independent business function, possibly spread across organizations. An SBA is different to, for example, a component-based application as the owner of an SBA generally does not own or control all of the services the SBA contains, whilst in

W. Abramowicz et al. (Eds.): ServiceWave 2011, LNCS 6994, pp. 206–219, 2011.

a component-based application the owner controls all the constituent parts [6]. Once built, SBAs are dynamic and may be *adapted* in response to changes in end-user requirements, service performance and/or the context of the service.

Shifting from monolithic application development to SBA service provision means traditional software engineering (TSE) [24,14] methodologies no longer meet the requirements for developing these service processes. This is because the engineering, composition, continuous adaptation and consumption of services involves:

1. New stakeholder types: In SOSE, business functions are delivered in the form of both complete SBAs (analogous to software systems and applications developed using TSE) and pools of reusable software services. Some TSE stakeholders, such as software designer, software architect and software developer, are often split into two types, one focusing on services and another focusing on SBAs (e.g., service designer and SBA designer, respectively). Moreover, some types of stakeholders are specific to SOSE and are not found in TSE; for example, service modelers, service monitors or adaptation designers are only found in SOSE. Note that in this paper, the term *stakeholder type* defines the specific function played by a stakeholder in SOSE.

2. Multiple stakeholder roles: SBAs are often composed of services owned by other stakeholders. This naturally increases the complexity of the development process as well as the execution environment. As discussed in previous work [8], due to the separation of service consumption and provision and the shift in ownership of services, a stakeholder may play multiple roles simultaneously, each with different goals and competencies. For example, in TSE software designers are responsible for software design and software developers are responsible for implementation. However, in SOSE a service designer in the role of *service provider* is concerned with the identification of services to provide to others whereas when they are in the role of *service consumer* she is concerned with the identification of services for integration purposes. As a result, a designer with a service provider's perspective should focus on requirements external to the organization, whereas a designer with the service consumer's perspective should pay particular attention to the constraints internal to the organization. In this work, the term *stakeholder role* defines the perspective taken by a stakeholder in SOSE.

Currently, there is no common understanding of these stakeholder types and roles and their relationship to service engineering. To help find these stakeholders, determine their role(s) and show where they are involved in the SBA lifecycle, we used the collective knowledge and experience of the EC's S-Cube NoE [21], a four-year project with the aim of establishing an integrated, multidisciplinary and vibrant research community in the field of SOSE. S-Cube[1] counts 16 academic partners, an industrial advisory board with 6 industrial partners and 11 industrial and academic associate members. In total the network contains approximately 200 researchers or experts in various SOSE-related fields.

---

[1] http://www.s-cube-network.eu/

Since S-Cube's participants work on different areas of software services and systems research and development, part of S-Cube's work is to integrate their research through the development of a methodology for the design, implementation and operation of SBAs. To ensure that methodology is relevant, this integration requires the identification of stakeholders who are involved in SOSE. This study of stakeholder types and roles are, therefore, important not only to the SOSE community but also to assist the S-Cube NoE as it seeks to tailor and promote its service engineering methodology to the correct audience.

This paper provides an initial taxonomy of these stakeholder types and roles and a description of the method used to collect and derive this information. The initial taxonomy contains nineteen stakeholder types and five roles we solicited from institutions within S-Cube. To demonstrate when each stakeholder and role is involved during the design, development and operation of an SBA we provide a context for our results by mapping them to the S-Cube service engineering lifecycle. Due to the nature, size and relevance of the information gathered, we feel these findings are important to the community, though it should be emphasized that this paper contains only one set of results (from the S-Cube NoE) and is not a comprehensive field study containing responses from many types of organizations. It is hoped this set of stakeholder roles and types will aid the future identification of the requirements for these stakeholders and contribute to the continuing research in service engineering methodologies.

This paper is structured as follows: Section 2 describes the S-Cube service engineering lifecycle we use to position and SOSE stakeholders; Section 3 describes the four-step method we used to determine the set of stakeholders; Section 4 describes the taxonomy of service engineering stakeholders we found using the research method; Section 5 shows how the taxonomy maps to the S-Cube service engineering lifecycle; Section 6 discusses related work in the identification of SOA stakeholders; Section 7 provides our conclusion.

2   The S-Cube Service Engineering Lifecycle

Figure 1 shows the SBA lifecycle model developed by S-Cube to capture the iterative process of continuously developing, implementing, and maintaining services. The development (right-hand) cycle addresses the classic development and deployment phases, including requirements and design, construction, operations and management. The entry-point to the lifecycle (the point where the SBA is conceived) is through the Early Requirements Engineering phase. The second (left-hand) cycle extends the first lifecycle by defining phases addressing changes and adaptations. This lifecycle is added to the traditional development cycle because a distinguishing feature of SBAs is that they are modified during their lifetime to satisfy new situations and requirements. The adaptation lifecycle can be broken into three phases: deciding if an adaptation to the SBA is needed (*Identify Adaptation Needs*); deciding how the system should be adapted (*Identify Adaptation Strategies*); and performing the adaptation (*Enact Adaptation*).

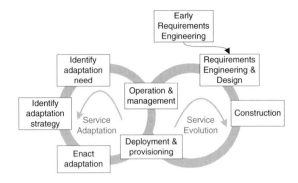

Fig. 1. The S-Cube Service Engineering Lifecycle

Other lifecycles, including SOMA [2], SOAD [26] and ASTRO [17], were evaluated by S-Cube. However these lifecycles cannot adequately explain the evolution and adaptation of SBAs and is why a new lifecycle was created [4]. In this work, we use the lifecycle to illustrate when a stakeholder is involved in the SBA lifecycle and provide another view of the connections between them. Further details on the S-Cube service engineering lifecycle can be found in [1].

3   Research Method

As described above, part of the work of S-Cube is to develop of a methodology for the design, implementation and operation of SBAs. Our motivation for identifying stakeholders was to provide this methodology with an initial set of stakeholders. To do this, we applied state-of-the-art research methods: a questionnaire survey [22] for step 1, content analysis [19] for steps 2 & 3, and a case-specific mapping study [12] for step 4. Due to space limitations this section provides an overview of how we used these methods to collect, collate and compile the stakeholder specifications gathered from S-Cube researchers.[2]

Step 1: Soliciting stakeholder types. Since each S-Cube partner performs research in one or more service engineering topics (e.g., service composition, service engineering, service design, etc.) to find the stakeholders relevant to S-Cube's engineering methodology we designed a questionnaire so S-Cube researchers could describe types of stakeholder, record which activities the stakeholder participates in, how the stakeholder relates to the S-Cube engineering lifecycle and why this stakeholder is particular to service engineering.

---

[2] The survey results and the information derived at each step of the methodology are available in a Microsoft Excel spreadsheet from
http://www.s-cube-network.eu/results/deliverables/
wp-ia-3.1/cd-ia-3.1.4/survey_results.xls. Each worksheet is numbered according to the steps in the methodology.

We asked S-Cube researchers to use the questionnaire to identify service engineering stakeholders from their own work and the literature and to provide justifications for their inclusion. We feel the data we collected is highly representative of the SOSE research community and their responses are highly relevant for other researchers, educators and industrial practitioners. In total 50 completed questionnaires were returned back to us. Nevertheless, we need to further generalize our results as reported in our conclusions (See Section 7).

Step 2: Classification of stakeholder types. The information in the questionnaires was used to classify the stakeholders based on the roles they take with the goal of finding which roles are played by different types of stakeholders and which types of stakeholders have multiple roles.

Initially, our classification schema was based on the four roles described in [7]: Service Provider, Service Broker, Service Consumer, and Application Builder. Within these roles, an Application Builder can be a Service Consumer when locating and executing services. When analyzing the data collected in Step 1, we identified another type of service consumer, the Service Composer. This role is different to the Application Builder (who builds applications using services) as the Composer builds composite services and provides them to other consumers. Since building applications requires different skills, expertise and knowledge to building services (e.g., the former activity collects requirements from the end-user while the latter collects requirements from its potential consumers) we explicitly differentiate between service composers an application builders. As a result, we split the role of Service Consumer from [7] into two specific consumer roles: Application Builder and Service Composer.

When categorizing the stakeholder types, some types could not be classified using the above roles. These types were either end-users (the initiators of SBA interactions) or experts that provide support during the service engineering lifecycle. As a result, we identified two more roles, the former as Application Clients and the latter as Supporting Roles to classify these types.

Finally, in this step we also found that none of the stakeholder types collected from the questionnaires acts as a Service Broker, an intermediary role between a service provider and service consumer that provides service location information from a service registry. We discuss this finding in detail in Section 4. The result of this step is the classification of stakeholder types according to the following five roles:

1. Service Providers: design, implement, own, publish and maintain services that can be invoked/executed.
2. Application Builders: integrate services into an application that meets the requirements of its end users.
3. Service Composers: provide composite services for internal or external usage and compose existing services or SBAs to achieve business goals.
4. Application Clients: use the application to achieve their goals.
5. Supporting Roles: are indirectly involved with the service lifecycle and provide auxiliary functions such as project management, technical advice and consultancy.

Step 3: Consolidation of stakeholder types. From the stakeholder questionnaires completed by the S-cube partners, we noticed that stakeholders with similar descriptions were often named differently. For example, in the questionnaires returned to us the stakeholder responsible for modeling the business process was called Business Modeler, Business Analyst and Domain Expert by different partners. To consolidate the types of stakeholders gathered and to obtain a list of unique types, in this step of the method we re-named the types of stakeholders when they had the same meaning but were named differently.

To do this we first determined the context and function for each classified stakeholder. For instance, the stakeholder Business Process Architect has the context *Business Process* and the function *Architect*. By analyzing the context and function of all stakeholders we identified synonyms that were used to rename stakeholders. For example, the Analyst function was treated as a synonym for Modeler, Designer was considered a synonym for Architect, Enterprise was judged a synonym for Business and Service-Based Application (SBA) was used as a synonym for System, End-point Service-Based System and Service Network.

We then compared the descriptions of stakeholders with the synonyms. If their descriptions were the same or very similar, the stakeholders types were given the same name. After renaming, we obtained the list of unique types of stakeholders (described in detail in the next section).

Step 4: Map stakeholder types to S-Cube lifecycle phases. In the previous step, stakeholder types with similar descriptions were given the same name. However, these stakeholders may participate in different phases of the service engineering lifecycle, therefore to provide information on where the consolidated stakeholder types mapped to S-Cube's service engineering lifecycle, we inspected the lifecycles of each of the submitted stakeholder types and for each type recorded the lifecycle phase(s) they apply to. If multiple specifications define the same stakeholder type but assert they belonged to different phases of the S-Cube lifecycle, we merge and record the coverage of the relevant S-Cube lifecycle phases for the consolidated stakeholder type. Using this method we obtained the consolidated list of the different types of stakeholders and how they participate in the S-Cube lifecycle, which we discuss further in Section 5.

4   A Taxonomy of Service Engineering Stakeholders

Table 1 shows the results of Steps 1-3 of the methodology. Taking the columns from left-to-right, the first column lists the stakeholder types found in the questionnaires returned in Step 1. Note the same type may appear more than once — this is because two partners may have returned questionnaires with the same name but not necessarily the same description. All responses received are included for completeness.

The second column of Table 1 lists the roles defined in Step 2 and shows how multiple stakeholder types are categorized. The third (final) column of the table shows the consolidated stakeholder types found in Step 3 of the method and how similarly named stakeholder types can be consolidated using the synonyms described above.

Table 1. Classified, sorted and consolidated stakeholders

Stakeholder	Role	Consolidated Stakeholder Type	Description
Application Architect Application Designer Business Process Engineer SBA Assembler SBA Developer SBA System Builder		SBA Architect	Creates structure and design of the SBA.
System Analyst Service Network Modeler Business Process Architect		SBA Modeler	Makes hypothetical descriptions of SBAs, possibly for use in testing.
Application Builder Application Developer	Application Builders	Application Developer	Concerned with facets of the application development process.
Business Analyst Business Analyst		Business Analyst	Analyzes operations to develop a solution to its problems.
Business Process Analyst Business Process Modeler		Business Process Analyst	Controls the configuration and operation of a process or organization.
Business Process Manager Business Process Owner		Business Process Administrator	Administers the operations of a process or organization.
Domain Expert Domain Experts Experts for User Interfaces		Domain Experts	Subject matter expert, or person with special knowledge or skills in a particular area.
Requirements Engineer Service Engineer		SBA Engineer	Uses their scientific knowledge to design SBAs.
End User End User		End User	The ultimate user for which the SBA is intended.
Direct User Indirect User Service Consumer Service Consumer	Application Clients	Service Consumer	Initiator and client for the SBA interaction.
Composition Designer Service Composition Designer Negotiation Agent	Service Composers	Composition Designer	Combines services and/or SBAs into more complex ones.
Enterprise Architect Service Architect SOA Domain Architect SOA Platform Architect		Service Architect	Creates structure and design of individual services.
Service Deployer		Service Deployer	Installs services into an operational environment.
Service Designer Service Designer Service Designer	Service Providers	Service Designer	Works out the 'form' of the service.
Service Developer Service Developer Service Developer Service Developer Service Developer/Provider		Service Developer	Involved with the creation or improvement of services.
Service Provider Service Provider		Service Provider	Supplies one or more services.
Change Manager Project Manager	Supporting Roles	Manager	Controls resources and expenditures
Technology Consultants & Suppliers Lawyers & Data Privacy Officers		Supporting Expert	Provides assistance in a particular area.

When looking at the results in the table, the categories with the largest number of stakeholder types are **Application Builders** and **Service Providers**. With respect to the **Application Builder** role, although this role has the primary task of building SBAs with services it also has the functions of a service provider and/or consumer depending on the service realization strategy. For example, [20] describes four strategies for realizing services: 1) in-house service design and implementation, 2) purchasing/leasing/paying for services, 3) outsourcing service design and implementation, and 4) using wrappers and/or adapters. In the first and fourth strategies the **Application Builder** functions as a **Service Provider** as it implements and publishes service for consumption. When taking the second and third strategies, the **Application Builder** acts as a **Service Consumer** that uses third-party services. Due to the broad scope of the **Application Builder** role — from design and implementation of services to integrating services to SBAs — it is natural that many types of stakeholders are required to perform this role.

The second role most present in our findings was the **Service Provider**, and we identified 5 types of stakeholder that perform this role. This is because in the engineering of SBAs it is not the design and development of integrated applications that are of most importance but on the engineering of services that can be reused by many, unknown service consumers. As a result, much of the research of the S-Cube NoE is focused on how to design, deploy and publish services to service consumers, all of which are a concern of the **Service Provider**.

As mentioned in Section 2, what we were not expecting is the non-identification of a stakeholder playing the role of a **Service Broker**. The benefit of a **Service Broker** is that they facilitate the discovery of (possibly third-party) services through a consumer sending a description of the requested service to the **Broker**, who selects a service that best fits the requirement and returns this information to the client [18]. There is a great deal of work on how service discovery can be realized, e.g., by matching between requests and services [13] or through context awareness [16]. However, in our experience, that work concentrates on service discovery mechanisms but not on their operation or use with service brokers. This observation is aligned with our survey on existing service engineering methodologies [9]: only two of the twelve methodologies we analyzed describe service discovery as an explicit part of the engineering process, demonstrating how service discovery and brokering are underrepresented in SOSE research.

5   Coverage of the S-Cube Service Engineering Lifecycle

Step 4 maps the consolidated stakeholder types to the phases of the S-Cube service engineering lifecycle. The results of the mapping are shown in Table 2. We now discuss the coverage of the S-Cube life phases by analyzing: 1) the stakeholder types, 2) the participation of each stakeholder type in the lifecycle and 3) the differences between the evolution and adaptation cycles.

Table 2. S-Cube lifecycle coverage by consolidated stakeholder types

| Role | Consolidated Stakeholder Type | Evolution Lifecycle | | | | Operation & Management | Adaptation Lifecycle | | |
		Early Requirements Engineering	Requirements Engineering & Design	Construction	Deployment & Provision		Identify Adaptation Needs	Identify Adaptation Strategies	Enact Adaptation
Application Builders	SBA Architect	✓	✓	✓	✓	✓	✓	✓	✓
	SBA Modeler	✓	✓		✓		✓	✓	
	Application Developer	✓	✓	✓	✓				
	Business Analyst	✓	✓				✓	✓	
	Business Process Analyst	✓	✓	✓			✓	✓	
	Business Process Administrator	✓	✓		✓		✓	✓	
	Domain Expert	✓	✓						
	SBA Engineer	✓	✓			✓			
Application Clients	End User	✓				✓	✓	✓	✓
	Service Consumer	✓	✓		✓	✓	✓		✓
Service Composers	Composition Designer	✓		✓			✓	✓	✓
	Negotiation Agent				✓	✓			✓
Service Providers	Service Architect	✓	✓	✓	✓	✓	✓	✓	✓
	Service Deployer				✓				
	Service Designer	✓		✓					
	Service Developer	✓	✓	✓	✓	✓			
	Service Provider				✓	✓	✓		✓
Supporting Roles	Manager	✓	✓	✓	✓	✓	✓	✓	✓
	Supporting Expert	✓	✓			✓	✓		
Coverage		84%	68%	42%	58%	53%	63%	48%	42%

5.1   Coverage of Lifecycle Phases by the Stakeholder Types

With reference to Table 2, we can see each phase of the lifecycle is covered but some more completely than others. The last row of the table shows the coverage of each lifecycle phase as a percentage relative to the total number of consolidated stakeholder types. Reviewing the figures we can see the lifecycle phase of Early Requirements Engineering has the greatest amount of coverage with respect to stakeholder types. This is understandable as ensuring the service or SBA being developed or built is useful to its intended end-users requires the input and experience of many stakeholder types, ranging from *Service Architect* to the eventual *End Users*. Only the *Negotiation Agent*, *Service Deployer* and *Service Provider* types, responsible for the provision of services, are not involved in collecting requirements at an early stage of the lifecycle.

It is interesting that the phase of Identify Adaptation Needs is covered by 63% of the stakeholder types identified in this work; dynamically adapting SBAs to meet changing requirements through the identification of adaptation requirements raised by stakeholders involved in the execution of SBAs, or generated by the technological environment in which the system is running is complicated as the adaptation requirements may be conflicting [15]. As more than half of the stakeholder types are involved in this phase this result shows the adaptation of SBAs is well covered by the research carried out within the S-Cube NoE.

The lifecycle phases of Construction, Enact Adaptation and Identify Adaptation Strategies have relatively less coverage (less than 50%). This can be interpreted as fewer stakeholder types are required or that insufficient research has been done in these phases. We feel that these phases may involve fewer types of stakeholders since implementing SBAs without the design, provisioning or enacting a adaptation strategy requires relatively fewer stakeholder types to complete, which is what we would expect.

However, for the Identify Adaptation Strategies phase we expected more stakeholder types. In this phase, the ways through which the adaptation requirements are satisfied are designed and an adaptation strategy is chosen based on the specific adaptation needs. In the stakeholder types derived, we didn't see any stakeholders that were specifically dedicated to these activities. From our survey of adaptation-related activities of sixteen service-oriented approaches [15], we found identifying adaptation strategies and selecting the most suitable strategy are generally not well supported and this finding reinforces this point.

5.2   The Participation of Each Type of Stakeholders

Table 2 shows how certain stakeholder types feature more prominently than others. Specifically, the *SBA Architect*, *Service Architect* and *Manager* types are omnipresent throughout the entire lifecycle, whilst *Service Designer* and *SBA Engineer* are present only in a few phases. It is understandable that the *Manager* may be involved throughout the whole lifecycle, taking care of management-related issues such as cost control and customer relationship management. We are not totally convinced the *SBA Architect* should be involved in all of the lifecycle phases, however, as an *SBA Architect* is responsible for the creation of structure and design of individual services or SBAs and should be active in the early stages of the lifecycle. This is because when a service or SBA has been implemented and deployed the operation and maintenance tasks should be dedicated to other stakeholders, such as the service monitor or adaptation designer, and should not be part of the *SBA Architect's* responsibilities.

5.3   Comparison between the Evolution and Adaptation Cycles

Looking at the differences between the stakeholders involved in the left-hand and right-hand side of Table 2 (i.e., differences between the stakeholders involved in adaptation and evolution phases of the lifecycle), we see that in the adaptation side of the S-Cube lifecycle a much broader range of roles are involved than in the evolution phases. E.g., it appears roles such as Application Clients and Service Composers are more present in the adaptation phase than in the evolution phase. Conversely, we find that roles such as Application Builders are represented to a greater extent in the evolution phases rather than the adaptation phases. We think this demonstrates how the evolution phase is focused much more on the engineering and design and implementation processes rather than the adaptation lifecycle which requires the input of the SBA's end-users, such as Application Clients and Service Consumers.

6   Related Work

The need for determining SOSE stakeholders has been recognized and initial research has been performed into their identification.[3] Kajko-Mattsson et al. [11] proposed a framework with an initial set of IT stakeholders adapted for the

---

[3] Note that in the literature stakeholders are often referred to as *actors* or *roles*.

development, maintenance and evolution of SBAs. Within the framework, 22 stakeholders are suggested and these are categorized into four groups: namely SOA support, SOA strategy and governance, SOA design and quality management and SOA development and evolution. Kajko-Mattsson's framework has a different focus to our work however, as it specifically takes into account business ownership and focuses on new concerns introduced by SOA (e.g., the understanding of the individual services and their cooperation with other services within a combined business process). As a result, many stakeholders (7 out of 22) are related to business, such as Business Process Support Engineer, Business Process Assistant, Business Process Architect, etc. Since we did not focus specifically on business-related tasks and responsibilities, these business-specific stakeholder types can be considered as complementary to our taxonomy.

Zimmermann & Mueller [27] propose a model for roles in a Web Services development project. Int it, the roles are divided into three categories, *existing roles* identified by TSE, *extended roles* that take additional Web services-related responsibilities and *extra roles* responsible for Web services-related tasks. The advantage of this model is that existing TSE stakeholders are explicitly differentiated from SOSE stakeholders. In our taxonomy, this difference is not obvious, although the description of each stakeholder and its participation in the service lifecycle helps make this distinction. The identification of service-specific aspects of stakeholders in our taxonomy is planned as a piece of future work.

The service delivery framework proposed by SAP [23] identifies five stakeholders; the service provider, service host, service gateway, service aggregator and service broker. However, SAP's framework only focuses on stakeholders involved in service provision and not the whole service engineering lifecycle.

The most important difference between previous work and the work presented here is that none of the related works describe *how* stakeholders were identified. Although Kajko-Mattsson et al. mention that they take traditional stakeholders as a starting point and use SOSE literature for reference, a systematic approach and methodology is missing. In this paper we have not only identified an initial set of SOSE stakeholders but also have described the structured approach we used to solicit, classify and consolidate the stakeholders found in the SOSE activities.

Another difference between the above work and ours is how stakeholders are classified: for instance, in the framework developed by Kajko-Mattsson et al. the stakeholders are classified by their function with the implication that these stakeholders need to collaborate more often and solve problems together; in [27] stakeholders are classified by their innovativeness, indicating that specific skills are required for performing certain roles. Our work contributes a new perspective by classifying stakeholders according to SOSE roles. In service engineering it is not uncommon for these roles (e.g., service provider, service consumer, etc.) to be distributed across multiple organizations. As a result, when engineering activities are performed collaboratively across organizational boundaries, additional concerns such as trust, governance and regulatory compliance must be considered [10]. Understanding the roles a SOSE stakeholder plays in this process aids the management of these issues.

Finally, identified stakeholders are associated to SOSE activities using the S-Cube service engineering lifecycle to provide them with a structure and context. This is different from the work we reviewed, which only identifies stakeholder responsibilities and skills and does not explain at which stage of the engineering lifecycle the stakeholders should participate. The lack of explicit links between stakeholders and SOSE engineering activities significantly reduces the applicability of SOSE methodologies, which was observed in our evaluation of a number of well-known SOSE methodologies [9]. The mapping of identified stakeholders to SOSE engineering activities provides an understanding of the stages where each stakeholder is expected to participate. This view is beneficial to the project management and governance of an SOSE project and is a contribution to the SOSE research community as it provides a precise instrument to identify the competencies required for specific service engineering lifecycle activities.

7   Conclusion

The development of SBAs requires more types of stakeholders than traditional software engineering and stakeholders may take multiple roles during the lifecycle of an SBA. In this paper we have reported our research to find information about these stakeholders from institutions within the S-Cube NoE and presented a taxonomy of nineteen stakeholder types performing five roles and a mapping between these stakeholders and the S-Cube service engineering lifecycle. However, despite the S-Cube NoE being the largest network of excellence in-the-field and hence containing broad SOSE know-how, we are aware that S-Cube does not represent the entire SOSE community. In particular, industrial practitioners have not directly participated in this survey; further investigation in industry is needed to validate this taxonomy and ensure generalization and completeness.

From the results it is clear that more types of stakeholders participate in the lifecycle of SBAs than in that of traditional applications and that stakeholders may play different roles depending on their focus on e.g. engineering services, SBAs, service provision or consumption. Moreover, we observed that: some types of stakeholders (such as *Service Architects*) are required in all of the lifecycle phases; there is a lack of stakeholders specifically dedicated to adaptation; and an absence of stakeholders playing the role of service broker. These observations will provide input for future research into these stakeholders that will concentrate on developing and tailoring service engineering methodologies for them.

Acknowledgments. These results has received funding from the European Community's Seventh Framework Programme FP7/2007-2013 under grant agreement 215483 (S-Cube).

References

1. Andrikopoulos, V. (ed.): Separate Design Knowledge Models for Software Engineering & Service-Based Computing. Deliverable CD-JRA-1.1.2, S-Cube Network of Excellence (December 2008)

2. Arsanjani, A.: Service-Oriented Modeling and Architecture (SOMA). IBM DeveloperWorks Article (November 2004)
3. Bass, L., Clements, P., Kazman, R.: Software Architecture in Practice. Addison-Wesley, Reading (2003)
4. Di Nitto, E. (ed.): State of the art Report on Software Engineering & Design Knowledge. Deliverable PO-JRA-1.1.1, S-Cube Network of Excellence (July 2008)
5. Freeman, R.E.: Strategic Management: A Stakeholder Approach. Pitman (1984)
6. Gehlert, A., Bucchiarone, A., Kazhamiakin, R., Metzger, A., Pistore, M., Pohl, K.: Exploiting assumption-based verification for the adaptation of service-based applications. In: Proceedings of the 2010 ACM Symposium on Applied Computing, pp. 2430–2437 (2010)
7. Gu, Q., Lago, P.: A Stakeholder-Driven Service Life-Cycle Model for SOA. In: Proceedings of the 2nd International Workshop on Service Oriented Software Engineering, pp. 1–7 (2007)
8. Gu, Q., Lago, P.: On Service-Oriented Architectural Concerns and Viewpoints. In: Proceedings of the 8th Working IEEE/IFIP Conference on Software Architecture, pp. 289–292 (2009)
9. Gu, Q., Lago, P.: A Service Aspects Driven Evaluation Framework for Service-Oriented Development Methodologies (2010) (submitted for publication)
10. Gu, Q., Lago, P., Di Nitto, E.: Guiding the Service Engineering Process: The Importance of Service Aspects. In: Poler, R., van Sinderen, M., Sanchis, R. (eds.) IWEI 2009. LNBIP, vol. 38, pp. 80–93. Springer, Heidelberg (2009)
11. Kajko-Mattsson, M., Lewis, G.A., Smith, D.B.: A Framework for Roles for Development, Evolution and Maintenance of SOA-Based Systems. In: Proceedings of the International Workshop on Systems Development in SOA Environments, International Conference on Software Engineering, pp. 117–123 (2007)
12. Kitchenham, B., Brereton, O.P., Budgen, D.: The value of mapping studies - a participant-observer case study. In: Proceedings of Evaluation and Assessment of Software Engineering, EASE 2010 (2010)
13. Klusch, M., Fries, B., Sycara, K.: Automated semantic web service discovery with OWLS-MX. In: Proceedings of the 5th International Joint Conference on Autonomous Agents and Multiagent Systems, pp. 915–922 (2006)
14. Kontogiannis, K., Lewis, G.A., Smith, D.B., Litoiu, M., Muller, H., Schuster, S., Stroulia, E.: The Landscape of Service-Oriented Systems: A Research Perspective. In: Proceedings of the International Workshop on Systems Development in SOA Environments, pp. 1–6. IEEE Computer Society, Los Alamitos (2007)
15. Lane, S., Gu, Q., Lago, P., Richardson, I.: Adaptation of service-based applications: A maintenance process? (2010) (submitted for publication)
16. Lee, C., Helal, S.: Context Attributes: An Approach to Enable Context-awareness for Service Discovery. In: Proceedings of the 2003 Symposium on Applications and the Internet, pp. 22–31. IEEE Computer Society, Los Alamitos (2003)
17. Marconi, A., Pistore, M., Traverso, P.: Automated Composition of Web Services: the ASTRO Approach. IEEE Data Engineering Bulletin 31(3), 23–26 (2008)
18. Massuthe, P., Reisig, W., Schmidt, K.: An Operating Guideline Approach to SOA. In: Proceedings of the 2nd South-East European Workshop on Formal Methods (2005)
19. Miles, M.B., Huberman, M.: Qualitative Data Analysis: An Expanded Sourcebook, 2nd edn. Sage Publications, Inc., Thousand Oaks (1994)
20. Papazoglou, M.: Service-Oriented Computing: Concepts, Characteristics and Directions. In: Proceedings of the 4th International Conference on Web Information Systems Engineering, pp. 3–12 (2003)

21. Papazoglou, M., Pohl, K.: S-Cube: The Network of Excellence on Software Services and Systems. In: At Your Service: An Overview of Results of Projects in the Field of Service Engineering of the IST Programme (2009)
22. Pfleeger, S.L., Kitchenham, B.A.: Principles of Survey Research: Part 1: Turning Lemons into Lemonade. SIGSOFT Softw. Eng. Notes 26(6), 16–18 (2001)
23. SAP. Service delivery framework - supporting service delivery for on-demand, business network, cloud environments on an internet-scale (2009),
http://www.internet-of-services.com/uploads/
media/SDF-Value-Proposition_01.pdf
24. Shan, T.C., Hua, W.W.: Service Spectrum for Service Engineering. In: IEEE International Conference on Services Computing, pp. 686–687 (2007)
25. Tarr, P., Ossher, H., Harrison, W., Sutton, S.M.: N Degrees of Separation: Multi-Dimensional Separation of Concerns. In: Proceedings of the 21st International Conference on Software Engineering, pp. 107–119 (1999)
26. Zimmermann, O., Krogdahl, P., Gee, C.: Elements of Service-Oriented Analysis and Design. IBM DeveloperWorks Article (June 2004)
27. Zimmermann, O., Mueller, F.: Web services project roles. IBM DeveloperWorks Article (January 2004)

Service Oriented Middleware for the Internet of Things: A Perspective*

(Invited Paper)

Thiago Teixeira, Sara Hachem, Valérie Issarny, and Nikolaos Georgantas

INRIA Paris-Rocquencourt, France

Abstract. The Internet of Things plays a central role in the foreseen shift of the Internet to the Future Internet, as it incarnates the drastic expansion of the Internet network with non-classical ICT devices. It will further be a major source of evolution of usage, due to the penetration in the user's life. As such, we envision that the Internet of Things will cooperate with the Internet of Services to provide users with services that are aware of their surrounding environment. The supporting service-oriented middleware shall then abstract the functionalities of Things as services as well as provide the needed interoperability and flexibility, through a loose coupling of components and composition of services. Still, core functionalities of the middleware, namely service discovery and composition, need to be revisited to meet the challenges posed by the Internet of Things. Challenges in particular relate to the ultra large scale, heterogeneity and dynamics of the Internet of Things that are far beyond the ones of today's Internet of Services. In addition, new challenges also arise, pertaining to the physical-world aspect that is central to the IoT. In this paper, we survey the major challenges posed to service-oriented middleware towards sustaining a service-based Internet of Things, together with related state of the art. We then concentrate on the specific solutions that we are investigating within the INRIA ARLES project team as part of the CHOReOS European project, discussing new approaches to overcome the challenges particular to the Internet of Things.

1 Introduction

The Internet of Things (IoT) is characterized by the integration of large numbers of real-world objects (or *things*) onto the Internet, with the aim of turning high-level interactions with the physical world into a matter as simple as is interacting with the virtual world today. As such, two types of devices that will play a key role in the IoT are sensors and actuators.

In fact, such devices are already seeing widespread adoption in the highly-localized systems within our cars, mobile phones, laptops, home appliances, etc. In their current incarnation, however, sensors and actuators are used for little more than low-level inferences and basic services. This is partly due to their highly specialized domains (signal

---

* This work is supported by the European Community's Seventh Framework Programme FP7/2007-2013 under grant agreement number 257178 (project CHOReOS - Large Scale Choreographies for the Future Internet - http://www.choreos.eu).

W. Abramowicz et al. (Eds.): ServiceWave 2011, LNCS 6994, pp. 220–229, 2011.

processing, estimation theory, robotics, etc.), which demand application programmers to assume the role of domain experts, and partly due to a glaring lack of interconnectivity between all the different devices.

To be truly useful, sensors and actuators must be ubiquitous rather than constrained to an area around a small set of personal devices, such as a mobile phone or a car. This translates to having a network with a massive number of *things*, spread over a large area — until it covers the entire world. But as the number of sensors and actuators in a network grows to millions and even billions, interoperability, scalability, and flexibility challenges arise. Many of these challenges are, at the surface, the same as those already observed in the existing Internet. However, as we contend later in this paper, these challenges are often significantly different when taking into consideration the complexity of handling physical-world information, especially at never-before-seen scales.

The goal of this paper is to discuss these challenges and propose new directions for solutions at the middleware layer. Throughout this discussion, we take a service-oriented view by abstracting a *thing* as a software service that also has a physical side: that is, *things* sense/actuate the physical world, and they carry physical attributes such as location and orientation in space. We start in Section 2 by stating what in our view are the foremost challenges of the IoT. Then, Section 3 surveys the existing IoT middleware in the literature. Section 4 continues by presenting an overview of our envisioned service-oriented middleware for the IoT, which aims to address the challenges posed by the IoT by leveraging well-studied characteristics of physical phenomena. Finally, Section 5 concludes the paper.

2   Challenges

Many of the challenges related to the Internet of Things are directly inherited from the existing Internet. However, when factoring in the massive scale of the IoT with the intricacies of handling the physical-world information (something that is not considered in the traditional Internet), we find that even some of the most commonly-studied challenges of the Internet appear with significant differences in their IoT manifestation.

In the discussion below, we describe those challenges that stand out, using minimalistic examples in an effort to pinpoint the fundamental cause of each of them. Note, however, that real-world uses of the IoT will no doubt be much more complex. As a result, these challenges will appear not in isolation, but rather as any number of different combination thereof. What we search is a system that can address these even when they occur simultaneously.

1. **Scale**—When performing a sensing or actuation task that pertains to millions of Sensors or Actuators (S&A), it is often infeasible to coordinate every one of the required devices due to constraints such as time, memory, processing power, and energy consumption. To put this into perspective, consider the simple case of an application that requires to know the average air temperature on the city of Paris at this very moment. The answer to this query can be "easily" found by calculating the mean value of the set of temperature readings of *all the thermometer-carrying devices* in the region. However, if there are millions of such devices in Paris, then this set of temperature readings quickly grows unmanageable. Thus even a simple-looking query such as this often leads to unattainable results when the massive

scale of the IoT is factored in. In this example, the solution taken by a domain expert might be to approximate the average temperature by selecting a small sample of temperatures uniformly-distributed within the city, using the well-known equations for the sampling distribution of the mean to calculate the optimal sample size. However, how can an IoT middleware bypass the need for a human expert in the loop, and perform this probabilistic sensor selection on its own?

2. **Deep Heterogeneity**—An important aspect of the IoT that is usually not emphasized enough is that services representing *things* are much more heterogeneous than typical services on the current Internet. For one, due to cost considerations, new sensing/actuating hardware *will often not replace* older generations in already-deployed networks — rather, different generations of devices will operate alongside one another. Likewise, it is probable that the future Internet will be composed of numerous sensor/actuator networks deployed by distinct entities, for distinct reasons. In all of these cases, these networks are bound to contain devices from an assortment of vendors, with highly varying sensing/actuating characteristics, such as error distributions, sampling rates, spatial resolution, and so on. All of these parameters (including functional and non-functional properties) lead to a *deep heterogeneity* that makes S&A networks extremely hard to work with, even for experts. And as networks increase in size, delegating these types of coordination tasks to humans will simply not be feasible. In such a dynamic environment, with so many unknowns, it is clear that fully automated methods for high level inference will become a necessity.

3. **Unknown Topology**—Much like the existing Internet, one of the IoT's main characteristics is the fact that its topology is both unknown and dynamic. As a consequence, applications will often end up depending on services which are not actually available from any single preexisting component of the network at that given time. For instance, if an application would like to obtain the value of the wind-chill factor at a certain location, it may happen that the network does not have a wind-chill sensor in that exact neighborhood. However, if instead the network does have temperature and wind speed sensors (i.e. anemometer), then a field expert could easily obtain the desired information through the composition of the temperature and wind speed readings using the well-known wind-chill equation. This is possible because the *function* of a wind-chill sensor is equivalent to the *function* provided by the thermometer/anemometer combination put together by the expert. The question is, then: can an IoT middleware perform these types of functional substitutions on its own without supervision? How can this type of service composition be performed in an optimal manner when the network is massive in scale, with unknown topology?

4. **Unknown Data-Point Availability**—A second consequence of the unknown topology is that sometimes there will be no suitable device at the desired geographical location or, other times, the device has not collected/stored the data-point that is desired. However, oftentimes the missing data-points can be estimated with a very high degree of accuracy. For instance, if an application would like to know the temperature at a location where no thermometer exists, then an expert should be able to estimate the result using the values of the temperature readings in the surrounding area (for example, with a Kalman filter). Or when the application requires access

to the location of a car at some time t_1, but only the locations at time t_0 and t_2 are known ($t_0 < t_1 < t_2$), then a user versed in Newton's laws of motion should be able to calculate the midpoint-speed t_1. But how can these estimations take place in an automated fashion, without the need for human intervention?

5. **Incomplete or Inaccurate Metadata**—The solution to many of the challenges above likely lies on the extensive use of metadata. However, since much of this metadata must be manually entered by a human operator at installation time, in a massive network this will surely result in a large amount of incomplete/inaccurate information due to human error. In addition, some of this information includes characteristics that change over time (e.g., calibration parameters). Therefore, even discounting human error, the state of the metadata in the network is bound to degrade until it no longer represents reality. In these scenarios, how can missing metadata be recovered? And how can existing information be monitored and updated when necessary?

6. **Conflict Resolution**—Conflict resolution is an issue that arises mainly with actuators, but not so much with sensors. Conflicts arise, for instance, when multiple applications attempt to actuate the same device in opposing ways, or when they would like to exert mutually-incompatible changes on the environment. For example, in a scenario where a smart building is able to adapt to people's personal temperature preferences, one person may want a choose a temperature of $17C$ while the other $25C$. A human mediator would likely resolve this conflict using the average of the two temperatures, $21C$. However, a much tougher example presents itself in the actuation of pan-tilt-zoom cameras: if one application requires the camera to turn left, and the other requires it to turn right, how can the network satisfy both applications — or at least gracefully degrade their quality of service?

3   Related Work

Most middleware solutions for the IoT adopt a service-oriented design in order to support a network topology that is both unknown and dynamic. But while some projects focus on abstracting the *devices* in the network as services (such as in HYDRA[1–3], SENSEI [4], SOCRADES[5], and COBIS[6]), other projects devote more attention to data/information abstractions and their integrations with services (among which are SOFIA[1] [7], SATware[8], and Global Sensor Networks GSN [9]). A common thread throughout all of these solutions, however, is that they handle the challenge of **unknown topology** through the use of discovery methods that are largely based on the *traditional* service/resource discovery approaches of the existing Internet, ubiquitous environments and Wireless Sensor & Actuator Networks [10–12]. For instance, SOCRADES provides discovery on two levels, the device level and the service level, which can employ either standard WS-discovery (for WS Web Service) or a RESTful discovery mechanism (for RESTful services). COBIS, on the other hand, uses its own service description language COBIL[2] (Collaborative Business Item Language) where service functions and keywords are annotated with a verbal description.

---

[1] http://www.sofia-project.eu
[2] http://www.cobil-online.de/cobil/v1.1/

Another point of agreement in the state-of-the-art in IoT middleware is in the widespread use of semantics and metadata to overcome **heterogeneity** challenges. Indeed it is standard practice to use ontologies to model sensors, their domains, and sensor data repositories [2, 13, 14]. Some projects even go a step further and also include context information[4], or service descriptions[5]. And as a type of service composition, many projects support the concept of virtual/semantic sensors (for instance, in HYDRA, GSN and SATware), i.e. entities that abstract several aggregated physical devices under a single service. A different implementation of a similar idea, though, is provided in the SATware project: in their work, virtual sensors actually correspond to transformations applied to a set of raw sensor streams to produce another semantically meaningful stream. Although it can be said that the concept of virtual sensors is a sort of service composition, one must be careful to point out that this composition is *not fully dynamic*, in that the services are first specified at *design time*, and only then are they dynamically mapped onto the network at run time. In contrast, a much more flexible type of composition is to perform both operations at run time, through the help of small predefined composition building blocks as supported by the SENSEI and SOCRADES projects.

Regarding **scalability**, most IoT projects address this challenge by pursuing modifications in the underlying network topology. At times, this is done by adopting fully-distributed infrastructures (such as in COBIS and SOFIA), and at other times through an architecture of peer-to-peer clusters (e.g., GSN). In our view, however, while these approaches work well for the existing Internet (where traffic is made up of a relatively small amount of service interactions) they are not fit for the complex weave of interactions that will be commonplace in the Internet of Things. In the IoT, a large number of requests will involve intricate coordination among thousands of *things* and services, whereas on today's Internet most requests are largely point-to-point. Therefore, the number of packets transmitted in the network will grow strongly nonlinearly as the number of available services increases. In such an environment, performing even a simple service discovery or composition may exceed acceptable time, processing, and memory constraints. For this reason, in Section 4, we propose to address the challenge of scalability by modifying the discovery and composition algorithms themselves, rather than focusing solely on designing optimal network topologies.

Finally, among the aforementioned projects, to the best of our knowledge, *none* considers the challenges of **data-point availability**, **inaccurate metadata**, and **conflict resolution**. To address such issues, in our proposed work, we rely on the highly-structured nature of physical information. We design our middleware to support not only semantic models but also *estimation models* that perform all of these tasks transparently, in the background, without ever burdening the application with the internal details of this process. In some ways, it can be said that this aspect of our approach bears some similarity with Google's Prediction API[3]. This is a web service which allows application writers to train and use classifiers on their own datasets without requiring any knowledge of machine learning or data mining. In our work, however, we do not aim to compete with the Prediction API, but rather provide the means by which these kinds of prediction services can be leveraged without the user or application-writer even knowing about it. The process, we claim, should be realized in a completely

---

[3] http://code.google.com/apis/predict/

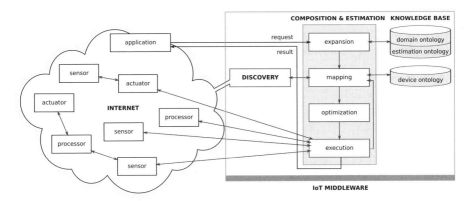

Fig. 1. Architecture of our IoT middleware

automated manner. To support all of these features, we envision an IoT architecture that is described in the next section.

4 Blueprints of a Solution

To address the challenges of the IoT, we take a service-oriented approach as commonly done in the literature, relying heavily on semantics to describe devices, their data, and their physical attributes. Building upon this semantic, service-oriented foundation, however, we also introduce the support for mathematical models capable of estimation, calibration, and conflict resolution. As a result, our proposed architecture produces a loose coupling of *things* and traditional services, all of which can contribute to resolving sensing/actuation requests, but none of which is strictly required. When one of these components is not available in the network, our middleware, then, makes use of estimations, approximations, and predictions.

Our envisioned IoT middleware, as shown in Figure 1, consists of three parts: a Discovery module, and Estimation & Composition module, and a Knowledge Base (KB). A description of these three modules, and the main innovations that we introduce in each of them, follows.

4.1 Discovery Module

The process of service discovery consists of two parts: registration and look-up. *Registration* is the process where each service connects to a server (called a registry) to give some information about itself, including a network address. *Look-up* can be described as finding the services that match a given set of desirable attributes (sensing modality, geographic location, error characteristics, etc.). However, to address the challenges of scale described in Section 2-1 we here introduce the concept of **probabilistic discovery** to provide, instead, *the set of services that can best approximate* the result that is being sought after. In the context of the example from Section 2-1, where a person would like to find out the average temperature in Paris, the middleware should proceed by first fetching the definition of "average" from the Knowledge Base, which includes a description of the well-known equation for the sampling distribution of the mean. This equation states that in a network of M sensors, we can afford to instead use only N sensors ($N < M$) to calculate the average temperature within some mean error of e. Then, with this information the middleware should perform the following actions:

1. Use the provided error equation to estimate the number N of sensors that will be needed for this request.
2. Produce a random sample of N points in time, space, and other dimensions (such as sensor/actuator orientation in space, their coverage area, or any other attribute of a device).
3. Discover N devices in the network that approximately match those N points.
4. Given this set of devices, recalculate the error estimate.
5. Repeat 2–5, depending on whether the new error estimate is satisfactory.

The steps above are an instance of what we call a *probabilistic lookup*. That is, an intelligently-constructed query that makes use of probabilities to find approximate sets of services when exact solutions would be too costly to compute. In a similar manner, another aspect of discovery that can also be made probabilistic is the registration process. In *probabilistic registration*, services use non-deterministic functions to determine (1) which registry they should register with, (2) at what times registration should take place, and (3) what attributes they should register with each registry. Part of our upcoming research will consist on characterizing the different combinations of probability distributions that can be used throughout the discovery process (during both lookup and registration), in order to establish the advantages and disadvantages of each discovery scheme.

4.2   Composition and Estimation Module

As can be seen in Figure 1, the component that is directly in charge of processing sensing and actuation requests is the Composition & Estimation module. Within this module, the process responsible for coordinating all tasks is the composition process. "Composition" consists of finding a dataflow graph that, given a description of the input parameters and the format of the desired output, connects the available services in order to produce the desired output from the parameters.

To clarify what this means, let us consider a brute-force implementation of the composition process, consisting of the following phases:

1. *Expansion*: This step expands the initial query by replacing each term with an equivalent expression, found by traversing the domain ontology. In this brute-force implementation, the final result of the expansion phase is a set of all possible combinations of service dataflows that answer the initial query.
2. *Mapping*: This step takes all dataflows produced by the expansion step and maps them to the actual network topology. As such, mapping is necessarily performed by interacting closely with the Discovery module. This phase also interacts with our device ontology (present in the KB) that models real world devices, to complement any information found to be missing during the discovery process. The output of the brute-force mapping step is the set of all possible mappings of the input dataflows onto the network topology.

3. *Optimal mapping selection*: Once all feasible dataflows have been mapped (in the mapping phase), the IoT middleware must choose one dataflow to enact. In this phase, therefore, a dataflow that is (in some predefined way) optimal is found and passed on to the execution block, below.
4. *Execution*: Now that the best composition of services has been determined for the query, in the execution step the services are actually accessed and the result is returned (or stored). In addition, during execution, the middleware must check for any conflicts that may arise at run-time, in a process that we call conflict resolution.

In an ultra-large-scale network with a large-scale Knowledge Base, seeking an optimal composition becomes an intractable problem. So instead of pursuing an exact solution as was done in the brute-force case above, in our research we will pursue the idea of **approximately-optimal composition**, where the concepts of *expansion* and *mapping* are modified as follows:

1. *Smart expansion*: To avoid exhaustively calculating all possible equivalent sets of dataflows, only one of which will eventually be selected during the optimization phase, a much smarter approach to expansion is to instead produce a reduced set of good candidate dataflows. These candidates are the dataflows that have the highest likelihood of having a matching overlay in the network that satisfies a set of predefined constraints. An example constraint could be that the predicted execution time should fall within a certain acceptable interval.
2. *Probabilistic mapping*: Taking as input the set of candidate dataflows from the previous phase, the probabilistic mapping phase differs from regular mapping in that it does not attempt to find all possible mappings of the input dataflows into the network topology. Instead, this phase will randomly pick a small subset of all implementable mappings by making small, atomic queries to the probabilistic Discovery module. The result is a much reduced set of dataflow mappings that are computed in considerably less time and using (hopefully) orders of magnitudes less resources.

So far, all of the new features mentioned above focus on addressing the way the challenges of scale, heterogeneity, and unknown topology magnify one another. However, in addition to these challenges, we also address the challenge of unknown data-point availability (Section 2-4), by injecting in the IoT middleware enough knowledge about sensing, actuation, physics, devices, etc., to be able perform the **automated estimation** of any missing data-points. This is possible through the use of physical/statistical models that are provided *a priori* by field experts and made available in a Knowledge Base. Then, when a missing data-point is detected, or when more accurate data is requested by an application, the middleware can apply the provided models onto the timeseries of measurements from a set of sensors, and therefore estimate the most likely true value of the data at the desired spatiotemporal point. This process takes place in three steps:

1. *Model discovery*: Look in the KB for models related to the desired devices.
2. *Optimal model selection*: Pick the most appropriate models based on a few parameters and a cost function (also specified in the ontology).
3. *Estimation execution*: Apply the models to the existing historical data from sensors, using as input parameters the sensor and deployment metadata. This will be done using pre-developed engines for each model.

Furthermore, it is likely that the same framework used for automated estimation can be extended to support *auto-calibration* and *conflict-resolution* techniques, given that all of them rely on enacting expert-provided models stored in the KB. This would address the challenges described in Sections 2-5 and 2-6. In the case of the former challenge, the same physical and probabilistic models employed during *estimation* could even be reused with little or no changes: here, however, the models would be executed *backwards*, to extract the parameters given the data (i.e. calibration), rather than estimate the data given the parameters (estimation).

4.3   Knowledge Base

A key piece that is fundamental to all others listed above is a comprehensive set of ontologies describing sensors, actuators, physical concepts, physical units, etc., as well as spatiotemporal and statistical correlation models of the data. This set of ontologies goes by the name "Knowledge Base", consisting of three parts:

The *Domain Ontology* carries information about how different physical concepts are related to one another. For instance, the "wind chill" concept can be described as a function two other concepts: "temperature" and "wind speed". This ontology also links each physical concept with a set of physical units ($"km/h"$, $"m/s"$, etc.) as well as with the known sensors/actuators that can measure/change them.

The *Device Ontology* stores information regarding actual hardware devices that may exist in the network, including manufacturers, models, type of device, etc., and connects each device to related concepts in other ontologies (for example, which physical units it uses when outputting data, what is the device's transfer function, etc.).

Finally, the *Estimation Ontology* contains information about different estimation models ("linear interpolation", "Kalman filter", "naïve Bayesian learning", etc.), the equations that drive them, the services that implement them, and so on.

Turning once again to the example from Section 2-3, what should be clear is that even the simplest-looking requests, upon closer inspection, end up requiring a rather complex composition of services in order to obtain an accurate result. However, it is likely that once the IoT infrastructure is in place, the most common requests will certainly be *much more complex* than the examples in this paper. Therefore, one of the greatest challenges in building a middleware for the IoT lies in envisioning an architecture that can grow and adapt to new, unforeseen situations. We believe that the system outline presented here fulfills this requirement. By deriving its composition and estimation decisions from models entered by domain experts in a Knowledge Base, our middleware is built from the ground up to evolve with the ever-changing demands of future IoT applications.

5   Conclusion

We have described the core challenges of the Internet of Things, and analysed the state-of-the-art within the context of these challenges. We, then, proposed an IoT middleware that addresses these challenges through probabilities and approximations. Our middleware adopts a service-oriented architecture to abstract all sensors and actuators as services in order to hide their heterogeneity, and relies heavily on a knowledge base that carries information about sensors, actuators, manufacturers, physical concepts, physical units, data models, error models, etc. To address challenges stemming from the IoT's massive scale and deep heterogeneity, we concentrate on three core research contributions: probabilistic discovery, approximately-optimal composition, and automated estimation. Together, these three contributions will allow our middleware to respond to sensing or actuation requests while managing the complex relationship between accuracy and time, memory, processing, and energy constraints.

References

1. Zhang, W., Hansen, K.: An evaluation of the NSGA-II and MOCell genetic algorithms for self-management planning in a pervasive service middleware. In: 14th IEEE International Conference on Engineering of Complex Computer Systems, pp. 192–201 (2009)
2. Eisenhauer, M., Rosengren, P., Antolin, P.: Hydra: A development platform for integrating wireless devices and sensors into ambient intelligence systems. The Internet of Things, 367–373 (2010)
3. Zhang, W., Hansen, K.: Semantic web based self-management for a pervasive service middleware. In: Second IEEE International Conference on Self-Adaptive and Self-Organizing Systems, pp. 245–254 (2008)
4. Presser, M., Barnaghi, P., Eurich, M., Villalonga, C.: The SENSEI project: Integrating the physical world with the digital world of the network of the future. IEEE Communications Magazine 47(4), 1–4 (2009)
5. Guinard, D., Trifa, V., Karnouskos, S., Spiess, P., Savio, D.: Interacting with the SOA-Based internet of things: Discovery, query, selection, and on-demand provisioning of Web Services. IEEE Transactions on Services Computing 3(3), 223–235 (2010)
6. CoBIs project, Cobis final project report deliverable 104 v 2.0, Tech. Rep. (2007), http://www.cobis-online.de/files/Deliverable_D104V2.pdf
7. Honkola, J., Laine, H., Brown, R., Tyrkko, O.: Smart-M3 information sharing platform. In: IEEE Symposium on Computers and Communications (ISCC), pp. 1041–1046 (2010)
8. Massaguer, D., Hore, B., Diallo, M., Mehrotra, S., Venkatasubramanian, N.: Middleware for pervasive spaces: Balancing privacy and utility. In: Bacon, J.M., Cooper, B.F. (eds.) Middleware 2009. LNCS, vol. 5896, pp. 247–267. Springer, Heidelberg (2009)
9. Aberer, K., Hauswirth, M., Salehi, A.: Infrastructure for data processing in large-scale interconnected sensor networks. In: International Conference on Mobile Data Management, pp. 198–205 (2007)
10. Al-Masri, E., Mahmoud, Q.H.: Investigating web services on the world wide web. In: Proceeding of the 17th International Conference on World Wide Web, pp. 795–804. ACM, New York (2008)
11. Zhu, F., Mutka, M., Ni, L.: Service discovery in pervasive computing environments. IEEE Pervasive Computing 4(4), 81–90 (2005)
12. Meshkova, E., Riihijarvi, J., Petrova, M., Mahonen, P.: A survey on resource discovery mechanisms, peer-to-peer and service discovery frameworks. Computer Networks 52(11), 2097–2128 (2008)
13. Eid, M., Liscano, R., El Saddik, A.: A universal ontology for sensor networks data. In: IEEE International Conference on Computational Intelligence for Measurement Systems and Applications, pp. 59–62 (2007)
14. Liu, J., Zhao, F.: Towards semantic services for sensor-rich information systems. In: 2nd International Conference on Broadband Networks, pp. 967–974 (2005)

Future Internet Apps: The Next Wave of Adaptive Service-Oriented Systems?

Andreas Metzger and Clarissa Cassales Marquezan

Paluno (The Ruhr Institute for Software Technology)
University of Duisburg-Essen, Essen, Germany
{andreas.metzger,clarissa.marquezan}@paluno.uni-due.de

Abstract. The Future Internet will emerge through the convergence of software services, things, content, and communication networks. Service-orientation is expected to play a key role as enabling technology that allows the provisioning of hard- and software entities and contents as services. The dynamic composition of such services will enable the creation of service-oriented systems in the Future Internet (FI Apps), which will be increasingly provided by third parties. Together with increased expectations from end-users for personalization and customization, FI Apps will thus face an unprecedented level of change and dynamism. Based on our understanding of adaptive service-oriented systems, this paper discusses the key adaptation characteristics for FI Apps (illustrated by a concrete application domain). The importance of each of those characteristics has been empirically assessed by means of a survey study. We provide the results of this study which can help in better understanding where future research and development effort should be invested.

1 Introduction

The Future Internet (FI) is expected to become a ubiquitous infrastructure that will overcome the current limitations of the Internet for what concerns interoperability, accessibility, resource efficiency, security, and trustworthiness, as well as integration with the physical world [9]. Specifically, the Future Internet will be built around four major areas: The IoS (Internet of Services) that relates to the provision, discovery, composition, and consumption of (software) services via the Internet. The IoT (Internet of Things) relates to embedded systems, sensors and actuators that collect and carry information about real-world objects via their interconnection with the Internet. The IoC (Internet of Content) relates to the discovery, distribution, combination, and consumption of all kinds of media objects (*e.g.*, text, 3D graphics and audio) which carry meta-information about their content and can be accessed via the Internet. Finally, NoF (Networks of the Future) relates to ubiquitous communication facilities (*e.g.*, mobile, broadband).

In the Future Internet setting, services are expected to play a key role as enabling technology and core building entities. These services will provide the right level of abstraction from hard- and software entities, extending from business functions to data storage, processing and networking, devices and content.

W. Abramowicz et al. (Eds.): ServiceWave 2011, LNCS 6994, pp. 230–241, 2011.

Service-oriented systems in the Future Internet, we call them *FI Apps*, will be dynamically composed from these service-based entities, operating on federated, open and trusted platforms exploiting the Future Internet areas.

The capabilities and features of FI Apps will be increasingly provided and "owned" by third parties. Examples include Internet-based software services, public sensor networks, and cloud infrastructures. Due to this "shared owner-ship" [1]), FI Apps will face an unprecedented level of change and dynamism. Further, expectations from end-users for what concerns the personalization and customization of those FI Apps are expected to become increasingly relevant for market success. For instance, a FI App should be able to adapt depending on the usage setting (*e.g.*, office vs. home) or based on the available communica-tion infrastructure (*e.g.*, sensors vs. WiMAX). It will thus become increasingly important to engineer FI Apps in such a way that those applications can dy-namically and autonomously respond to changes in the provisioning of services, availability of things and contents, as well as changes of network connectivity and end-user devices, together with changes in user expectations. Ultimately, this means that *adaptation* will become a key capability of FI Apps.

There has been significant progress for what concerns principles and tech-niques for building adaptive service-oriented systems. For example, many solu-tions have been developed within S-Cube[1]. However, if we consider the Future Internet setting, those solutions will need to be significantly augmented, im-proved and integrated with a complete systems perspective. Specifically, this requires significant progress towards novel strategies and techniques for adap-tation, addressing key characteristics of adaptive FI Apps. To enable the next wave of adaptive service-oriented systems in the Future Internet, it will thus be critical to understand the importance of the various adaptation characteristics to specifically target research and development activities.

This paper, therefore, identifies and analyses key characteristics of adaptive FI Apps (Section 3). Those characteristics are illustrated with examples from a scenario of the application domain of transport and logistics (Section 2). The paper scrutinizes the relevance of those different characteristics through an em-pirical study (Section 4). As a research method we have employed an exploratory survey study, involving 51 respondents from the Future Internet community.

2   The Transport and Logistics Scenario

Modern transport and logistics processes are characterized by distributed inter-organization activities often spanning several countries and continents. An illus-tration of current transport and logistics process associated with the construction of an offshore wind energy plant is presented in Figure 1. Based on this example, we describe some of the limitations of current processes and present insights on how Future Internet can contribute to overcome those limitations.

---

[1] The EU Network of Excellence on Software Services and Systems.
  http://www.s-cube-network.eu/

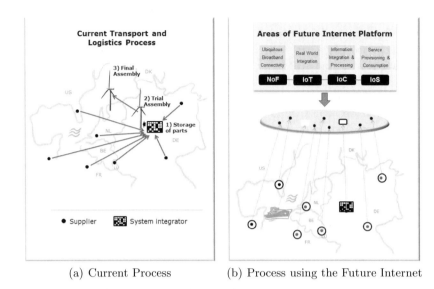

(a) Current Process   (b) Process using the Future Internet

Fig. 1. Offshore Wind Energy Plant Example

Figure 1(a) shows the stages required currently to accomplish the construction of a wind energy engine. The individual components are produced by various suppliers that typically are geographically distributed and in the first stage they are delivered to the manufacturer (*i.e.*, the system integrator) of the wind energy station who is responsible for storing these components. To ensure that all resources and semi-finished goods are available on time at the production line, this structure of the supply chain requires a considerable amount of buffer and warehousing space at the sites of each supplier as well as at the system integrator. This inefficient and highly cost intensive process results from the fact that current logistic processes lack the required end-to-end visibility of the supply chain, which itself results from insufficient integration between IT systems of the various logistics stakeholders.

After component production and supply management, the complete wind energy station is constructed in a trial assembly for a full operational test (stage 2). This is required to ensure defect-free operation as expected by the end-customer, and can avoid any costly and time-consuming delivery requirements for missing or defective parts when assembly occurs at the final destination. From the business perspective, the trial assembly is necessary because the information provided throughout the supply chain is often incompatible, so that operational reliability cannot be guaranteed by merely inspecting the documentation of the delivered components. After the trial assembly and a final operational test, the plant is disassembled and shipped to the intended destination (stage 3).

This example shows that current transport and logistics processes face obstacles that prevent the achievement of a more reliable, lower cost and environmentally friendly industry. Solutions for these obstacles must be characterized by:

integration of different ICT environments, better integration among systems and the real world, reduction of manual intervention and guarantees of ubiquitous access to information among the partners. The Future Internet is an alternative that can encompass all these characteristics. Indeed, the employment of Future Internet areas, as illustrated in Figure 1(b) can enable the end-to-end visibility of the supply chain, where information derived from the real world (*e.g.*, data retrieved from sensors or cameras in the vessel) can be ubiquitously accessed by all the partners of the chain (using for this any kind of network connectivity) and the service based applications of those partners are able to exchange information, negotiate and collaborate in order to accomplish the business goals of the supply chain. The environment aforementioned constitute, indeed, the so called Future Internet application. In such heterogeneous environment, dynamic and unexpected changes can happen and, thus, adaptive characteristics become of great importance for Future Internet applications.

3   Adaptive Characteristics of FI Apps

In this section, we elaborate key characteristics for adaptive FI Apps. Those characteristics have been identified jointly by S-Cube, the EU Network of Excellence on Software Services and Systems [7], and FInest (the EU FI PPP Use case project on transport & logistics). Figure 2(a) shows the projects' shared understanding of the the layers of the Future Internet. This will be used to explain the different adaptation characteristics and their relationships that are presented in Figure 2(b) and described further below.

The *Future Internet Platform* layer (in Figure 2(a)) constitutes generic technology building blocks from various Future Internet areas (IoS, IoC, IoT and NoF). Those building blocks can be instantiated to platform instances on top of which FI Apps can be executed. The *Future Internet Application* layer constitutes domain-specific technology building blocks, as well as domain-specific FI Apps. As illustrated in Figure 2(a), possible application domains are transport

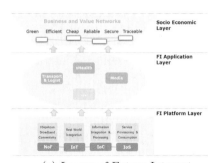

(a) Layers of Future Internet

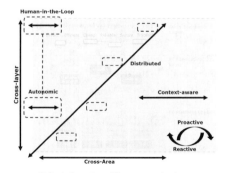

(b) Adaptive Characteristics

Fig. 2. Future Internet Layers and Adaptation

& logistics, eHealth and media. The *Socio-Economic* layer constitutes networks of people and organizations, which can benefit from the FI Apps.

3.1 Cross-Layer Adaptation

The proposals in the research literature highlighted fundamental aspects of cross-layer adaptation in service-oriented systems [7,1]. These proposals considered the interaction among the SOA layers (business process management, service composition and service infrastructure). For FI Apps, however, the cross-layer adaptation is expected to gain a much broader meaning. An example of how cross-layer adaptation might have to be reconsidered can be derived from the scenario presented in Section 2. Consider that sensors are used to monitor the conditions of the wind engine parts transported by the vessel (Figure 1(b)) and this information is used by the supply logistic chain to organize and synchronize the collaboration among the parties (all suppliers, warehousing and transport providers). Now, if the vessel informs that goods inside of the containers have been damaged, this information must be escalated up to the Socio-Economic Layer so that the parties can adapt their applications and business values and networks in response to a change in the FI Platform layer. Therefore, future service-oriented systems need to expand on the concept cross-layer adaptation.

3.2 Cross-Area Adaptation

As motivated in the introduction to this paper, the Future Internet will enable end-users to experience an ubiquitous and transparent access to applications, services and information using any kind of device at any time. One important consequence of this vision is thus the anticipated need for FI Apps to adapt not only considering the changes and resources in one specific area (*e.g.*, service availability in the IoS), but also regarding other areas (*e.g.*, adapting according to sensor information availability in the IoT). In our running example, for instance, if the sensors of the vessel stop sending information for the transport & logistics application, it is necessary to start adaptive actions to gather information about the status of the containers in the vessel from other sources. One possible solution would be to exploit the capabilities of the IoC, *e.g.*, by processing the video streams from the surveillance cameras of the vessel. Cross-area characteristics of adaptation, thus, can lead to many new research questions. One of such questions, is related to understand the limits and the interactions between the adaptive capabilities in each of the FI areas.

3.3 Distributed Adaptation

Most of current solutions for adaptation in the scope of service-oriented application (*i.e.*, based on third-party services) typically employ a central entity for gathering information from distributed sources and taking the decisions. This leads to at least two critical problems. First, in a third-party scenario, the central entity will only have limited access to information from the third-party service providers (*e.g.*, the load of the computing infrastructure at the providers' side is unknown to the service user). Second, a central entity will present classical problems like single point of failure, lack of scalability, and bottlenecks which will not be acceptable once the scale of the Future Internet. In our view, distribution is not only about retrieving information from distributed entities, but it is also about the distribution of the actual decision-making process. This need is expected to be exacerbated if we also take into account the relevance of cross-layer and cross-area characteristics in FI Apps. In our example, for instance, once the vessel informed to the collaborative supply chain (Figure 1(b)) that a container is damaged and the parts of the wind engine are compromised, the service-oriented application of each partner in the supply chain has to adapt, for instance, by re-negotiating contracts (*e.g.*, delaying the actual physical transport and requesting more warehouse space). In this case, the service-oriented applications could distribute and negotiate the decision of which parts of the supply chain should adapt because in such a distributed business network it will not possible to collect complete information from all the parties (e.g., due to privacy or IP concerns). Thus, distributed decision-making would help to avoid unilateral and isolated adaptations in the supply chain.

3.4   Context-Aware Adaptation

The information about the context in which service-based systems are executed as well as their users impact on the expected behaviour and quality of the systems [7]. For the Future Internet, not only information about the users' context will impact on the applications, but also other context aspects from the FI areas related to the application will gain importance; e.g., information about the environment (from IoT) or about the geographic region (from IoC). For example, if the service-oriented applications of the supply chain of the wind energy plant do not receive the expected report from the vessel, they cannot assume that adaptation actions are needed because no status of the wind engine parts was received. It is necessary to check the context of the vessel. For instance, because of a very strong storm, the radio and satellite communications might have been interrupted. One possible manner to become aware of such a context change would be through the combination of information from GPS and weather forecasts. Another context-aware adaption issue in the transport and logistics scenario is associated with country-specific regulations. In this case, if some change occurs and the freight needs to be delivered through another country, the documents and delivery processes need to be adapted to reflect that country's regulations.

3.5   Autonomic and Human-in-the-Loop Adaptation

One important perspective of Future Internet applications will be the involvement of different user roles in the adaptation activities. Although many adaptation decision can be performed autonomously (e.g., communication networks and computing infrastructures are furnished with self-* capabilities), there will be a certain limit for such an automation. Specifically, once adaptation decisions can impact on the business strategy and success of an organization, or it involves creative decision making, humans need to be involved in the adaptation process. This means that there will be a range of adaptation strategies from completely automated (*autonomous*) to interactive and manual (*human-in-the-loop*), as illustrated in Figure 2(b). In the wind energy scenario, for example, when the vessel informs the application that parts of wind engine are damaged, there might be the option to automatically contract an alternative provider for those parts. However, a more effective decision would have been to change the assembly order of the parts, thereby saving the costs incurred in starting a new procurement process with an alternative provider. When designing adaptive FI Apps, we thus need to find a proper balance between these two characteristics.

3.6   Reactive and Proactive Adaptation

The adaptation of service-oriented applications mostly occurs reactively, *i.e.*, the application is re-configured due to changes in the context or due to faults of third-party services [7]. In contrast to reactive adaptation, preventive and proactive adaptation offer significant benefits. Preventive adaptation is associated with the case in which an actual local failure is repaired before its consequences become visible to the end-user, while proactive adaptation predicts future failures and changes, and modifies the application before those changes impact[2]. For instance, if a problem is discovered before it impacts on the actual application, no compensation or roll-back actions have to be performed (cf. [5,8]). For the FI Apps proactive adaptation is expected to gain further importance, mainly because of the heterogeneity of elements involved in the design of such applications and the intensification of the inter-organizational dependencies. Thus, a local fault can lead to a chain of reactive adaptations across organizations. For example, in the construction of the wind energy plant, the transport and logistics application must be very well synchronized in order to avoid extra costs with transport and warehousing in case of delays. A proactive supply chain application for this scenario (as illustrated in Figure 1), could predict – e.g., based on weather forecasts – if deviations along some of the transport routes might occur (e.g., when severe thunderstorms impact on air-traffic situations). If such a deviation is predicted, the FI App could either modify the transport processes by using alternative transport modes (such as trains), or schedule further warehouse capacity.

4   Survey Study

Currently, there are few empirical studies for what concerns assessing the importance of characteristics of FI Apps. The NESSI membership survey (published in May, 2011) is one of those. That survey has identified "adaptable" and "self-manageable" as being among the top 7 characteristics. However, no further details on what kind of "self-management" or "adaptiveness" would be expected has been provided. Therefore, to gain insight into the practical importance of the various characteristics of adaptive FI Apps (as the ones identified in Section 3), we have performed an exploratory survey study involving practitioners

---

[2] In this paper, preventive adaptation is subsumed in proactive adaptation.

and researchers involved in Future Internet activities. This section reports on the design and the results of this survey study, for which we follow the recommendations for empirical research by Kitchenham et al. [2].

4.1 Context

The survey study was performed by involving the participants of the 6th Future Internet Assembly, which was held in Budapest from 17-19 May, 2011. The Future Internet Assembly serves as a forum, where European and international practitioners, academics and policy makers come together to discuss emerging issues in the Future Internet. More specifically, the survey study was carried out as part of a dedicated session on "Adaptive Future Internet Applications", co-organized by the authors[3]. We consider the FIA event as an ideal setting for our survey, as its participants are representative for the FI community.

The research question that we aimed to answer with this survey study were associated with the importance of the different characteristics of FI Apps. In addition, we wanted to explore the relative importance of adaptation for the various layers, areas and application domains that we see emerging in the Future Internet (see Section 4.3 for details). We believe that the outcomes of the survey can give insights that contribute to a better understanding of the practical relevance of the issues addressed in this empirical study and ultimately can lead to more targeted research activities (as analyzed in Section 3).

4.2 Design, Execution and Data Collection

Concerning the design of our survey questionnaire, we specifically took into account the following findings from psychology as reported by Krosnick [3].

(i) Based on the observation that ranking can be very time consuming and that people enjoy ratings more than rankings, we asked participants to rate the various characteristics. We decided to determine the ranking based on the rates by applying a simple weighing function to the responses.

(ii) Concerning the answer choices, we did not offer a "no opinion" choice. This was based on the observation that offering a "no opinion" choice, can compromise data quality. Further, we used verbal scale labels, as numeric labels might convey the wrong meaning. Following a recent survey study presented by Narasimhan and Nichols [6], we used their five-point scale employing the following labels: unimportant, of little importance, somewhat important, important, very important. Finally, we started with the negative options first, as studies have shown that people tend to select the first option that fits within their range of opinion. By doing so, our study will thus lead to more "conservative" results.

The questionnaire has been pretested by 10 researchers from our institute. This pretest lead to significant improvements for what concerns the understandability

---

[3] http://www.future-internet.eu/home/future-internet-assembly/
budapest-may-2011.html

of questions and options. Specifically, questions that have been perceived as difficult to understand have been augmented with examples. In addition, the context in which the survey was carried out (the session at FIA) started with a short introductory presentation that explained the key terminology. Further, three different application domains have been presented to further illustrate adaptive FI Apps. Those included media, eHealth, as well as transport and logistics (the last one being described in Section 2 of this paper).

Each of the participants has been handed a survey questionnaire (see Section 4.2) during the course of the FIA session. Altogether we received responses from 19 of the 51 of the registered participants of the session[4], *i.e.*, we achieved a response rate of 38%. As we have distributed the questionnaire only to the participants of the FIA session on "adaptive services", we can assume a general interest and knowledge about the topic and thus can expect good data quality. Further, as Table 1 shows the respondents demographic distribution closely matches that of the population, which implies that respondents constitute a representative sample.

Table 1. Demographic Distribution (Organization Type)

Population (% of TOTAL)	Academia	Industry	Other	TOTAL
Registered Participants	26 (51%)	24 (47%)	1 (2%)	51
Survey Respondents	10 (53%)	8 (42%)	1 (5%)	19

4.3   Analysis, Findings and Validity Threats

The results of our survey are presented along the four questions that we asked the participants:

Q.1 How important are the following adaptation characteristics for Future Internet applications?

Q.2 How important are adaptation capabilities within the following Future Internet areas?

Q.3 How important are adaptation capabilities on the following layers?

Q.4 How important are adaptive FI applications for the following application domains?

The adaptation characteristics and the rating for each one of them are illustrated in Figure 3. The three most important characteristics are context-aware, human-in-the-loop and cross-layer, which indicates the need to better understand the role of users for what concerns adaptation of FI Apps. Usage settings constitute a relevant context factor, human-in-the-loop adaptation relies on the critical decision making capabilities of humans, cross-layer adaptation involves the business and socio-economic layers, where human interaction starts to play an important role. Reactive and proactive adaptation capabilities have been

---

[4] Organizers and speakers did not answered the survey in order not to bias the results.

rated roughly similarly, indicating that both characteristics need to be considered for FI Apps. Interestingly, distributed and cross-area adaptation have been ranked least important. Although the recent research literature points out some proposals towards distribution in service-oriented systems [4], it seems that this is not perceived yet as an important feature. We perceive the low rating of cross-area adaptation as a consequence of the fact that each one of the FI areas are not consolidated and well established (in terms of their specification foundations). Therefore, it is comprehensible that the need for this type of cross-area adaptation is not perceived as important.

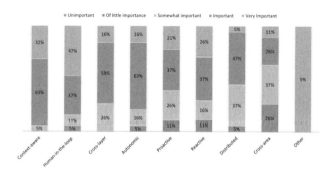

Fig. 3. Replies to Question Q1: Relevant Adaptation Characteristics

The left side of the Figure 4 illustrates the importance rating of question "Q2". Adaptation has been deemed to be most relevant for software services (IoS) and for security, privacy and trust (SPT) aspects, followed right behind by communication networks (NoF). Interestingly, adaptation in the IoT has been deemed least important, which might be attributed to the fact that so far, the IoT has been perceived a rather static entity, only now becoming increasingly dynamic (*e.g.*, due to the increased use of nomadic devices).

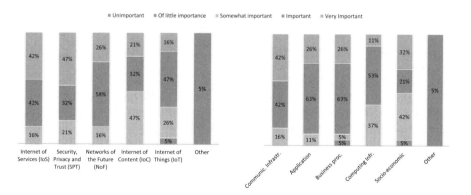

Fig. 4. Replies to Questions Q2 & Q3: Layers & Areas for Adaptation

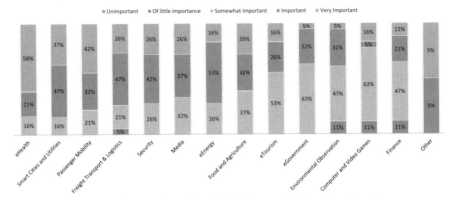

Fig. 5. Replies to Question Q4: Relevant Application Domains

The observations associated with question "Q3" are presented in the right side of Figure 4. The communication infrastructure layer has been deemed most important, followed by the application and the business layers. Although the high rank of the communication layer might contradict the findings that the IoS is the most important area, one needs to understand that the adaptation of services can be strongly impacted by network connectivity. Interestingly, adaptation at the computing infrastructure layer (such as cloud) ranks as less important, although one would expect that with increasing demands for cloud computing (such as provisioning of SaaS for multiple tenants), adaptation should be more relevant.

Figure 5 shows the results related to question "Q4". In this survey study, eHealth with quite some difference from other domains, has been deemed the application domain where adaptive capabilities will be most important. Smart cities and utilities, as well as mobility, transport and logistics follow right behind.

The analysis of validity threats to our survey is also an important issue to be discussed. We believe that the construct validity has been addressed by the carefully design of the survey questionnaire as discussed in Section 4.2. The questionnaire itself is accessible at `http://www.s-cube-network.eu/fia`. Another issue is the internal validity. In this survey study, one should be careful in interpreting the results for question *Q.4*, as three application domains, *viz.*, eHealth, transport & logistics and media have been elaborated during the FIA session, thus possibly leading to biased answers. Finally, the we also analyze the external validity threat, and we believe that Section 4.3 demonstrated that the respondents of our session, during the FIA event, show a demographic distribution that is very close to the one of the whole population of registered session participants. Still, the participants in our survey study have not been selected randomly, which implies that generalization of results should be done with caution [3,2].

Based on the aforementioned, therefore, we believe that the results of this survey study can contribute to understand where adaptation can play a key role for FI Apps. It also demonstrates which are the research fields where adaptation issues can to be further explored, like human-in-the-loop, cross-area adaptation.

5   Conclusions

This paper has introduced and discussed key characteristics for service-oriented systems in the Future Internet (FI Apps). In addition to identifying such characteristics based on the state of the art, we have performed an empirical study to assess the importance of those characteristics. The survey has confirmed some of the typical expectations (*e.g.*, the importance of adaptation for service-oriented systems). However, the survey also lead to unexpected outcomes. Specifically, distributed and cross-area adaptation capabilities have been deemed least important, although one would have expected those characteristics to become highly relevant in the Future Internet. We believe this deserves further investigation.

Acknowledgments. We thank the participants of our survey at FIA 2011, the speakers and panelists of the FIA session on "Adaptive Services", our fellow co-organizers, as well as our Paluno members for participating in the pretest of the survey. We would like to thank the kind provisioning of demographic data about the FIA session participants by Anne-Marie Sassen from the EC. The research leading to these results has received funding from the European Commission's 7th Framework Programme FP7/2007 2013 under grant agreements 215483 (S-Cube) and 285598 (FInest).

References

1. Di Nitto, E., Ghezzi, C., Metzger, A., Papazoglou, M., Pohl, K.: A journey to highly dynamic, self-adaptive service-based applications. Automated Software Engineering (2008)
2. Kitchenham, B.A., Pfleeger, S., Pickard, L., Jones, P., Hoaglin, D., El Emam, K., Rosenberg, J.: Preliminary guidelines for empirical research in software engineering. IEEE Transactions on Software Engineering, 721–734 (2002)
3. Krosnick, J.: Survey research. Annual Review of Psychology 50(1), 537–567 (1999)
4. de Lemos, R., Giese, H., Müller, H., Shaw, M.: Software Engineering for Self-Adpaptive Systems: A second Research Roadmap. In: Software Engineering for Self-Adaptive Systems. Dagstuhl Seminar Proceedings, vol. 10431 (2011)
5. Metzger, A., Sammodi, O., Pohl, K., Rzepka, M.: Towards pro-active adaptation with confidence?: Augmenting service monitoring with online testing. In: Proceedings of the ICSE 2010 Workshop on Software Engineering for Adaptive and Self-managing Systems, SEAMS 2010, Cape Town, South Africa (2010)
6. Narasimhan, B., Nichols, R.: State of cloud applications and platforms: The cloud adopters' view. IEEE Computer 44(3), 24–28 (2011)
7. Papazoglou, M., Pohl, K., Parkin, M., Metzger, A. (eds.): Service Research Challenges and Solutions for the Future Internet: Towards Mechanisms and Methods for Engineering, Managing, and Adapting Service-Based Systems. Springer, Heidelberg (2010)
8. Sammodi, O., Metzger, A., Franch, X., Oriol, M., Marco, J., Pohl, K.: Usage-based online testing for proactive adaptation of service-based applications. In: COMPSAC 2011 – The Computed World: Software Beyond the Digital Society. IEEE Computer Society, Los Alamitos (2011)
9. Tselentis, G., Domingue, J., Galis, A., Gavras, A., Hausheer, D.: Towards the Future Internet: A European Research Perspective. IOS Press, Amsterdam (2009)

Using Services and Service Compositions to Enable the Distributed Execution of Legacy Simulation Applications

Mirko Sonntag[1], Sven Hotta[1], Dimka Karastoyanova[1],
David Molnar[2], and Siegfried Schmauder[2]

[1] Institute of Architecture of Application Systems,
University of Stuttgart, Universitaetsstrasse 38, 70569 Stuttgart, Germany
{sonntag,hotta,karastoyanova}@iaas.uni-stuttgart.de
[2] Institute of Materials Testing, Materials Science and Strength of Materials,
University of Stuttgart, Pfaffenwaldring 32, 70569 Stuttgart
{david.molnar,siegfried.schmauder}@imwf.uni-stuttgart.de

Abstract. In the field of natural and engineering science, computer simulations play an increasingly important role to explain or predict phenomena of the real world. Although the software landscape is crucial to support scientists in their every day work, we recognized during our work with scientific institutes that many simulation programs can be considered legacy monolithic applications. They are developed without adhering to known software engineering guidelines, lack an acceptable software ergonomics, run sequentially on single workstations and require tedious manual tasks. We are convinced that SOA concepts and the service composition technology can help to improve this situation. In this paper we report on the results of our work on the service- and service composition-based re-engineering of a legacy scientific application for the simulation of the ageing process in copper-alloyed. The underlying general concept for a distributed, service-based simulation infrastructure is also applicable to other scenarios. Core of the infrastructure is a resource manager that steers server work load and handles simulation data.

Keywords: Service compositions, simulation workflows, distributed simulations, BPEL, Web services.

1 Introduction

The importance of computer simulations increases steadily. Nowadays many scientific institutes utilize computer simulations for their research. Due to achievements in information technology it is possible to use more and more complex and hence realistic simulation models. Nevertheless, there is still potential to improve existing solutions. In collaborations with scientific institutes in the scope of our research project we perceived that many simulation applications are based on legacy software that was developed over years and is still in development process. Many authors contributed to the software and may already have left the institute or organization. Usually, there is no time, money or knowledge to re-implement the tools in a modern programming language. The software is simply enhanced with new

W. Abramowicz et al. (Eds.): ServiceWave 2011, LNCS 6994, pp. 242–253, 2011.

features. We experienced that there are many simulation tools in use that do not benefit from multi-core CPUs, distributed computing, Grid computing or computer clusters. The programs often cannot deal with parallel invocations, e.g. because they do not organize the result files appropriately. The simulation applications are monolithic or consist of only a few applications with simple, usually command line-based interfaces. It is even common that simulations are programmed and compiled into an executable (e.g. simulations based on Dune, http://www.dune-project.org). In this case, the simulation parameters are hard-coded and can only be changed by programming and re-compilation. There are a lot of manual tasks for scientists, such as copying result files between the participating applications, starting these applications, or merging results. These and other problems leave room for improvements of existing scientific simulation applications.

In this paper we present a conceptual architecture for a distributed simulation environment based on SOA and service compositions. In the last 5 to 10 years much research has been done to apply workflows for scientific applications (e.g. [1, 2, 3, 4]). We are convinced that workflows and service compositions possess great potential to improve the tool support for many scientists. These are the tools scientists work with every day. There is a need to automate and optimize simulation processes, to exploit recent developments in hard- and software, and to improve user-friendliness and flexibility of simulation applications. This can be done if modern IT and software engineering technologies and techniques are used. At the same time, scientists do not want to re-write existing code or re-implement applications for simulation tasks. The proposed concept addresses these and other requirements.

The main contributions of the paper are follows: (1) based on a scenario for the simulation of solid bodies and on our experience on software projects with scientists we have conceived a concept for a service-oriented simulation infrastructure. Major part of the infrastructure is a resource manager that steers work distribution between the scientific services and that handles simulation data. (2) we have implemented the concept for the simulation of solid bodies with Web services (WS) and BPEL [5]. Where possible we adopt existing concepts, e.g. from Grid computing.

The paper is structured as follows. Section 2 presents the real use case for the simulation of solids. In Section 3 we discuss related work. In Section 4 we describe the service composition-based simulation infrastructure using the example of Section 3. Section 6 closes the paper with a conclusion.

2   Related Work

Using service compositions to orchestrate scientific applications is not new. E.g. for BPEL the applicability in the scientific domain is shown in [1, 6, 7], for YAWL in [8]. To the best of our knowledge no service-oriented scientific workflow system makes use of a resource manager as middleware for load balancing and simulation context storage.

The Message Passing Interface (MPI) [9] is a specification of a programming model that allows parallel computing in Grids or computer clusters by exchanging messages, accessing remote memory or by parallel I/O. MPI provides a set of operations to implement the communication between applications. MPI-based programs mix process (or communication) logic and domain logic which is the main difference to our approach with workflows/service compositions. This minimizes the communication overhead but increases the programming effort for scientists. Our service-based solution relieves scientists from the knowledge about other applications when implementing their modules/services, increases reusability of their applications, allows monitoring of the simulation process and load balancing in the infrastructure.

Grid middleware (e.g. the Globus Toolkit (http://www.globus.org/toolkit/), Unicore [10]), especially in combination with Grid workflows, provide features similar to our approach, e.g. load balancing and distributed computing. The main difference is that we foresee a resource manager as first-class citizen in our infrastructure that handles and correlates simulation data. In Grids such a data storage is not a standard component. With OGSA [11] and the WSRF [12] Grid resources can be made available as services. Grid services provide operations to clients to steer their life time and to reserve computing time. These existing concepts had an impact on our ticket-based approach to issue or deny computing power. Nevertheless, a middleware is needed to steer work distribution on Grid services based on the processor load of resources. This task is addressed by the resource manager proposed in this paper. In fact, our general concept allows using Grid services to conduct scientific simulations and to combine Grid and Web services for simulations.

Pegasus [13] is a system to compile and run workflow-like graphs in Grids. Pegasus makes use of different catalogues that are conceptually similar to our resource manager. The site catalogue lists all participating servers; the transformation catalogue lists the software installed on these servers; and the replica catalogue contains the data items in the system. The difference to our resource manager is that Pegasus' replica catalogue does not correlate data items to a specific simulation run. The user has to know or find out himself which items are associated.

In a SOA environment, the enterprise service bus (ESB) has the task to find and bind services which are stored in a service registry [14]. ESBs do not account for the server load and for data correlation issues because business services are usually not resource-demanding and can serve many requests in parallel. The resource manager in this paper can be seen as a lightweight ESB and service registry with extensions to manage long-running, resource-demanding scientific services and the simulation data. In [15] the open source ESB Apache ServiceMix (http://servicemix.apache.org/) was extended with WSRF functionality so that resource properties can be used as service selection criteria besides the usual functional and non-functional service requirements. Simulation data storage features or fault handling patterns (e.g. service availability checks) are not implemented as foreseen in the proposed infrastructure.

In [16] the authors propose a concept for passing arbitrary data by reference in BPEL (e.g. files, database tuples). This keeps huge data sets out of the BPEL engine if not needed for navigation through the workflow (as is usually the case in scientific simulations). The data storage of the resource manager in this paper does the same but in a more light-weight fashion: Passing references is not reflected in the workflow itself, data items are *always* passed by reference. Currently, we support only data because many simulation applications rely on data stored in files. In future, we should extend the data handling towards relational databases.

3   Use Case: Simulation of Solid Bodies

The macroscopic mechanical properties of metals strongly depend on their underlying atomistic structures. Copper-alloyed α-iron, e. g., changes its material behavior during the ageing process, especially when operated at high temperatures of above 300°C. In that case, precipitates form within the iron matrix, yielding to precipitation strengthening of the material [17] followed by a decrease of the material strength as the precipitates grow further in time. In order to model this complex behavior, the growth process of precipitates, which is a diffusion based mechanism, is accounted for by a Kinetic Monte-Carlo (KMC) approach [18, 19].

A number of copper atoms is placed into a fixed body-centered cubic (bcc) iron lattice by exchanging an iron atom with a copper atom. This yields a solid solution crystal as starting configuration.

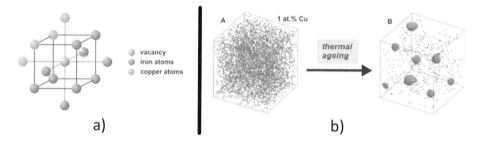

Fig. 1. Body-centered cubic crystal lattice nearest neighbors and a vacancy for one possible atom configuration (a). KMC simulation of precipitation (b). Iron atoms are transparent for better visualization. Solid solution: copper atoms are randomly distributed (A). Precipitates form during the thermal ageing process (B) [20].

The chemical interaction between atoms is described by nearest neighbor binding energies. A vacancy within the simulation box allows the movement of an atom by site exchange between the vacancy and a neighboring atom (iron, copper) (Fig. 1a). The jump activation energies depend on the local atom configuration around the vacancy. For each of the eight first neighbours of the vacancy the corresponding jump frequencies are calculated. By applying a rejection-free residence time algorithm, one of these eight possibilities is selected as the new position of the vacancy. In the long run, a series of vacancy jumps during the simulation yields the formation of precipitates with mean radii above 1 nm (Fig. 1b).

The time scale is adjusted according to the number of Monte-Carlo steps and the vacancy concentration. Periodic boundary conditions are applied in all directions in order to approximate a bulk single crystal. A more detailed description can be found in [21]. At desired time steps the atom configuration is analyzed yielding particle size distributions, mean radii of particles and the degree of supersaturation of the remaining solid solution.

3.1 Simulation Application

The simulation application opal (Ostwald-Ripening of Precipitates on an Atomic Lattice) [21] consists of five monolithic Fortran programs where the individual programs require manually created input data and are started manually. Two of them (*opalbcc* and *opalabcd*) build up the starting configuration and calculate the input values such as interaction energies, respectively. In addition to iron and copper, two more atom species can be incorporated. The precipitation process is simulated by the main application *opalmc*. After specified time intervals, opalmc generates output files containing the atom configuration (snapshot). The analysis of these atom configurations at different time steps, i.e. after specified amounts of vacancy jumps, is performed by the two programs *opalclus* and *opalxyzr* which identify the clusters within the matrix and determine size distributions and mean radii, respectively. After the analysis, the results are visualized applying commercially available software like MatLab, VMD, Rasmol, POV-Ray or Gnuplot. All in all, the overall simulation can be subdivided into four phases: preparation, simulation, analysis and visualization.

4 Service-Based Distributed Simulation Environment

Due to increasingly complex simulation models, computer simulations consume more and more computing power and storage capacity. Although the information technology improves steadily, many legacy simulation programs cannot benefit from these advancements (e.g. the opal simulation application).

Usually, computer simulation makes use of multiple tools, e.g. for calculations, visualizations, or analysis. Simulations often require manual tasks such as creation of input files, copying files between different applications that participate in a simulation, or transformation of data (e.g. merging of files). The simulation applications can conduct CPU-intensive calculations and hence exclusively engross the CPU of a machine. Using computer clusters or (public) Grids to run simulation applications would help but these infrastructures are rare and highly demanded (i.e. computing hours are difficult to obtain). In contrast, scientific institutes usually have a sufficient inventory of commodity hardware (ordinary desktop PCs). The typical work of employees (e.g. working on documents) does not use the workstations to full capacity allowing for the operation of simulation tasks in the background.

4.1 Using Services and Service Compositions to Improve This Situation

The application of SOA concepts and service compositions in these scenarios is beneficial to scientists. When scientific programs are provided as services, they can be invoked over a network using appropriate middleware. Thus, it is easy to implement distributed applications by orchestrating scientific services that are located on different resources. These resources do not have to be high-end servers—connected commodity hardware is sufficient. Furthermore, different application types can be integrated, e.g. the invocation of a visualization tool after a simulation run is finished. This contributes to the automation of manual steps, too. Thus the overall execution of an application can be sped up and can be made more efficient. Common service composition languages provide fault handling features. These can increase the robustness of simulation applications, especially if the simulation functions are implemented with a programming language that offers only restricted fault handling mechanisms. Service compositions have an additional benefit because they can also be used as (graphical) documentation of the simulation logic and help new employees and programmers to understand the overall simulation process. This is necessary due to the relatively high fluctuation of employees in scientific institutes.

4.2 Simulation Infrastructure

These above-mentioned advantages of a service-based re-engineering of legacy applications are well-known to the SOA community in theory and practice. But legacy *simulation* applications provided as services differ from services that implement business functions. The reason is that simulation applications can be long-running and processing power-demanding. Running simulation programs can easily allocate a complete computer processor. Thus, natively invoking scientific services results in the problem that busy services can get crammed with requests they cannot serve (Fig. 2a). In business environments an ESB is employed to prevent from these cases. The ESB would recognize that server A is busy because it does not respond. If the communication is asynchronous, it might be impossible for the ESB to perceive that the service is used to capacity. In both cases, the ESB *reacts* to the unavailability of a service, which means loss of time. It would be better to have a mechanism that conducts load balancing based on the processor load of servers. A resource manager that acquires services on behalf of a client can perform this task (Fig. 2b).

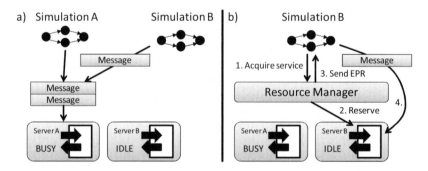

Fig. 2. Invocation of a scientific service natively (a) and with a resource manager (b)

Existing work on service compositions for scientific applications does not report on how to deal with long-running, resource-demanding services. We claim that a service-based infrastructure for scientific simulations needs a resource manager that knows the participating servers and services as well as their current load and that works as mediator between the clients and the services (Fig. 3). Note that the components can be arbitrarily distributed on participating servers and workstations. Nevertheless, having the simulation client and simulation manager installed on different engines has the advantage that the scientists can shut down their workstations without affecting the started, possibly long-running simulations. Please consider [22] for a demonstration of the prototype that implements this architecture.

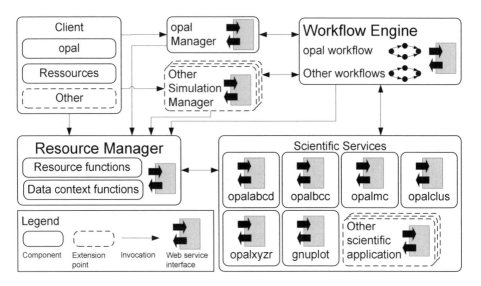

Fig. 3. Architecture of the service-based simulation infrastructure

4.3 Simulation Applications

Providing the *simulation applications* as services does not imply that existing code has to be re-implemented. However, there are cases where modifications of the simulation code are needed. This strongly depends on the granularity and the interface of the application. As a first step, it should be examined if the application consists of logical units that may be separated. This step is tedious but improves the resulting simulation application enormously [23]. The probability increases that the logical units can be reused and the simulation workflow is finer-grained. The latter enables a more detailed monitoring and more options to adjust the workflow in order to create new or adapted simulations without the need for programming and code re-compilation. Additionally, the simulation logic can be optimized with workflow analysis techniques [24]. Besides modularization of the application optimization of its interface may also be needed. It should at least be possible to invoke the application with parameters instead of hard-coding these parameters or configurations [25].

The second step is to make the application units remotely accessible as services. When using the WS technology [26], a thin WS wrapper is needed. The WS wrapper can be tailored to the application or a reusable, generic wrapper can be used that is able to invoke the application [25]. Note that the former is only possible if the simulation application is implemented in a language that allows native invocations. A WS wrapper has to be deployed on the server that offers the simulation applications. Now the simulation application can be registered with the resource manager.

With five Fortran programs and Gnuplot the simulation application opal already has an acceptable granularity (Fig. 3); there was no need to subdivide the programs into smaller units. But we extended the Fortran applications with interfaces that allow their invocation with parameters. That eliminates the need to re-compile them if the simulation configuration changes. Since there is no WS toolkit for Fortran programs, we implemented a JAVA-based WS wrapper. The approach with Java Native Access (https://jna.dev.java.net/) failed because Fortran had difficulties to process parallel write operations on files spread over several threads in a single Java process. (Curiously, this happened even for writes on different files.). The way to invoke the Fortran programs over file system commands solved these problems as each invocation creates a new Java process for execution. The re-engineering of this use case took approximately one person month for a student developer unfamiliar with Fortran 77.

4.4 Resource Manager

Besides its registry and load balancing functionality the *resource manager* (RM) also works as storage for simulation data. It provides functions to register and manage servers and scientific applications prior to or during the execution of simulations. Clients that want to use a simulation application have to ask the RM for permission. If the RM cannot find a requested service in its registry, it sends an appropriate fault message to the client. If the RM could allocate a requested service (i.e. an implementation of the service is registered and the corresponding server has computing capacities), it creates a service ticket and responds to the client with the ID of that ticket, the endpoint reference (EPR) to the service implementation, and the ticket validity in seconds. A service ticket warrants exclusive usage right to the client. The RM can recall this permission by invalidating the ticket (e.g. to enable other clients the usage of the application). This usage permission mechanism is comparable to advanced reservation techniques in Grid Computing [27]. The goal of the RM is to ensure that a server is not overloaded with requests (i.e. load balancing). If a server provides two logical processors, then it can deal in parallel with two requests for simulation applications where each allocates one processor. If the ticket validity runs out, the service is released automatically by the RM. Service clients can reset the validity time to its maximum by calling an appropriate operation of the RM. Note that the validity countdown is stopped during usage of a service. This prevents the loss of a service ticket during long-running operations. Furthermore, the RM checks the infrastructure on network partitions. A network partition between RM and a service is recognized when the service cannot acknowledge the start of an operation to the RM. The service ticket then times out; the RM removes the corresponding server and its services from the registry; and the client gets informed about ticket expiry so that it can react accordingly (e.g. by requesting the service again). A network partition might separate a service from the RM after the start of an operation was acknowledged. The RM would perceive this because we implemented a periodical availability check that would fail in this case. Again the service client is informed about the failure. The simulation applications have to implement and provide a set of operations in order to facilitate allocation, de-allocation and observation by the RM.

   Additionally, the RM can be used as storage for simulation data (e.g. simulation parameters, configuration, results). The data may be distributed among the servers, but the RM provides a logically centralized view on them. Each simulation run gets its own simulation context where data can be saved, organized and deleted. The context correlates data items that belong to the same simulation run. This improves reproduction of simulations because the configurations and input data as well as result data are assembled and can be observed by scientists at a glance. The data items do not have to be searched for and correlated later on, which may not be possible at all since simulation applications may not have a sophisticated storage mechanism (e.g. legacy simulation applications might overwrite simulation data of former runs). Furthermore, collaboration between scientists is fostered because simulation configurations and results can easily be exchanged. Another advantage of the data storage within the simulation infrastructure is that data can be accessed and thus transmitted by reference. Only those components that are interested in a data item can load its value from the storage.

4.5   Workflow Engine, Simulation Manager and Simulation Client

The *workflow engine* executes the scientific service compositions. Due to the data RM's storage the engine is relieved of holding huge simulation data. Usually, this data is not needed for workflow navigation and it is thus sufficient to keep only the references to this data in the engine. Each simulation workflow has to be tailored to the specific simulation applications. We use Apache ODE (http://ode.apache.org/) as workflow engine and have implemented the opal workflow with BPEL. The workflow automates formerly manual tasks (e.g. starting post-processing, invocation of Gnuplot) and parallelizes the post-processing of the lattice snapshots. We have created reusable BPEL snippets for scientific service acquisition, service usage and release. This simplifies modeling workflows for other use cases or even for other BPEL-based workflow system, e.g. Sedna [6].

The *simulation managers* offer functions specific to the corresponding simulation application and workflow. With the opal manager, e.g., the client can create and manage global simulation data such as initial lattice configurations. This data is stored in the RM and can be used for several simulation runs. The opal manager can start new simulations by sending an appropriate message to the workflow engine and creates a new simulation context in the RM. All related data is stored in this context. For an asynchronous communication with the workflow engine the opal manager provides a callback were acknowledgements and other information can be sent to (e.g. the information that an error occurred in the simulation workflow). For the deletion of a simulation, the opal manager deletes the context and related data in the RM and terminates the simulation workflow instance to clean up the simulation environment.

The *simulation client* is a GUI for scientists to interact with the simulation environment. We have experienced that simulation tools are often command line-based and lack an acceptable UI. Some even have to be re-compiled if parameters change (e.g. opal, Dune). The client improves the usability of such simulation tools. The domain-specific part of the simulation client makes use of the opal manager or other simulation managers to create new simulations, provide them with input data, run and monitor the simulations, steer the simulation runs (e.g. termination, deletion), and observe intermediate and final results. The opal client allows storing input data in the RM as profile for other simulation runs (Fig. 4a). We have implemented a file explorer that shows all files related to a selected simulation run in a tree view. Additionally, we have realized a two-colored rotating 3D visualization of the lattice snapshots with the help of Java 3D (Fig. 4b). That makes it possible for scientists to observe the convergence of the simulation results during run time.

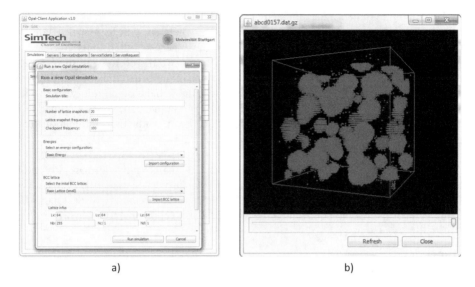

a)   b)

Fig. 4. The simulation client with the dialog to start a new opal simulation (a) and the 3D preview of the simulation snapshots (b)

Further, the RM functions of the client enable scientists to administrate the simulation infrastructure, e.g. registering servers and installed simulation applications. For each server it can be specified how many CPU cores are enabled for simulations. For each simulation service the scientist can set how many CPU cores are allocated by the service during execution. For monitoring purposes we have implemented a view that shows all service ticket requests sent to the RM and a view that lists all issued service tickets. This enables scientists to observe the status of the simulation environment and existing problems (e.g. a long list of open service requests may indicate too few available instances of a simulation service in the system).

5   Conclusions

In this paper we applied services and service compositions to re-engineer a legacy scientific application for the simulation of solid bodies. The resulting solution improves the existing application and speeds up the overall simulation by automating manual tasks and parallelizing formerly sequential work. A new GUI increases the ease-of-use for the scientists, especially with the visualization of intermediary results. The general concepts behind this use case and the extension points allow an application to other legacy simulation tools. Due to the difference between business and scientific services we had to introduce a component that steers the work distribution in the infrastructure, the resource manager. Its functionality is in parts orthogonal to that of ordinary ESBs since it accounts for the server occupation during service selection and works as storage for correlated simulation data. To the best of our knowledge none of the existing scientific workflow systems that enable the orchestration of scientific services make use of such a resource manager.

The simulation client hides the actual service compositions from the scientists. On the one hand the non-IT scientists do not get overwhelmed with technical details of the implementation. On the other hand they have to use other tools to see the workflow progress or change the workflow. In future we therefore want to integrate the simulation client in a workflow modeling and monitoring tool. Extending the resource manager so that it can install the services on demand on an idle server (with the help of provisioning techniques [27, 28]) is another open issue. Finally, a comparison of the service and workflow overhead with the automation and parallelization speedup needs to be done.

Acknowledgments. The authors would like to thank the German Research Foundation (DFG) for financial support of the project within the Cluster of Excellence in Simulation Technology (EXC 310/1) at the University of Stuttgart. We thank Peter Binkele who contributed the MC simulation code opal to our work.

References

1. Akram, A., Meredith, D., Allan, R.: Evaluation of BPEL to Scientific Workflows. In: Proc. of the 6th IEEE International Symposium on Cluster Computing and the Grid (2006)
2. Barga, R., Jackson, J., Araujo, N., et al.: The Trident Scientific Workflow Workbench. In: Proc. of the IEEE International Conference on eScience (2008)
3. Goerlach, K., Sonntag, M., Karastoyanova, D., et al.: Conventional Workflow Technology for Scientific Simulation. In: Yang, X., Wang, L., Jie, W. (eds.) Guide to e-Science, Springer, Heidelberg (2011)
4. Sonntag, M., Karastoyanova, D., Deelman, E.: Bridging the Gap Between Business and Scientific Workflows. In: Proc. of the 6th IEEE Int. Conf. on e-Science (2010)
5. OASIS: Business Process Execution Language (BPEL) Version 2.0 (2007), http://docs.oasis-open.org/wsbpel/2.0/OS/wsbpel-v2.0-OS.pdf
6. Wassermann, B., Emmerich, W., Butchart, B., Cameron, N., Chen, L., Patel, J.: Sedna: A BPEL-Based Environment For Visual Scientific Workflow Modelling. In: Taylor (ed.) Workflows for e-Science, pp. 428–449. Springer, Heidelberg (2007)
7. Scherp, G., Höing, A., Gudenkauf, S., Hasselbring, W., Kao, O.: Using UNICORE and WS-BPEL for Scientific Workflow Execution in Grid Environments. In: Lin, H.-X., Alexander, M., Forsell, M., Knüpfer, A., Prodan, R., Sousa, L., Streit, A. (eds.) Euro-Par 2009. LNCS, vol. 6043, pp. 335–344. Springer, Heidelberg (2010)
8. Wassink, I., Ooms, M., van der Vet, P.: Designing Workflows on the Fly Using e-BioFlow. In: Baresi, L., Chi, C.-H., Suzuki, J. (eds.) ICSOC-ServiceWave 2009. LNCS, vol. 5900, pp. 470–484. Springer, Heidelberg (2009)
9. MPI Forum: MPI: A Message-Passing Interface Standard Version 2.2 (2009), http://www.mpi-forum.org/
10. Streit, A., Bala, P., Beck-Ratzka, A., et al.: UNICORE 6 – Recent and Future Advancements. Forschungszentrum Jülich Zentralbibliothek (2010) ISSN 0944-2952
11. Foster, I., Kesselman, C., Nick, J.M., Tuecke, S.: The Physiology of the Grid: An Open Grid Services Architecture for Distributed Systems Integration (2002), http://www.globus.org/alliance/publications/papers/ogsa.pdf
12. Foster, I., Frey, J., Graham, S., et al.: Modeling Stateful Resources with Web Services (2004), http://www.ibm.com/developerworks/library/ws-resource/ws-modelingresources.pdf

13. Deelman, E., Blythe, J., Gil, Y., Kesselman, C., Mehta, G., Patil, S., Su, M.-H., Vahi, K., Livny, M.: Pegasus: Mapping Scientific Workflows onto the Grid. In: Dikaiakos, M.D. (ed.) AxGrids 2004. LNCS, vol. 3165, pp. 11–20. Springer, Heidelberg (2004)
14. Chappell, D.: Enterprise Service Bus. O'Reilly Media, Sebastopol (2004)
15. Wiese, A.: Konzeption und Implementierung von WS-Policy- und WSRF-Erweiterungen für einen Open Source Enterprise Service Bus. Diploma Thesis No. 2664, University of Stuttgart (2008)
16. Wieland, M., Goerlach, K., Schumm, D., Leymann, F.: Towards Reference Passing in Web Service and Workflow-based Applications. In: Proc. of the 13th IEEE Enterprise Distributed Object Conference (2009)
17. Kizler, P., Uhlmann, D., Schmauder, S.: Linking Nanoscale and Macroscale: Calculation of the Change in Crack Growth Resistance of Steels with Different States of Cu Precipitation Using a Modification of Stress-strain Curves Owing to Dislocation Theory. Nuclear Engineering and Design 196, 175–183 (2000)
18. Schmauder, S., Binkele, P.: Atomistic Computer Simulation of the Formation of Cu-Precipitates in Steels. Computational Materials Science 24, 42–53 (2002)
19. Soisson, F., Barbu, A., Martin, G.: Monte-Carlo Simulations of Copper Precipitates in Dilute Iron-Copper Alloys During Thermal Ageing and Under Electron Irradiation. Acta Materialia 44, 3789–3800 (1996)
20. Molnar, D., Binkele, P., Hocker, S., Schmauder, S.: Multiscale Modelling of Nano Tensile Tests for Different Cu-precipitation States in α-Fe. In: Proc. of the 5th Int. Conf. on Multiscale Materials Modelling, pp. 235–239. Fraunhofer Verlag (2010)
21. Binkele, P., Schmauder, S.: An atomistic Monte Carlo simulation for precipitation in a binary system. International Journal for Materials Research 94, 1–6 (2003)
22. Sonntag, M.: Workflow-based Simulation of Solid Bodies. Prototype demo (2010), http://www.iaas.uni-stuttgart.de/forschung/projects/simtech/downloadsE.php#opalVideo
23. Rutschmann, J.: Generisches Web Service Interface um Simulationsanwendungen in BPEL-Prozesse einzubinden. Diploma Thesis No. 2895, University of Stuttgart (2009)
24. Leymann, F., Roller, D.: Production Workflow – Concepts and Techniques. Prentice Hall, Englewood Cliffs (2000)
25. Hotta, S.: Ausführung von Festkörpersimulationen auf Basis der Workflow Technologie. Diploma Thesis No. 3029, University of Stuttgart (2010)
26. Weerawarana, S., Curbera, F., Leymann, F., et al.: Web services platform architecture: SOAP, WSDL, WS-Policy, WS-Addressing, WS-BPEL, WS-Reliable Messaging and more. Prentice Hall, Englewood Cliffs (2005)
27. Foster, I., Kesselman, C.: The Grid 2: Blueprint for a New Computing Infrastructure, 2nd edn. Morgan Kaufmann, San Francisco (2004)
28. Mietzner, R., Leymann, F.: Towards Provisioning the Cloud: On the Usage of Multi-Granularity Flows and Services to Realize a Unified Provisioning Infrastructure for SaaS Applications. In: Proc. of the Int. Congress on Services (2008)

A Semantic Rule and Event Driven Approach for Agile Decision-Centric Business Process Management

(Invited Paper)

Adrian Paschke

Freie Universität Berlin
Institut for Computer Science
AG Corporate Semantic Web
Königin-Luise-Str. 24/26, 14195 Berlin, Germany
paschke@inf.fu-berlin.de
http://www.corporate-semantic-web.de

Abstract. The growing importance of Web-based service organizations and agile enterprise service networks creates a need for the optimization of semi- or unstructured, decision-centric service processes. These decision-centric processes often contain more event-driven and situation-aware behavior, more non-standard knowledge intensive cases and event-driven routings, and more variability and agility than traditional processes. Consequently, systems supporting these decision-centric service processes require much more degrees of freedom than standard BPM systems. While pure syntactic BPM languages such as OASIS WS-BPEL and OMG BPMN addresses the industry's need for standard service orchestration semantics they provide only limited expressiveness to describe complex decision logic and conditional event-driven reaction logic. In this paper we propose a heterogenous service-oriented integration of rules (decision rules and complex event processing reaction rules) into BPM to describe rule-based business processes. This leads to a declarative rule-based Semantic BPM (SBPM) approach, which aims at agile and adaptive business process execution including enforcement of non-functional SLA properties of business services via rules.

1 Introduction

Typical business processes often include a number of decision points which effect the process flow. For example, in OMG's Business Process Management Notation (BPMN), decision points are represented by a diamond and choices in the flow forks. However, the expressiveness of the current purely syntactic BPM standards, such as the OASIS Web Services Business Process Execution Language (WS-BPEL 2.0 or BPEL for short) and BPMN 2.0, for explicitly representing more complex decision logic is rather limited to simple qualifying truth-valued conditions (without e.g. explicitly representing the decision goals, decision structures and decision types by declarative rule chaining, variable binding with backtracking over multiple solutions, etc.). Although more complex decision can be

W. Abramowicz et al. (Eds.): ServiceWave 2011, LNCS 6994, pp. 254–267, 2011.

included as a decision activity or as an (external) decision service in BPMN and BPEL, in a large number of the modern agile Internet of Services business cases, the entire process flow is controlled by semi-structured decisions which are evaluated based on complex events and knowledge-intensive (situation) conditions. Decisions are often based on knowledge intensive decision criteria, require multiple subdecisions, use a complex event/situation based decision technique, and conclude one or more results, etc. For instance, a process can try to optimize on-demand the enterprise service network, according to the service levels defined in the service provider's service level agreements (SLAs). Other decision criteria can focus, e.g., on the end-to-end optimization from the customers point-of-view, or on the minimization of the information flow reducing communication overhead and information requests, or focus on decision criteria based on the organizational and collaboration structures, etc. These decision-centric processes need higher levels of semantic understanding of the decision goals and structures, the real-time process situations (including non-functional properties, e.g. SLA enforcement), and the complex events which happen internally and externally and influence the decision-centric process flow. Such agile processes require higher levels of declarative semantic expressiveness, then the pure syntactic orchestration languages such as BPEL provide.

In recent years we have seen the rise of a new type of software called business rule management systems (BRMS) which allow enterprize architects to easily define, manage, update and run the decision logic that directs enterprize applications in a business rules engines (BRE) without needing to write code or change the business processes calling them. This addresses an urgent need businesses do have nowadays: to change their business rules in order to adapt to a rapidly business environment, and they contribute to agility in Service Oriented Architectures (SOAs) by enabling reduced time to automate, easier change, and easier maintenance for business policies and rules. Early manifestations of BREs which have their roots in the realm of artificial intelligence and inference systems were complex, expensive to run and maintain and not very business-user friendly. New rule standards such as OMG SBVR, RuleML (W3C RIF) and improved technology providing enhanced usability, scalability and performance, as well as less costly maintenance and better understanding of the underlying semantics and inference systems makes the current generation of BREs and rules technology more usable. Business rules have been used extensively in enterprizes, e.g., to implement credit risk assessment in the loan industry (what is the interest rate for my car loan?), yield management in the travel industry (what price to sell a ticket?), operations scheduling in manufacturing (what should we build today to maximize throughput and keep customers happy?), etc.

In this paper we describe a heterogeneous service-oriented combination of BPM technology and rule technology which incorporates BREs as inference / decision web services into the BPEL process logic (BPEL + Rules). While BPM enables automated and flexible business processes, declarative rules enable decision logic, reaction logic for processing complex events (CEP) and for reacting to them, and various types of constraints. The declarative rules address the event-based, message driven, decentralized choreography semantics, while BPEL manages the overall orchestration execution of the business process. The inference services, which run a BRE (implemented in Prova), are deployed on an enterprize service bus (the RuleML Rule Responder ESB) and can be invoked by the BPEL process as semantic web services (SWS), using one of the many transport protocols supported by the Rule Responder middleware.

This service-oriented rule-based approach has the potential to profoundly change the way IT services are used and collaborate in business processes. Akin to multi-agent systems (MAS) the rule-based logic inference layer which wraps the existing web services and data sources allows for semi-autonomous decisions and reactions to complex events detected by the rule-based event processing logic. The combination of rules with ontologies gives precise semantics to used concepts such as processes, events, actions, tasks, state, time etc. Different rule inference services can communicate in (agent-based) conversations via messaging reaction rules, which enables them to build agent-based choreography workflows, that can be used as external subprocesses in the main orchestrated BPEL process. Potential application scenarios of BPEL+Rules for BPM are, e.g.:

- Dynamic processing
  - Intelligent routing
  - Validation of policies within process
  - Constraint checks
- Ad-hoc Workflows
  - Policy based task assignment
  - Various escalation policies
  - Load balancing of tasks
- Business Activity Monitoring
  - Alerts based on certain policies and complex event processing (rule-based CEP)
  - Dynamic processing based Key Performance Indicator (KPI) reasoning

In this paper we contribute with a declarative rule-based service-oriented business process execution approach exploiting WS-BPEL in combination with Corporate Semantic Web (CSW) technologies (semantic rules, ontologies and events/actions) and a scalable ESB middleware to operationalize such a distributed rule-based approach. Rule-based reaction logic for event processing and event messaging, and rule-based decision logic in combination with ontologies play a central role in connecting the various IT resources, human and knowledge resources, and Web-based services to agile business service networks. Ultimately, our novel rule-based design artifact might put the vision of highly flexible and adaptive Internet of Services supply chains / enterprize service networks into large scale practice and will lead to a highly flexible and agile BPM.

This combination of semantic technologies, i.e. declarative rules, ontologies and semantic event/action logics, with BPM, which leads to Semantic Business Process Management (SBPM) promises:

- enhanced automation in semantic discovery, configuration and composition
  of appropriate process components, information objects, and services (including human agents)
- automated mediation between different heterogeneous interfaces (e.g. semantic web services) and abstraction levels
- targeted complex queries on the process space and the process flow and state
- much more agile business process management via expressive rule-based decision and reaction logic

The key benefits of our approach are:

- use of complementary technologies: semantic technologies for representing
  rules, events, actions, state, etc. + BPM technologies
- standard-compliant use of WS-BPEL for orchestration of services as well as
  people and partners implemented as external semantic web services or semantic agents (having a precise meaning/semantics defined for their interfaces)
- clear separation of concerns:
  - BPEL is used for orchestration in the business process
  - rules for declarative specification of constantly changing business policies
    and regulations
  - rules focus on decision making, policies and rule-based event processing
    for building complex events of higher level of abstraction and relevance
    for the business process
  - rules can be used to integrate choreography sub-workflows in orches-
    trated BPEL processes
- enables business users to participate in business processes and in adapting
  business rules
- modify and apply new business rules without redeploying processes
- declarative semantics for processing events, actions, rules, state etc. (including logic for transactions, compensations etc.)

The rest of the paper is organized as follows: In section 2 we discuss related
work and describe what is missing in current BPM standards with respect to
semantics and rules. In section 3 we introduce the heterogenous service-oriented
integration approach for adding rules to BPEL. In section 4 we implement this
integration approach with a highly scalable and efficient rule-based inference
ESB middleware, called Rule Responder. Section 5 concludes this paper and
gives an outlook on our ongoing efforts to integrate humans by means of rule-
based agents.

2   Enhancing Non-semantic BPM to Semantic BPM

Current BPM languages, such as BPMN 2.0 for modeling and WS-BPEL 2.0
for execution, are mostly syntactic process specification languages without a
precise declarative formal logic semantics. This allows for ambiguities in the
interpretation of models and specific functionalities such as compensations or

exceptions. It hinders the integration of, e.g., rule inference services or humans via people link interactions. Modeling languages and models become incompatible and are no longer interchangeable. For instance, there are problems with model-to-model transformations and round-tripping, e.g. between BPMN and BPEL and vice versa. There is also a semantic gap between the business world and the IT world which use different vocabularies to describe the models and have different requirements on the abstraction level. The inner semantics of activities and their effects cannot be represented semantically in the current BPM approaches, which makes it hard to analyze and understand the business process behavior and the effects on the process states, beyond the pure functional description of the orchestration flow and the invoked web service interfaces. Agile business decisions in terms of business rules, complex event-driven behavior, and choreography interactions cannot be semantically integrated into BPEL.

What it missing for the semantic enrichment of BPM, i.e. for SBPM, is the integration of rules for declaratively representing the decision and reaction logic and the integration of ontologies for events, processes, states, actions, and other concepts that relate, e.g., to change over time into the BPEL definitions. With rules and ontologies the processes and their causalities and roles would be precisely defined by logic. This would also make rules or logic that govern processes or react to events truly declarative knowledge which can be used in the processes for decisions and ad-hoc reactions. It would increase the ability to interchange semantic models across major BPM and BRMS vendors and would allow reusable, enterprize-relevant knowledge such as business policies and business vocabularies to be used in BPM models.

In the last years, Semantic Web Services (SWS) as a combination of ontologies and Web services have been extensively studied in several projects in the Semantic Web community and different approaches exist such as RBSLA (Rule-based Service Level Agreements), OWL-S (former DAML-S), WSDL-S, SAWSDL, SWWS / WSMF, WSMO / WSML, Meteor-S, SWSI . They are all aiming at semantically describing the interfaces of Web services, their functional and non-functional properties, and policies such as SLAs. Several extensions to WS-BPEL using SWS approaches have been proposed - see e.g. the SUPER project[1]. These works mainly address the execution layer of business processes, where the semantics solves the discovery and integration of services into business process execution, but also semantic mapping problems between the business oriented modeling and management of processes, e.g. in BPMN, and the translation into an execution syntax such as BPEL. In [1] we have described an approach which uses ontologies and rules to incorporate semantic bridges between cross-organizational business process models.

In this paper we will mainly focus on the heterogenous integration of rules technology with BPEL in order to enhance its expressiveness for representing and declaratively executing decision-centric businness processes. We will not specifically address ontologies for BPM and CEP which must relate processes, events, states, and actions, must include tense (past, present and future; perfected and

---

[1] http://www.ip-super.org/

progressive), time intervals with quantities (units, duration, composition, conversion and accuracy), etc. However, since our rule language allows using ontologies as type system for the rules, existing ontologies for semantic BPM and CEP [11] can be easily used.

3   Integration of Rules in Business Processes Execution

In this section we describe a heterogenous integration approach of rules into service-oriented BPEL processes. Rules are integrated as external distributed rule inference services. This means they are not directly part of the BPEL process (homogenous integration), but are integrated by invoking the inference service (heterogenous integration) which runs a rule engine and executes the rule logic.

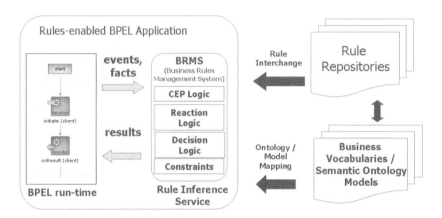

Fig. 1. Heterogenous Integration of Rule Inference Services into BPEL Processes

Figure 1 illustrates this integration approach. A BPEL decision activity invokes a rule inference service sending event or fact data (e.g. queries) to the rule engine. The rule engine processes the received data according to its internal rule-based logic. The results might be, e.g. derived answers (e.g. decisions) on the queries of the BPEL process, or they might be actions which are triggered by the reaction rule-based processing of the events from the BPEL process.

The concrete steps in this approach are

1. Create a rule inference service with rule repository and define the semantic interface description of the inference service
2. Create a new inference service Partnerlink, choose a rule connection and choose an interaction pattern and the parameter bindings
3. Add a rules Activity which invokes the rule inference service; Bind BPEL variables to parameters of the Partnerlink

During the process execution the BPEL engine will invoke the rule inference service mapping the BPEL variables to the input facts / events and the result from the rule inference service. It is possible to implement different stateful and stateless interaction patterns between the BPEL process and the inference service.

4 Implementation of the BPEL+ Rules Approach

In this section we will implement the proposed heterogenous BPEL+Rules integration approach and describe the main technical components with a focus on the expressiveness of Prova, which is used as the underlying semantic rules engine.

4.1 Rule-Based Semantic Decision Services

In order to use rules for BPEL a BRMS, which manages and executes the rule logic with an internal BRE, is provided as Semantic Web Services (SWS). A SWS is a Web Service which in addition to its syntactic interface description (WSDL) is extended with semantic information, for semantic discovery, selection, invocation and composition. In [7,9] we have implemented a rule-based SWS approach which in addition to the semantic interface descriptions of the service allows representing non-functional properties of the service, in terms of a Rule-based Service Level Agreement (RBSLA) - see figure 2.

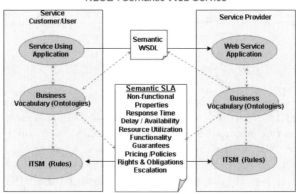

Fig. 2. RBSLA Semantic Web Services

For instance, a rule set from a Service Level Agreement might define three different IT Service Level Management schedules (see ITIL ITSLM process):

```
if current time between 8am and 6pm then prime schedule.
if current time between 6pm and 8am then standard schedule.
if current time between 0am and 4am then optional maintenance schedule.

if prime schedule then the service level "average availability"
has a low value of 98%, a median of 99% and a high value of 100%
```

```
and a response time which must be below 4 seconds.
...
if standard schedule then the responsible role for service outages
is the second admin.
```

As shown in the RBSLA (Rule-based Servicel Level Agreements) project [7,9] such rule sets can be adequately represented as logic programs and easily extended with further rules, e.g. rules describing escalation levels and deontic norms such as certain obligations if service levels are missed.

The additional semantic information provided by RBSLA service descriptions is used for effectively invoking the inference services from the BPEL process, e.g. invoke an inference service which provides the requested decision functionality and the required quality of service (QoS). [9] Furthermore, in cross-organizational business processes, RBSLA's support for semantic ontologies, which are used as type system for the rules, allows for semantic mediation in of the information flow in cross-organizational business process models. [1] The monitoring and enforcement events from the validation of hierarchical SLA chains of the involved partner services can be used on-demand to decide and restructure the service supply chains used to execute the business process. [3,4]

4.2 Prova - A Semantic Rule Engine

Prova (http://prova.ws) [5,7] is both a Semantic Web rule language and a highly expressive distributed rule engine which supports declarative (backward reasoning) decision rules, complex reaction rule-based workflows, rule-based complex event processing (CEP), and dynamic access to external data sources such as databases, Web services, and Java APIs. It has a typed logic approach which allows using external ontologies or Java class hierarchies as type system for the rules. Prova follows the spirit and design of the W3C Semantic Web initiative and combines declarative rules, ontologies (vocabularies) and inference with dynamic object-oriented programming and access to external data sources via query languages such as SQL, SPARQL, and XQuery. One of the key advantages of Prova is its separation of logic, data access, and computation as well as its tight integration of Java, Semantic Web and event processing technologies.

For instance, the following rule defines a discount policy of ten percent for gold customers. The example shows how variables (starting with upper case letters) and constants (starting with lower case letters) can be typed with concepts defined in external ontologies, e.g., a business ontology defining the type *business:Customer* or a math ontology defining a type *math:Percentage*. The type ontologies are typically provided as Web ontologies (RDFS or OWL) where types and individuals are represented as resources having an webized URI. Namespaces can be used to avoid name conflicts and namespace abbreviations facilitate are more readable and compact language.

```
% A customer gets 10 percent discount, if the customer is a gold customer

discount(X^^business:Customer, 10^^math:Percentage) :-
    gold(X^^business:Customer).

% fact with free typed variable acts as instance query on the ontology A-box
gold(X^^business:Customer).
```

Prova's semantics draws on backward-reasoning logic programming (LP) concepts to formalize decision logic in terms of derivation rules and combines them with forward-directed messaging reaction rules for distributed event and action processing in order to exploit the benefits of both worlds. The following syntactic and semantic instruments in Prova 3.0 capture the basics and offer unique advanced features for implementing rule-based workflows and business processes:

- reactive messaging;
- inherent non-determinism for defining process divergences;
- concurrency support, including partitioned and non-partitioned thread pools;
- built-in predicate spawn for running tasks;
- process join;
- predicate join;
- reaction groups combining event processing with workflows;
- support for dynamic event channels;
- guards

Messaging reaction rules in Prova describe processes in terms of message-driven conversations between inference agents / services and represent their associated interactions via constructs for asynchronously sending and receiving event messages. Choreography interaction flows between distributed Prova inference agents/services are defined by the order of sending and receiving message constructs in messaging reaction rules. Messaging reaction rules maintain local conversation states which reflect the different activity flows and support performing them within in simultaneous conversation or sub-conversation branches.

The main language constructs of messaging reaction rules are: *sendMsg* predicates to send outbound messages, reaction *rcvMsg* rules which react to inbound messages, and *rcvMsg* or *rcvMult* inline reactions in the body of messaging reaction rules to receive one or more context-dependent multiple inbound event messages:

```
sendMsg(XID,Protocol,Agent,Performative,Payload |Context)
rcvMsg(XID,Protocol,From,Performative,Paylod|Context)
rcvMult(XID,Protocol,From,Performative,Paylod|Context)
```

where *XID* is the conversation identifier (conversation-id) of the conversation to which the message will belong. *Protocol* defines the communication protocol such as JMS, HTTP, SOAP, Jade etc. *Agent* denotes the target party of the message. *Performative* describes the pragmatic context in which the message is send. A standard nomenclature of performatives is, e.g. the FIPA Agents Communication Language ACL or the BPEL activity vocabulary. *Payload* represents the message content sent in the message envelope. It can be a specific query or answer or a complex interchanged rule base (set of rules and facts).

For instance, the following messaging reaction rule waits for an inbound query which might come from the invoke request of a BPEL activity: (variables start with upper case letters)

```
% receive query and delegate it to another inference agent
rcvMsg(CID,esb, Requester, acl_query-ref, Query) :-
    ... some conditions finding e.g. another inference agent ...,
    sendMsg(Sub-CID,esb,Agent,acl_query-ref, Query),
    rcvMsg(Sub-CID,esb,Agent,acl_inform-ref, Answer),
    ... (other conditional goals)...
    sendMsg(CID,esb,Requester,acl_inform-ref,Answer).
```

Via logical unification the data from the received inbound message is bound to variables and is used by the conditions in the body of the rule, which act as goals on other derivation rules in the local rule base (so called rule chaining). In the example the rule sends the query in a new sub-conversation (with the unique id *Sub-CID*) to another agent and waits for the answer. That is, the rule execution blocks at the *rcvMsg* condition in the body until an answer message is received in the inlined sub-conversation (or some timeout occurs), which activates the rule execution flow again, e.g., to prove further subsequent conditions (subgoals) of the rule or start other sub-conversations. Data from the received answers is bound to variables including backtracking to several variable bindings as usual in logic programming. Finally, in this example the rule sends back the answer to the original requesting party, which would be the BPEL process and terminates (finitely succeeds).

By using the conversation id to distinguish different processing branches Prova includes a mechanism (inspired by Join-calculus) for creating diverging branches (parallel gateway) and process join points (inclusive gateways). For instance, the following two rules, will create two parallel processing streams for a task and will join the received results.

```
fork(CID):-
    sendMsg(CID,self,0,reply,task(X),corr_a),
    rcvMsg(CID,self,Me,reply,task(X),corr_a).
fork(CID):-
    sendMsg(CID,self,0,reply,task(X),corr_b),
    rcvMsg(CID,self,Me,reply,task(X),corr_b),
    join(Me,CID,join,task(X)).
```

CEP-based Event-driven gateways for event-driven BPM (edBPM) can be programmed in Prova using reaction groups which allow correlation of event reactions.

```
fork(CID):-
    @group(ab)
    rcvMsg(CID,Protocol,From,command,runTaskA), ... .
fork(CID):-
    @group(ab)
    rcvMsg(CID,Protocol,From,command,runTaksB), ... .
fork(CID):-
    @or(ab)
    rcvMsg(CID,Protocol,From,or,_).
```

In the above example the two event processing handlers for the events *runTaskA* and *runTaskB* are grouped (correlated) by defining a reaction group *@group(ab)*. The OR reaction group *@or(ab)* in the third reaction rule waits for either of the two events to arrive. When either event arrives, due to the semantics of *OR*, the group as a whole is terminated (i.e. the alternative reaction is also terminated).

While an event-driven gateway is a simplified version of a reaction group, the general concept of reaction groups provides much more expressiveness for defining Complex Event Processing (CEP) patterns. Prova 3.0 includes a large collection of annotations for reaction groups that help with defining expressive correlated complex events and designing sophisticated event-driven workflows. For instance, consider the following example which defines a complex event pattern which detects suspicious logins from different IPs.

```
% Start detection on each new user login
rcvMult(XID,Protocol,From,request,login(User,IP)) :-
    service(XID).

service(XID) :-
    @group(g1)
    rcvMsg(XID,Protocol,From,request,logout(User,IP)),
    @group(g1) @timeout(1000)
    rcvMsg(XID,Protocol,From,request,login(User,IP2)) [IP2!=IP].
service(XID) :-
    @and(g1) @timeout(2000)
    rcvMsg(XID,Protocol,From,and,Events),
    println(["Suspicious Login Pattern detected: ",Events]," ").
```

Once the initiator event (a user login) is detected by the global *rcvMult* in the first rule, the predicate *service* creates two reactions that simultaneously wait for subsequent events. For each new initiator event, more reactions will become active.[2] The two sub-event reactions in the first *service* rule belong to the group *g1*, indicated by the reaction group annotation *@group(g1)*. They concurrently detect the follow-up event sequences of a *logout* followed (again) by a *login* from another *IP* which is detected by the pre-conditional guard $[IP2! = IP]$. Additionally, a *@timout* annotation of 1 second is defined in milliseconds, which starts at the moment the second *rcvMsg* statement is executed (and consequently, an inline reaction for a second login from another IP is created). After the timeout elapses, the inline reaction is purged and is no longer active. The third reaction is the result (composite) reaction corresponding to the operator *AND* *(@and(g1))* applied to the two event handlers waiting for a logout followed by a login event from another IP. This means that the whole group will terminate when both composed reactions are detected or the (global group) timeout expires after 2 seconds.

In summary, the declarative rule-based approach provides an expressive and compact declarative programming language to represent complex event processing logic in arbitrary combination with conditional decision logic implemented in terms of derivation rules. Via sending and receiving event messages it is possible to implement (complex) event-driven choreography workflows that span several communicating (messaging) rule inference agents / services. With that approach it is possible to implement e.g. petri-net style conversation flows, and all complex event-based workflow patterns (as described, e.g. by Van der Aalst et al. [12]) such as Join, Simple Merge, Cancel Activity, Multi-Choice, Structured Loop, Milestone

---

[2] However, it should be noted, that Prova does not block on any active reactions but instead keeps them in real-time memory ready to match when new qualifying inbound messages are detected.

can be implemented including also patterns like Deferred Choice which cannot be implemented by orchestration flows. The major benefit of the described rule-based approach is the tight integration of standard derivation rules for implementing complex decision logic and messaging reaction rules for implementing behavioral event message based reaction logic, conversation-based interactions and choreography workflows. Complex (business) decision logic, such as business rules, can be implemented in a declarative way in terms of derivation rules (as logic programs) and used to prove conditional goals mixed in arbitrary combinations with send and receive message constructs in messaging reaction rules.

4.3   Rule Responder Enterprise Service Bus Middleware

To deploy and execute distributed Prova inference agents as semantic web services an enterprise service bus based middleware, called Rule Responder [10], is used. We focus on the technical aspects of the middleware and on the machine-to-machine communication between automated rule inference agents. Figure 3 illustrates the architecture of the ESB middleware.

Several Prova rule engines [5] are deployed as distributed semantic web-based services. Each service runs a local rule base which implements the decision and reaction logic. The rules have access to local applications, data sources (e.g. web services, Java object representations such as EJBs, databases etc.), etc. and use them as local fact bases. The rule agents react to incoming events messages (requests) according to the defined rule-based execution logic. To communicate between the rule inference agents, Reaction RuleML [8] [2], the current de-facto standard language for reactive web rules, is used as common rule interchange

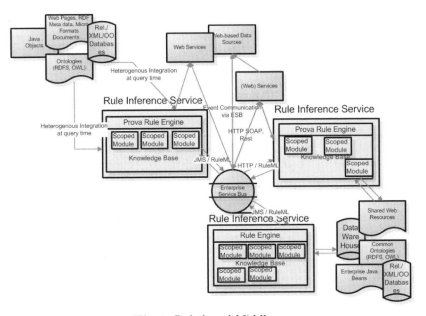

Fig. 3. Rule-based Middleware

format. Translator services translate from Prova execution syntax into Reaction RuleML and vice versa.

To seamlessly handle asynchronous message-based interactions between the Prova rule inference services and with other applications and web-based services an enterprise service bus (ESB), the Mule open-source ESB [6], is integrated as communication middleware. The ESB allows deploying the rule-based agents as distributed rule inference services installed as Web-based endpoints in the Mule object broker and supports the Reaction RuleML based communication via arbitrary transport protocols such as JMS, HTTP, SOAP, REST (more than 30 protocols are supported) between them. That is, the ESB provides a highly scalable and flexible event messaging framework to communicate synchronously but also asynchronously between services.

5   Conclusion

In this paper we have examined how the logic of decisions in business processes can be semantically represented by using rules. We have proposed a declarative rule-based approach for executable decision-centric business processes descriptions in BPEL, where complex conditional decisions, complex event processing (CEP) logic, and choreography workflows are implemented in terms of declarative logic-based rules. The rules are heterogeneously integrated into the BPEL process by invoking and executing them as semantic inference services. The rule based logic language combines derivation rules as means to represent conditional decision logic such as business rules with messaging reaction rules to describe conversation based process flow between agents. The conversational interactions take place via event messages. We have implemented a rule-based ESB middleware called Rule Responder which deploys Prova rule engines as distributed inference services. At the platform-independent level it uses Reaction RuleML as a compact, extensible and standardized rule and event interchange format between the platform-specific Prova services. A highly scalable and efficient enterprize service bus is integrated as a communication middleware platform and web-based agent/ service object broker. The realization of decision and reaction logic in business processes by means of rules provides an expressive enhancement of the syntactic BPEL orchestration language which forms the technical foundation to integrate the business rules technology with the enterprize service and BPM technology. In summary the key benefits of our rule-based SBPM approach are:

- BPEL for orchestration of services , people and partners
- Rules focus on decision making and policies
- Rules can be used to integrate choreography sub-workflows in orchestrated BPEL processes
- Declarative specification of constantly changing business decisions, policies and regulations
- Enables business users to participate in business processes via adapting business rules
- Modify and apply new rules without redeploying processes

The agent model of our rule-based approach in Prova (with distributed event-based conversations) can be used to implement (distributed) event processing agent networks and for distributed problem solving by rule-based choreography of multi-agent services. It also provides promising means to integrate people into the BPEL process via intelligent agent interfaces providing semi-automated decision services and self-autonomous reactions. While we have focused on the declarative logic-based programming expressiveness of the underlying rule-based approach on the platform specific execution layer in this paper, we have also worked on the computational independent modeling layer extending BPMN with rules and ontologies [1] and on the platform independent description of process services and their SLA properties [3,4,7,9].

Acknowledgements. This work has been partially supported by the "Inno Profile-Corporate Semantic Web" project funded by the German Federal Ministry of Education and Research (BMBF) and the BMBF Innovation Initiative for the New German Länder - Entrepreneurial Regions.

References

1. Barnickel, N., Böttcher, J., Paschke, A.: Incorporating semantic bridges into information flow of cross-organizational business process models. In: I-SEMANTICS (2010)
2. Boley, H.: The ruleML family of web rule languages. In: Alferes, J.J., Bailey, J., May, W., Schwertel, U. (eds.) PPSWR 2006. LNCS, vol. 4187, pp. 1–17. Springer, Heidelberg (2006)
3. Ul Haq, I., Paschke, A., Schikuta, E., Boley, H.: Rule-based workflow validation of hierarchical service level agreements. In: GPC Workshops, pp. 96–103 (2009)
4. Ul Haq, I., Schikuta, E., Brandic, I., Paschke, A., Boley, H.: Sla validation of service value chains. In: GCC, pp. 308–313 (2010)
5. Kozlenkov, A., Paschke, A.: Prova (2006), http://prova.ws
6. Mule. Mule enterprise service bus (2006), http://mule.codehaus.org/display/mule/home
7. Paschke, A.: Rule-Based Service Level Agreements - Knowledge Representation for Automated e-Contract, SLA and Policy Management. Idea Verlag GmbH, Munich (2007)
8. Paschke, A., Kozlenkov, A., Boley, H., Kifer, M., Tabet, S., Dean, M., Barrett, K.: Reaction ruleml (2006), http://ibis.in.tum.de/research/reactionruleml/
9. Paschke, A., Bichler, M.: Knowledge representation concepts for automated sla management. Decision Support Systems 46(1), 187–205 (2008)
10. Paschke, A., Boley, H., Kozlenkov, A., Craig, B.L.: Rule responder: Ruleml-based agents for distributed collaboration on the pragmatic web. In: ICPW, pp. 17–28 (2007)
11. Teymourian, K., Paschke, A.: Towards semantic event processing. In: DEBS (2009)
12. van der Aalst, W.M.P., ter Hofstede, A.H.M., Kiepuszewski, B., Barros, A.P.: Workflow patterns. Distributed and Parallel Databases. MIS Quarterly 14(1) (2003)

Web Services Trustworthiness Model
(Invited Paper)

Radosław Hofman[1,2] and Andrzej Bassara[1]

[1] PayU S.A., ul. Marcelinska 90, 60-324 Poznań, Poland
[1] Polish Attestation and Standardization Organization (SASO),
pl. Wolnosci 18, 61-739 Poznań, Poland
{Radoslaw.Hofman,Andrzej.Bassara}@payu.pl

Abstract. Proper selection of a Web Service for a particular business process from a set of services offered by external parties is a complex task that involves significant level of risk. It requires extensive knowledge not only on service capabilities but also on specific business context of its use as well as ability to compare contexts with capabilities. This article presents shortcomings of existing approaches to service discovery and selection in this area. Based on these observations, it proposes a vision of solution to this problem in terms of trustworthiness calling for the further research in this subject.

Keywords: Web Services, trustworthiness, service discovery, service selection.

1 Introduction

A decade ago fully automated business processes that span boundaries of one organization were domain of large and wealthy enterprises. Only these organization could afford to carry out necessary large scale integration projects, as integration was complex at that time. Open standards were uncommon and proprietary protocols were the norm. Know-how on integration technologies and knowledge on best practices in integration patterns were scarce. Moreover, the legal environment was not helping ether. It did not encourage and sometimes forbade electronic interchange of information.

It all began to change with emergence of domain specific platforms for electronic information interchange (EDI, SWIFT etc.) as well as with increasing popularity of open standards. The biggest enabler for inter-company automated processes are however internet technologies. Web Services (as understood by WS-I (WS-I 2011)) but also much more simpler approaches to integration based on exchange of XML or JSON documents via HTTP protocol (so called WebAPI) drastically broadened the scope of companies that can exchange electronic information with their business partners.

Required tools can be acquired free of charge (not counting the cost of related work). Acquisition of required know-how is fairly cheap as these technologies are open, relatively simple and popular. Moreover, we may also observe gradual changes in legal environment that not only acknowledges the validity of electronic information interchange, but also starts to facilitate progress in this area.

This all leads to the situation, where the number of inter-company automated business processes is unprecedented. Companies of every size are buying and selling their

W. Abramowicz et al. (Eds.): ServiceWave 2011, LNCS 6994, pp. 268–277, 2011.

services in electronic form. These services are then relatively easy (from technical standpoint) composed into complex processes (companies are focusing on their core capabilities and acquire many non-core capabilities in form of electronic services from external vendors).

It is also worth to note, that due to low technical complexity of integration, these processes can be composed dynamically (often partial automation of these composition may be supported). Furthermore, due to low cost of integration, these processes can be short-lived or frequently reconfigured/recomposed. For instance, a particular service in a dynamically reconfigurable process may be automatically selected from a pool of available substitutive services provided by different vendors. Additionally, this selection can be performed at every process invocation (or even at the time of service invocation, i.e. the service is selected just prior to its execution, not at the beginning of the process), therefore every process instance may be based on different services.

However, the dynamic service selection poses new challenges related to the selection of the most suitable one. Suitability of an service for a particular business process covers many different dimensions: the basic function of the service, required parameters, expected output, quality attributes, security attributes etc. The problem with the selection is even more demanding, as there is no single source of trustworthy information regarding this information. In this context, methods and tools that facilitate proper selection of service providers and selection of particular services are more vital than ever before.

2 Related Work

2.1 Web Services Quality

From 1960's development of software was perceived as discipline of engineering. These was also the beginning for all attempts to define goals and measures for software. One of the most important measures was software quality. Unfortunately, since the beginning it has been more than difficult to create unambiguous definition of quality. It remains an open issue up to the present day (compare the works of ISO/IEC JTC1/SC7/WG6 on SQuaRE model (ISO/IEC25010 FDIS 2011)).

Since first publications on quality appeared, it has been known that quality related issues are often a mixture of different quality meanings. Important work in these area was made by Kitchengam et al. (Kitchenham and Pfleeger 1996), where five quality views have been identified:

- quality as an abstract, meta-physical term – unreachable ideal, which shows the direction where to products are heading but will never get there,
- quality as a perspective of a user considering attributes of software in special context of use,
- quality as a perspective of a manufacturer, seen as compliance with stated requirements and following ISO 9001 series view,
- quality as a product perspective understood as internal characteristic, resulting from measures of product attributes,
- quality as a value based perspective, differing in dependence on stakeholder for whom is defined.

Special case of software quality, relates to quality of Web Services. The software itself is said to be different from other human craft products, mainly because it is intangible (Basili 1993). It should be noted, that Web Services for the user are even more intangible, as their quality is being assessed only on the basis of the results of their invocation. These invocations are in turn dependent on software which provides the service, underlying infrastructure, maintenance procedures etc. (compare (Abramowicz, et al. 2009)). Therefore in the context of Web Services "quality" means the whole spectrum of attributes related to the service.

Web Services Quality attributes, quality characteristics or quality models have been presented in literature since the beginning of the 21st century. Large number of researchers perceive quality of Web Services as an abbreviation of Quality of Service (QoS). In this case, typically proposed quality attributes are similar to those used for low level telecommunication services (compare (Kalepu, Krishnaswamy and Loke 2004), (Evans and Filsfils 2007)). An extensive review of attributes appearing in literature was presented in (Abramowicz, et al. 2009). The conclusion is similar to the one related to the legacy software product - there is no commonly accepted understanding of QoS, nor even quality related attributes of Web Services.

2.2 Web Services Selection

Problem of proper, preferably automated, selection and composition of services have been already discussed in literature a number of times and different models have been presented. Most of these models deals specifically with Web Services (as understood by WS-I). They also share many similarities among themselves. They all relay heavily on services descriptions. This is a natural choice, as service description should be the only place, where details related to a service usage should be defined. However, as (Abramowicz, et al. 2008) points out, Web Service description expressed in a well-defined and widely accepted notation Web Service Description Language (WSDL) is insufficient, as it limits itself only to technical interface description - structure (but not semantics) of exchanged documents, a list of supported operations, available endpoints etc.

Therefore, if services are to be selected solely based on service descriptions, these descriptions must be enhanced with additional information on:

- real-life results of service invocation. In many cases, service invocation results in changes to the state of real life. It may be change in obligations or responsibilities between parties involved or sometimes it leads to physical changes like movements of goods. Therefore, service description should precisely state its goal, impact on the state of the world, preconditions for service invocation etc.,
- terms and conditions of service usage. Service description should not only covers technical details or rules governing service invocation but also state clearly what are the mutual obligations of the service provider and the client with respect to the service usage,
- service level, i.e. certain measurable goals describing important and relevant aspects of service performance.

The discrepancy between information present in WSDL descriptions and information required for automatic service selection and invocation led to the emergence of Semantic Web Services, which is a general term for approaches to development of infrastructure that would enable automation of Web Services provisioning and usage (which according to (Friesen and Altenhofen 2005) covers: publication, discovery, selection, composition, mediation negotiation, invocation, monitoring, composition and recovery), by means of semantic technologies. Semantic Web Services involves, among many others, development of replacements or extensions to WSDL, which enhances services descriptions with additional, business-oriented information. Notable examples in this area includes, such frameworks as: OWL-S (Ontology Web Language for Web Services) (Martin, et al. 2004), WSMO (Web Services Modeling Ontology) (Roman, et al. 2005) and SAWSDL (Semantic Annotations for WSDL) (Farrell and Lausen 2007). All these frameworks are constructed in a way, that service description should contain all information necessary for automatic service discovery and execution. Input and output parameters, goals as well as state of the real-world before and after successful service execution should be presented and encoded in machine readable format.

These frameworks are however limited when it comes to other, non-functional aspects of service invocations. This limitations raised motivation for another wave of research on selection and composition of services based on their quality attributes (this research is thoughtfully summarized in (Abramowicz, et al. 2008)). However, due to the lack of common understanding of non-functional parameters definitions, proposed approaches to discovery and selection of Web Services based on their quality information are highly limited (see the review in (Abramowicz, et al. 2009)). Moreover, basing the selection of services on explicitly declared quality, rises the concerns of trust towards QoS attributes values (even if one assumes that there are commonly understood definitions), which is usually neglected.

3 Problem Statement

A business entity considering usage of Web Services for their business processes faces several sources of uncertainty. It has to consider if the service, it is to choose provides:

 — adequate level of quality of results (the service delivers what it promises to deliver). The main concern of the customer is getting the result which is relevant to the desired purpose of the Web Service invocation. For example, if one needs to get translation from English to Hungarian, he is interesting in finding a service providing such function with the highest available quality of translation,
 — adequate level of quality of service. In many cases, the Web Service call has to be fast or reliable enough to use the service. For example, an agent using Web Services for ongoing analysis of stock market for the purpose of trading decision, may suffer significant loss if the Web Service provides information with a delay or does not provide them at all,
 — acceptable business terms.

In (Abramowicz, et al. 2009) authors also point out that in the selection process the aspects related to the provision of the service should be considered as well. These aspects may include hosting and network related issues.

Unfortunately, even if all the above criteria have been analyzed and proved to be satisfactory for a particular scenario, it still does not guarantee that the service would be suitable for end-to-end process, which is being executed by service customer. To illustrate this limitation, let us consider a sample scenario. Let us assume, that there are two Web Services (WS1 and WS2), each providing weather forecast for geographic location (exemplary call: N: 52° 24' 23", E: 16° 55' 5", Radius: 10 km, Date: 28.10.2011, Hour: 12:00, Forecast: 12h). Let us also assume that there are two customers which would invoke any of these two services: a travel agency and air-traffic operations center. Both customers are using the same invocation method therefore on the technical level both services are considered to be equivalent. It may be further assumed that both services are provided by competing providers aiming to attract as many customers as possible, therefore both services are described with all possible tags related to weather forecasting. Furthermore, both providers assure the same level of QoR, QoS and terms of service (including price).

Which service should be then chosen for air-traffic planning, and which should be used for holiday planning? If any of the two services mentioned above is suitable for one of these contexts of use, then it is almost certain that it will be useless for the other one and vice versa (for holiday planning one needs the overview of complete situation, while air traffic planning requires information related to detailed situation in the air – for example the temperature and wind parameters 10 km above the sea level).

Similar problem is related to security and safety of the service and their impact on the overall process. It is commonly stated, that the security level is as high, as the worst cell in the chain. However, it may be shown, that combining several services, each with acceptable level of security, may result in overall security level which is unacceptable for the whole process. Therefore, selection of a Web Service should take into consideration context as well as security and safety requirements for the overall process. An example of such situation may include a service, which contains a security vulnerability, which is not dangerous in itself, however when is combined with another vulnerability in the end-to-end process it introduces some side off effects which make the whole process prone to data disclosure.

The problem described above may be presented from another perspective as well. In this perspective it should be assumed that services are similar, have indifferent QoR, QoS and business parameters, however the access to the services uses different network routes. The routing is independent from both: the service provider and the customer (it is assumed that the impact on the access to the service may be made somewhere between). It is natural that customer cannot expect from the provider that they will ensure the complete route, however in the selection process the customer should be aware that there is another set of parameters, not related to service description, which affect the execution.

The common denominator for the above parts of the problem is the lack of trustworthiness of Web Services, what is completely reasonable, because provided descriptions may be misleading for the process of service selection. The trustworthiness cannot be based solely on service description (what is neglected by most of service frameworks). Therefore, if the customer is to decide to use a Web Service, then he would need enough proofs that the service is adequate to what he is looking for.

The consequences of the problem of limited trustworthiness are significant. Professional customers are unable to select (manually, not to mention automatically) Web Services that are adequate to their end-to-end processes requirements, to their context of use. As a consequence, they cannot allow their crucial processes to be delivered by many different providers (they typically select statically service provider, sign up an agreement and use the idea of SOA only for the technical integration layer).

In conclusion, dynamically composed intercompany business processes requires solution to the above-presented problem. The fundamental question presented in this paper is, if introduction of context of use to the service selection process will improve trustworthiness of the Web Services from business perspective?

4 The Vision of Solution

In the beginning of this section the term "trustworthiness" has to be defined. The term has developed for decades, however, in the context of IT, trustworthiness was described by Bishop as the degree of conformance to a given set of requirements and the evidence for this conformance. The term is being used mainly by history researchers, where trustworthiness refers to the reliability and authenticity of records (Minnesota State Archives 2011) or in linguistic approach, where trustworthiness is an attribute of an entity deserving of trust or confidence, being dependable and reliable (Suryn 2011). The understanding of trustworthiness is therefore based on conformity with defined requirements and the evidence corroborating this conformity. Roughly speaking, trustworthiness may be perceived as the degree of certainty that the service will deliver what the user expects, based on prior experience of all users.

The models of reliability assessment of the Web Services based on customer feedback or RES agency were already proposed (see (Abramowicz, et al. 2009) for the review), however these solutions leave the problem defined in the previous section intact. The first issue results from service descriptions limitations. In the example provided in the previous section, both Web Services could be described in exactly the same way, but each of them was relevant to different contexts of use. Addressing this issue calls for building up an ontology of business contexts of use. This ontology should allow expressing the end-to-end processes in which the service can be used. However, as previously noted, service providers might act in a way, which may mislead potential customers while maximizing provider's traffic (and potentially his revenue). In this situation, both services could still use the same list of ontology tags making the descriptions indifferent.

The second issue could be solved using analogous ideas, to those proposed for QoS reliability propagation - a common institution holding information regarding calls and users automatic feedbacks. Contrary to solutions proposed in literature, it should be assumed that the information regarding calls and feedbacks contains not only technical parameters, but also end-to-end process context involved in the service call. A new customer, knowing their own end-to-end process, would be able to search for a Web Service which proved to be adequate for a similar context of use. After the call, the information regarding this particular context of use and the feedback, should be stored.

In the previous section not only the context of use was described as the potential source of inefficient service selection, but also security (as the separate dimension of parameters) and the technical location of the caller (in the meaning of network route). In general the number of dimension may be unlimited, however in this article, the three mentioned above are used to describe the vision of context aware model. The applicability of these dimensions is analogous to the flow described for end-to-end context: the caller searches for a service knowing their location and security parameters and leaves the feedback with this information after the call.

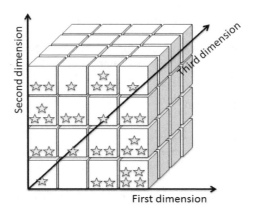

Fig. 1. Three dimensions of WS descriptions with rankings

The degree of similarity measurement statutes the third pillar of the vision. Beginning from the most easy to describe – the technical location, it could be measured by comparison of the route necessary to call the service to routes ranked previously by user feedbacks. Comparison process should focus on the first common node, assuming that the route from common node to the same service is similar. For example if the route necessary to call the service requires the use of A, B, C, D, E network infrastructure elements (lines, switches etc.), and there are ranked calls X, Y, C, D, E, and Z, B, C, D, E then it may be concluded that both rankings are similar to desired route. This example is presented on Fig 2.

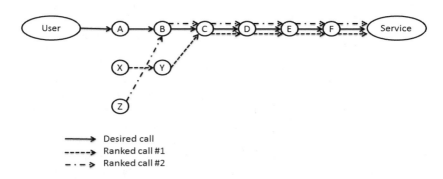

Fig. 2. Network path similarity assessment

It is not known what impact on the ranked calls came from X, Y or Z nodes, however if overall feedbacks are positive it may be expected that:

— if A works properly then the second ranked call supports the positive probability of reaching the service
— if A and B works properly then the first ranked call supports the positive probability of reaching the service

The first corollary contains only the uncertainty about A, since B was already ranked.

The measurement of end-to-end context similarity is more complicated. The main challenge, as it was mentioned at the beginning of this section, is an adequate ontology, which should describe and categorize end-to-end contexts. The similarity degree could be based on simple ontology-based similarity measures (such as (Resink 1999) or (Araújo i Pinto 2007)). These measures are simple and general, however having knowledge regarding details of desired end-to-end context, one may use their own algorithm for the similarity assessment.

Security context, on the other hand, seems to consist of several binary attributes which are provided (or not) by the service. For example, in a search for payment service one may require the service to provide "Payment from link", while the other one may require the same future to be disabled (for instance, if an entity is providing direct sales they could use payments from links sent via email, while other merchants, which are unable to validate variables during the call, may perceive payments from link as the door for cross-site-scripting (XSS) vulnerability). If the desired service must provide certain parameters, then the user will evaluate binary attributes relevant for their call or adopt other selection pattern.

In summary, the vision proposed in this article consists of three pillars:

— context awareness of the user, expressing their requirements in common terms (using ontology for end-to-end context, network infrastructure information and ontology for security parameters etc.),
— common information source containing information on the context of calls and user feedbacks,
— similarity assessment method or selection algorithm.

It is beyond the scope of this article to propose the details of the implementation of the vision, however it should be the subject of further research, in order to make SOA dynamic service composition more acceptable for the business.

5 Further Research

In has been shown above, that proper selection of a service for a particular business process from a set of services delivered by external parties is a complex task. It requires extensive knowledge not only on service capabilities but also on specific business context of its usage. Since existing approaches to service discovery and selection are limited in this area, a sketch of sample solution to this problem based on trustworthiness was presented. This model needs however to be detailed and its major underpinning concepts further refined. Major areas of concern for further research are presented in the remaining part of this section.

The importance of the trustworthiness problem may be presented in the context of user experience influence on the evaluation process. Hofman (Hofman, 2011) proposes a quality assessment model that takes into account not only the direct attributes, but also associated attributes, user mental state and knowledge. The experiment results shown in this article reveals that software quality assessment is based on memories of users.

This observation should be considered as a crucial factor for trustworthiness building. User, who will become not satisfied with the service, may never change their mind. Therefore Web Service providers should plan their maintenance and service development activities in such a way, that in any time all users will be handled appropriately. Adequate trustworthiness framework should be designed in such a way, which will maximize the reliability of the model. In other words, trustworthiness framework will deliver services reflecting trustworthiness degree of evaluated services. However the service delivering these ranks in acoordance with trustworthiness framework should also be trustworthy.

It is also worth to note, that the methodology regarding trustworthiness certification of software (especially COTS[1]) is actually in its experimental phase. It has been developed in international cooperation among three scientists: Dr. Yuyu Yuan from Beijing University of Posts and Telecommunication, Dr. Witold Suryn from École de technologie supérieure, Montréal, Canada and Mr. Jørgen Bøegh from TERMA, Denmark (Suryn 2011). It is expected that currently the ISO/IEC JTC1/SC7 will launch a new project aiming to research the area, and prepare the standard of trustworthiness certification of software.

It should be noted that the general aim of this project addresses the issues related to complete product, however the discussion regarding trustworthiness of Web Services may fall beyond software related framework. Mainly because of intended context of call, which does not affect the evaluation of product as much, as the evaluation of single service invocation. The model of trustworthiness of Web Services assessment seem to be important challenge for both: the research and implementation into market.

One should also consider challenges that appear in intra-organizational setting. Processes that span boundaries of organizations may often lead to their suboptimal composition. For instance, if more than one entity is involved in business process and each entity acts independently, then the selection process may be expressed in concepts of the game theory. In this case, every entity (taking into consideration proper risk management and limited trustworthiness) should select services in a way, that would maximize its benefit but also should take into account uncertainty, possible conflicting of interests with other entities as well as their possible actions. As a result, every entity should select services in a way that would yield optimal result for this particular entity no matter what are the actions of other entities. In consequence, process composition may not be optimal. For instance, if we have two entities that buy services in a process, they would probably optimize their cost locally, it does not imply however that the overall cost of services in a process is optimal.

This situation calls for development of service composition frameworks that take into account the whole end-to-end process as well as existence of many independent parties with limited trust and often conflicting interests.

References

1. (WS-I), Web Services Interoperability Organization (July 31, 2011),
   http://www.ws-i.org
2. Abramowicz, W., Haniewicz, K., Hofman, R., Kaczmarek, M., Zyskowski, D.: Decomposition of SQuaRE-Based Requirements For The Needs Of SOA Applications. In: Ao, S.-I., Huang, X., Alexander, P.-k. (eds.) Trends in Communication Technologies and Engineering Science, Wai, vol. 33, pp. 81–94. Springer, Netherlands (2009)

---

[1] Commercial Off The Shelf.

3. Abramowicz, W., Hofman, R., Suryn, W., Zyskowski, D.: SQuaRE based Web Services Quality Model. In: International Multiconference of Engineers and Software Scientsts IMECS 2008 (2008)

4. Araújo, R., Sofia Pinto, H.: Towards Semantics-Based Ontology Similarity. In: Ontology Matching Workshop, OM 2007(2007)

5. Basili, V.R.: The experimental paradigm in software engineering. In: Rombach, H.D., Selby, R.W., Basili, V.R. (eds.) Experimental Software Engineering Issues: Critical Assessment and Future Direction. LNCS, vol. 706, pp. 1–12. Springer, Heidelberg (1993)

6. Evans, J., Filsfils, C.: Deploying IP and MPLS QoS for Multi-service Networks: Theory and Practice. Morgan Kaufmann, San Francisco (2007)

7. Farrell, J., Lausen, H.: Semantic Annotations for WSDL and XML Schema. W3C Recommendation (2007)

8. Friesen, A., Altenhofen, M.: Semantic Discovery Optimization: Matching Composed Semantic Web Services at Publishing Time. In: WEBIST 2005, Proceedings of the First International Conference on Web Information Systems and Technologies (2005)

9. Hofman, R.: Behavioral economics in software quality engineering. In: Empirical Software Engineering, pp. 278–293 (April 2011)

10. ISO/IEC25010 FDIS. Software engineering-Software product Quality Requirements and Evaluation (SQuaRE) Quality model. International Standardization Organization, Geneve (2011)

11. Kalepu, S., Krishnaswamy, S., Loke, S.-W.: Reputation = f(User Ranking, Compliance, Verity). In: Proceedings of the IEEE International Conference on Web Services, San Diego, California (2004)

12. Kitchenham, B., Pfleeger, S.: Software Quality: The Elisive Target. IEEE Software (1996)

13. Martin, D., et al.: OWL-S: Semantic Markup for Web Services. W3C Member Submission (2004)

14. Minnesota State Archives (July 31, 2011),
   `http://www.mnhs.org/preserve/records/index.htm`

15. Resink, P.: Semantic similarity in a taxonomy: an information-based measure and its application to problems of ambiguity in natural language. Journal of Artificial Intelligence Research (1999)

16. Roman, D., et al.: Web Service Modeling Ontology. Journal Applied Ontology (2005) 1st edn.

17. Suryn, W.: Trustworthiness of Software - Challenge of the 21st Century (2011) (unpublished)

Identification and Specification
of Generic and Specific Enablers of the Future Internet –
Illustrated by the Geospatial and Environmental Domain
(Invited Paper)

Arne J. Berre[1], Thomas Usländer[2], and Sven Schade[3]

[1] SINTEF, Norway
arne.j.berre@sintef.no
[2] Fraunhofer IOSB, Germany
thomas.uslaender@iosb.fraunhofer.de
[3] European Commission - Joint Research Centre, Italy
sven.schade@jrc.ec.europa.eu

Abstract. The identification and specification of generic and specific enablers of the Future Internet is based on a use-case oriented methodology taking into account life cycle and architectural constraints. The approach is illustrated by examples from the geospatial and environmental domain that are both elaborated in the ENVIROFI usage area project as part of the Future Internet Public Private Partnership program. The approach claims to be applicable to other thematic domains and usage areas.

Keywords: Future Internet, Architecture, Enablers, Geospatial, Environmental.

1 Introduction

The presented approach for identification and specification of generic and specific future internet enablers has been developed and applied in the context of the ENVIROFI usage area project [1] as part of the Future Internet Public Private Partnership (FI PPP) program. ENVIROFI addresses, in particular, the geospatial and environmental domain. However, the suggested methodology for enabler identification and specification is designed to be independent of thematic domains and usage areas, and thus claims to be applicable more broadly. The methodology starts with use case modeling, potentially linked with user stories from an agile modeling approach. It continues with a use case analysis activity that is closely related to a system description approach using RM-ODP, including a mapping to enablers that takes into account life cycle and architectural constraints.

In section 2 we first present the methodology. Section 3 describes the life cycle-based approach whereas section 4 focuses on the architectural approach for the identification of enablers. Section 5 presents conclusions and outlines further work.

2 Methodology for Enabler Identification and Specification

This section provides an overview of the methodology illustrated for geospatial and environmental usage areas. It is based on use case modeling and combines the

W. Abramowicz et al. (Eds.): ServiceWave 2011, LNCS 6994, pp. 278–289, 2011.

SERVUS methodology [2] with agile modeling and SoaML. SERVUS is a Design Methodology for Information Systems based upon Geospatial Service-oriented Architectures and the Modelling of Use Cases and Capabilities as Resources.

2.1 Use Case Modelling

The methodology requires that requirements for enablers are elaborated in a first step as user stories and use cases by the experts of thematic domains. Applying an iterative approach, the use cases are matched in a second step with the capabilities of the emerging Future Internet platform, encompassing both generic enablers (to be provided by the FI-WARE project as part of the core platform) and specific enablers, provided by usage area projects, e.g. environmental enablers to be provided by ENVIROFI as illustrated in Figure 1.

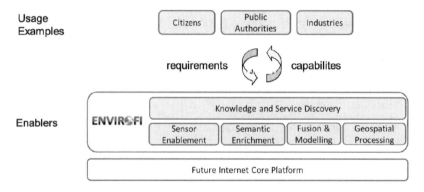

Fig. 1. Overall Idea of the ENVIROFI Use Case Analysis

Use case modelling has been proven to be an efficient and powerful approach to reach a common understanding of the system itself and its behaviour. In interdisciplinary projects, involving thematic experts from different domains (e.g., air and water) as well as software experts, it is as challenging as essential to reach consensus on a common terminology. Use cases represent the most common practices for capturing and deriving requirements. The requirements of the system are described in a narrative way with minimal technical jargon. In a nutshell, "a use case describes who can do what with the system and for what" [3]. Those quotes of Cockburn indicate that the most important basis to implement case studies is use case modelling.

We propose that use cases are described in a semi-formal way, with a use case template based on a structured textual description in tabular form. Furthermore, the SERVUS design methodology argues that additional information about the requested information resources (e.g. type and format of needed data) is necessary to completely describe a use case from both a user's and system's point of view. This small extension with respect to a classical use case approach heavily facilitates the transition to the abstract design step (e.g., the specification of the information model in the Unified Modelling Language UML) but is still very easy to understand by thematic experts. Furthermore, requirements (for enablers) should be derivable from the use cases. Three types of requirements can be identified:

- Functional requirements,
- Informational requirements,
- Non-functional requirements.

Functional requirements can be derived from the sequence of actions (main success scenario, extensions and alternative paths) as part of the use case description. The informational requirements address data that is exchanged between two communication partners, i.e. between users and the system or between system components. Here, the identification of requested information resources already as part of the use case description is quite helpful. Finally, the non-functional requirements cover all requirements that do not alter the foreseen functionality of the system, e.g. the quality of data and results.

2.2   Use Case Analysis Process

Figure 2 illustrates the use case analysis process [4]. As part of the project planning there needs to be some agreement of how to document use cases. For this continuous activity a project space has to be created which preferably should be supported by a use case server that is accessible by all participants of the analysis process. In ENVIROFI, this use case server is provided in the form of a web-based collaborative tool.

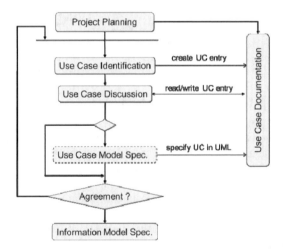

Fig. 2. Procedure of the ENVIROFI Use Case Analysis

As a first step of the analysis iteration loop a set of preliminary use cases (UC) is identified, mostly by those thematic experts who drive the effort. For each of them an entry in the project space has to be generated. As described above, the methodology proposes that use cases are initially described in structured natural language but already contain the list of requested resources. This description is the language which is used in the UC discussion that takes place in workshops that are facilitated by the system analyst. Depending on the level of agreement that can be reached the iteration loop is entered again in order to refine or add new use cases.

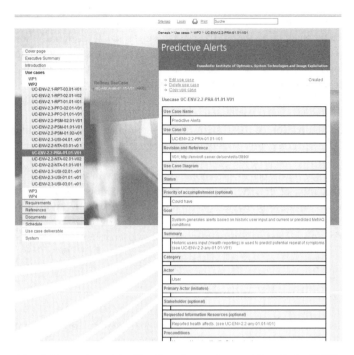

Fig. 3. Screenshot of the Use Case Server (source: Fraunhofer IOSB)

In order to identify inconsistencies and check the completeness of the UC model, the system analyst may transform the semi-structural UC description into formal UML specifications. However, these UML diagrams should still be on a high abstraction level such that a discussion with the end-user is possible. It is the advantage of this formal transition step already in an early analysis phase to detect inconsistencies and missing information as quickly as possible. The UML specification helps to (re-) discuss and check the use cases with the thematic experts.

However, in addition to the usual UML use cases they already comprise the links to the set of requested (information) resources, their representation forms and the requirements to create, read, write or delete them[1]. Once an agreement is reached about the set of use case descriptions and related UML specifications it is then up to the system analyst to specify the resulting information model taking the resource model as a modeling framework.

2.3 Reference Model based on ISO RM-ODP

The identification and discussion about enabler requirements analysis cannot take place without having in mind a common reference model of a Future Internet system architecture. Here, we propose to rely upon agreed international standards such as ISO RM-ODP. Inspired by "distributed processing systems based on interacting objects", ISO defined the Reference Model for Open Distributed Processing (ISO/IEC

---

[1] Inspired by the resource-oriented architectural style as used by RESTful web services [4].

10746-1:1998). The RM-ODP standards have been adopted widely. They constitute the conceptual basis for the ISO 191xx series of geospatial standards from ISO/TC211. The viewpoints of RM-ODP are applied as follows. The *Enterprise viewpoint* describes the purpose, scope and policies of that system and contains the use cases described above. The *Information viewpoint* describes the semantics of information and information processing and contains the information resources identified as the use case extension. The *computational viewpoint*[2] describes the functional decomposition of the system into components and objects which interact at interfaces. The *Engineering viewpoint* describes the mechanisms and functions required to support distributed interaction between objects in the system. The *Technology viewpoint* describes the choice of technology in that system.

The identification of generic and specific enablers is done based on a combination of top down and bottom up analysis using a complete life cycle approach as well as a complete end to end architectural approach. The two following sections describe the framework for the identification of life-cycle based enablers and architectural based enablers.

3 Life-Cycle Based Enablers

In this section we describe a life-cycle based perspective for the identification of enablers with both a service centric and data centric view.

We re-use components which have been identified in a recent activity of the European Committee for Standardisation (CEN), Technical Committee (TC) 287 for building a reference model for spatial data infrastructures (SDI) [5], see also Fig. 4. Notably, the Service Centric View could be applied to any service-oriented system. Only the Data Centric View contains instantiations, which are specific for the geospatial and environmental domains. Likewise, GeoPortals are a specific type of geospatial applications.

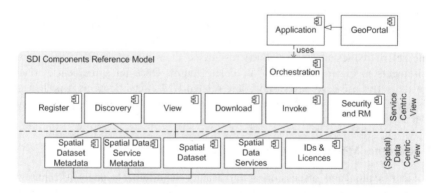

Fig. 4. Core Components of the SDI Reference Model ([5], modified)

---

[2] Sometimes also referred to as „Service Viewpoint" acknowledging its application in (geospatial) service-oriented architectures [2].

The primary organizing structure is determined by the following generic core life cycle components (corresponding to the service centric view in the figure):

- *Register*: for describing and publishing resources.
- *Discovery*: for searching for and discovery of resources.
- *View*: for visualising of resources.
- *Download*: for downloading and exchanging resources.
- *Invoke*: for interacting with resources.
- *Orchestration and Composition*: for providing aggregated resources including in particular workflows for service composition.
- *Security and Rights Management*: for managing access rights to resources.

Related to the data centric and service centric view shown in figure 4 we illustrate the requirements of the environmental usage area following a life-cycle centric approach. First, we introduce the roles, which are involved in generating knowledge about our environment and define the overall added-value chain. In a second step, we present common requirements for future eEnvironment services. In doing so, we provide a bridge between practical environmental applications and the wider political framework. The presented findings could equally be applied to other geospatial and non-geospatial domains beyond the environmental domain.

3.1 The Value Chain of Environmental Knowledge Generation

Analyzing the requirements of eEnvironment services for the terrestrial, atmospheric and marine sphere, we could extract a total of six roles, which contribute to the generation of environmental knowledge [6]:

1. *Observer*, being the initial source of information about the environment. This may reach from sensor measuring weather conditions to citizen observing species occurrences.
2. *Publisher*, making a resource, such as an observation, discoverable to a wider audience, e.g. by providing required resource descriptions (metadata).
3. *Discoverer*, being the entity that finds a resource, e.g. species occurrence data, based on all available descriptions.
4. *Service Provider*, making information or an environmental model accessible to (and usable by) the wider audience, e.g. by offering a standard based service for data download.
5. *Service Orchestrator*, being responsible for combining existing services in a way that they create information for a distinct purpose, i.e. environmental application focusing on a particular sphere, such as terrestrial biodiversity.
6. *Decision Maker*, consuming an environmental application in order to retrieve decision supporting material and making a final decision based on the information available, e.g. designating a new protected area.

Consequently, the process workflow can be summarized as in the figure below (Fig. 5). Notably, following this workflow services may themselves get published in order to serve as building blocks for more complex eEnvironment solutions.

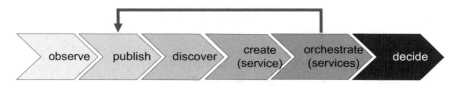

Fig. 5. Added value chain of environmental knowledge generation [6]

3.2 Overview of Stakeholders

The tasks identified above (section 3.1) are played by a variety of individuals and organizations. Those have been again extracted from requirements of eEnvironment. In a nutshell, those can be defined as:

- *Citizens* of a particular social, political, or national community;
- *Environmental agencies* on sub-national, national and European level;
- *Public authorities* of national and regional and other level;
- *Industries* from the primary, secondary and service sector;
- *Platform providers* offering frameworks on which applications may be run;
- *Infrastructure providers* offering physical components and essential services;
- *Sensor network owners* holding the sensor and basic communication hardware.

Table 1. Added-value chain of environmental knowledge generation [6]

	observe	provide	discover	create	orchestrate	decide
Citizens	x	x	x	x	x	x
Environmental agencies	x	x		x		x
Public authorities		x		x		x
Industries			x	x	x	x
Platform providers				x		
Infrastructure providers				x		
Sensor network owners	x	(x)		(x)		x

Table 1 provides an overview of the manifold mappings between these stakeholders and the different roles in the value chain of environmental knowledge generation. Notably, citizens can play all roles, they may even discover available information and provide new services (mash-ups). The decisions they may take are on individual level, such as "Should I travel through an area with bad air quality?".

3.3 Requirements for a Next Generation of eEnvironment Services

Given the above, we can now identify the requirements for a next generation of eEnvironment services in Europe. They can be summarized as follows:

- publication, discovery, access and visualization of environmental data sets;
- planning, publication, discovery, access and visualization of measurements;

- publication, discovery, access and visualization of objective, semi-objective and subjective observations by end users;
- transformation of data sets and fusion of observations;
- publication, discovery and access to environmental models and simulations;
- composition and invocation of workflows;
- support and enforcement of data and service policies based on identity, licenses, trust chains, etc.;
- publication, discovery, access, visualization and annotation support for controlled vocabularies, taxonomies, and ontologies;
- integration with the Semantic Web and Web 2.0; and
- interoperability with existing and planned infrastructures in the context of:
  - the most relevant initiatives at international level, such as INSPIRE [7], GMES [8], SEIS [9], GEOSS[10],
  - relevant well-established communities, including research and e-government infrastructures [11], and
  - the mode relevant policies on international level, above all related to Public Sector Information (PSI) [12].

Specific components (environmental enablers) should support these requirements. They should be designed and developed leveraging existing architectural approaches and technical specifications, and re-using/extending existing tools. Particular attention should be paid to open international standards and communities-of-practice specifications, and to open source components in order to make the resulting system more flexible and scalable (see also [13]).

4   Architectural Based Enablers

The life cycle based enablers and relevant applications can further be described in terms of their architectural components and enablers/services. The following figure shows how the different types of enablers can be related in the context of a complete end-to-end ICT architecture.

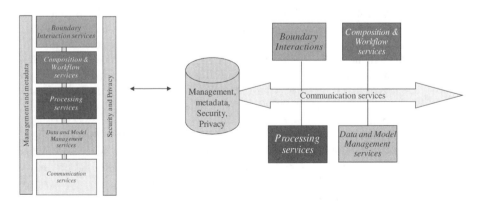

Fig. 6. Relationships of enablers in both a layered and a bus architecture

Figure 6 shows the relationship of different enabler categories both in a layered architecture and also as a bus architecture. The taxonomy of the enabler types is in accordance with ISO 19119 Geographic information – Services, clause 8.3. [14]. The approach is to define both generic domain independent and specific enablers, such as geospatial and environmental specific enablers, in each of the following six groups, color coded in the figure:

- **Boundary Interaction Enablers** are enablers for management of user interfaces, graphics, multimedia and for presentation of compound documents. Boundary Interaction services have been defined to not only include human interaction services, but also other system boundaries like sensor and actuator services. Specific enablers focus on providing capabilities for managing the interface between humans and Geographic Information Systems and location based sensors and actuators. This class includes also graphic representation of features, as described in ISO 19117.
- **Workflow/Task Enablers** are services for support of specific tasks or work-related activities conducted by humans. These enablers support use of resources and development of products involving a sequence of activities or steps that may be conducted by different persons. The specific enablers focus on workflow for tasks associated with geographic and environmental information — involving processing of orders for buying and selling of geographic information and services. These services are described in more detail in ISO 19119.
- **Processing Enablers** perform large-scale computations involving substantial amounts of data. Examples include enablers for providing the time of day, spelling checkers and services that perform coordinate transformations (e.g., that accept a set of coordinates expressed using one reference system and converting them to a set of coordinates in a different reference system). A processing service does not include capabilities for providing persistent storage of data or transfer of data over networks. The specific enablers focus on processing of geographic information. ISO 19116 is an example of a processing service. Other examples include services for coordinate transformation, metric translation and format conversion.
- **Model/Information Management Enablers** are enablers for management of the development, manipulation and storage of metadata, conceptual schemas and datasets. The specialization of this class of enablers focuses on management and administration of geographic information, including conceptual schemas and data. Specific services within this class are identified in ISO 19119. These services are based on the content of those standards in the ISO 19100 series that standardize the structure of geographic information and the procedures for its administration, including: ISO 19107, ISO 19108, ISO 19109, ISO 19110, ISO 19111, ISO 19112, ISO 19113, ISO 19114 and ISO 19115. Examples of such services are a query and update service for access and manipulation of geographic information and a catalogue service for management of feature catalogues.
- **Communication Enablers** are enablers for encoding and transfer of data across communications networks. The specific enablers focus on the transfer

of geographic information across a computer network. Requirements for Transfer and Encoding services are found in ISO 19118.

- **System Management and Security Enablers** are enablers for the management of system components, applications and networks. These services also include management of user accounts and user access privileges. The specific enablers focus on user management and performance management, and on Geo Right Management.

The six categories of enablers have been identified through an end-to-end architectural analysis. Since the initial version of this approach in the ISO 19101 and 19119 standards around 2001 they have been found sufficient for most identified service types and enablers, with the escape mechanism that many new instances will be put into the processing category. There are also situations where tools and applications are composite and contain components that will span multiple categories, and also for this reason the life cycle based classification has been found useful as an additional classification. In general, multiple classification schemes from different perspectives should be supported.

The different service types can also be categorized according to their relevance for emerging cloud services, starting with a classification for the application level and software as a service (SaaS), but also further down to platform as a service (PaaS) and infrastructure as a service (IaaS).

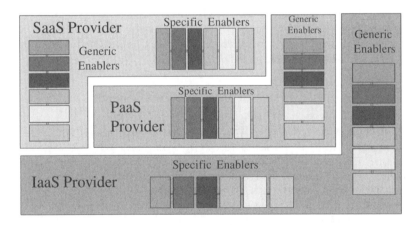

Fig. 7. Generic and specific enabler types for SaaS, PaaS and IaaS

The initial generic enabler areas identified by the FI-WARE project is targeted at providing further support in many of the areas identified through the life cycle based perspective and the architectural perspective here. The initial six areas can be mapped to the architectural areas as follows:

1. *Cloud hosting (IaaS)* is addressing generic enablers in particular related to processing and model/information management on the IaaS level.
2. *Data/Context management (with intelligent services)* is related to model/information management enablers on the SaaS and PaaS level.

3. *Application Services framework* – is related to processing and system management enablers on the PaaS level.
4. *IoT Service enablement* – is related to boundary enablers on the SaaS and PaaS level
5. *Interface to Network and Devices (I2ND)* is related to communication enablers on the PaaS and IaaS levels.
6. *Security* is related to System management/Security enablers on the SaaS and PaaS level.

In the ongoing FI PPP activities about the identification of further generic and specific enablers, it is assumed that more enablers will be found for all of the different enabler areas across all of the cloud levels from SaaS to PaaS and IaaS.

5   Conclusions and Further Work

The presented methodology and approach for the identification and specification of generic and specific Future Internet enablers is currently being used in the ENVIROFI project for the purpose of identifying and specifying enablers in the FI PPP program.

A broader initiative has been started for the further identification of enablers through the ENVIP community and CEN TC287. It is an aim that this approach can be further applied also in other domains and usage areas.

Acknowledgments. We thank the ENVIROFI (FP7 – 284898) project consortium for the lively discussions we had. This paper is based on our common findings, extended from our previous work in previous European research projects and in the context of ISO/TC211, CEN/TC287, OMG and OGC.

References

1. The Environmental Observation Web and its Service Applications within the Future Internet (ENVIROFI) project homepage, http://www.envirofi.eu/
2. Usländer, T.: Service-oriented Design of Environmental Information Systems. PhD thesis of the Karlsruhe Institute of Technology (KIT), Faculty of Computer Science, KIT Scientific Publishing (2010) ISBN 978-3-86644-499-7
3. Cockburn, A.: Writing Effective Use Cases. Addison-Wesley, Reading (2001) ISBN-13 978-0-201-70225-5
4. Usländer, T., Batz, T.: How to Analyse User Requirements for Service-Oriented Environmental Information Systems. In: Hřebíček, J., Schimak, G., Denzer, R. (eds.) Environmental Software Systems. IFIP AICT, vol. 359, pp. 161–168. Springer, Heidelberg (2011)
5. European Committee for Standardization (CEN): TR15449 Geographic information — Spatial data infrastructures — Part 1: Reference model. Technical Report (2011)
6. Schade, S., Fogarty, B., Kobernus, M., Schleidt, K., Gaughan, P., Mazzetti, P., Berre, A.-J.: Environmental Information Systems on the Internet: A Need for Change. In: Hřebíček, J., Schimak, G., Denzer, R. (eds.) Environmental Software Systems. IFIP AICT, vol. 359, pp. 144–153. Springer, Heidelberg (2011)

7. The European Parliament and of the Council: Directive 2007/2/EC of the European Parliament and of the Council of 14 March 2007 establishing an Infrastructure for Spatial Information in the European Community (INSPIRE). Official Journal on the European Parliament and of the Council (2007)

8. Commission of the European Communities: Communication COM(2009) 223 - GMES and its initial operations (2011-2013) (2009)

9. Commission of the European Communities: Communication COM(2008)0046 - Towards a Shared Environmental Information System (SEIS). 2008/0046 (2008)

10. Group on Earth Observations (GEO): The Global Earth Observation System of Systems (GEOSS) 10-Year Implementation Plan (2008)

11. European Commission: Communication COM(2010)743 - The European eGovernment Action Plan 2011-2015: Harnessing ICT to promote smart, sustainable & innovative Government (2010)

12. The European Parliament and the Council: Directive 2003/98/EC of the European Parliament and of the Council of 17 November 2003 on the re-use of public sector information, PSI Directive (2003)

13. Interoperable Solutions for European Public Administrations (isa): European Interoperability Strategy (EIS) for European public services (December 16, 2010)

14. International Organization for Standardization (ISO): 19119 Geographic information – Services. ISO Standard (2005)

Future Internet Technology for the Future of Transport and Logistics

(Invited Paper)

Rod Franklin[1], Andreas Metzger[2], Michael Stollberg[3], Yagil Engel[4], Kay Fjørtoft[5],
René Fleischhauer[3], Clarissa Marquezan[2], and Lone Sletbakk Ramstad[5]

[1] Kühne + Nagel Management AG, Schindellegi, Switzerland &
Kühne Logistics University, Hamburg, Germany
rod.franklin@kuehne-nagel.com
[2] Paluno (The Ruhr Institute for Software Technology)
University of Duisburg-Essen, Essen, Germany
{andreas.metzger,clarissa.marquezan}@paluno.uni-due.de
[3] SAP Research, Dresden, Germany
{michael.stollberg,rene.fleischhauer@sap.com}@kuehne-nagel.com
[4] IBM Research Labs, Haifa, Israel
yagile@il.ibm.com
[5] MARINTEK (Norwegian Marine Technology Research Institute), Trondheim, Norway
{Kay.Fjortoft,LoneSletbakk.Ramstad}@marintek.sintef.no

Abstract. International freight transport is the foundation of global trade, representing a large and growing industry where various stakeholders collaborate to transport goods around the world. The ICT infrastructures currently employed throughout logistics business networks are limited and the use of manual systems is common. This drastically hampers the operational efficiency of logistic service providers, carriers, and the various other stakeholders involved in transport processes. This paper presents an initial conceptual architecture for an ICT platform to overcome these deficiencies. The architecture is built on top of Future Internet technologies that provide generic capabilities for the efficient and effective development of cloud-based applications based on the Internet of Services, Internet of Things, and Internet of Contents with integrated security and privacy mechanisms.

Keywords: Future Internet, Transport, Logistics, Conceptual Architecture, Business Collaboration, E-Contracting, Event Handling, Transport Planning.

1 Introduction and Motivation

The efficient operation of international transport and logistics networks is a critical success factor for sustainable growth in global trade. Such inefficient operation creates barriers to trade by causing shipment delays and raising trading costs. Since transport and logistics activities account for 10% to 20% of a country's Gross Domestic Product, increases in the efficiency of these activities can dramatically improve a country's competitiveness. In addition, environmental impacts resulting from the operation of transport

W. Abramowicz et al. (Eds.): ServiceWave 2011, LNCS 6994, pp. 290–301, 2011.

and logistics activities are significant, so any improvement in efficiency within a logistics network positively contributes to sustainability objectives.

While the transport and logistics industry has made great strides in attempting to improve its efficiency, limitations in technology, transport infrastructure and regulatory regime incompatibilities have created significant barriers to future improvements. Overcoming these barriers requires new information and communications technologies that allow organizations to rapidly assemble collaborative logistics networks that can efficiently and effectively execute international trading activities. The Future Internet, with its promise of ubiquitous operation and information access, provides a potential platform for overcoming the limitations of current ICTs.

Building on the proposed capabilities of the Future Internet being developed under the European Union's Future Internet Public Private Partnership program (FI PPP), the FInest Use Case project (www.finest-ppp.eu) is designing a collaboration and integration platform for the transport and logistics industry. The *FInest platform* leverages generic capabilities, so called generic enablers, provided by the Future Internet and implements a domain-specific configurable set of services for the transport and logistics domain.

This paper presents the initial conceptual architecture of the FInest platform. In Section 2 the high level architecture of the platform is introduced. Section 3 refines this architecture by describing the initial set of services which are being implemented for the transport and logistics domain.

2   FInest High Level Architecture

The FInest platform consists of three layers shown in Figure 1. The layers and modules that reside within these layers are interconnected by using service-oriented technology. Service-oriented technology facilitates interoperability, openness and extensibility through standard interfaces. The use of integrated security and privacy management mechanisms ensures the secure and reliable exchange of confidential and business-critical information.

In the following we outline the three layers of the FInest architecture and discuss how we envision to exploit Future Internet technologies for the implementation of the platform.

2.1   Front End Layer

The front end layer of the FInest platform provides users with role specific, secure, ubiquitous access from different devices to information concerning the operation of the transport and logistics network. Roles that are supported through this front end layer include, but are not limited to, the following:

- end-users (customers) – can issue or trace their orders.
- transport planners – can develop, monitor and update transport plans based on end-user/customer orders. Transport plans may include the individual legs of a shipment, the mode used for that leg of the shipment and the provider of the transport service for that leg of the shipment.

- logistics service providers – can provide offers for transport and logistics services and retrieve demands for these services via dedicated marketplaces.

2.2 Back End Layer

The back end layer of the FInest platform provides access to, and integration with, legacy systems, third party services and any Internet of Things (IoT) devices that may provide information during the transport lifecycle. Legacy system integration is facilitated by service-oriented technology, e.g., by exposing features of legacy systems as services, or by offering access to legacy systems via the "Software as a Service" [1, 2] delivery model.

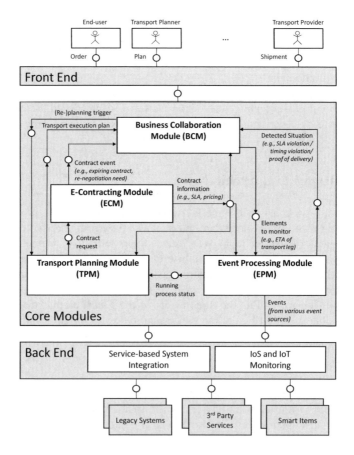

Fig. 1. FInest platform high level conceptual architecture[1]

---

[1] The notation used throughout this document is TAM (Technical Architecture Modeling), see http://www.fmc-modeling.org/fmc-and-tam

2.3   Core Modules Layer

The core layer of the FInest platform is composed of independent transport and logistics service modules integrated through the Business Collaboration Module. The independent service modules are "cloud-based" applications that provide essential domain services for the shipment of goods. The initial set of core modules that are being developed for the FInest platform include the following:

- **Business Collaboration Module (BCM)** – the central module of the FInest platform that supports the inter-organizational collaboration between transport and logistics network partners and acts as an integration service between these partners and the various cloud based components selected to manage the efficient flow of goods between the partners.
- **E-Contracting Module (ECM)** – this module provides computer support for service provider selection, contract negotiation and agreement, contract management and the provision of contract related service requirements to other modules that utilize this information for ensuring the effective and efficient network operation.
- **Event Processing Module (EPM)** – this module provides end-to-end visibility of shipments through event-driven monitoring across domains and transportation modality. The module is also responsible for SLA monitoring (based on data from the ECM) and triggers transport re-planning when needed.
- **Transport Planning Module (TPM)** – this module provides support for dynamic transport planning and re-planning activities, exploiting real time event data provided through the EPM and with respect to contracts between business partners that are managed within the ECM component. Re-planning of shipments occurs when real-time signals from the EPM indicate that a current transport plan cannot be achieved because of some event that has arisen in the shipment process.

2.4   Usage of Future Internet Technologies

The FInest Platform will be developed using Future Internet technologies that provide a foundation for cost-efficient and rapid development of cloud-based end-user applications based on emerging techniques for the Internet of Services, Internet of Things, and Internet of Content. The following list describes the Future Internet technologies of primary importance for implementing the FInest Platform. Most of these are addressed within the FI-WARE project, which develops the Future Internet Core Platform within the FI PPP program (www.fi-ware.eu):

- **Infrastructure, methodology, and tools for cloud-based platform and application development**, including an infrastructure for deploying the FInest Platform and its components on public or private clouds along with methodology and tool support for developing additional end-user services for individual transport and logistics stakeholders;
- **Language and tool support for the Internet of Services**, including a service description language that covers both technical and business requirements along with integrated tool support for the provisioning, management, and

consumption of services; this shall be used for realizing the back-end layer of the FInest platform and for managing the interaction of the FInest core modules;

- **Access to real-world data from the Internet of Things,** enabling the integration and technical handling of real-world data obtained from sensor networks for real-time monitoring and tracking during the execution phase of transport and logistics processes;
- **Facilities for data and event processing in the Internet of Contents**, allowing to process huge amounts of data to retrieve insights into relevant scenarios, as well to analyse real-time event data to quickly determine relevant situations and instantly trigger actions.

- **An integrated framework for security and privacy management for the Future Internet**, including identity management, authentication and authorization facilities, non-repudiation services and policy management for user profiles as the basis for ensuring the security, privacy and confidentiality of information exchanged between business partners, which is a pre-requisite for employing the FInest Platform in real-world business environments.

3   FInest Platform Core Modules

The details for each of the FInest platform core modules, as introduced above, are further elaborated in the following sections. The focus in these descriptions is on the conceptual architecture and the main capabilities of the core modules; the technical realization and actual usage of Future Internet technologies is subject to future work.

3.1   FInest Business Collaboration Module (BCM)

Logistics processes are distributed and involve numerous different stakeholders. Stakeholders may include customers (such as the consignor and the consignee), one or more transport planners, a set of actual transport providers (carriers or shippers), insurance companies and other legal parties, governance authorities (e.g., customs or border control) as well as other partners. Each one of these parties needs information about the goods being shipped in order to successfully conduct a transport process. However, currently employed ICT systems have been developed for intra-organizational management and do not provide easy access for external partners. Coordination between the different stakeholders, therefore, requires manual intervention in order to share information. The large amount of manual intervention required hampers effective supply chain management and increases the likelihood of errors as well as shipping costs.

The FInest Business Collaboration Module (BCM) provides transport and logistics network partners with the ability to securely manage their end-to-end networks by integrating component based services for e-contracting, planning and event monitoring. The BCM is the central module of the FInest platform for interaction with business partners. It holds all necessary information about the logistics processes and provides specialized user interfaces so that necessary information can be presented while confidential information remains undisclosed.

To enable this, the BCM uses so-called Collaboration Objects (CO) which implement a data-centric modelling approach [3, 4]. Each CO encapsulates information about a certain aspect of the overall transport and logistics chain (e.g., a certain transportation leg or an involved carrier) and the process fragment associated with this aspect. Hence, a CO consists of two different elements: a data element and a process or lifecycle element. The combination of different COs describes the end-to-end transportation process and establishes a global view of the entire process. In addition, the distribution of information about the various aspects of the transport process over multiple COs enables privacy management due to the fact that only the information that is contained in the particular process aspect which a stakeholder is authorized to see is actually presented to this very stakeholder.

The general functionality of the BCM can be described as follows and is depicted in the conceptual architecture shown in Figure 2 below:

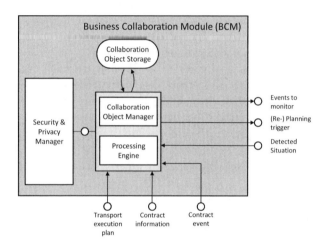

Fig. 2. Business Collaboration Module (BCM) conceptual architecture

- Create a representation of the end-to-end transport and logistics process – To create a representation of the end-to-end process the BCM initializes the COs by integrating data from existing business (legacy) systems, transport plans from the transport planning system and end-user inputs.
- Store the CO-based process representation – The BCM stores the CO-based representation of the end-to-end process in a shared database.
- Provide secure access to process data – Business partners have access to the shared database, but only to those stored COs that their user rights allow. The BCM uses the scattering of information among the COs to ensure security and only discloses the necessary objects to the client.
- Provide value added services – The BCM provides stakeholders with access to other FInest modules enhancing their ability to manage their network. Access

to information about the current status of a logistic process is provided by the EPM, which can be integrated to automatically update the status of the logistic process. Planning and re-planning information for the logistic process can be obtained through the integration of the TPM by the BCM. Information about contract details can be obtained through the integration of the ECM.

3.2 FInest E-Contracting Module (ECM)

Contracting within the transport and logistics domain for complex international move-ment of goods is currently a manual and time consuming process. The process begins with the identification of a need to ship something. Needs identification is followed by partner identification and qualification, partner bid development and bidding, bid evalua-tion and tentative partner selection. Once a tentative partner has been selected a contract is negotiated and agreed between various members of the contracting parties. The con-tract specifies all legal terms and conditions for the carriage of goods and SLA conditions such as: escalation processes for those occasions when problems arise, payment sched-ules and service level requirements. Unfortunately, all of this information is contained in a paper based document that is not generally available to the downstream individuals who are responsible for executing the contract.

The FInest E-Contracting Module (ECM) is being designed to address the highly manual nature of transport and logistics contracting and the problem of downstream transparency to contracted SLA conditions by exploiting solutions from e-contracting [7, 8]. It is important to remark that the legal terms and conditions of a contract are not in the focus of the ECM. The e-contracting module is envisioned as providing support for:

- A dynamic marketplace to support partner selection, bidding and spot market requirements;
- Semi-automated execution of contract negotiation, establishment and man-agement;
- Electronic distribution of contract-specified execution information (e.g., SLAs, pricing, escalation processes, etc.);
- On-line management and review of contracts with automatic notification of contract end dates and renegotiation time fences.

The key architectural elements that are planned for the ECM include:

- Contract Repository – data repository for all established transport and logis-tics contracts, including a set of contract primitives (such as general attrib-utes that characterize transport and logistics contracts);
- User Contract Demand Manager – single interface where actors (human or electronic) interact with the ECM and inform it of the type of contract (e.g., blanket, spot, etc.) to be negotiated;
- Blanket Contract Manager – service responsible for assembling the elec-tronic form of a blanket contract, selection of partners (via auctioning or other processes) and contract creation;

- Spot Market Contract Manager – service responsible for selecting qualified bidding partners for a spot contract, developing and establishing the spot contract;
- Spot Marketplace – space for executing an auction process (offering, bidding, selecting, etc.);
- Special Contract Manager – service responsible for handling user requests associated with SLA violations or requests to handle special issues not covered under blanket contracts;
- Data Extractor – service responsible for generating information about/from contracts for other external modules.

A high level architecture of the ECM is shown in Figure 3 below.

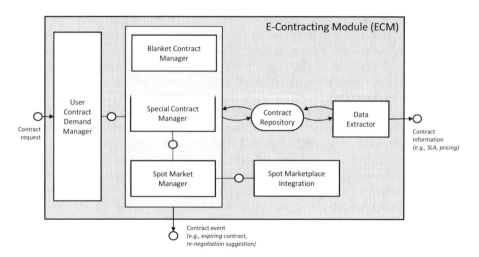

Fig. 3. E-Contracting Module (ECM) conceptual architecture

3.3 FInest Event Processing Module (EPM)

Event-driven architectures support applications that are reactive in nature, ones in which processing is triggered in response to events, contrary to traditional responsive applications, in which processing is triggered in response to an explicit request [5]. In FInest, an event-driven architecture is employed for the purpose of end-to-end monitoring of a logistics process and to facilitate immediate and proactive response to problems and potential deviations occurring during execution time. The functionality can be described at three levels.

- On the surface, event processing provides visibility into the current status of the logistics process: the location of a shipment, whether it is on a carrier or in a warehouse, whether or not it was customs-cleared, etc.
- Beyond the functionality of mere track-and-notify, event-processing employs rules that encapsulate specific logic applied to events. The basic functionality of rules exists in indicating whether or not the logistics process progresses as it should, or whether something has gone wrong.

- At a deeper level, events potentially provide insights regarding parts of the scenario that have not yet been reached; for example, stormy weather near a seaport may indicate that a ship carrying the managed containers will be delayed in entering the port. Security alerts at an airport may imply flight delays. Detecting those events relevant to the scenario at an early stage allows the system to respond to events *before* they occur, and thus to surface *proactive event-driven computing* functionality [6].

The Event Processing Module (EPM) can be characterized according to four elements, which are identified in Figure 4:

- Event Sources – FInest differentiates between two types of event sources. The first type refers to various existing (but usually incompatible) systems. These include airport systems, sea freight systems employed by ports and vessels, scanning and tracking systems of packages, and others. The second type refers to sources that will be provided by the Future Internet infrastructure and will allow more accurate monitoring, as well as predictive capabilities; these include, for instance, RFID tags, smart cameras on roads and other smart items.
- Events – FInest also distinguishes between two types of events: the events emitted by existing sources and events emitted from Internet of Things artefacts. While the latter must be defined and characterized in order to generate requirements from the Future Internet, existing events are described by domain sources such as *Cargo 2000*, which is an airline industry standard.
- Run-time Engine – The run-time engine exploits a set of rules to determine situations. Rules can either be permanent (for any scenario) or instantiated for a specific scenario, e.g., according to SLA parameters provided by the ECM or according to information about the execution of the transport plan (e.g., ETA for individual transport legs).
- Determined Situations – In FInest, the results of event processing can be directed either to the human interface, and / or to one of the other technical components in order to trigger actions. The TPM should get information regarding future events that might trigger re-planning. The ECM and BCM should be notified of potential breaches of SLAs.

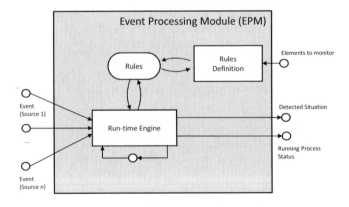

Fig. 4. Event Processing Module (EPM) conceptual architecture

3.4 FInest Transport Planning Module (TPM)

Efficient and effective transport planning and re-planning is all about making sure that relevant information is available at the right time and place to support supply chain operations. Planning consists of resource and information requirements which are tightly linked to resource status, availability, and configurability. Resources can be found both inside a logistics service provider (LSP) and outside an LSP, e.g., in ports or customs agencies. The ability to incorporate or "wrap-in" this information into the planning process is essential. Today this is mainly done through manual inter-organizational collaboration processes [9, 10].

The FInest Transport Planning Module (TPM) will make real-time information about resource status available across actors and organizational boundaries, which constitutes a significant improvement in planning and optimization processes [11, 12]. The TPM considers all elements that are part of an end-to-end supply chain planning process, structured according to the following four stages:

- Stage 1: Marketing of services – Relevant information includes: service category and type (vehicle services, terminal services, sea services, etc.); operation areas (location or district that the service should cover); environmental profile of the service; service capacities such as weight restrictions, dangerous goods limitations, availability; price information.
- Stage 2: Planning of a shipment – Relevant information includes: selection and negotiation of transport services to be included; pre-booking and booking of services; contracting with the service providers and with customs; reservation of space on the transport mean(s); definition of transport items (goods to be transported); split and joint booking activities; stuffing and stripping activities.
- Stage 3: Execution – Relevant information includes: status information and deviation reporting; information reporting to authorities.
- Stage 4: Completion – Relevant information includes: proof of delivery; invoicing; claims and deviation management; contract evaluation.

The TPM is being developed in order to support the planning processes regarding all these information aspects while being supported by the other modules of the FInest platform. For instance, the ECM will provide capabilities for contracting with service providers, as well as selection and negotiation of transport services. The EPM, as a further example, allows monitoring of progress and obtaining status information and deviations from the plan.

The TPM architecture includes several service components as shown in Figure 5 below:

- Service search – This component supports searching for available services by interacting with the ECM. If no contracts are available, additional contracts (e.g., spot market contracts) can be requested.
- Transport chain composition – This component is used to create an end-to-end transport plan in which many services are included.
- Stuffing and stripping – This component assists in planning the stowage of goods, e.g., in a container on a ship.
- Planning handler and data extractor – These components provide statuses and can be used to store information based on the planned transport.

Based on the information processed through the TPM, a Transport Execution Plan is created that provides a complete overview of the planned transport for both the items to be transported and the services to be used that together make up the transport plan [13,14].

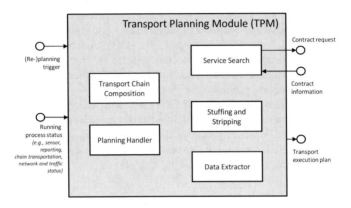

Fig. 5. Transport Planning Module (TPM) conceptual architecture

4 Conclusion

This paper has introduced the FInest platform, a Future Internet based services platform for the transport and logistics domain that addresses many problems that currently exist with ICTs employed in this domain. The FInest platform integrates various value added "cloud-based" components through a Business Collaboration Manager. Cloud-based service components for contracting, visibility and pro-active event management, and planning are integrated to provide transport and logistics domain actors with access to real-time statuses on shipments. The platform facilitates the dynamic re-planning and contracting of services for domain participants providing a clear step forward in capabilities over existing technologies and processes. The FInest services are realized by leveraging Future Internet services based on the Internet of Things, Internet of Services and Internet of Content currently under development through the European Union's Future Internet Public Private Partnership (FI PPP) program. Refinement of the FInest platform will occur as the platform services move beyond the conceptual stage described in this paper and are deployed in live use case pilots.

Acknowledgements. The research leading to these results has received funding from the European Community's Seventh Framework Programme FP7/2007-2013 under grant agreement 285598 (FInest).

References

1. Turner, M., Budgen, D., Brereton, P.: Turning Software into a Service. Computer 36(10) (2003)
2. Mietzner, R., Metzger, A., Leymann, F., Pohl, K.: Variability modeling to support customization and deployment of multi-tenant-aware Software as a Service applications. In: Proceedings of the ICSE 2009 Workshop on Principles of Engineering Service Oriented Systems, PESOS (2009)

3. Meijler, T.D., et al.: Coordinating Variable Collaboration Processes in Logistics. In: 13th International Conference on Modern Information Technology in the Innovation Processes of Industrial Enterprises, Trondheim, Norway (2011)
4. Hull, R., et al.: Introducing the Guard-Stage-Milestone Approach for Specifying Business Entity Lifecycles. In: 7th International Workshop WS-FM 2010, Hoboken, USA (2010)
5. Etzion, O., Niblett, P.: Event Processing in Action. Manning (2010)
6. Engel, Y., Etzion, O.: Towards Proactive Event-Driven Computing. In: 5th ACM International Conference on Distributed Event-Based Systems, DEBS (2011)
7. Papazoglou, M., Pohl, K., Parkin, M., Metzger, A. (eds.): Service Research Challenges and Solutions for the Future Internet: S-Cube – Towards Mechanisms and Methods for Engineering, Managing, and Adapting Service-Based Systems. Springer, Heidelberg (2010)
8. Nitto, E.D., Ghezzi, C., Metzger, A., Papazoglou, P., Pohl, K.: A journey to highly dynamic, self-adaptive service-based applications. Autom. Softw. Eng. 15(3-4) (2008)
9. Stevens, G.C.: Integrating the Supply Chain. International Journal of Physical Distribution & Logistics Management 19(8) (1993)
10. Al-Mashari, M., Al-Mudimigh, A., Zairi, M.: Enterprise resource planning: A taxonomy of critical factors. European Journal of Operational Research 146(2) (2003)
11. Fjørtoft, K., et al.: MIS - Identification and organization of MIS users and processes, Delivery A, MARINTEK (2010)
12. Sleire, H., Wahl, A.M.: Integrated Planning - One road to reach Integrated Operations. In: SPE Bergen Conference (2008)
13. The FREIGHTWISE project, http://www.freightwise.info/cms/
14. The TCMS project,
    http://www.sintef.no/Home/MARINTEK/
    Software-developed-at-MARINTEK/TCMS/

ICT Enablers for Smart Energy
(Invited Paper)

Johannes Riedl[1], Kolja Eger[1], Werner Mohr[2], and Ludwig Karg[3]

[1] Siemens AG, Corporate Technology, Otto-Hahn-Ring 6,
81739 Munich, Germany
{Johannes.Riedl,Kolja.Eger}@siemens.com
[2] Nokia Siemens Networks GmbH & Co. KG, St. Martinstrasse 76,
81541 Munich, Germany
Werner.Mohr@nsn.com
[3] B.A.U.M. Consult GmbH, Gotzinger Str. 48/50,
81371 Munich, Germany
l.karg@baumgroup.de

Abstract. Almost all innovative applications in usage areas like energy, transport & logistics, healthcare rely on specific Information & Communication Technologies (ICT). These often need to fulfill very stringent requirements which cannot easily be fulfilled by today's technologies. Developing usage area specific ICT solutions is not the solution since this prohibits benefiting from an economy of scale. Initiated by the European Commission (EC) the Future Internet Public Private Partnership (FI-PPP) has been setup to systematically identify ICT requirements from different usage areas and address as many of them as possible by so-called generic Future Internet / ICT enablers. Obviously, Smart Energy is a very important usage area which is addressed by the FI-PPP project FINSENY. This article will provide a detailed description of the project setup and its methodology.

Keywords: Future Internet, ICT, Smart Energy, Smart Grid.

1 Introduction

Sustainable energy supply is currently one of the most important and critical topics. It is heavily discussed at technical and political level. Consequently energy from renewable sources like wind and solar are playing a very critical role. Beside sustainability, also reliability and affordability of energy are two dimensions which are in the focus. In fact optimum trade-offs need to be found between sustainability, reliability and costs. One of the challenges is the volatility of many of those energy sources. Another challenge will be unpredictable loads e.g. from electric vehicle loading. It is commonly understood that this requires significant use of Information and Communication Technologies (ICT) which fit to the corresponding requirements.

Innovative applications in many other usage areas, like intelligent transport systems, logistics or smart city applications, will also require ICT functions. And many of these requirements are expected to be quite similar so that they should be

W. Abramowicz et al. (Eds.): ServiceWave 2011, LNCS 6994, pp. 302–308, 2011.
© Springer-Verlag Berlin Heidelberg 2011

provided in a generic way; such functions are called generic ICT enablers. This avoids the development of similar ICT functions in a different way for different usage areas which finally would end up in breaking the economy of scale. In order to avoid fragmentation and a lack of interoperability, the Future Internet Public Private Partnership (FI-PPP) [1; 2] has been recently installed by the EC.

Within the FI-PPP all ICT requirements will be identified for a certain set of usage areas. An understanding will be commonly achieved, which of them need to be addressed in a generic way and which must be taken care of by every usage area itself. Large-scale trials will be prepared for a later phase of the program to be able to demonstrate that finally generic ICT enablers and specific ICT enablers are indeed the enablers of innovative and impact creating applications in the respective usage areas. In this context, the usage area project dealing with Smart Energy is FINSENY, Future INternet for Smart ENergY. This article provides a detailed overview of the work being done in FINSENY. Due to the start of the project on 1st April 2011, no project results can be provided yet, but the approach and methodology will be described in detail.

2   Smart Energy – Key Drivers and Challenges

Increasingly, renewable decentralised energy generation will be used in order to limit climate change and to replace nuclear power generation. Renewable energy generation is depending on changing weather conditions and the energy system has to cope with this volatility. The entire system has to optimally use existing grid infrastructures and adapt to the new requirement. That is not only a question of electrical engineering but also a question of bringing more intelligence to the entire power system. In addition, the liberalisation of the energy market allows for and even calls for new services and new market roles. These developments require a combination of action fields like smart grid and smart home as well as smart grid and electric mobility. A key enabler for the smart energy world is ICT – Information and Communication Technology.

The ICT challenge of Smart Energy is to exchange information across multiple domains, among devices and between subsystems of diverse complexity. In addition to interoperable communications between such elements, future Smart Energy systems will rely on the availability of access to and correct configuration of systems across ownership and management boundaries (such as the boundaries between energy management systems, energy markets, electricity distribution with distributed resources and the boundaries between interactive customers with smart meters, energy management devices, smart appliances and electric vehicles).

3   FINSENY's Approach

The FINSENY project represents a European consortium with partners from the ICT domain, the energy utility and manufacturing domain, SMEs, Associations, R&D centres and universities.

FINSENY will use scenario techniques to identify the prominent ICT challenges. The term 'scenario' refers to an application domain in the evolving Smart Energy landscape, expected to be of significant importance, and requiring advanced ICT technologies. The following five smart energy scenarios will be addressed in the project:

- Distribution network,
- Microgrid,
- Smart buildings,
- Electric mobility, and
- Electronic market place for energy.

To focus work on each individual scenario, FINSENY will assume that energy transport and energy distribution takes place solely as electricity. For every considered scenario four main tasks have been identified:

3.1 Scenario Evaluation

Every scenario will be evaluated in detail by describing the framework conditions, the roles and players as well as the detailed most relevant use cases. Obviously there are quite some activities ongoing in these fields which will be taken into account. This will avoid repeating work and allows for making use of it. The relevance of the use cases will be evaluated according to their potential to induce remarkable ICT requirements. Finally, selected use cases will be described according to common templates.

3.2 ICT Requirements

Based on the use case descriptions the ICT requirements will be identified. These will be described along a certain template which needs to be agreed upon not only within the FINSENY project but within the entire FI-PPP program. In the following there are two different stages of ICT requirements consolidations required: first between all the scenarios within the FINSENY project, and second between all usage area projects within the FI-PPP. Finally, a detailed understanding will be available, which of the ICT requirements will be addressed by generic ICT enablers and which ones require domain-specific ICT enablers that each usage area needs to take care by itself.

3.3 Functional ICT Architecture

Based on the detailed understanding of the respective scenario, the generic ICT enablers being made available by the ICT industry, and the domain-specific ICT enablers taken care of by the energy & ICT industry, a functional ICT architecture will be developed. This will result in an architecture, which describes how the scenario use cases shall be supported and equipped with the available ICT enablers. This will also require coordination between the scenarios, since they are obviously not disjoint. Where scenarios are interfacing to each other or even overlapping, the respective functional ICT architectures need to be consistent.

3.4 Trial Candidates

Following the overall process of the EC's FI-PPP, pan-European trials will be prepared, which – after a further Call for Proposal in the European Framework Programme 7 – are expected to start in April 2013. To prepare for such a suitable trial in the Smart Energy domain, every FINSENY scenario will propose candidates and work out a potential field trial design in more detail. Thus, the FINSENY proposal for a Smart Energy trial will involve existing and promising demonstration projects as well as new approaches at various test sites all over Europe.

Intensive cooperation on all levels will be an important success factor. This is on the one hand side organized through a Smart Grid Stakeholder Group as described below and on the other hand side via interactions with other projects in the field and the FI-PPP. This includes European funded projects (like ADDRESS, BeAware, FENIX, PREMIO, SAVE ENERGY, Web2Energy, etc.), national programs (like E-Energy in Germany, Energy@Home in Italy, SG Model Regions in Austria, etc.), and further industrial initiatives. For this purpose projects and initiatives are being collected, stored and assessed in the FINSENY database.

4 FINSENY's Scenarios

All five smart energy scenarios investigated by FINSENY are large domains. As mentioned before, a detailed evaluation of them is the first step FINSENY is working on. Just to give a rough impression what the scenarios are about this section shortly summarizes the most relevant aspects in terms of ICT requirements and in terms of the progress beyond state-of-the-art which shall be achieved by FINSENY.

4.1 Scenario Distribution Network

Advanced automation, control and management of distribution networks are needed in order to meet the anticipated increase in distributed energy generation and to tackle new challenges such as the charging of electrical vehicles. This involves new methods of load prediction and demand side management as well as interfaces with the existing and new markets.

4.2 Scenario Microgrid

The large scale introduction of distributed generation supports the establishment of local or regional microgrids. Using techniques like virtual power plants or virtual power systems they strive for aggregating and autonomously controlling their own supply and demand side resources to balance production and consumption in as small as possible entities. Interaction with the surrounding distribution network and with the connected production, storage and consumption appliances is the key to the efficient control of such grids.

Table 1. Advancements Beyond State-of-the-Art for the scenarios "Distribution Network" & "Microgrid"

Distribution Network & Microgrid	
State-of-the-Art	*Beyond State-of-the-Art*
Supervision and Control of primary substations and their periphery only	Supervision and control of all active components in the Distribution Network, e.g. to assure power quality even with high percentage of renewable energy
Indirect fault detection and vague fault localization	Extensive use of sensor data and of an ICT-based control infrastructure for fast fault detection, precise fault localization and automatic restoration
Standard profiles to predict consumption and adapt generation	Detailed consumption information and means to adapt consumption to production (demand side management)
Uncontrolled feed in from (volatile) distributed power generators	Controllable inverters including ability to provide system services (e. g. reactive power)
in particular for Microgrid: Island control only for object networks (small-scale) and transmission systems (large-scale)	Independent operation in case of macrogrid connection-loss, assurance of power quality even with high percentage of renewable energy generation

4.3 Scenario Smart Building

Efficient energy management in buildings requires extensive use of communication network infrastructure to and in buildings as well as the provision of the necessary interfaces to local appliances, local distributed generation and energy and service providers.

4.4 Scenario Electric Mobility

The large scale introduction of electrical vehicles will have an impact on the energy infrastructure. Providing the necessary charging points requires interaction between the energy infrastructure, the transport infrastructure, the vehicle information systems and the communication network infrastructure in order to collect, process and deliver the needed information, e.g. for charging and billing.

4.5 Scenario Electronic Market Place for Energy

The introduction of Smart Energy Grids and deregulation results in a transformation of the European energy market. New players are appearing and the roles of incumbent players are changing. An electronic market place for energy must support all these players and roles by providing the necessary interfaces and information exchange. It should also be open to support new applications, players and roles.

Table 2. Advancements Beyond State-of-the-Art for the scenario "Smart Building"

Smart Building	
State-of-the-Art	*Beyond State-of-the-Art*
Legacy buildings and legacy equipment within these buildings cannot easily be equipped with or adapted to advanced ICT technologies for building automation	FINSENY together with the Technology Foundation will provide a shared open platform for building-based ICT services (including building-scale energy management, building automation, building security services), even in legacy buildings. This platform will allow for the integration of legacy equipment in a comprehensive building energy management system.
Separation of Building Management System (BMS) and " ICT infrastructure for "regular" ICT services (telephony, internet).	Integration of BMS and other ICT services on the same platform allows for economies of scale and more efficient energy management. Availability of additional context data for BMS
High Complexity of setting up, configuring and maintaining building energy management systems, experts know-how required	Self-configuration and self-management of integrated and shared ICT infrastructure for building energy management and building automation is the long-term objective that FINSENY will strive to achieve;
Brittle centralized and difficult to scale / analytical energy optimization solutions	Minimal manual programming, scalability and adaptability of building energy optimization engines, using such technologies as multi-agent systems

Table 3. Advancements Beyond State-of-the-Art for the Scenario "Electric Mobility"

Electric Mobility	
State-of-the-Art	*Beyond State-of-the-Art*
Focus on single energy provider and national / small-scale scenarios → proprietary solutions	Full integration of energy management systems for electric mobility and the grid operation
	Pan-European solution, involvement of all mobility and energy providers ("roaming")
Missing common solution for business-process interaction between all different actors of electric mobility	Standardized ICT Support to enable Business-relationship handling between all actors of electric mobility throughout business domains

Table 4. Advancements Beyond State-of-the-Art for the Scenario "Electronic Market Place for Energy"

Electronic Market Place for Energy	
State-of-the-Art	*Beyond State-of-the-Art*
Current energy market dynamics is not accessible for many energy stakeholders.	Access to an extended virtual marketplace for all energy stakeholders.
Missing tools for all energy transactions being available to the energy stakeholders	Advanced ICT Tools for enabling Energy Transactions: real-time, reliable, secure
Today, energy trading happens with low granularity in terms of amount of energy and time	

5   Smart Grid Stakeholder Group

Due to the large scope of Smart Energy, one project partnership alone cannot host all relevant stakeholders. Therefore intensive cooperation is required far beyond the FINSENY consortium. Therefore, the Smart Grid Stakeholder Group (SGSG) has been established in June 2010 to foster the information exchange between ICT and energy industry and thus to better understand each others views.

The organization of the SGSG is a task in FINSENY. At least three workshops are planned to present and discuss project findings and to identify further cooperation opportunities. This group is open for all industrial organizations which are interested in Smart Grid / Smart Energy topics. In case of interest to join that group, please contact the authors of this article.

6   Conclusion

There is common sense that there is a need to act now and to assure that the energy systems become smarter with the help of ICT. FINSENY has been setup to contribute to this goal and to deliver a clear understanding within the coming two years which ICT enablers – generic ones and domain-specific ones – are required and how they fit into the functional ICT architecture of a Smart Energy system. It is expected that this will successfully lead into a Smart Energy trial activity which will show that the identified concepts lead to and maintain sustainable, reliable and cost-efficient energy solutions in a large scale.

Acknowledgement. The authors gratefully acknowledge the contributions of all FINSENY project partners. The FINSENY project is partly funded by the European Commission within the FI-PPP which is part of the Framework Program FP7 ICT.

References

1. Future Internet Public Private Partnership (FI-PPP),
   http://ec.europa.eu/information_society/activities/foi/lead/fippp/index_en.htm
2. Future Internet PPP – The future now, http://www.fi-ppp.eu/

SLA Translations with a Model-Driven Business Impact Analyses Framework

Ulrich Winkler and Wasif Gilani

SAP Research, The Concourse, Queen's Road, Belfast BT3 9DT
{ulrich.winkler,wasif.gilani}@sap.com

Abstract. A Business Continuity Management (BCM) Impact Analysis derives business-level BCM Service Level Agreements (SLAs) which need to be translated at service-level, infrastructure-level and facility-level. However, translation and optimization of SLAs across a large and distributed service-oriented system is not an easy task. In this demo we will present our Stochastic-Petri-Net based approach to automatically translate and optimize BCM SLAs for large service oriented systems. We will do the demo in the context of a business use-case.

Keywords: SLA Translation, Business Continuity Management.

1 Introduction

Business process disruption could lead to financial and legal losses as well as damage to reputation [1]. Business Continuity Management (BCM) aims (1) to identify critical business processes, resources and internal/external dependencies (2) to identify potential threats to services, operations and critical business processes and (3) to evaluate potential damages that may be caused by a threat. Business Continuity Expert (BCEx) refers to this activity as Business Impact Analysis (BIA). In this demo we present our Stochastic-Petri-Net based approach to automatically translate and optimize BCM SLAs for large service oriented systems.

A BIA is done three phases. First, the BCEx has to understand the business, business processes and the impact of business disruptions. He has to take into account financial and non-financial indicators, such as legal requirements or external reputation. Moreover, large and global organizations deploy hundreds of cross-functional business processes in a number of regional variants [2].We explain how our approach helps to conduct a sound and systematic BIA [3]. Second, the expert has to determine various Business Continuity Metrics for every business process and business function. We elaborate how the BCEx uses our methodology to determine the Maximum Tolerable Outage Time (MTO) of business functions and first level services. A first level service is directly consumed by a business function. Third, the BCM dependency and risk graph is used to determine service level requirements. We discuss how our methodology supports the expert to select optimal SLA offers from service providers.

W. Abramowicz et al. (Eds.): ServiceWave 2011, LNCS 6994, pp. 309–310, 2011.

2 Demo Story

The demo video is uploaded in YouTube at the following link: http://www.youtube.com/watch?v=NjPTNcxhSp4

Step 1:
The BCEx uses modelling tools, such as the SAP NetWeaver BPMN modeller [2], to model and compose business process out of enterprise services.

Step 2:
The Business Process Expert (BPX) annotates business process requirements, such as "Business Impact", against business process activities. Business Impacts are the consequences that a business faces if it fails to execute certain process activities within given time frames.

Step 3:
The BCEx uses IT Topology models (provided by IT experts) and facility models (provided by facility managers) to construct an IT BCM Model.

Step 4:
The BCEx adds risks information, recovery times and impact delays.

Step 5:
The resources required to execute business process activities are annotated from the business process resource list.

Step 6:
Once resources are assigned to a business process, the BCEx is able to generate the BEAM model. The BEAM model editor enables the BCEx to refine the behaviour model at a very detailed level if needed.

Step 7:
The BEAM model is used for performing business continuity analysis. The BCEx initiates the process by pushing a button. This launches the Business Impact Analyses, Dependency Analyses, and Risk Analyses.

Step 8:
Once the analysis run is completed, the business continuity analysis results are shown to different stakeholders in their respective modelling environments. For some stakeholders, such as the Line of Business Manger or external BCM auditors, who do not have a specific modelling environment, our solution generates a set of reports.

References

1. Wijnia, Y., Nikolic, I.: Assessing business continuity risks in IT. In: IEEE International Conference on Systems, Man and Cybernetics, pp. 3547–3553 (2007)
2. Silver, B.: SAP NetWeaver BPM White Paper (2009), http://spedr.com/d73s
3. Winkler, U., Fritzsche, M., Gilani, W., Marshall, A.: A Model-Driven Framework for Process-Centric Business Continuity Management. In: QUATIC 2010 Proceedings of the Seventh International Conference on the Quality of Information and Communications Technology (2010)

OFELIA – Pan-European Test Facility for OpenFlow Experimentation

Andreas Köpsel and Hagen Woesner

EICT GmbH, Berlin
Firstname.lastname@eict.de

Abstract. The demonstration will show the live access to the control framework of a pan-European OpenFlow testbed. The testbed spans five islands all over Europe, allowing experimenters access not only to virtual machines but to the switches interconnecting them. This extends the control of networking experiments beyond best-effort overlays to a real control of the network, its routing and forwarding functions itself. A first video explaining the registration process and the setup of a slice for a new network experiment can be found here: http://www.youtube.com/watch?v=p482T9O9HOg.

A tutorial explaining (in short video sequences) the registration and use of the testbed is online on http://www.fp7-ofelia.eu.

Keywords: OpenFlow, FIRE facility, networking experiments, SFA.

1 OpenFlow Test Facility in the FIRE Context

The limitations of the legacy Internet architecture have been studied by the scientific and industrial community now for a decade leading to a wide variety of proposals for architectural extensions. However, introducing such extensions into the "production" Internet has proven to be a tedious task due to the closed nature of today's network elements' designs. OpenFlow introduces a fundamental split between user and control plane decoupling a networking element's forwarding engine from its controlling logic, thus allowing a separate evolution of user and control plane, and offering an opportunity to study new control architectures in the field.

OFELIA is an FP7 Call 5 project aiming towards creation of an OpenFlow test facility allowing researchers from academia as well as industry to develop new control protocols in controlled networking environments on dedicated OpenFlow enabled carrier-ready hardware devices.[1] However, OFELIA's scope is wider and more diversified than just offering yet another testing environment: the OpenFlow architecture with its flow based approach simplifies network virtualization, allowing various control planes to co-exist in parallel and each control plane to handle flows individually; and, it flattens the differences among network elements, e.g. switching and routing devices.[2] The network slice in OFELIA consists of

- Traffic sources and sinks (currently, Xen-based VMs or students' traffic)
- Commercial switches (partially virtualized through OpenFlow and FlowVisor)
- Virtualized links (in project phase II links of dedicated bandwidth will be used)

W. Abramowicz et al. (Eds.): ServiceWave 2011, LNCS 6994, pp. 311–312, 2011.

This network virtualization approach is key to deploying experimental control planes in parallel to production control planes on the same physical network infrastructure. OFELIA consists of autonomous OpenFlow enabled islands each intended to serve as a nucleus for an OpenFlow enabled campus network at their local organization and site. These core networks demonstrate maturity and stability of OpenFlow hardware and software components, potentially paving the way towards OpenFlow deployment in NREN operated networks or in the long-term even operator networks.

2   Description of the Demonstration

The control framework to be demonstrated is based on the SFA-oriented Expedient, a tool that was developed at Stanford University in the eGENI project.[3] OFELIA has enhanced this tool by the capability to dynamically create virtual machines and assign these to experimenter-defined slices, improved the work flow and stabilized the implementation. The OFELIA demo as shown at the Service Wave 2011 event is demonstrating these core features of OpenFlow and OFELIA:

1. Dynamic creation of control place slices suitable for deployment of existing or emerging control plane protocols and architectures for the Future Internet.
2. Co-existence and co-operation of different control planes on the same physical network infrastructure including research and production slices.
3. Dynamic creation of virtual machines for acting as data sinks and/or sources or for hosting control plane entities.
4. Assignment of end systems and users to different network slices each controlled by a different control plane based either on user or network decision.

The demonstration will cover the "OpenFlow domain" and the "Virtual technology manager" (VTM) aggregate managers and show their use how to control the OpenFlow domain as well as how to create, deploy and use virtual machines for functional or performance testing.

References

[1]   OFELIA FP7 project, http://www.fp7-ofelia.eu
[2]   McKeown, N., Anderson, T., Balakrishnan, H., Parulkar, G., Peterson, L., Rexford, J., Shenker, S., Turner, J.: OpenFlow: Enabling Innovation in Campus Networks, White paper, to be found at, http://www.openflow.org/documents/openflow-wp-latest.pdf
[3]   Enterprise GENI (eGENI) project:
      http://groups.geni.net/geni/wiki/EnterpriseGeni

Coverage and Capacity Extensions by Means of Opportunistic Networks in the Future Internet

Panagiotis Demestichas[1], Nikos Koutsouris[1], Dimitris Karvoynas[1],
Andreas Georgakopoulos[1], Vera Stavroulaki[1], Jens Gebert[2], and Markus Mueck[3]

[1] University of Piraeus, Department of Digital Systems, Piraeus, Greece
[2] Alcatel-Lucent, Stuttgart, Germany
[3] Intel Mobile Communications, Munich, Germany
{pdemest,nkouts,dkarvoyn,andgeorg,veras}@unipi.gr,
Jens.Gebert@alcatel-lucent.com,
markus.dominik.mueck@intel.com

Abstract. Our work showcases how opportunistic networks can be used for expanding the coverage and the capacity of infrastructures in a Future Internet context. Opportunistic networks are managed by cognitive systems, which collaborate through control mechanisms. The demonstration of these technologies shows enhanced service provision capabilities, higher resource utilization, lower transmission powers, and "green" network operation.

Keywords: Opportunistic networks, cognitive management, coverage, capacity.

1 Introduction

This document is a summary of a proposed demonstration. The next section includes a short description of the system and demonstrated features. Section 3 is a summary of the novel characteristics.

2 Short System Description – Features Demonstrated

Our *system* includes three main technologies [1]: opportunistic networks, cognitive management systems, and control channels [2] for the cooperation of the cognitive systems. These are applied for achieving efficient coverage and capacity extensions of a network infrastructure in a Future Internet (FI) context, which comprises relevant applications (related to social networking, machine-to-machine and the Internet of Things), networking technologies and device capabilities. The *features* demonstrated through our system include coverage extensions [3,4], for mitigating infrastructure failures or compensating for node mobility, and capacity extensions by means of femtocells [5].

In our work, *opportunistic networks* are operator-governed. They can be dynamically and automatically created, in places and for the time they are needed to deliver multimedia flows to mobile users, in a cost-efficient manner. They can

W. Abramowicz et al. (Eds.): ServiceWave 2011, LNCS 6994, pp. 313–314, 2011.

comprise nodes of the infrastructure, and terminals/devices potentially organized in an ad-hoc network mode. Therefore, opportunistic networks can entail cost-efficiency in terms of operational expenditures (e.g., due to the "dynamic" and "automated" creation), as well as capital expenditures (e.g., as the need for investments in permanent infrastructures is reduced). Operator governance is materialized through the designation of resources (e.g., spectrum, transmission powers, etc.) that can be used, and the provision of policies, information and knowledge.

Cognitive systems are used for the management. Cognition is required for the following main reasons: (i) self-management enables the automated determination of suitability, creation, modification and release of opportunistic networks; (ii) learning improves the speed and reliability of respective management decisions.

Control channels [2] convey information and knowledge on the context encountered, the profiles of users/applications/devices involved, the relevant policies of various stakeholders and decisions.

3   Summary of Novel Characteristics

The following novel characteristics are included: (i) Enhanced capabilities for application/service provision in an FI context; (ii) An ecosystem of distributed cognitive functionality and interfaces.

Efficiency derives from: (i) the higher utilization of resources, and therefore, the resulting savings in the capital expenditures; (ii) the use of lower transmission powers, and therefore, the lower energy consumption in the infrastructure; this means lower operational expenditures; (iii) the "green" footprint of the application delivery model.

Acknowledgments. This work is performed in the project OneFIT which is partially funded by the European Community's 7th Framework programme. This paper reflects only the authors' views. The Community is not liable for any use that may be made of the information contained herein. The contributions of OneFIT colleagues are hereby acknowledged.

References

1. OneFIT (Opportunistic networks and Cognitive Management Systems for Efficient Application Provision in the Future Internet) project, http://www.ict-onefit.eu
2. European Telecommunication Standardization Institute (ETSI), Technical Committee on "Reconfigurable Radio Systems" (RRS),
   http://www.etsi.org/website/technologies/RRS.aspx
3. Opportunistic Coverage Extension for Infrastructure Failure Mitigation,
   http://www.youtube.com/watch?v=R831ByciSzc
4. Opportunistic Coverage Extension for Mitigation of Outages due to Node Mobility,
   http://www.youtube.com/watch?v=wNQpPF4_TrU
5. Opportunistic Capacity Extension through Femtocells,
   http://www.youtube.com/watch?v=Bq9cJP8HFGQ

REMICS- REuse and Migration of Legacy Applications to Interoperable Cloud Services

REMICS Consortium

Andrey Sadovykh[1], Christian Hein[2], Brice Morin[3],
Parastoo Mohagheghi[3], and Arne J. Berre[3]

[1] SOFTEAM, France
[2] Fraunhofer FOKUS, Germany
[3] SINTEF, Norway
{Parastoo.Mohagheghi,Arne.J.Berre}@sintef.no

Abstract. The main objective of the REMICS project is to specify, develop and evaluate a tool-supported model-driven methodology for migrating legacy applications to interoperable service cloud platforms. The migration process consists of understanding the legacy system in terms of its architecture and functions, designing a new SOA application that provides the same or better functionality, and verifying and implementing the new application in the cloud. The demonstrations will cover the following REMICS research topics: model-based analysis and testing and model-driven interoperability with the tools by Fraunhofer FOKUS and SINTEF. Video is published at http://goo.gl/ExV38.

Keywords: Cloud computing, service-oriented architecture, legacy systems, ADM, model-based analysis, model-based testing, model-driven interoperablity.

1 REMICS Approach and Demonstrations[1]

The REMICS[2] project will provide tools for model-driven migration of legacy systems to loosely coupled systems following a bottom up approach; from recovery of legacy system architecture (using OMG's ADM-Architecture Driven Modernization) to deployment in a cloud infrastructure which allows further evolution of the system in a forward engineering process. The migration process consists of understanding the legacy system in terms of its architecture, business processes and functions, designing a new Service-Oriented Architecture (SOA) application, and verifying and implementing the new application in the cloud. These methods will be complimented with generic "Design by Service Composition" methods providing developers with tools simplifying development by reusing the services and components available in the cloud.

---

[1] Video is published at YouTube http://goo.gl/ExV38
[2] http://remics.eu/; funded by the European Commission (contract number 257793) within the 7th Framework Program.

W. Abramowicz et al. (Eds.): ServiceWave 2011, LNCS 6994, pp. 315–316, 2011.

In order to instrument the migration process, the REMICS project will integrate a large set of metamodels and will propose several dedicated extensions. For the architecture recovery the REMICS will extend the KDM metamodel. On Platform Independent Model (PIM) level, the components and services are defined using SoaML (SOA Modeling Language[3]) which is developed in the SHAPE project[4]. The REMICS project will extend this language to address the specific architectural patterns and model driven methods for architecture migration, and to cover specificities of service clouds development paradigm. In particular, the PIM4Cloud Computing, model-driven Service Interoperability and Models@Runtime extensions are intended to support the REMICS methodology for service cloud architecture modeling. Furthermore, REMICS will investigate existing test notations such as the UML2 test profile (UTP) for their application to the SOA and Cloud Computing domain and refine and extend them.

The demonstrations focus on two aspects covered in the project: (1) the model-based analysis and testing and (2) model-driven interoperability.

The first demonstration shows two toolkits which are being developed within the REMICS. The toolkit consists of a model analysis workbench and a model-based testing workbench. The analysis workbench focuses on static aspects of all kind of engineering models. The workbench can be used to define and compute metrics for static analysis of the REMICS models. The measurement can be used to determine a certain degree of quality of the recovered and migrated models. In contrast to analysis workbench the model-based testing part is focusing on dynamic aspects of the models, for instance the generation of test specification and test data out of the behavioral description of the models is a typical activity with respect to model-based testing. These generated tests can be used by a test execution engine to validate specific behavioral properties of a system under test.

When the legacy system has been migrated to the cloud, it can leverage other services already deployed in the cloud to:

- Extend some of its services to provide some added value to migrated services
- Replace some of its services to use some similar services which provide better QoS, are cheaper to use, etc.

This leads to interoperability issues:

- How to exchange data between the migrated services and the "external" services available in the clouds?
- How to synchronize protocols (exchange of messages)?

In this second demo, we will focus on the first issue while the second issue is covered in the future research. Many tools (Semaphore, MapForce) already exist to define mappings between data-structures, and generate code out of these mappings to actually realize the mapping of data. However, some mappings are trivial, and explicitly specifying then is a waste of time. But some mappings are much more difficult to identify. Designers should thus be guided during this task. The tool to be presented in the demo provides guidance for designers to identify semantic mappings.

---

[3] http://www.omg.org/spec/SoaML/
[4] http://www.shape-project.eu/

Towards Governance of Rule and Policy Driven Components in Distributed Systems

Pierre de Leusse and Krzysztof Zieliński

AGH University of Science and Technology, Faculty of Electrical Engineering, Automatics,
Computer Science and Electronics, Department of Computer Science,
Distributed System Research Group, Al. Mickiewicza 30, 30-059 Krakow, Poland
{pdl,kz}@agh.edu.pl
http://www.ki.agh.edu.pl/

Abstract. The rule and policy technological landscape is becoming ever more complex, with an extended number of specifications and products. It is therefore becoming increasingly difficult to integrate rule and policy driven components and manage interoperability in distributed environments. The described work presents an infrastructure going towards the governance of heterogeneous rule and policy driven components in distributed systems. The authors' approach leverages on a set of middleware, discovery protocol, knowledge interchange and consolidation to alleviate the environment's complexity.

Keywords: Rule and policy driven component, Distributed systems, Governance, Knowledge interchange, RIF.

1 Introduction

Over the years, rule and policy driven systems are becoming increasingly popular. This evolution can mostly be attributed to three factors, 1) better separation of concerns between the knowledge and its implementation logic in contrast to a hard-coded approach; 2) repositories that increase the visibility and readability of the knowledge represented in rule and policies artifacts and 3) graphical user interfaces that render these artifacts more usable while bridging the gap between users (e.g. domain experts) and IT specialists.

Influenced by this increased interest, the technological landscape is becoming more and more complex. This is partly due to the number of technologies that have been developed and the frequency in which they appear. In particular, the amount of platforms implemented as well as the various specifications related to rule and policy expression and enactment have rendered this domain more opaque.

This abundance of technologies and products can be beneficial as different approaches attempt to address a variety of problems. However, it greatly impacts the usability of distributed systems that are built upon components using these technologies to specify their behaviors. Indeed, the behavioral and functional complexities reduced by rules and policies at the component level translate into management and interoperability issues at the distributed application plane. The main

W. Abramowicz et al. (Eds.): ServiceWave 2011, LNCS 6994, pp. 317–318, 2011.

contribution of this paper and the demonstration system it presents is a set of functionalities aimed at facilitating the governance of rule and policy driven components involved in distributed systems. This demonstration addresses challenges in the domains of rule and policy driven components discovery, interoperability, rule and policy interchangeability and knowledge consolidation in the context of distributed systems.

2   Anatomy of a Governance Infrastructure for Rule and Policy Driven Components in Distributed Systems

In order to simplify the demonstration, in this experiment the authors assume that no semantic translation is needed – i.e. an "Order" for one component has the same meaning, but not necessarily the same data structure, as in the other components.

Component discovery: to permit the discovery and storage of the different artifacts (e.g. rule engines, translators) the authors make use of a central repository. In this experiment, the repository is implemented using the Atom Publication Protocol (APP) and eXist DB. The authors have implemented a dedicated OSGi Service Tracker and a Service Location Protocol agent that automatically register the components with the global or a local APP repository. The repositories are interconnected allowing the discovery to span across multiple component containers, servers and domains.

Component interoperability: the extendable middleware model designed by the authors allows exposing components' adaptation engine (i.e. rule engine or policy decision and enforcement points) in a flexible manner. Thus, by default, two sets of functionalities are expected for each component, enabling control and evaluation of the rules and policies. The *'Management'* oriented functionalities allow administration type operations while the *'Functional'* ones allow operations on rules or policies and facts. It is noticeable that additional types of functionalities can be provided such as access control and reliability (e.g. heartbeat) depending on the component.

Rule and policy interchangeability: for the purpose of this experiment, the authors have chosen to investigate rule interchange between Drools and Jess using the Rule Interchange Format (RIF) production language as platform neutral language. Drools and Jess were chosen for their popularity and similarities.

Knowledge consolidation: the authors have designed algorithms to correlate facts and combine rules and policies. In addition, a basic conflict detection system has been implemented for mathematical operator contradiction. Please note that at this stage, the validation is performed only after translation at the interchange stage, against the rule engine or policy decision point. The authors are aware of the need to validate the knowledge during the consolidation stage and this aspect is currently being investigated.

Short video of the demonstration: http://www.youtube.com/watch?v=i2PTbrTpNpY

Acknowledgements. This work is part of the IT SOA project founded European Regional Development Fund program no. POIG.01.03.01-00-008/08 and UDA-POKL.04.01.01-00-367/08-00.

SLA-enabled Enterprise IT

Michael Nolan[1], Andy Edmonds[1], John Kennedy[1], Joe Butler[1], Jessica McCarthy[1],
Miha Stopar[2], Primoz Hadalin[2], and Damjan Murn[2]

[1] Intel Labs Europe, Collinstown Industrial Park, Leixlip, Co. Kildare, Ireland
{Michael.Nolan,AndrewX.Edmonds,John.M.Kennedy,Joe.M.Butler,
Jessica.C.McCarthy}@intel.com
[2] XLAB d.o.o., Pot za Brdom 100, 1000 Ljubljana, Slovenia
{miha.stopar,primoz.hadalin,damjan.murn}@xlab.si

Abstract. The SLA@SOI project has researched and engineered technologies
to embed SLA-aware infrastructures into the service economy. It has published
models, defined architectures, developed an open-source framework and driven
open standards such as the Open Cloud Computing Interface. In this demo the
application of SLA@SOI in an enterprise IT use case will be demonstrated. The
presentation will cover the SLA-aware negotiation, scheduling, provisioning,
and monitoring of virtual machines.

Keywords: SLAs, Cloud-computing, IaaS, Infrastructure, Enterprise IT.

1 Introduction

Fundamental limitations exist with today's service-based offerings, including those
hosted by cloud infrastructure. Typically the customer has to accept boiler-plate high
level Service Level Agreements (SLAs), and violations are difficult if not impossible
to detect and disposition. It is infeasible for service providers to create customized
service offerings or negotiate with customers individually, and translating from
business requirements into specific internal provisioning manifestations consumes
valuable time and resources. Internally, the economies of optimizing deployment
landscapes whilst maintaining customized SLAs is largely unachievable. The
opportunity exists for a comprehensive, holistic, SLA-management framework.

SLA@SOI has researched and engineered technologies to embed SLA-aware
infrastructures into the service economy. A consortium of 11 key players, this
European Commission funded project has created a comprehensive, extensible model
in which arbitrary SLAs can be described, defined a flexible component-based SLA-
enabling architecture, and has integrated and is validating the results in four industry-
led use cases. It has also championed the development of open standards, co-chairing
the recently published Open Cloud Computing Interface (OCCI). In this demo the
application of SLA@SOI in an enterprise IT use case will be demonstrated. The
presentation will cover the SLA-aware negotiating, scheduling, provisioning, and
monitoring of virtual machines.

The **Enterprise IT** use case focuses on SLA-aware provisioning of compute
platforms, pursuing the most efficient resource selection at provisioning time based

W. Abramowicz et al. (Eds.): ServiceWave 2011, LNCS 6994, pp. 319–320, 2011.

on infrastructure policies, the optimal infrastructure landscape at run time, and informing future investment decisions. The ultimate goal is to illustrate how provisioned IT infrastructure can dynamically reflect and react to the changing priorities of the enterprise.

This demo will introduce core concepts of SLA@SOI, including:

- A high level scenario in which machine readable SLAs can operate
- The architecture of the open-source framework that has been developed
- The flexible and extensible SLA model that has been published

A live deployment of the Enterprise IT use case will be available to illustrate the concepts in a relatively realistic deployment. Visitors will be able to browse a reference SLA template, personalize an SLA, provision the service in real time and observe live monitoring data. When VM's are manipulated through an administrators interface, the implications for the SLA terms being monitored and the detection of SLA violations are observable.

Two videos of the SLA@SOI Enterprise IT use case are available on YouTube and illustrate the scope of the proposed demo.

For the video illustrating the provisioning of an SLA-Aware service please see: http://www.youtube.com/watch?v=tD7WyOWYoTc

For the video illustrating the automatic detection of an SLA violation please see: http://www.youtube.com/watch?v=jF5UFwsWzN4

For complete information on SLA@SOI including links to the various open source projects spawned or contributed too, please visit http://www.sla-at-soi.eu.

SeCMER: A Tool to Gain Control
of Security Requirements Evolution*

Gábor Bergmann[1], Fabio Massacci[2], Federica Paci[2],
Thein Tun[3], Dániel Varró[1], and Yijun Yu[3]

[1] DMIS - Budapest University of Technology and Economics
{bergmann,varro}@mit.bme.hu
[2] DISI - University of Trento
{fabio.massacci,federica.paci}@unitn.it
[3] DC - The Open University
{t.t.tun,y.yu}@open.ac.uk

Abstract. This paper presents SeCMER, a tool for requirements evolution management developed in the context of the SecureChange project. The tool supports automatic detection of requirement changes and violation of security properties using change-driven transformations. The tool also supports argumentation analysis to check security properties are preserved by evolution and to identify new security properties that should be taken into account.

Keywords: security requirements engineering, secure i*, security argumentation, change impact analysis, security patterns.

1 Introduction

Requirements change continuously making the traceability of requirements hard and the monitoring of requirements unreliable. Moreover, changing requirements might have an impact on the satisfaction of security properties a system design should satisfy.

In this paper we present SeCMER[1], a tool for requirement evolution management which provides three main features: a) *Modelling requirement evolution*: The drawing of requirement models in different state of the art requirement languages such as SI* [5], Problem Frames (PF) [7] and SeCMER[2] is supported; b) *Argumentation-based security analysis* [7]: it allows the requirement engineer to check that security properties are preserved by evolution and to identify new security properties; c) *Change management based on evolution rules* [3]: it allows to detect changes into the requirement model, to check argument validity, to automatically detect violations or fulfilment of security properties, and to issue alerts prompting human intervention.

---

* Work parly supported by the project EU-FP7-ICT-FET-IP-SecureChange.
[1] A detailed description of the tool implementation is reported in [4], and a demonstrating screencast is presented at http://www.youtube.com/watch?v=OWwzcNeSuJM
[2] SeCMER is a requirement language that includes concepts belonging to SI*, PF and security such as asset.

W. Abramowicz et al. (Eds.): ServiceWave 2011, LNCS 6994, pp. 321–322, 2011.

These capabilities of the tool are provided by means of the integration of Si* [5] as a graphical modeling framework for security requirements, OpenPF [6] which supports argumentation analysis, and EMF-INCQUERY [2] which supports change detection.

2 Demo Scenario

We illustrate the features supported by our prototype using as example the ongoing evolution of ATM systems planned by the ATM 2000+ Strategic Agenda [1] and the SESAR Initiative. We focus on the introduction of the Arrival Manager (AMAN), which is an aircraft arrival sequencing tool to support air traffic controllers, and an IP based data transport network called System Wide Information Management (SWIM) that should replace actual point-to-point networks.

1. **Requirements evolution.** We show how the tool allows to model the evolution of the requirement model as effect of the introduction of the SWIM.
2. **Change detection based on evolution rules.**
   a *Detection of a security property violation based on security patterns.* We show how the tool detects that the integrity security property of the resource "Meteo Data" is violated due to the lack of a trusted path.
   b *Automatically providing corrective actions based on evolution rules.* We show how evolution rules may suggest corrective actions for the detected violation of the integrity security property.
3. **Argumentation-based security analysis.** We show how argumentation analysis is used to provide evidence that the information access property applied to the meteo data is preserved by evolution.

References

1. EUROCONTROL ATM Strategy for the Years 2000+ Executive Summary (2003)
2. Bergmann, G., Horváth, Á., Ráth, I., Varró, D., Balogh, A., Balogh, Z., Ökrös, A.: Incremental evaluation of model queries over EMF models. In: Petriu, D.C., Rouquette, N., Haugen, Ø. (eds.) MODELS 2010. LNCS, vol. 6394, pp. 76–90. Springer, Heidelberg (2010)
3. Bergmann, G., et al.: Change-Driven Model Transformations. Change (in) the Rule to Rule the Change. Software and System Modeling (to appear, 2011)
4. Bergmann, et al.: D3.4 Proof of Concept Case Tool,
   http://www.securechange.eu/sites/default/files/deliverables/
   D3.4%20Proof-of-Concept%20CASE%20Tool%20for%20early%20requirements.pdf
5. Massacci, F., Mylopoulos, J., Zannone, N.: Computer-aided support for secure tropos. Automated Software Engg. 14, 341–364 (2007)
6. Tun, T.T., Yu, Y., Laney, R., Nuseibeh, B.: Early identification of problem interactions: A tool-supported approach. In: Glinz, M., Heymans, P. (eds.) REFSQ 2009 Amsterdam. LNCS, vol. 5512, pp. 74–88. Springer, Heidelberg (2009)
7. Tun, T.T., et al.: Model-based argument analysis for evolving security requirements. In: Proceedings of the 2010 Fourth International Conference on Secure Software Integration and Reliability Improvement (2010)

FIRE OpenLab IP Testbed and Tool Demo

Timur Friedman[1] and Anastasius Gavras[2]

[1] UPMC Sorbonne Universités and CNRS
[2] Eurescom GmbH

Abstract. The demonstration provides an insight into a sub-set of available testbeds and management tools available in the OpenLab project. These are available for experimentation by researchers that are seeking experimental environments for trying out their innovative Future Internet related algorithms, protocols, services or applications.

Keywords: Future Internet Research and Experimentation, OpenLab.

Description

We demonstrate testbeds and tools that are available in the OpenLab [1] project that is part of the European Future Internet Research and Experimentation (FIRE) initiative. These testbeds and tools are subject to further development by the OpenLab integrating project according to requirements expressed by its users. The starting date of the project is September 2011.

The demonstration focuses on the emulation capabilities of PlanetLab Europe (PLE) [2], an overlay and distributed systems testbed of the OneLab experimental facility [3]. PLE is the most used testbed for Future Internet experimentation in Europe today, and counts over 140 universities and industrial research labs as members that contribute and maintain computing resources for the testbed. OneLab's PLE public statistics page indicates that there are over 190 active experiments being run at any given time by some of the testbed's more than 1500 registered users. Among other use cases [4], the experiments range from examination of innovative overlay routing systems to tests of new geolocation algorithms. The demonstration will show PLE's novel emulation feature and will show how to access PLE.

In addition to PLE, further testbeds and tools that are available in the OpenLab project are demonstrated, such as the Teagle control framework that is used for brokering heterogeneous testbed resources and for constructing custom testbed configurations [12].

Functions and Features Demonstrated

The demonstration presents to potential users the opportunity for conducting experiments in a hybrid real-world and emulated environment. It provides a rationale for doing so, and describes use cases. It guides users through the simple steps required for deploying an experiment on PlanetLab Europe.

W. Abramowicz et al. (Eds.): ServiceWave 2011, LNCS 6994, pp. 323–324, 2011.

Furthermore the demonstration includes a sample session of constructing a custom testbed by interoggating the Teagle resource repository and drawing the so called Virtual Customer Testbed (VCT) in a drag-and-drop manner.

Several videos available online explain the context and relevance (i.e. "WHY") [8] of the PLE emulation capabilities as well guide the users through the use of the PLE capabilities (i.e. "WHAT" and "HOW") [9].

Further videos illustrated how the Teagle control framework is used to construct custom testbeds [7].

Example Novel Characteristics

As Professor Luigi Rizzo, a member of the OpenLab team, describes in his recent Google Tech Talk, *New Developments in Link Emulation and packet Scheduling in FreeBSD, Linux, and Windows* (available on YouTube) [5], emulation is a standard tool in protocol and application testing. It provides the researcher:

- ease of configuration and setup,
- reproducibility, and
- more realistic results than simulation.

PLE exposes experiments to the real world environment of todays Internet, however by integrating Rizzo's dummynet [6] emulator the experimenter can incorporate emulated links with characteristics (delay, bandwidth, loss rate) of future technologies, such as new wireless protocols that are not available yet in deployed network equipment.

References

1. http://www.ict-openlab.eu/
2. http://www.planet-lab.eu/
3. http://www.onelab.eu
4. http://onelab.eu/index.php/services/testbed-access/use-cases.html
5. http://www.youtube.com/watch?v=r8vBmybeKlE
6. http://info.iet.unipi.it/~luigi/dummynet/
7. http://www.fire-teagle.org/tutorials.jsp
8. http://www.dailymotion.com/video/xf6oet_onelab-emulation_tech
9. http://www.dailymotion.com/video/xd3249_using-emulation_tech
10. Carbone, M., Rizzo, L.: An emulation tool for PlanetLab. Elsevier, Amsterdam (2011), http://dx.doi.org/10.1016/j.comcom.2011.06.004
11. Fdida, S., Friedman, T., Parmentelat, T.: OneLab: An open federated facility for experimentally driven future internet research. In: Tronco, T. (ed.) New Network Architectures. SCI, vol. 297, pp. 141–152. Springer, Heidelberg (2010), http://dx.doi.org/10.1007/978-3-642-13247-6_7
12. Wahle, S., et al.: Emerging testing trends and the Panlab enabling infrastructure. IEEE Communications Magazine 49(3), 167–175 (2011), http://dx.doi.org/10.1109/MCOM.2011.5723816

Distributed Spectrum Sensing in a Cognitive Networking Testbed

Stefan Bouckaert[1], Peter Van Wesemael[2], Jono Vanhie-Van Gerwen[1],
Bart Jooris[1], Lieven Hollevoet[2], Sofie Pollin[2],
Ingrid Moerman[1], and Piet Demeester[1]

[1] Ghent University - IBBT,
Gaston Crommenlaan 8 bus 201 - 9050 Ghent - Belgium
[2] Imec, Kapeldreef 75 - 3001 Leuven - Belgium

Abstract. In this demonstration, we show how the IBBT w-iLab.t wireless testbed, combined with multiple spectrum sensing engines designed by imec, can be used for experimentally-supported design and evaluation of cognitive networking protocols. Functionalities include the advanced characterization of the behavior of a cognitive solution under test, and characterization of the wireless experimentation environment itself.

Keywords: experimentation, testbed, wireless, cognitive radio, cognitive networking, spectrum sensing.

1 Introduction

The field of experimentally supported research in wireless networks receives increasing attention from the international research community. Multiple well-established wireless networks such as TWIST, w-iLab.t, Motelab, or Orbit have now been in use for multiple years, and many of these testbeds are now also putting effort in federating their facilities. One of these federations, the CREW (Cognitive Radio Experimentation World) federation (www.crew-project.eu), is bringing together the hardware, software, and expertise from multiple European wireless testbeds, with the aim of facilitating experimental research in the field of cognitive radio, cognitive networking and advanced spectrum sensing.

2 System Description and Novel Characteristics

The presented demonstration is an evolution of our contribution at the Service-Wave 2010 conference, entitled "Spectrum Sharing in Heterogeneous Wireless Networks: An FP7 CREW Use Case". In last year's demonstration, we showcased both a cognitive networking experiment that was remotely deployed on the IBBT w-iLab.t (a heterogeneous ISM testbed with 200 Wi-Fi and Zigbee based wireless nodes deployed over three floors of an office environment), and the real-time use of the imec sensing engine in the exhibition area. Since then, the imec sensing engine has considerably progressed: while processing of the received wireless signal used to be done in Matlab, it is now running in real-time on a newly

W. Abramowicz et al. (Eds.): ServiceWave 2011, LNCS 6994, pp. 325–326, 2011.

developed ASIP, called the DIFFS (Digital Interface for Sensing). The DIFFS enables flexible processing through a wide variety of sensing algorithms, including cyclostationary detection for DVB-T, resource allocation detection for LTE, and energy detection. As a result, we will now be able to showcase a portable version of the sensing solution, equipped with a USB interface.

Furthermore, we have now integrated this new version of the spectrum sensing engine in the w-iLab.t testbed: currently, the sensing engine is configured to scan the entire 2.4GHz ISM band, and continuously puts power spectral density (PSD) values in a database. This information is then visualized in real-time on the w-iLab.t GUI and may also be used during or after the experiment by the experimenter. Soon (during the demo), ten configurable spectrum sensing engines will be installed permanently throughout the w-iLab.t testbed.

In addition to showcasing the new sensing hardware and the integration, we demonstrate the use of these multiple distributed sensing engines inside the w-iLab.t environment, in an example cognitive networking use case where a Zigbee-based wireless sensor network reconfigures its transmission parameters in order to better coexist with a co-located Wi-Fi network.

The availability of distributed sensing components in a wireless testbed, brings many new possibilities, including (i) defining metrics based on the acquired PSD values when evaluating wireless (cognitive) protocols; (ii) capturing the state of the wireless environment in the testbed, before, after and during an experiment, thus increasing the meaningfulness and comparability of experimental results; (iii) developing novel cognitive networking protocols, which are using the detailed distributed spectral measurements to optimize their transmission parameters. We will showcase the above use case by setting up a repeatable, emulated home environment: first, a set of devices in the w-iLab.t testbed is configured as access points and clients; second, the reliability of a simple, non-optimized, sensor network solution is characterized in terms of packet loss and spectral efficiency. Third, the experiment will be repeated, but now with the sensor network performing cognitive channel selection. Again, the reliability and spectral efficiency of the solution will be evaluated.

To summarize, this demonstration complements and extends last year's demonstration, by presenting the completed integration of our cognitive networking testbed and our updated, more compact and faster spectrum sensing engine. Moreover, we demonstrate how this combination enables us to emulate a repeatable house environment and how our example coexistence experiment can be monitored and evaluated in real-time.

A short demonstration video can be found at:
http://users.atlantis.ugent.be/sbouckae/hidden/crew.

Acknowledgement. The research leading to these results has received funding from the European Union's Seventh Framework Programme (FP7/2007-2013) under grant agreement n 258301 (CREW project).

DTN Simulation Tool for N4C Integration Support

Witold Hołubowicz[1], Łukasz Kiedrowski[2], and Krzysztof Romanowski[2]

[1] Adam Mickiewicz University, Poznań, Poland
[2] ITTI, Poznań, Poland

Abstract. The demonstration presents a simulation tool developed in the N4C project. The project involved development, integration, and deployment of delay-tolerant networks (DTN) and applications in remote areas. The simulation tool supports system integration and testing by connecting real and virtual hardware and software network nodes via DTNs simulated with the aid of the *ns-3* network simulator. The examples shown illustrate node discovery and message transport – direct as well as using a data mule service.

Keywords: delay-tolerant networks, network simulation, N4C.

1 Motivation

The *Networking for Communications Challenged Communities* (N4C [1]) project, carried out in the years 2008-2011, addressed the needs of communities in remote areas where providing permanent Internet connections was infeasible and the only communications facilities were opportunistic networks, devised to be delay- and disruption-tolerant (DTN [2]). The project aimed at developing Internet-like services for such networks and testing them in actual communications challenged regions (CCRs), with the testbeds themselves also offered as a sustainable service for research and development activities beyond the project.

Considering the resources (time, manpower, cost) necessary to perform tests in CCRs (some of them reachable only by helicopters or several days' hiking), the possibility of testing the services to be deployed in a simulated environment is important both for system integration and for deployment planning. A number of network simulators have been developed in the context of DTN, including the DTNSim [3], DTNSim2 [4], and ONE [5], some (the former two) no longer maintained, some (the latter) actively developed. They focus on DTN protocol research and some of them require sizeable computing resources. The needs of system integration in the N4C project called for a simple tool tailored to simulating the physical layer of the DTNs – with the protocols implemented entirely by the actual tested software – and to observation of the real hardware and software nodes being integrated.

W. Abramowicz et al. (Eds.): ServiceWave 2011, LNCS 6994, pp. 327–328, 2011.

2 Description of the System

The simulation tool uses the *ns-3* network simulator [6]. The communications channel is modelled in *ns-3* as WiFi-type, including topology and mobility patterns, data transfer ranges, rates, and error characteristics. The tool adds connections to network nodes, which are all external to *ns-3*, and may be virtual machines (*VitrualBox* [7]), Linux containers (*lxc* [8]), or real hardware – the latter connected to the simulator host locally or remotely over a VPN. The software on the nodes is actual DTN networking stacks and service applications being integrated or tested. The tool adds facilities for networking setup and replication, system configuration and automation.

3 Demonstration

The video demonstration first illustrates sending files in a simple simulated DTN including one real (Nokia N900) and three virtual (LXC) nodes, with their mobility controlled manually. The demonstration shows node discovery, message transport – both direct and via a data mule service (where a node transports data bundles destined for some other node) – as well as integrating real hardware in the simulated network and interacting with the running simulation. Then a simulation of a complex network setup of 50-90 LXC nodes, 2 VirtualBox nodes, and one remote VPN node is presented. The nodes are arranged in a number of stationary remote groups and a pool of mobile nodes providing data mule services. The demonstration shows node discovery and data transfer in a scenario with predefined data mule mobility patterns: one of a scheduled bus round trip and the other of random movement. The demonstration video file can be found as http://torn.itti.com.pl/n4c/video/sw2011.avi or – with the keywords "dtn n4c sw2011" – at http://www.youtube.com.

Acknowledgements. This work was co-funded by the European Community Seventh Framework Programme as part of project N4C (Networking for Communications Challenged Communities: Architecture, Test Beds and Innovative Alliances), under grant no. 223994.

References

1. N4C project home page, http://www.n4c.eu
2. Farrel, S., Cahill, V.: Delay- and Disruption-Tolerant Networking. Artech House, Boston (2006)
3. Jain, S., Fall, K., Patra, R.: Routing in a delay tolerant network. In: Proc. SIGCOMM 2004, pp. 145–158. ACM, New York (2004)
4. DTNSim2 project home page, http://watwire.uwaterloo.ca/DTN/sim
5. Keränen, A., Ott, J., Kärkkäinen, T.: The ONE Simulator for DTN Protocol Evaluation. In: Proc. SIMUTools 2009, pp. 55:1–55:10. ICST, Brussels (2009)
6. NS-3 project home page, http://www.nsnam.org
7. VirtualBox home page, http://www.virtualbox.org
8. LXC project home page, http://lxc.sourceforge.net

Testing and Profiling Internet Services in Mobile Devices

Almudena Díaz Zayas and Pedro Merino Gómez

Dpto. Lenguajes y Ciencias de la Computación,
University of Malaga,
Campus Teatinos, Malaga, Spain
{pedro,almudiaz}@lcc.uma.es
http://www.lcc.uma.es/~pedro/mobile

Abstract. UMA proposes a novel testing facility based on normal mobile devices as testing nodes, exposing their functionalities through a
new technology agnostic control node (*UMA controller*). This solution
will provide a scheme to deploy experiments not only on top of current
mobile technologies (e.g. UMTS, HSPA...) but also over the upcoming
LTE or LTE-Advanced standards as they are introduced in the market.

Keywords: testing, facility, connectivity, performance, mobile services.

1 Introduction

Recently, the interest in packet data mobile services has grown driven by key applications such as VoIP or video streaming, as opposed to circuit switched legacy
voice services. This trend is also in line with the evolution of 3GPP mobile technologies, as there has been a clear move towards All-IP mobile networks. Also
mobile data services have been shown to provide high added value to citizens,
complementing traditional services provided by fixed networks. In this context
it is key to ensure than the new improvements in the architecture of cellular networks provide appropriate capabilities for supporting advanced mobile Internet
services assuring optimum levels of user experience.

UMA (University of Malaga) is developing a testing facility for supporting the
complete development process of Internet services and applications for mobile
devices.The facility is based on the instrumentation of commercial mobile devices
and their use as measurement tools. Currently the facility enables the execution
of manual measurement campaigns during the execution of data services on
the instrumented mobiles, however the purpose is to provide a remote access
to schedule and perform unattended measurement campaigns. The facility is
envisioned to targets data connectivity and performance over cellular networks
(GSM, GPRS, UMTS, HSPA and LTE), mobility procedures analysis, IP traffic
monitoring, code inspection, energy consumption and location. At present the
functionality offered focuses on network, traffic, battery and location monitoring.
In future extensions of the facility it is envisioned the need to include code related
information as part of the reports provided by the devices. With the inclusion of

W. Abramowicz et al. (Eds.): ServiceWave 2011, LNCS 6994, pp. 329–330, 2011.

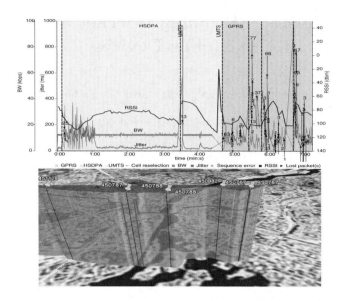

Fig. 1. Cross layer data correlation

code inspection all the stages of the mobile development and deployment process would be covered by the facility.

Measurements and post-processing. The output provided by instrumented devices is a set of correlated traces with information from all levels: radio technology in use, cell id, gps localization, signal strength received, handovers and IP traffic. Instrumented mobile nodes are based on commercial devices running advanced monitoring software developed by UMA, in which area have an extensive background. Monitoring software is available for Symbian, Android and Blackberry OS platforms.

Data post-processing will enable to find the source of particular events observed at application level matching different information sources. Fig. 1 is an example of the likelihood of the correlation of data collected at different levels. The upper figure shows the correlation of the bandwidth and jitter observed during a audio streaming session in a vehicular environment with radio access technology in use, signal received, packet losses and cell reselections.

Also the correlation of data collected with the geographical context is key to detect areas with poor coverage or QoS. The bottom figure plots RSSI and cell changes over a geographical map, which enables to associate degradation in the strength of the received signal in the vicinity of a river.

Conclusions. The main objective of the facility is the provision of a mechanism which enable to obtain perfectly tuned services and applications for mobile devices. Video demo available at: http://www.youtube.com/watch?v=TH3ez6UM9Y8.

Demonstration of the OPTIMIS Toolkit for Cloud Service Provisioning

Rosa M. Badia[5], Marcelo Corrales[11], Theo Dimitrakos[7], Karim Djemame[6],
Erik Elmroth[3], Ana Juan Ferrer[2], Nikolaus Forgó[11], Jordi Guitart[5],
Francisco Hernández[3], Benoit Hudzia[9], Alexander Kipp[10],
Kleopatra Konstanteli[8], George Kousiouris[8], Srijith K. Nair[7],
Tabassum Sharif[12], Craig Sheridan[12], Raül Sirvent[5], Johan Tordsson[3],
Theodora Varvarigou[8], Stefan Wesner[10], Wolfgang Ziegler[1], and Csilla Zsigri[4]

[1] Fraunhofer Institute SCAI, Sankt Augustin, Germany
wolfgang.ziegler@scai.fraunhofer.de
[2] Atos Origin, Barcelona, Spain
ana.juanf@atosresearch.eu
[3] Dept. Computing Science, Umeå University, Sweden
{hernandf,tordsson,elmroth}@cs.umu.se
[4] The 451 Group, Barcelona, Spain
csilla.zsigri@the451group.com
[5] Barcelona Supercomputing Center, Barcelona, Spain
{Raul.Sirvent,jordi.guitart,rosa.m.badia}@bsc.es
[6] School of Computing, University of Leeds, UK
karim@comp.leeds.ac.uk
[7] British Telecom, London, UK
{theo.dimitrakos,srijith.nair}@bt.com
[8] National Technical University of Athens, Greece
{gkousiou,kkonst,dora}@telecom.ntua.gr
[9] SAP Research Belfast, United Kingdom
benoit.hudzia@sap.com
[10] High Performance Computing Center Stuttgart, Germany
{kipp,wesner}@hlrs.de
[11] Institut für Rechtsinformatik, Leibniz Universität Hannover, Germany
{corrales,nikolaus.forgo}@iri.uni-hannover.de
[12] Flexiant Limited, Livingston, UK
{tsharif,csheridan}@flexiant.com

Abstract. We demonstrate the OPTIMIS toolkit for scalable and dependable service platforms and architectures that enable flexible and dynamic provisioning of Cloud services. The innovations demonstrated are aimed at optimizing Cloud services and infrastructures based on aspects such as trust, risk, eco-efficiency, cost, performance and legal constraints. Adaptive self-preservation is part of the toolkit to meet predicted and unforeseen changes in resource requirements. By taking into account the whole service life cycle, the multitude of future Cloud architectures, and a by taking a holistic approach to sustainable service provisioning, the toolkit provides a foundation for a reliable, sustainable, and trustful Cloud computing industry.

W. Abramowicz et al. (Eds.): ServiceWave 2011, LNCS 6994, pp. 331–333, 2011.
© Springer-Verlag Berlin Heidelberg 2011

1   Introduction

Contemporary Cloud computing solutions have mainly focused on providing functionalities at levels close to the infrastructure, e.g., improved performance for virtualization of compute, storage, and network resources, as well as necessary fundamental functionality such as Virtual Machine (VM) migrations and server consolidation. In the cases when higher-level concerns are considered, existing solutions tend to focus on functional aspects only. Furthermore, existing Platform as a Service environments are typically offered through proprietary APIs and limited to a single infrastructure provider. In order to move from a basic Cloud service infrastructure to an improved Cloud service ecosystem the European project OPTIMIS focuses on five higher-level concerns that we address for a wider adoption of Cloud computing: 1) Service life cycle optimization, 2) The non-functional Quality of Service parameters Trust, Risk, Eco, Cost, 3)Adaptive self-preservation, 4) Multi-Cloud architectures, and 5) Market and legislative issues.

2   OPTIMIS Innovations

The OPTIMIS toolkit supports the construction of multiple coexisting Cloud architectures. The focus of the toolkit is on Cloud infrastructure and service optimization throughout the service life cycle: *construction, deployment, and operation* of services. In the toolkit all management actions are harmonized by overarching policies that consider trust and risk assessment to comply with economical and ecological objectives without compromising operational efficiencies. The tools enable developers to enhance services with non-functional requirements regarding allocation of data and VMs, as well as aspects related to performance (elasticity), energy consumption, risk, cost, and trust. The toolkit incorporates risk aspects in all phases of the service life cycle and uses trust assessment tools to improve decision making in the matching of Service Providers (SPs) and Infrastructure Providers (IPs). Furthermore, the ecological impact of service provisioning is integrated in all relevant decision making. The toolkit also ensures that the desired levels of risk, trust, or eco-efficiency are balanced against cost, to avoid solutions that are unacceptable from an economical perspective. The tools enable SPs and IPs to compare different alternative configurations in terms of business efficiency. Legislative and regulatory aspects are also incorporated in the toolkit, e.g., to address data privacy legislation. The toolkit enables and simplifies the creation of a variety of provisioning models for Cloud computing, including Cloud bursting, multi-Cloud provisioning, and federation of Clouds.

3   Demonstration

- SP running a three tier Web-application in a private Cloud and adding more external Cloud resources dynamically when the local load exceeds a threshold

- SP simultaneously using resources offered by two independent Cloud providers for service deployment
- The non-functional Quality of Service parameters initially requested by the SP and their influence in decision making for all scenarios

The short video can be found here: www.optimis-project.eu

Travel eCommerce Experiment – Through TEFIS, a Single Access Point to Different Testbed Resources

Jérérmie Leguay[1], Annika Sällström[2], Brian Pickering[3], E. Borrelli[4], and F. Benbadis[1]

[1] Thales Communications and Security, Colombes, France
[2] Luleà University of Technology - Centre for Distance-spanning Technology, Luleà, Sweden
[3] University of Southampton, IT Innovation Centre, Southampton, UK
[4] INRIA, Sophia Antipolis, France

Abstract. This demonstration will show how the TEFIS portal is used to plan a Future Internet service experiment, to request testbed resources, to configure and provision them, and to run single or multiple testruns, checking monitoring output and results in the process. We will show a live demonstration of a Future Internet service, using a very complex Travel eCommerce application to provide insights into how TEFIS meets experimenter's service requirements via a single access point. Moreover, we will show how to specify and plan for a Future Internet experiment to optimise for the best results.

Keywords: Service development lifecycle, Iterative service development, Experimental testing Facilities, Testbeds, Living Labs, Experimentation.

1 Introduction

There have been a number of initiatives across the world in recent years with a view to providing support and resources for experiments in and around the Future Internet. In this demonstration we want to show the TEFIS solution for multi-faceted testing [1] and its support for service researchers and engineers in testing and experimentation with new service technologies. TEFIS is a Future internet testing service that provides a number of capabilities to allow experimenters to design effective tests which involve different resources and which can make use of the design and results of previous work, assuming appropriate levels of access have been assigned. Via TEFIS Future Internet experimenters get access to multiple test facilities offering different services and capabilities, from large, computer clusters to highly distributed systems and network simulators as well as end-user testing environments (Living Labs) for the design and evaluation phases of the service lifecycle.

2 Demonstration Description

In this demonstration we will show an experiment with a commercial application designed to run within a Service Oriented Architecture (SOA). Specifically, the test application represents a backend dedicated to the support of a significant Travel eCommerce platform. The application itself brings together many independent services for database

W. Abramowicz et al. (Eds.): ServiceWave 2011, LNCS 6994, pp. 334–336, 2011.

access, log files and other dedicated tools. All these services are orchestrated as a function of the life of the frontend application, i.e. new features to be published, bug fixes to be applied and even existing or potential bugs to be identified need to be processed resulting in the quasi constant update of the application.

An important part of this application is the processing of the large amounts of technical and functional log data (terabytes) generated by the system. For the experiment, it is necessary to extract and produce a high level representation of user sessions in order to analyze the behaviour of the system (tracking efficiency and capacity to conform to the service level agreement, or SLA) and track customer behaviour when bugs are reported.

So this Travel eCommerce experiment demonstrates the following:

- Many complex services to be orchestrated;
- Services requiring different environments (different OS, applications, amount of memory and storage, hardware and others);
- Critical services with specific SLA terms to respect;
- Using a number of testbeds to achieve large scale and mass experiments for different kinds of services;
- Large scale experiments;
- Complex SOA applications with large numbers of services running;
- Parallel Web Services requiring a backend Grid for their execution; and
- Performance measurements.

Three different testbeds are involved in the experiment: (i) ETICS [2] to build the application(s) and check functional coverage, (ii) PACA Grid [3] and (iii) PlanetLab [4] to evaluate performance in different client environments.

In the demo, we will show how the TEFIS portal is used for planning an experiment, to request testbed resources on demand, to configure and initialise those resources, to deploy them and to manage and run/re-run individual testruns and then to monitor and access results from the test. The demo will be a live demonstration of an effective test in runtime which involves three different testbed resources independent of place. As the Future Internet service to be deployed, the Travel eCommerce service is a very complex application, and so spectators will gain insights into how TEFIS supports and satisfies the user requirements of service experimenters via a single access point. Moreover we will also demonstrate how to specify and plan for a Future Internet experiment and the various factors which should be taken into account for the best results.

3 Videos to Show Experiment

We provide [5] two videos to give a short glimpse of what will be demonstrated. The video entitled 'ETICS_TEFIS demo' shows how the ETICS testbed is used for the Travel eCommerce experiment. This part of the demonstration shows how a real experiment is supported on one of the TEFIS testbeds, from its inception to the actual execution of the tasks in the test run. TEFIS provides a single port of call, therefore, to be able to plan, configure and execute experiments using remote resources that are appropriate to the specific task or subset of tasks for an experiment. In the second video 'TEFIS demo experimental data management', experimental data management in TEFIS is described. The demonstration shows how the TEFIS community of experimenters can find related work, based on natural language searches; how experimental data are stored and referenced for seamless execution across whatever resource is required; and how performance monitoring can be viewed as part of an experiment and its output.

References

1. Tefis project, http://www.tefisproject.eu
2. Etics, http://etics.cern.ch/eticsPortal/
3. Paca grid, http://proactive.inria.fr/pacagrid/
4. Planetlab, http://www.planet-lab.org
5. Demo videos, http://staff.www.ltu.se/~annika/TEFIS_demos/

Author Index